New Frontiers in the Philosophy of Intellectual Property

Are intellectual property rights a threat to autonomy, global justice, indigenous rights, access to life-saving knowledge and medicines? The chapters in this volume examine the justification of patents, copyrights and trade marks in light of the political and moral controversy over TRIPS (the Agreement on Trade-Related Aspects of Intellectual Property Rights). Written by a distinguished international group of experts, the volume draws on the latest philosophical work on autonomy, equality, property ownership and human rights in order to explore the moral, political and economic implications of property rights in ideas. Written with an interdisciplinary audience in mind, these essays introduce readers to the latest debates in the philosophy of intellectual property, whether their interests are in the restrictions that copyright places on the reproduction of music and printed words or in the morality and legality of patenting human genes, essential medicines or traditional knowledge.

ANNABELLE LEVER is Associate Professor of Normative Political Theory in the Political Science Department at the University of Geneva. She has previously held teaching and research appointments at Harvard University, the Massachusetts Institute of Technology, the University of Rochester, the London School of Economics and, latterly, at the Institute of Science, Ethics and Innovation at Manchester University and at the Chaire Hoover, Université Catholique de Louvain.

Cambridge Intellectual Property and Information Law

As its economic potential has rapidly expanded, intellectual property has become a subject of front-rank legal importance. *Cambridge Intellectual Property Rights and Information Law* is a series of monograph studies of major current issues in intellectual property. Each volume contains a mix of international, European, comparative and national law, making this a highly significant series for practitioners, judges and academic researchers in many countries.

A list of books in the series can be found at the end of this volume

New Frontiers in the Philosophy of Intellectual Property

Edited by

Annabelle Lever

CAMBRIDGE
UNIVERSITY PRESS

CAMBRIDGE UNIVERSITY PRESS
Cambridge, New York, Melbourne, Madrid, Cape Town,
Singapore, São Paulo, Delhi, Mexico City

Cambridge University Press
The Edinburgh Building, Cambridge CB2 8RU, UK

Published in the United States of America by Cambridge University Press, New York

www.cambridge.org
Information on this title: www.cambridge.org/9781107009318

First published 2012

Printed in the United Kingdom at the University Press, Cambridge

A catalogue record for this publication is available from the British Library

Library of Congress Cataloguing in Publication data

ISBN 978-1-107-00931-8 Hardback

Contents

List of contributors

LAURA BIRON Research Fellow, Queens College, Cambridge and Greenwall Fellow in bioethics and health policy, Georgetown University and Johns Hopkins University, USA

JOHN CHRISTMAN Professor of Philosophy, Political Science and Women's Studies, Pennsylvania State University, USA

GEERT DEMUIJNCK Professor of Business Ethics, EDHEC Business School, Lille, France

ABRAHAM DRASSINOWER Associate Professor and Chair in the Legal, Ethical and Cultural Implications of Technological Innovation, University of Toronto Faculty of Law, Canada

GRAHAM DUTFIELD Professor of International Governance, School of Law, University of Leeds, UK

DAVID LAMETTI Director, Centre for Intellectual Property Policy and Associate Professor of Law, McGill University, Canada

ANNABELLE LEVER Associate Professor of Normative Political Theory, Department of Political Science and International Relations, University of Geneva, Switzerland

KATHLEEN LIDDELL Senior Lecturer, Faculty of Law, Cambridge University, UK

STEPHEN R. MUNZER Distinguished Professor of Law, UCLA Law School, USA

ALEX ROSENBERG R. Taylor Cole Professor of Philosophy, Duke University, USA

JORN SONDERHOLM Visiting Researcher, Department of Philosophy, The George Washington University, USA

JAMES WILSON Lecturer in Philosophy and Health, Centre for Philosophy, Justice and Health, and Comprehensive Biomedical Research Centre, UCL, UK

Acknowledgements

We gratefully acknowledge the assistance of Blackwell Publishing for permission to reprint Jorn Sonderholm's 'Ethical Issues Surrounding Intellectual Property Rights', which was originally published in *Philosophy Compass* Vol. 5, Issue 12, (2011) 1107–15 and Palgrave Macmillan's permission to reprint substantial parts of Geert Demuijnck's 'Is P2P Sharing of MP3 Files An Objectionable Form of Free Riding?', published in Axel Gosseries, Alain Marciano and Alain Strowel (eds.), *Theories of Justice and Intellectual Property* (Basingstoke and New York: Palgrave Macmillan, 2008).

We are also happy to acknowledge the assistance of the following institutions which helped to fund the conference, 'Philosophy and Intellectual Property', which inspired this book: The Mind Association, The Society for Applied Philosophy, the Aristotelian Society, the Department of Philosophy, Logic and Scientific Method, the London School of Economics and Political Science and the Institute of Philosophy, University of London. Without their help, the conference would not have been possible and, without the conference, there would have been no book.

We would like to thank Kim Hughes, Joanna Breeze our editor, Richard Woodham and Cambridge University Press, for their willingness to publish this collection and for their help in overcoming the numerous obstacles between contract and publication. We are extremely grateful to Lynn Aitchison, our copy-editor, for bringing order to such a large and diverse text, and to Kate Mertes for creating the index.

Finally, the editor would like to thank John Harris and the Institute of Science, Ethics and Innovation, Manchester University School of Law, for appointing her to an Interdisciplinary Bioethics Research Fellowship, and for their encouragement and support of this book. The Institute is a model of interdisciplinary research and John's love of a good argument, wide interests and support for junior colleagues gives the Institute its distinctive character and ethos. It is a wonderful place to work. Above all, thank you to my husband, Dan Grecu, who helped with this book and the conference from start to finish.

Table of cases

Australia

Milpurrurru v. *Indafurn Party Ltd* (1994) 130 ALR 659 66

Canada

CCH Canadian Ltd v. *Law Society of Upper Canada* [2004] 1 SCR 339 207n.9, 218n.3, 291n.32
Cusenaire v. *S. W. Imports Ltd* (1969) SCR 208 19
Euro-Excellence Inc. v. *Kraft Canada Inc.* [2007] 3 SCR 20, 2007 SCC 37 218n.19
Harvard College v. *Canada (Commissioner of Patents)* 2002 SCC 76 196n.*d*, 199n.91

Court of Justice of the European Union

Case C-34/10 *Brüstle* v. *Greenpeace*, Opinion of the Advocate General, 10 March 2011; Judgment 18 October 2011 140, 166–9, 170–1

European Patent Office

Edinburgh Patent EP 06953351 (Opposition Division) 21 March 2003 147n.27
T0866/01 *Euthanasia Compositions*, 11 May 2005 148n.33, 150n.34
T19/90 *HARVARD/Oncomouse* [1991] EPOR 525 140, 152, 154
T0315/03 *HARVARD/Transgenic Animals* [2006] 1 OJEPO 15 147n.30, 148n.32, 149, 150n.34, 154, 162
T0272/95 *HOWARD FLOREY/Relaxin* (Opposition Division) [1995] EPOR 541; Decision of Technical Board of Appeal 3.3.4 [1995] EPOR 357 150n.36, 152, 153, 154, 162, 201n.95
G0001/98 *NOVARTIS/Transgenic Plant*, 20 December 1999 150n.34

Inter-American Court of Human Rights

United Kingdom

United States

World Trade Organization

Table of legislation and treaties

Africa

Australia

Canada

Europe

Latin America

United Kingdom

United States

Introduction: Philosophy of intellectual property – incentives, rights and duties

*Annabelle Lever**

The new frontiers in the philosophy of intellectual property lie squarely in territories belonging to moral and political philosophy, as well as legal philosophy and the philosophy of economics – or so this collection suggests. Those who wish to understand the nature and justification of intellectual property may now find themselves immersed in philosophical debates on the structure and relative merits of consequentialist and deontological moral theories, disputes about the nature and value of privacy, or the relationship between national and global justice. Conversely, the theoretical and practical problems posed by intellectual property are increasingly relevant to bioethics and philosophy and public policy, as well as to more established areas of moral and political philosophy.

Perhaps this is just to say that the philosophy of intellectual property is coming into its own as a distinct field of intellectual endeavour, providing a place where legal theorists and philosophers can have the sorts of discussions – neither reducible to questions about what the law is, nor wholly divorced from contemporary legal problems – which typify debates about freedom of expression, discrimination and human rights. These are all areas in which legal and philosophical ideas influence each other at the level of method as well as of substance. My hope is that this collection of essays will appeal to those who, whatever their professional specialty or training, share an interest in the philosophy of intellectual property, and

* With thanks to Laura Biron, Geert Demuijnck and Abraham Drassinower for commenting on parts of this Introduction, and with special thanks to Stephen Munzer for kindly reading and editing several drafts. Any errors, unfortunately, are all mine. However, without the help and support of John Harris, and the wonderful Institute for Science, Ethics and Innovation, The University of Manchester Law School, I would not have been able to see this volume to publication. It is a pleasure to be able to thank John and the Institute for appointing me to their Senior Wellcome Biomedical Ethics Fellowship, and for the help and support – and enjoyably energetic arguments – from which I profited as a member of iSEI.

that it will build upon and advance existing interdisciplinary dialogue and research in this complex, fascinating, and important area.[1]

Most of the chapters in this collection were specially written for a conference on the philosophy of intellectual property which took place at the Institute of Philosophy, London, in May 2009. In organising that conference I had been hoping to learn what, if anything, unites patents, copyright, trade marks and trade secrets and distinguishes them from other forms of property. As a political theorist working on privacy, I had come to be interested in intellectual property as a way of thinking about the relationship between privacy and property rights, on the one hand, and of private and collective property on the other. Finding this hard going, I was keen to have a bunch of experts on hand to answer my questions for me.

My hopes for a ready answer to my questions, however, were dashed by the conference. It quickly became apparent that issues which have been so central to philosophical and legal theorising about privacy seem largely irrelevant to legal theorists and philosophers interested in intellectual property. In the course of editing these chapters for publication, and of thinking about their points of agreement and tension, I have again been struck by how little the nature and justification of property concerns our authors, with the notable exception of John Christman, and how far the idea of patents and copyright as *property* seems either irrelevant to, or actively at odds with, the conception of rights which they seek to defend.

This might suggest that it is unnecessary to clarify what makes intellectual property a form of property – albeit one distinct from the property that we might have in material objects, animals, labour and relationships. Certainly, the quality and interest of the chapters here suggest that such clarification is often unnecessary. But it is also possible that there are puzzles in the theory and practice of intellectual property which we will not be able to solve without a better sense of the ways in which familiar forms of intellectual property are property, and of the advantages, as well as the limitations, of thinking about our interests in ideas this way. My hunch is that the puzzles thrown up by the different chapters suggest that

[1] See, for example, Stephen R. Munzer (ed.), *New Essays in the Legal and Political Theory of Property* (Cambridge University Press, 2001); Axel Gosseries, Alain Marciano and Alain Strowel (eds.), *Intellectual Property and Theories of Justice* (New York and Basingstoke: Palgrave Macmillan, 2008); Charles Beitz, 'The Moral Rights of Creators of Artistic and Literary Works' *Journal of Political Philosophy* 13(3) (2005): 330–58, hereinafter 'The Moral Rights of Creators'; Thomas Pogge, 'The Health Impact Fund: Better Pharmaceutical Innovations at Much Lower Prices', in Thomas Pogge, Matthew Rimmer and Kim Rubenstein (eds.), *Incentives for Better Global Public Health: Patent Law and Access to Medicines* (Cambridge University Press, 2010); Allen Buchanan, Tony Cole and Robert O. Keohane, 'Justice in the Diffusion of Innovation' *Journal of Political Philosophy* 19(3) (2011): 306–32.

this, too, is a real possibility. But in order to tell whether it is or not, it will help to look at the chapters in this collection one by one.

Control rights and income rights in ideas

The collection starts with John Christman's 'Autonomy, social selves and intellectual property claims', a piece which builds on his prior work on autonomy, and on an egalitarian interpretation of property rights. In an important article in *Philosophy and Public Affairs*,[2] Christman argued that we can think of the bundle of rights that makes up full property ownership in terms of two different groups of rights: one set he called control rights, and the other income rights. The former include familiar property rights, such as the rights to use, destroy, acquire, alienate and exchange a property, whereas the latter include familiar property rights such as the right to profit financially from the use, acquisition, alienation and destruction of one's property.

Distinguishing control rights from income rights, Christman argued, gives us a way to think about our autonomy and equality interests in property, and to see how they might be reconciled, rather than pitted against each other, as is often the case. In particular, Christman argued, if we care about autonomy and equality, we will want to distinguish the moral and political importance of control rights from income rights, because there is no particular level of income from property which is necessary to our autonomy or equality with others, whereas we cannot think of ourselves as autonomous beings, or as the equal of others, if we are treated simply as objects, or are denied the ability to distinguish our treatment of objects based on our beliefs about what is useful, beautiful, valuable and meaningful. In his chapter for this collection, Christman examines whether this way of thinking about property illuminates the claims by indigenous peoples to intellectual property (IP) in traditional knowledge (TK) and, therefore, how far his understanding of the links between autonomy and control support the claims of people who have often been denied the status of property owners, and legal rights in their ideas and artefacts.

Accordingly, a major part of Christman's chapter concerns his conception of autonomy, and the ways in which it might explain the importance of control over cultural artefacts and knowledge by indigenous peoples. Importantly, Christman wants to challenge the idea that autonomy is a problematically individualist value, and therefore inimical to claims to

[2] John Christman, 'Distributive Justice and the Complex Structure of Ownership' *Philosophy and Public Affairs* 23(3) (1994): 225–50.

self-determination made by people who value their unchosen ties to others. Suitably understood, Christman argues, autonomy need not imply or reflect an individualistic picture of self-determination. However, while a link can be made between autonomy and cultural survival in ways that might ground control rights in cultural artefacts, he claims that this is insufficient to justify IP rights in TK, because our interests in autonomy, whether individualistic or not, rarely justify the *income* rights which are part of IP rights.[3] Hence, he concludes, claims of autonomy will not justify IP rights in TK, not because there is something wrong with autonomy (it's too individualistic, or indifferent to culturally specific claims) or because there is something about TK that means people cannot have property rights in it, and certainly not because indigenous peoples lack interests in self-determination. The problem, rather, is that *no-one*'s autonomy normally justifies the income rights implicit in IP rights, although Christman thinks that indigenous groups might be able to substantiate their claims to income rights in TK based on claims of distributive justice, rather than autonomy.

This is an interesting and helpful argument. It suggests both that indigenous peoples' claims in TK are more complex than is often thought – and that what is true of indigenous peoples' claims is likely true of others' claims in their non-traditional forms of knowledge. However, Christman's ideas highlight two long-standing puzzles in the philosophy of IP. The first concerns the justification for *monopoly* rights in ideas, and the second the relationship between the control and income aspects of IP. Because Christman takes the familiar package of IP rights as given, he argues that our claims to autonomy will only justify IP rights if they show that we have an *exclusive* right to control access and use of a resource. This, as he says, is extremely difficult to substantiate, even in the case of indigenous groups, and is likely to be all but impossible to substantiate for most other people.[4]

Precisely because you can use my ideas without depriving me of the ability to use them, it is difficult to show that my autonomy as an inventor requires me to have exclusive control of my ideas, even if it requires me to have a determinative say in cases where, for example, conscientious objections or deep-seated moral or religious commitments would make some uses of my ideas anathema to me. On the face of it, therefore, Christman's reasons for doubting that our autonomy supports exclusive income rights in our ideas are also reasons for doubting that it supports exclusive control rights in them, too: because experience suggests that

[3] John Christman, 'Autonomy, social selves and intellectual property claims', Chapter 1 below.

[4] Ibid.

autonomy requires us to have a *share* in resources or decisions more often than *exclusive control* over them.

Second, Christman's suggestion that claims of distributive justice, rather than claims to autonomy, might justify income rights in ideas, raises questions about the relationship between justice and autonomy. As Christman puts it: 'restrictions on licensing fees in various forms and degrees in many cases will leave untouched the autonomy of the holders of the IP, as long as the use and publication of the product can be controlled by the creator in ways that are consistent with continued autonomy'.[5] This is plausible, but the point seems to cut both ways. If, on the one hand, it suggests that the combination of autonomy and distributive justice might justify income rights as well as control rights, it also suggests that the links between our autonomy and the ability to profit from our ideas may be tighter than it first seemed.

Although it is rarely the case that people's autonomy requires them to obtain income from *this* resource, rather than *that* one, it matters to most people's autonomy that they should be able to support themselves by their ideas and ingenuity, and not merely through hard slog and mechanical effort. So the ability to generate income from our ideas, artefacts and knowledge may be necessary for our autonomy, even if autonomy rarely turns on the ability to gain income from *this* particular idea or from *that* specific artefact. Christman's chapter, therefore, points to the way our interests in ideas intersect with basic political, civil and personal rights: because the ability to share in decisions can be as critical to our autonomy as the ability to make them unilaterally; and we can have interests in supporting ourselves through our intellectual and cultural endeavours even though we have no right to income from any particular idea.[6]

Restorative justice, autonomy and intellectual property

Stephen Munzer, too, is interested in the ways that IP rights can reflect and promote the autonomy of indigenous peoples. However, his interest is less in the philosophical elucidation of links between the concept of

[5] Christman, ibid., pp. 54–5.

[6] An interesting example of this might be the protection for future earnings by a statutory '*droit de suite*', or resale royalty right, referred to in Beitz, 'The Moral Rights of Creators', at 332, in order to distinguish it from the non-pecuniary moral rights recognised by some copyright systems, such as the French. As Beitz says, even if they are not motivated by economic concerns, moral rights affect the economic interests of creators and of actual and potential owners of creative works. Hence, he thinks, 'Any attempt to justify a system of Moral Rights . . . should at least take account of their impact on these interests, even if, in the end, it turns out that other considerations should be overriding', 339.

autonomy and the different types of rights which make up a typical package of IP rights, than with whether or not there are compelling arguments to justify including protections of IP in legally enforceable reparations for the unjust treatment of indigenous peoples by governments and corporations. Munzer's argument is that there are, because: 'Indigenous peoples have frequently suffered great wrongs – murder, enslavement, rape, torture, theft, forced relocation – at the hands of outsiders. They have autonomy-based reasons for seeking intellectual property IP rights in their TK. There is ample warrant for recognising these rights as a matter of corrective justice.'[7]

Corrective justice is mainly backward-looking, in that it seeks to right past wrongs. However, Munzer notes that it has at least one forward-looking dimension: 'If reparations are justified, we want to have reparations that work.'[8] Hence, he thinks, six steps are necessary to make a successful argument for IP rights part of a reparations package: that some harms have been committed against an indigenous group or its members; that the wrongdoers are identifiable as a group, or as individual members of a group; that the wrongs unjustifiably harm the indigenous group or its members; that the harmed are identifiable as an indigenous group, or as members of such a group; that the wrongdoers have a moral duty to rectify the wrongs and harm that they caused, and so have no excuses or other factors which remove this duty; and that recognising IP rights in TK would, in principle, form part of an effective package of measures offering compensative or restorative justice to the indigenous group or its members.

As these six steps make clear, familiar problems from the literature on restorative and compensatory justice form much of the subject matter of Munzer's chapter. These include the difficulty of identifying the victims of injustices and of determining who, if anyone, counts as their contemporary representatives and, therefore, the beneficiary of successful claims to compensation. Similarly, there is the familiar difficulty of determining how best to identify and describe the wrongdoers and their contemporary descendants. Here one must bear in mind that if victims and perpetrators are not simply a random bunch of individuals, but members of an identifiable group, that group may no longer exist in its earlier form and, quite possibly, may not exist at all. So, in addition to the potentially complex causal claims involved in determining who did what to whom in the past, arguments for reparations appear also to face potentially irresolvable metaphysical and

[7] Stephen R. Munzer, 'Corrective justice and intellectual property rights in traditional knowledge', Chapter 2 below, p. 58.

[8] Ibid.

conceptual problems in explaining what counts as an individual or a member of a group, what counts as a contemporary representative of a past individual or group, and so on. Then, of course, there are the important questions of whether and, if so, how IP rights could form part of an adequate restorative or compensatory package for gross violations of human rights, such as murder, enslavement, rape and torture.

As Munzer argues, from a legal perspective many of these problems are more apparent than real. So, he explains, the fact that bits of property, however precious, are no compensation for murder and other serious crimes, does not mean that they cannot be parts of a package that seeks to rectify injustices that are now beyond the reach of criminal justice – national or international. The appropriate point of comparison for IP rights, in other words, is not *criminal* trial and punishment, but *civil* remedies, which are normally the only forms of legal remedy available to rectify wrongs from long ago. Moreover, some of the wrongs suffered by indigenous peoples at the hands of outsiders include the expropriation and theft of indigenous labour and culture, and the disparagement of indigenous knowledge, artefacts and culture. So IP rights in TK have the great virtue of recognising indigenous peoples' claims in these, and the importance of denouncing and rectifying the wrongs that were done to them in the past.

Similarly, the fact that contemporary members of wronged indigenous groups have a metaphysically complex relationship to their predecessors, as do contemporary descendants of those who perpetrated the wrongs, need not determine the legal status of the respective rights and duties. As in debates over affirmative action, so in debates over restorative justice, we have good moral and political reasons to accept that debts of justice can be owed across generations. These reasons remain, even though there is no perfect way to identify debtors and beneficiaries such that only wrongdoers, or those who benefited from wrongdoing, bear the burden of rectification. Although arguments for affirmative action are often forward-looking in ways that distinguish them from arguments for restorative justice, the fact that both typically concern the current disadvantaged status of members of historically disadvantaged groups means that what matters morally and politically is not the precise way in which people came to be members of one group rather than another, or in virtue of which characteristics individuals can be distinguished into philosophically distinct groups, but what follows from membership, understood as a *socio-political* fact, rather than a *metaphysical* or *biological* one.[9]

[9] See, for example, Anne Phillips, *The Politics of Presence* (Oxford University Press, 1995); Melissa S. Williams, *Voice, Trust and Memory: Marginalised Groups and the Failure of Liberal Representation* (Princeton University Press, 1998); Iris Marion Young, *Inclusion*

In light of Christman's distinction between control and income rights in ideas, an interesting question raised by Munzer's argument concerns whether there would be something wrong – morally, politically or legally – with granting indigenous peoples IP rights to *non-traditional* forms of knowledge, as part of a package of reparations. For Munzer it matters greatly that IP rights recognise the capacities for autonomy of indigenous peoples, and the ways that those capacities have been developed and used to cultivate specific lands, and to produce specific cultural artefacts such as songs, pottery, medicines and food. Precisely because IP rights recognise people's creativity, and that creativity has so often been denied, denigrated or threatened in the case of indigenous peoples, they can be a particularly appropriate form of recognition and compensation. Because IP rights enable indigenous groups to have exclusive access to their land and artefacts, or to decide whether or not to share them with others, they give indigenous groups the sort of legally enforceable options that may help them to exercise their autonomy in a world that is often threatening or callously indifferent.

But it does not follow that it is only IP rights in *indigenous* knowledge that would be justified by these arguments, or that there would be something wrong in supposing that a share in the IP of companies who owe debts of reparations might not *also* be parts of legally enforceable compensatory agreements. Rather, it is important to ensure that these not be regarded as *replacements* for IP rights in TK, where those are desirable and possible. Munzer appears to be unsympathetic to such ideas, at least when formulated as an objection to granting IP rights in TK.[10] However, it seems a merit, rather than a demerit, of his argument, that it suggests a greater variety of remedies for historical injustice than we might otherwise consider, including ones which speak both to the symbolic and the practical aspects of reparations.

Welfare, efficiency and idealisation

Effectiveness is critical, if not determinative, in instrumental justifications of legal rights, although effectiveness is a relative, as well as absolute standard, reflecting the alternatives before us and the nature of our objectives. In previous work, Alex Rosenberg had argued on welfarist grounds that we are justified in having stringent protections

and Democracy (Oxford University Press, 2002). For French light on these debates, see *French Politics, Culture and Society*, 26(1) (Spring, 2008), a special issue devoted to the subject, organised by Daniel Sabbagh and Shanny Peer.

[10] Munzer, 'Corrective justice and intellectual property rights in traditional knowledge', Chapter 2 below.

for patent rights because of the importance of good new ideas to human well-being, and the importance of stringent protections for IP to the supply of good new ideas.[11] However, in 'Designing a successor to the patent as second best solution to the problem of optimum provision of good ideas', Rosenberg concludes that internal and external threats to the international system of patent rights require us to seek a new 'second best' way of promoting good new ideas, and that the model for that second best solution can be found in the reward structure of pure science.

Key elements in Rosenberg's chapter include the following claims:

(1) Good new ideas, unlike more traditional factors of production, such as land, labour and capital, do not suffer from diminishing marginal productivity and, therefore, 'Insofar as welfare is contingent on the total amount of output – the size of the pie, holding shares in it constant – increases in welfare will be subject to diminishing marginal productivity' unless we can find compensating increases in the supply of good new ideas.[12]

(2) The capacity of patents optimally to foster good new ideas is threatened by piracy, which constitutes an *external threat* to patents, and reflects the lack of an enforceable global system of IP rights.[13]

(3) The capacity of patents to foster the optimal level of good new ideas faces an *internal threat* to the patent system: namely, that the holders of patents, which are limited monopolies, may in time be able to use these to build up so much dominance in the market that they are able to manipulate the price for other goods in ways that suit themselves. In other words, they are able to become 'price-setters' rather than 'price takers' and to avoid the competitive pressures which make the grant of temporary monopolies in a market economy an optimally effective way to promote the supply and use of good new ideas.[14]

(4) The reward system of pure science is, essentially, a prize system in which first discoverers reap all of the prizes of fame and fortune, compared to later competitors. This makes for a maximally efficient use of intellectual resources, and provides the basis for an alternative model to patents, albeit a second best solution, namely, the use of public and privately funded prizes.

[11] Alex Rosenberg, 'On the Priority of Intellectual Property Rights, especially in Biotechnology' *Politics, Philosophy and Economics* 3(1) (2004): 77–95.

[12] Alex Rosenberg, 'Designing a successor to the patent as second best solution to the problem of optimum provision of good ideas', Chapter 3. Hereinafter referred to as 'Designing a successor to the patent'.

[13] Ibid. [14] Ibid.

> The availability of the internet makes it feasible easily and cheaply to put together large coalitions of small contributors to establish prizes for particular inventions ... the feasibility of this proposal turns on the willingness of large numbers of people to provide others with a quasi-public good, even when others free-ride on the costs of the good. Evidence from experiments in game theory suggests that when the amounts individuals pay are low, the number of cooperating individuals is very large, and the benefit is great and non-rivalrous the participants are prepared to tolerate free-riders even when exclusion is feasible.[15]

With Rosenberg's chapter, the philosophy of IP lands bang in the middle of the philosophy of economics and in what we might call the philosophy of regulation.[16] It raises important questions about how far arguments for protecting IP should be understood as arguments in ideal theory, and how far as arguments about what is practicable and justified, given the world we live in. Rosenberg believes that the patent system would be close to optimally welfare promoting were it not for piracy and the problem of monopolies. Hence, his arguments for replacing patents by prizes need to be distinguished from the arguments of those who think that patents exacerbate existing forms of inequality, national and global, or that they lead us wrongly to commodify humans, animals and the natural world, or to confuse discoveries with inventions.[17] It is equally noteworthy that Rosenberg does not appear to believe that there is anything intrinsically wrong with pirating patented inventions and ideas, or trying to obtain the benefits of another person's ideas, labour and investments for oneself. So if it turned out that piracy helped to curb or discipline would-be monopolists, and thereby to solve the 'internal' problem threatening the patent system, it would seem that Rosenberg would have no moral objection to it, and might even wish to promote it in certain areas of the economy, while pursuing it more vigorously in others.

In general, the threat to one's market position posed by cheaper competitors can be met in various ways. One can try to lower one's prices, though, given the need to recoup the costs of research and development, it is unlikely that pharmaceutical companies, for example, will be able to compete on price with their unlicensed competitors. Or one can compete on other terms that might seem to justify the higher price one charges for

[15] Rosenberg, ibid., pp. 105–6.

[16] See also Shuba Ghosh, 'When Property is Something Else: Understanding Intellectual Property Through the Lens of Regulatory Justice', in Gosseries, Marciano and Strowel (eds.), *Intellectual Property and Theories of Justice* ch. 5, pp. 106–21.

[17] For a discussion of such concerns, see Annabelle Lever, 'Is It Ethical to Patent Human Genes?', in ibid., ch. 12, pp. 246–64.

one's product: on the reliability and superior quality of one's product; on the service and training that one supplies to those who use it, and the speed with which one responds to customer needs and complaints; and it is sometimes possible to trade on brand loyalty or, paradoxically, to make the expensiveness of one's product part of its appeal. Given the importance of the placebo effect in medical treatment, the last strategy may be less ridiculous than it seems, although there are, presumably, limits to the extent to which drug manufacturers can treat their products as the equivalent of an especially soothing bedside manner, let alone of an expensively branded handbag or beauty product.

The threats posed by piracy and the limits of international enforcement of patent rights, then, may be less potent and inevitable than Rosenberg suggests.[18] But that does not mean that prizes might not be an attractive supplement for patents. Nor does it meant that we should ignore the ways that prizes might be more attractive than patents, even when the latter work as intended. If prizes mean that good ideas immediately become a public resource, freely available to anyone with the means to understand and use them, then perhaps prizes are really better at promoting welfare than patents? At any rate, prizes would seem to have moral, political and economic advantages which patents lack in the short term.

Of course, if prizes are to replace, or even supplement patents, they must be large enough to attract resources that would otherwise go into the creation of patentable inventions, and that may not be possible. Whether or not it is would probably be a matter of individual and collective will. But once one considers the role of political will in combating over-mighty companies, it is hard to see why the internal threats that Rosenberg identifies could not adequately be met by the sorts of anti-monopolistic

[18] According to Rosenberg, 'the absence of an internationally enforceable patent right is close to the same as no patent right at all'. 'Designing a successor to the patent', p. 90, n. 2. If the American experience is anything to go by, the deliberate promotion of some forms of unlicensed copying can be economically rational, even as one seeks stringently to prevent other forms. Nor, if Zorina Khan is right, is it self-evident that British authors, for example, suffered economically from American piracy, although it is possible that in the short term the pirating of better quality foreign products slowed down the production of home-grown products of comparable quality. See B. Zorina Khan, *The Democratisation of Invention: Patents and Copyrights in American Economic Development, 1790–1920* (Cambridge University Press, 2005), ch. 9 on American copyright piracy and, particularly, p. 273, with its discussion of the way that foreign authors, such as Charles Dickens, made their money from well-paid tours of America, where they read their books aloud to a mass market of readers generated by cheap, unlicensed editions of their work. The same advantages may be possible for spin-offs from the unlicensed use of patented goods, whether cosmetics, medicines or car products.

legislation and public policies that are usually used (or that *could be* used) to prevent monopolies from undermining economic competition.[19]

Rosenberg's chapter therefore asks us to consider the nature of the ideals we use to evaluate IP rights and, in particular, the relationship between the idealised models of markets, which characterise neo-classical economics, and the idealised models of norm-governed behaviour, characteristic of contemporary moral and political philosophy. There is nothing in free market theory, for example, that requires governments to be democratically elected rather than authoritarian, and there is nothing in a commitment to increase people's welfare that says we should hold current shares in the national or international pie constant. How, therefore, should we evaluate the alternatives to patents if we want to factor the differences between democratic and undemocratic governments into our analysis? And how should we describe the main policy alternatives from a welfarist perspective, given that the way we distribute shares in national income has complex effects on its future size? In short, the challenges raised by Rosenberg's chapter are not merely at the level of substance, but at the level of methodology as well.

Invention, law and morality

The chapters by Jorn Sonderholm, James Wilson, Kathleen Liddell and Graham Dutfield shed an interesting light on the preceding chapters and on the methodological and substantive issues which they raise. If, on the one hand, they suggest that utilitarian considerations may, indeed, provide the best justification for legally enforceable patent rights, they forcefully raise the problem of how deontological concerns for justice, liberty and equality fit into this framework morally and legally.

For example, in 'Ethical issues surrounding intellectual property rights', Sonderholm suggests that patents may have to be supplemented by prizes or schemes, such as Thomas Pogge's Health Impact Fund, in order to avoid two moral problems which are as endemic to patents as the threat of permanent monopolies, which worries Rosenberg. Because it is intrinsic to the patent system that funds for socially useful research come from the profits generated by temporary monopolies, it

[19] In chapter 2, 'The Patent System in Europe and America' and chapter 4, 'Democratization and Patented Inventions', Zorina Khan shows how differences in patent fees and the ease with which patents could be submitted, affected the relative balance amongst individuals, small and large companies, and amongst patent-holders, and not merely the rate at which inventions were patented. It also affected what was patented, and the focus of both inventive activity and patenting. Chapters 5 and 6 on women inventors in America are particularly interesting in these respects: B. Zorina Khan, *The Democratisation of Invention.*

is inevitable that the patent system will under-supply good new ideas and products for problems where the market is small, or where it is large, but made up of people with limited incomes. Hence the problem of 'orphan drugs' – drugs for diseases that affect relatively few people, and the problem of drugs for the diseases that ravage millions of people in developing countries.[20] Likewise, because it is the profits of temporary monopolies which must pay for the costs of past and future research, the price of goods under these temporary monopolies is often so high – and necessarily so – as to price all but the wealthy out of the market for these drugs.[21] However, Sonderholm notes, the main way to respond to these problems is generally thought to require supplementing, rather than replacing patents, on the assumption that these play a critical role in incentivising desirable research.

Perhaps it is true that patents provide critical incentives for desirable research, despite Rosenberg's concerns. Still, patents have rarely been the sole means to generate investment in socially useful ideas and technologies. For most of their history patents have been supplemented by a wide range of additional forms of funding and support for new ideas – whether government subsidies or direct investment in education, research and technology, or government efforts to shield favoured companies or areas of research from outside competition. So Sonderholm's helpful account of ethical objections to intellectual property rights (IPRs), and of their possible solutions, reminds us that at least some of the problems which surround IPRs have their counterparts in other areas of public policy, because the problem of how to pay for public goods is no more unique to ideas than are moral concerns with the structure of markets.[22]

Indeed, debates about the moral limits of the market underpin James Wilson's argument in 'On the value of the intellectual commons'. He contends both that inventors have no special moral rights in their ideas, and that utilitarian justifications for IP may have to exclude medicines. Wilson's reasoning is as follows: we cannot justify special rights for inventors based on their need to have continued access to their ideas, because *your* ability to use my ideas in no way diminishes *my* ability to use them.

[20] Jorn Sonderholm, 'Ethical issues surrounding intellectual property rights', Chapter 4 below.

[21] Ibid.

[22] For some classic examples of the latter which shed an interesting light on moral debates about patents, see Elizabeth Anderson, *Value in Ethics and Economics* (Cambridge, Mass.: Harvard University Press, 1995); Margaret Jane Radin, *Contested Commodities: The Trouble with Trade in Sex, Children, Body Parts and Other Things* (Cambridge, Mass.: Harvard University Press, 1996); and Deborah Satz, *Why Some Things Should Not be For Sale: The Limits of Markets* (Oxford University Press, 2010).

And, he thinks, I have no moral right to exclude you from ideas unless you are willing and able to pay me for their use because *your* use of my ideas does not diminish *my* ability to use them.[23] Nor, Wilson argues, do I have a moral right that you should not benefit from my creative efforts when you can do so without imposing extra costs on me. So, he concludes, inventors cannot have moral rights in their ideas *qua* inventors, because there is nothing about being the person who made up a good idea which means that other people should not be able to share in it. Hence, the justification for private property in ideas cannot be the moral rights of inventors, but must be utilitarian or consequentialist, if such rights are justified at all.

Wilson's accessible and elegant argument appears to support the justificatory assumptions of Rosenberg and Sonderholm, and to fit well with Christman's belief that income rights from TK (and income rights more generally) cannot usually be justified by people's claims to autonomy. However, they seem at odds with Christman's belief that people can have moral rights to exclusive control of their knowledge, and it may therefore be helpful to stop and consider the question of inventors' rights more closely.

It is essential to Christman's argument that indigenous peoples have been excluded or threatened with exclusion from their TK and that, if their moral rights in that knowledge are not properly acknowledged, this loss may undermine a way of life that is, in other respects, viable, satisfying and a reflection of their autonomy. By contrast, Wilson's argument works on the assumption that authors will have the same rights in their ideas as everyone else, and therefore do not need private control rights in order to secure access to their own ideas and inventions.

The differences in these assumptions point to the ways in which ideas are private, as well as public goods and private, as well as public ills. Though in principle it is true that my use of traditional patterns or medicines need in no way diminish your use of them, there are two ways in which this may not be the case. The first is where I am able to translate my use of these ideas into control of resources that you need to use the ideas. Because knowledge or ideas are usually embodied in objects, they are vulnerable to the mistaken, as well as deliberate, destruction and expropriation of their object and purpose. Second, because people can have different and mutually inconsistent purposes, my use of our shared ideas can undermine the value of your use of them, and may even come to prevent you using them at all. So, for example, if my invention of a new

[23] James Wilson, 'On the value of the intellectual commons', Chapter 5 below.

weapon is designed expressly to protect people struggling against unjust domination, then your use of it on behalf of those would-be dominators will diminish the value of my ideas to me and, if you are successful, may wreak so much destruction that my side, over time, is unable ever to use them again.

Wilson assumes that the competitive aspect of ideas is a reason why I should usually have the right to keep my ideas to myself.[24] However, he thinks, once I have agreed to share them with other people, I have no moral claim to decide who should use my ideas or how they should be used. Once you have agreed to work for all, so to speak, by making your ideas public, maybe you are no longer in a position to object if some uses of your labour are at odds with your fundamental convictions.[25] But there is nothing about ideas which requires us to assume this, or to suppose that their aspect as *public goods economically* should dominate their aspect as *private goods morally*. Indeed, doing so would seem to be at odds with familiar justifications for freedom of religion, expression and personal choice, which entitle people to act on personal considerations, even self-interested ones, instead of collective ones. So an implication of Wilson's arguments, perhaps, is that some legal protections for the *producers*, as well as the *consumers* of ideas, may have to figure in a normatively appealing scheme of patent rights, because the interests of these two groups are not identical, and neither should be left wholly to the whims of the market.

Respect for human dignity, liberty and equality place moral limits on patents, conceived as devices to promote well-being. However, how the deontological and consequentialist claims on patents are to be combined in practice, or philosophically, is far from clear, and these difficulties are legal as well as moral or economic. Indeed, these are the legal problems which motivate 'Immorality and patents: The exclusion of inventions contrary to *ordre public* and morality', Kathleen Liddell's spirited defence

[24] Ibid. I say 'usually' in deference to the fascinating – but disturbing – case of the Chamberlen family who, Wilson explains, were able to keep 'the discovery of the obstetrics forceps secret for more than 100 years in order to protect their midwifery business'. While the point of patents is to discourage such forms of trade secrecy, the moral question of whether or not one is entitled to keep such life-saving knowledge secret is not settled by the legal availability of patents. Instead, one faces the question of whether it is ethical to prefer secrecy to claiming a patent on such knowledge, and of licensing it on terms that make it widely available. The example is particularly interesting given Wilson's belief that medicines should sometimes be unpatentable on moral grounds. For details of the Chamberlen case Wilson refers us to W. Moore, 'Keeping Mum' *British Medical Journal* 334(7595) (2007). For Wilson's reservations about patenting medicines, see pp. 135–6.

[25] The idea that one's only choice is to reveal and/or share one's ideas, or to keep them secret has the same structure as the idea that once a woman has agreed to have sex with *some* man she can be assumed to consent to sex with *any* man. Hence my scepticism that IP rights require such a dichotomy.

of the morality exclusions from patent protection found, for example, in European IP law.

Liddell's aim, it should be said, is not to defend any particular formulation of those exclusions, nor does her argument imply that all forms of morality exclusion are wise or desirable. But she does want to argue that some standard objections to them – characteristic of Anglo-American lawyers – are ill-founded, and that morality exclusions can usefully be understood as a way to fulfil the utilitarian objectives which justify private property rights in ideas. So understood, she thinks, we will be better placed to reflect on what their content should be, and on how best to interpret and apply such legal exclusions. Indeed, she thinks, properly understood, we will see that morality exclusions are not simply a useful addition to patent law, but that the role they fill is sufficiently important that we should seek to add such exclusions to our law books if they are not on them already.

As Liddell says, it is now fairly uncontroversial that no sharp distinction exists between law and morality. So the people who object to the idea that patent law should not apply to certain things, such as medicines, life forms, or human genes, cannot avail themselves of the idea that morality has nothing to do with law. After all, if you think that the best justification for patent rights is that they facilitate socially desirable outcomes, it seems that you would have to object to patent rights that undermined such outcomes, all else being equal. So why not prevent certain things from being patentable if you have reason to believe that this would be counter-productive? As Liddell says, morality exclusions do not require legal decision makers to 'define immorality with philosophical rigour. Far from solving the puzzles that have troubled and divided philosophers for centuries . . . they simply have to grapple openly and conscientiously with a lower-order goal of responding reasonably to moral pluralism and the empirical information [about people's beliefs about morality] that is currently available'.[26]

Liddell's chapter persuasively shows that many of the objections to morality exclusions in patent law are overstated or unpersuasive. However, when you consider the political manoeuvring, and the forms of inequality and exclusion which underpin the process of granting morality exemptions, it is hard to know what moral respect to accord *actual* morality exclusions, or whether explicitly building such exemptions into law is such a good idea.

[26] Kathleen Liddell, 'Immorality and patents: The exclusion of inventions contrary to *ordre public* and morality', Chapter 6 below, hereinafter 'Immorality and patents'.

One area in which the role of morality is most interesting and controversial legally concerns the 'threshold test' for a patent – namely, the proof that one's brilliant new ideas are an *invention*, rather than a *discovery*. This is the subject of Dutfield's chapter, 'The genetic code is 3.6 billion years old: it's time for a rewrite: Questioning the metaphors and analogies of synthetic biology and life science patenting'. According to Dutfield, there are two problems with contemporary applications and justifications of patents by scientists: the first arises from the difficulty of explaining cutting-edge ideas to non-specialist audiences.[27] The second problem is one of scientific hubris, which leads us systematically to denigrate or disparage the role of nature – or pre-existing facts – in our creative activities – as in the quotation from Tom Knight, head of MIT's Artificial Intelligence Laboratory, from which Dutfield takes his title. According to Knight, synthetic biology is getting ready to rewrite our DNA, because 'the genetic code is 3.6 billion years old. It's time for a rewrite!'[28] In both cases, the use of metaphor and analogy to facilitate the understanding and communication of complex ideas, Dutfield suggests, makes it difficult for us effectively to police the line between discoveries and inventions and to ensure that patent rights are limited to the latter, as the law requires.

As Dutfield shows, the problem is not metaphor or analogy *per se*, as these are inseparable from creative thinking and the effective exposition of new ideas, but the danger of taking them literally, especially when figures of speech draw on highly specialised bodies of technical knowledge. 'Frequently we explain a phenomenon, such as the way that something works, by reference to something else that is unrelated. The more complicated the phenomenon, the more likely we are to have to resort to analogy for us to make sense of it.'[29] However, when people fail adequately to understand the analogies that are being used, or to recognise the differences between analogical and homological reasoning, Dutfield suggests, they fall prey to manipulation, deception and self-deception.

The implication of Dutfield's argument is that these difficulties are inevitable features of scientific communication and inevitable in legal judgments about the validity of patent claims. So are there moral, economic or legal reasons to persist with the idea that patents apply only to

[27] Graham Dutfield, ' "The genetic code is 3.6 billion years old: it's time for a rewrite": Questioning the metaphors and analogies of synthetic biology and life science patenting', Chapter 7 below, hereinafter 'The genetic code'.
[28] Ibid. [29] Ibid.

inventions, rather than to discoveries with industrial application?[30] The question is especially pressing because the exclusion of mathematical ideas from patent protection, as Liddell implies, may be better understood as a *moral* judgment about the resources to which everyone should have access than as a *conceptual* claim about the nature of inventions, or an *economic* judgment of the best way to promote them. Hence, Liddell and Dutfield force us to consider whether moral concerns for fair access to ideas justify the discovery/invention distinction, despite its difficulties and, if not, whether it has any justification at all.

Copyright, freedom and communication

How far, if at all, do the concerns animating thinkers on patents affect those whose primary concern is copyright? In 'Copyright infringement as compelled speech', Abraham Drassinower advances a deontological account of the nature and purposes of copyright law. Taking aim at what he sees as the mistaken reification and commodification of authorship, he argues that the point of copyright is not to promote some optimal level of creative work, let alone to promote economic development, but to protect 'an author's autonomy as a speaking being'.[31]

In an innovative and influential series of articles, Drassinower has developed a perspective on copyright which seeks to present it as a system, or legal regime, rather than as the terrain for *ad hoc* acts of balancing, compromise and conflict amongst people's disparate interests in ideas. He therefore asks us to turn away from debates about the best way to reward or promote creativity and, instead, to consider the nature of authorship as an act, and copyright as the body of law which recognises and protects that act. So understood, the point of copyright is not to regulate the production of ideas or to distribute benefits or rewards, but to give legal status and protection to a morally fundamental feature of persons, namely, their capacities to originate, or author, works.

Critical to Drassinower's argument is the claim that, for copyright purposes, authors and users of ideas are not two random groups of people,

[30] For example, Sir Hugh Laddie questions whether the legal test of 'non-obviousness' in UK patent law serves any useful purpose, given that the main obstacles to producing new products appear to be the expense of research, rather than the intrinsic difficulty or non-obviousness of the ideas and techniques involved. See, 'Patents – What's Invention Got to Do With it?', in David Vaver and Lionel Bently (eds.), *Intellectual Property in the New Millenium: Essays in Honour of William R. Cornish* (Cambridge University Press, 2004), p. 94.

[31] Abraham Drassinower, 'Copyright infringement as compelled speech', Chapter 8 below, hereinafter 'Copyright infringement'.

engaged in unrelated acts of using and producing ideas. Instead, this body of law concerns authors *as* users of other people's works, and users are of legal significance *as* actual or potential authors. Seen in this way, Drassinower contends, the unity or integrity of familiar features of copyright law becomes visible, and it becomes easier to understand aspects which might otherwise seem unmotivated or *ad hoc*, such as the treatment of simultaneous invention, fair use and the non-communicative use of ideas.

As Drassinower explains, copyright is not concerned with the originality of works in the sense of their *novelty*, but with their *origin*. Therefore, there is no reason why 'simultaneous creators' should be denied legal protection for their independent acts of authorship. On the contrary, *qua* authors, they are entitled to precisely the same degrees and kinds of protection as the most popular, innovative or prolific authors. Similarly, because authorship is impossible in a world without ideas to draw on and respond to, Drassinower argues that fair use is an integral part of copyright, not some exception tacked onto it.[32] The point of copyright is to protect authorship and therefore, he claims, authors own their work for some purposes, but not others. In particular, they do not own their works for the purposes of criticism, as in this respect their works are part of the public domain, freely available to all.[33] 'By asserting his copyright, the author seeks to be treated as a person, and not a mere puppet . . . By the same token, his work, as copyright subject matter, is addressed to persons, and not mere puppets, and so contemplates the responses of its audience.'[34]

According to Drassinower, a proper understanding of copyright also helps us to understand why authors do not own their works in ways that entitle them to monitor or license acts of private copying for personal enjoyment, instruction or discipline, or to constrain their non-communicative use, whether we are baking pies or engaged in the act of accounting. Such uses involve works as tools, rather than as acts of communication, Drassinower explains, in an analysis of the classic case of *Baker* v. *Selden*.[35] They therefore have no bearing on the protection of authorship,

[32] Abraham Drassinower, 'Authorship as Public Address: On the Specificity of Copyright vis-à-vis Patent and Trade-mark' *Michigan State Law Review* 1 (2008): 199–232, esp. 208–10, hereinafter 'Authorship as Public Address'. See also 'Copyright infringement'.

[33] Drassinower, 'Authorship as Public Address', 221.

[34] Drassinower, 'Copyright Infringement', p. 220.

[35] *Baker* v. *Selden*, 101 US 99 (1879). For the example of baking pies, see Abraham Drassinower, 'Authorship as Public Address', 219, n. 57 and the decision in *Cusenaire* v. *S. W. Imports Ltd.* (1969) SCR 208, repudiating the possibility that 'everybody who made a rabbit pie in accordance with the recipe of *Mrs. Beeton's Cookery Book* would infringe the literary copyright in that book'.

or communication, and so are irrelevant to the law of copyright, although the use of ideas as tools is central to the law of patents. As Drassinower puts it, 'Authors hold rights in respect of their work not as owners but as authors ... Thus copyright is less an exclusive right of reproduction than an exclusive right of public presentation.'[36] It prevents copying not as an end in itself, but as a means to other ends: the protection of our ability to author communicative acts.

How do these claims help us to understand the distinctive point and justification of copyright as a systematic body of law? Here Drassinower's presentation of a rights-based justification of copyright, in this volume, provides a helpful clarification and elucidation of his ideas. In particular, it illuminates the differences between copyright and privacy law in ways that reflect the unity of the former; and it shows how the form/content distinction, so familiar to scholars and lawyers, explains why legal protections for copyright are not reducible to protections for an author's privacy or reputation, nor for the integrity or financial value of a work.

Copyright, Drassinower argues, prevents the unauthorised publication of unpublished work, not because it is unpublished, but because it is *unauthorised*.[37] So while copyright helps to ensure that authors are not forced to speak when they wish to remain silent, legal protections for privacy are no substitute for copyright – no more than rights against self-incrimination would be.

Legal protections for privacy are pre-eminently concerned to prevent the unauthorised publication of personal facts, especially where these were previously unpublished. Copyright, by contrast, is unconcerned with the degree of intimacy or self-revelation involved in a text, but merely with its origin or authorship.[38] Copyright therefore protects authors from unauthorised *re-publication* of their works, not just unauthorised *publication*, and takes the latter as seriously as the former. By contrast with laws protecting us from misrepresentation, copyright is concerned as much with the accurate, albeit unauthorised, publication of works as it is with ones that are inaccurate, bowdlerised, misleading or deceptive.[39] Finally, as distinct from laws protecting us from exploitation and theft, copyright seeks to protect us from unauthorised publication, whether or not unauthorised publication would harm us financially.[40] In short, Drassinower contends, because copyright protects the *form*, not the *content* of our ideas, it is necessarily indifferent to features of them that are essential to other bodies of law. Because its concern with form is a reflection of its concerns with *origin* or *authorship*, Drassinower explains, we miss the point of

[36] Drassinower, 'Authorship as Public Address', 221.
[37] Drassinower, 'Copyright infringement'. [38] Ibid. [39] Ibid. [40] Ibid.

copyright if we see it as a way to protect our property right in *things* – books, letters, manifestos, posters – rather than as a system of protections for *acts* of authorship.

But why is authorisation important in the absence of harms to our wallets, our reputations, or our privacy? Here we come to an intriguing feature of Drassinower's account of copyright: namely, the claim that unauthorised publication 'amounts to forcing another to speak. Unauthorized publication is wrongful because it is compelled speech.'[41] Capturing the sense that unauthorised publication is something to be prevented, if possible, rather than compensated *post facto*, the idea that unauthorised publication is compelled speech reflects the fact that publication can *wrong* us, whether or not it also harms our work, our status, or our finances. It helps to account for the sense that unauthorised publication wrongs *authors*, whoever else it wrongs, and therefore captures the reasons why our legal rights in ideas are not simply emanations of our duties to others – important though the latter may be. Finally, it raises interesting questions about the relationship between the harms of copyright infringement and the harms of forced oaths,[42] or the forced extraction of information under torture, for these rights against compelled speech are inalienable and cease at our death.[43]

In 'Public reasons, communication and intellectual property', Laura Biron, like Drassinower, turns to Kant in an effort to provide an alternative to economistic models of copyright.[44] Distancing herself from what she sees as misreadings of Kant in authors such as Neil Netanel and Leslie Kim Treiger-Bar-Am, she aims to develop a communicative account of copyright. Biron's chapter reflects Onora O'Neill's philosophical work on Kant and on the creation, storage and use of information.[45]

[41] Ibid., p. 212.

[42] The classic American legal case is *West Virginia State Board of Education* v. *Barnette*, 319 US 624 (1943), protecting the right of Jehovah's Witnesses not to pledge loyalty to the US flag. In 1962, the US Supreme Court struck down requirements that state employees affirm allegiance to the national and state constitutions, and disclaim membership of the Communist Party and other 'subversive' organisations. See Eric Barendt, *Freedom of Speech* (Oxford University Press, 2005), pp. 93–8 for a sensitive discussion of 'rights not to speak' bearing on union dues, trade advertisements, licence-plate slogans and gay rights. However, for a sobering assessment of employees' free speech rights in America, see Matthew W. Finkin's Piper Lecture of 1996, published as 'Employee Privacy, American Values and the Law' *Chicago-Kent Law Review* 72 (1996–7): 221–69.

[43] See Beitz, 'Moral Rights of Creators', 346–50. Beitz thinks that making moral rights inalienable is hard to justify, and often reflects the scope for conflict between two social interests underpinning moral rights: the interest in promoting or encouraging creativity, and the interest in preserving a cultural or artistic heritage.

[44] Laura Biron, 'Public reason, communication and intellectual property', Chapter 9 below, hereinafter 'Public reason'.

[45] Ibid.

According to Biron, reflections on Kant should lead to a justification of copyright grounded in the ethics of communication and, in particular, in a communicative ethics aimed at a potentially universal, rather than circumscribed, audience. As Biron describes it, 'the idea that thinking for oneself and communicating publicly are inextricably linked is fundamental to Kant's account since, as he argues, acts of thinking presuppose audiences of some kind, as we endeavour to think "in community with others, to whom we communicate our thoughts and who communicate their thoughts to us" '.[46] As with Drassinower, Biron also believes that this aspect of Kant's thought explains why the existence of a public domain is internal to copyright – rather than as a set of *ad hoc* constraints imposed on it from outside. Moreover, according to Biron, attention to the communicative aspects of patents and trade marks can illuminate their commonalities with copyright.

For instance, Biron, like Drassinower, believes that the existence of a rich and varied public realm, permitting critical and transformative uses of copyrighted materials, is necessary to the communicative rationale of copyright itself. So reflections on the normative point of copyright help to explain why copyright cannot extend indefinitely, why it cannot cover content, rather than expression, and why it must allow fair comment as well as satirical and transformative uses of the way that one has framed one's communication.[47] In the case of trade marks, Biron believes that a communicative approach to patents will help us to distinguish their *informative* function from their *persuasive* or emotional one, so that the reasons to protect the former are not confused with reasons to protect the latter.[48] Likewise, in the case of patents, she believes, attention to their communicative, rather than proprietary aspects, reminds us that 'mere disclosure of information is not sufficient for communication to meet the standards of public reason [suggested by Kant] – other standards besides accessibility are needed. . . . In addition to innovators disclosing information about patents, they must also do so in a way that makes such information intelligible by relevant audiences.'[49] Hence, Biron believes, a communicative approach puts the burden of proof on would-be patent-holders, to show that they have adequately disclosed the details of their invention, by contrast with the contemporary situation where the onus is on others to prove that disclosure has been inadequate.

Biron's account is extremely interesting, both in the links it suggests amongst different forms of IP, and between the justification of IP and

[46] Ibid., p. 237; the quotation from Kant can be found at p. 247. [47] Ibid.

[48] For Abraham Drassinower's views on trade marks and patents, see his 'Authorship as Public Address', 229.

[49] Biron, 'Public reason', p. 257.

political and moral ethics more generally. It reminds us that the deontological elements of a philosophical justification of legal rights need not, themselves, be rights-based but might, rather, reflect our moral duties and the importance of our ability to fulfil them. Not surprisingly, therefore, Biron's approach raises many questions about the nature and justification of copyright, and its relationship to other rights we might have in ideas.

The most pressing of these questions concerns the content of the communicative ethics which best makes sense of copyright norms. Although Biron looks to Kant for inspiration, others might look to Habermas, where the effort to work out a communicative ethics suitable for democratic societies still influences Anglo-American as well as continental moral and political thought.[50] Or, presumably, one might look to Derrida for inspiration and to ideals of communication that are playful, actively invite challenge, seek to evade, rather than to justify stable power relations, and so on.[51]

Once one reflects on the different ways one might try to develop an ethics of communication, and the different forms that it might take, the difficulties of justifying legal rights this way become apparent. If we try to formulate those norms sufficiently thinly, or abstractly, to capture what is common to different ethics of communication, our moral foundation is likely to be too thin to answer practical questions about the legal rights we should have. If, on the other hand, we try to define our communicative ethics with sufficient detail so as to provide legal guidance, 'where guidance is needed' (to paraphrase Rawls), we risk ending up with a body of IP law that is unappealingly sectarian, or that arbitrarily accords great protection to some of our interests in ideas, while neglecting or actively disparaging the significance of others. For example, Biron's distinction between the informative and persuasive aspects of trade marks assumes that the former is more important ethically than the latter. However, it is unclear why this should be so, or what this distinction implies about IP protections for the plastic arts, as well as for music.[52]

These are familiar problems in political philosophy – whether one is concerned with debates on Rawls and Habermas, for example, or the

[50] See, for example, Seyla Benhabib and Fred Dallmayr, *The Communicative Ethics Controversy* (Cambridge, Mass.: MIT Press, 1990).

[51] See, for example, Judith Butler, *Excitable Speech: A Politics of the Performative* (New York: Routledge, 1997).

[52] I do not think the informative/persuasive distinction can be seen simply as a reflection of the lesser constitutional protections offered for commercial speech under US constitutional law. This is partly because trade marks presumably fall within the realm of commercial speech, and because American constitutional protections cut across Biron's distinction.

definition of women's rights against harassment and verbal abuse.[53] No magic wand seems likely to make these problems disappear, nor are they susceptible to a purely philosophical solution, in so far as they arise from the need to justify legally enforceable rights and duties, and legally constructed conflicts of interest and balances of power. Hence, a counterpart to a communicative perspective on copyright, it would seem, is an account of the scope for political choice in the formulations of legally enforceable rights, duties and permissions, and the alternatives to these as a way to protect our interests. Attention to the role of political choice is especially important, because a deontological perspective on IP need not be rights-based, and might therefore draw the line between the legal and the moral in ways quite different from those with which we are familiar.[54] In short, Biron's chapter is a salutary reminder that our moral duties may have a role in determining our legal rights, and that these duties are potentially as important for our 'control' rights in ideas as they are for our rights to gain income from them.

Morality, sharing and free riding

Our collection of chapters closes with two qualified defences of free riding, motivated by reflections on peer-to-peer (P2P) sharing in the music industry. Updating and extending an earlier piece on copyright, Geert Demuijnck's 'Illegal downloading, free riding and justice' takes a look at the economics of the music industry in order to explain why the unlicensed copying of the latest hits is often fair.[55] Inspired by Demuijnck's chapter,

[53] See, for example, Samuel Freeman (ed.), *The Cambridge Companion to Rawls* (Cambridge University Press, 2003) and Stephen K. White (ed.), *The Cambridge Companion to Habermas* (Cambridge University Press, 1995); and for a debate concerning its bearing on women's rights, see Wendy Brown, 'Suffering Rights as Paradoxes' and Annabelle Lever, 'The Politics of Paradox: A Response to Wendy Brown' *Constellations: An International Journal of Critical and Democratic Theory* 7(2) (2000): 208–29 and 242–54, respectively.

[54] The race to make the human genome publicly available, in order to pre-empt Venter's effort to patent parts of it, suggests that we can cause harm by failing to defend our patents and copyrights against others, and the same may be true in cases where our ideas would be used for immoral purposes unless we seek actively to stop them. See, for example, John Sulston and Georgina Ferry, *The Common Thread: A Story of Science, Politics, Ethics and the Human Genome* (Washington DC: John Henry Press, 2002). Generally, our laws do not require people to defend their reputations or their assets, nor their rights in their ideas. But that does not mean that the best justification of IP would support this status quo, or the conditions of alienability which characterise existing IP rights.

[55] Geert Demuijnck, 'Illegal downloading, free riding and justice' chapter 10 below, hereinafter 'Illegal downloading'. The earlier piece is Geert Demuijnck, 'Is P2P Sharing of MP3 Files an Objectionable Form of Free Riding?', in Gosseries, Marciano and Strowel (eds.), ch. 7, *Theories of Justice and Intellectual Property*, pp. 141–59.

David Lametti turns to virtue ethics in order to illuminate the morality of file sharing, and its place within a scheme of IP.[56]

Free riding is possible whenever the behaviour of others generates positive externalities – or good side-effects – from which people can benefit without having to contribute. Demuijnck gives the example of his enjoyment of his neighbour's violin playing, which wafts towards him as he sits in the garden. Or one might think of the enjoyment one gets, as a tourist, driving through the beautifully kept villages in France. So understood, it is clear that the enjoyment of positive externalities is not intrinsically immoral – just as there is nothing intrinsically praiseworthy with putting up with negative externalities, such as noise, dirt, or insecurity. When free riding is morally wrong, therefore, it seems to have particular properties, reflecting moral condemnations of ingratitude, selfishness or amorality, which may be particularly appropriate to cases of free-riding on cooperative schemes, as these are often difficult to create and maintain.

However, drawing on Garrett Cullity's analysis, Demuijnck suggests that there are three cases where free riding is morally acceptable:

(1) where paying for the benefits generated by a cooperative scheme would leave me worse off than I would be without the scheme. In such cases I am not refusing to pay my fair share for a collective good but, at most, refusing to contribute to a scheme whose costs considerably outweigh any gains I might receive from it;
(2) where a cooperative scheme is so poorly conceived or run that it is unable to generate the collective benefits which would make free-riding immoral. In such cases the refusal to contribute looks more like a refusal to throw one's money away than an unwillingness to do one's fair share to provide a collective good; and
(3) where the collective scheme is immoral in its means, and/or in the ends which it hopes to achieve, since I can hardly be blamed for refusing to contribute to an immoral enterprise, even if it might work in my favour.[57]

So, Demuijnck supposes, it is morally wrong to take a free ride on an institutional scheme designed to cope with the problem of supplying public goods if the scheme is morally irreproachable, one would benefit from the scheme even if one had to contribute to it, and the scheme is sufficiently well conceived and run that it is likely to achieve its morally attractive goals.

[56] David Lametti, 'The virtuous p(eer): Reflections on the ethics of file sharing', Chapter 11 below, hereinafter 'The virtuous p(eer)'.

[57] Demuijnck, 'Illegal downloading'.

What does this mean for the music industry? According to Demuijnck, it means that a lot of unlicensed copying is morally harmless, even if it is illegal, so those who wish to prosecute such unlicensed copying cannot wrap themselves in the mantle of morality in order to justify their behaviour.

In the first place, the popular music market is a 'winner-takes-all market', which means that a lucky few receive rewards that bear no relationship to the costs of their creative efforts, or to the benefits those efforts bring to others. As Demuijnck explains, in a winner-takes-all market, 'reward depends heavily on relative, and not absolute performance. When a farmer is slightly less productive than his neighbour, he will have a slightly smaller income. In the world of music there is no such proportionality. The system of excessive reward creates '"a few big winners and lots of losers who have wasted their time"'.[58] It is not true, then, that everyone benefits from current arrangements for financing popular music, as most musicians make no money from copyright. So unlicensed copying is not the same as free riding on a collectively beneficial scheme, Demuijnck contends, because there is no collectively beneficial scheme which copyright in popular music is currently protecting.

Moreover, Demuijnck argues, because winner-takes-all markets are essentially unfair, we cannot say that copyright is protecting a fair cooperative arrangement – albeit one that fails to benefit everyone. In the case of the music industry that unfairness is particularly marked, as it is copyright itself which makes it the case that the rewards to winners are very large relative to costs and to the benefits conferred, and that these exceptionally large rewards for a few coexist with almost no rewards for most. As Demuijnck notes, the structure of the music industry accentuates the problem, because it is highly concentrated, and the major players own the channels through which content is distributed, as well as the content itself. This makes it economically profitable to mass-market heavily promoted, but otherwise similar products, but very difficult to finance the production either of niche music or of music with a potentially very large market of relatively poor people.[59] These, in the artistic world, are the equivalent of the market failures Jorn Sonderholm describes in the case of orphan drugs and drugs for diseases in poor countries.

Demuijnck concludes that if people only download the music of those who have won in the lottery that is success in the music industry, they

[58] Ibid., p. 270. He is quoting Mark Lemley, 'Property, Intellectual Property and Free Riding' *Texas Law Review* 83 (2005): 1031–75.

[59] Demuijnck, 'Illegal downloading'.

cannot be accused of wrongful free riding on the productive efforts of the artists whose work they use without licence. These artists do not deserve their reward, nor are such extravagant rewards required to motivate artists to produce the works which most people copy for free. If unfairness exists, he thinks, 'it is unfairness with respect to the paying consumers who finance the production' of CDs and other artefacts, rather than unfairness to the big stars whose music is copied illicitly.[60] Finally, he notes that in so far as the people who download CDs illegally are too poor to pay for them, their failure to buy music at the going rate leaves the market for CDs unaffected. So while copyright serves a legitimate purpose, it is wrong to say that all free riding is immoral, although in practice it may be hard – even impossible – to determine which cases of unlicensed copying are morally blameless.

Demuijnck, then, uses economic theory and facts about the structure of the music industry to reach moral conclusions about free riding. His analysis of the morality of free riding, therefore, raises interesting questions about the relationship between economics and political morality on the one hand, and economics and private morality on the other. For example, perhaps one has duties to contribute to public goods, even if their production is inefficient, or their costs are high, if a failure to do so would leave other people even worse off than oneself. Even in cases where one currently has no duty to contribute to the provision of a public good, one might have duties to criticise the failure to provide public goods, to demonstrate one's readiness to pay for them, and to share in the process of determining how best to organise their provision. Demuijnck's chapter, therefore, forces us to consider the difference between public goods and collective goods, and to consider how far it matters to our views on free riding that consumers of music span countries, and even continents, and are often too young to be citizens, with the chance to vote or to stand for election themselves.

Moreover, the differences between Demuijnck and Rosenberg over winner-takes-all competitions raise interesting questions about the

[60] Similarly, in response to efforts to show that non-voters are free riders, and that free riding is so morally wrong that we should make voting legally compulsory, I show that non-voting is often justified and that, even where it is morally wrong, the harms that it causes are not really to fellow citizens who vote, but to those who are affected by the action of our country but are unable to vote because they are not yet born, are too young, or are not citizens. If the appeal of free riding-based arguments for coercion, then, is that they seem to work no matter one's particular values or concerns, their weakness is that they frequently fail to capture our intuitions about morality *precisely because* they avoid any strong assumptions about what is just or of value. See Annabelle Lever, 'Compulsory Voting: A Critical Perspective' *British Journal of Political Science* 40(4) (2010): 897–915, esp. 913–15.

assumptions of fact and value that we bring to moral evaluation. It is possible that Rosenberg accepts the justice and efficacy of the winner-takes-all aspect of patents, as in the distribution of fame in pure science, because the 'losers' are generally well placed to support themselves financially through salaries paid for by companies, research labs or university teaching.[61] By contrast, Demuijnck's hostility to winner-takes-all competitions may reflect the economics of the music and literary industries, in which a great many people struggle to survive on very low wages and on piece-work of various sorts because of the way the industry and copyright combine to structure the economics of the creative professions.

However, it is possible that their contrasting attitudes to winner-takes-all competitions reflect a difference of opinion about the tightness of fit between the financial rewards which IPRs bring and what is necessary to motivate creativity. Rosenberg supposes that, by and large, the patent system would approach the optimum production of good new ideas were it not for piracy and the problem of monopolies. Thus, his working assumption is that the income rights from patents generally reflect the costs of production and the risks of failure. By contrast, Demuijnck clearly supposes that copyright forms part of a system of rewards which provides little or no benefit to most musicians – who will earn most of their music-generated income from live performances – while offering extravagant rewards to a few, though these are generally unnecessary to motivate creative effort. So reflecting on the differences between Demuijnck and Rosenberg leads us to consider whether a tight fit between reward and creative outcome is necessary to the justification of IPRs and, if so, how tight that fit should be.[62]

At first blush, this seems to be an issue only for those who subscribe to instrumental justifications of IPRs. However, deontological approaches face their own version of this question, for what is at issue is the relationship between the income and control rights which make up the IPRs

[61] Rosenberg, 'Designing a successor to the patent', pp. 101–4 on the reward structure of pure science, and pp. 104–9 on prizes.

[62] Of course, the differences could just be explained by the fact that Rosenberg is concerned with patent rights, whereas Demuijnck is concerned with copyright, as Stephen Munzer reminded me. But it is unclear why this difference, in and of itself, should explain why the structure of winner-takes-all competitions should be acceptable in the one case and not the other. It is true that copyright in music does not involve the research costs and trials involved in the production of medicines, but such factors should affect the size of the reward, not how it is distributed. Moreover, public taste is arguably as fickle as the human body is surprising, so success in the music industry seems no more a foregone conclusion than success in pharmacology. The only difference, presumably, is that one does not risk being sued because one's drug had unforeseen side effects, although the flip side of this is that music producers never get an unexpected surge of orders because, surprisingly, their drug turns out to have secondary, patentable, uses that no one foresaw.

package, and what reasons, if any, we have to suppose that the latter implies the former. Clearly, for Drassinower and Biron, the justification for income from one's copyrighted ideas follows if it does, only from one's claims to control the public presentation of ideas which one has authored. But there is nothing in their account of authorship which implies that authors must be able to benefit financially from their ability to license the reproduction or use of their work, or that seems to shed light on the morality of winner-takes-all competitions. So reflection on the disagreement between Demuijnck and Rosenberg highlights the difficulty of justifying the income which IPRs generate, and the way that that income is distributed, whatever one's favoured type of justificatory strategy.

In light of these questions, it is particularly appropriate that our collection closes with David Lametti's reflections on the ethics of file sharing. Lametti believes that any plausible justification of IPRs must make room for the personal dimensions of music, and the private acts of copying, transformation, sharing and communication which reflect its social meaning. In 'The virtuous p(eer): Reflections on the ethics of file sharing', Lametti argues that the norms which should govern copyright must take account of human flourishing, which is not reducible either to the promotion of creativity or to an ethics of public communication. Instead, he argues, we need to reflect on the role of music in people's lives and, in particular, on the way that the sharing of music, and the creation of copies and compendia sustain ethically important relationships, such as friendship, and a sense of one's personal and social identity.

Music has a social dimension, Lametti argues, which gives personal acts of copying an ethical significance that is not well captured either by talk of theft or piracy, or by legal protections for the transformative use of works in public communications. When we make copies and compilations for friends, after all, we are not usually trying to take something without paying, but trying instead to share what we have, and to make it available to others in a form that they will appreciate. In some cases, the effort of making the copy, rather than buying an original, is what gives the present added value, even in cases where the selection of music to be copied, or the order in which it is presented, are no different from those in the original. Hence, Lametti argues, attention to how people use music suggests that copying has an ethics which makes digital 'locks' on music immoral, and precludes the aggressive pursuit of unlicensed copying by the young.[63]

[63] Lametti, 'The virtuous p(eer)'.

That is not to say that anything goes, or that Lametti believes that all acts of unlicensed copying are moral. Rather, he thinks that 'if you are in the habit of sampling music in order to decide what music you will later purchase, that practice is ethically justifiable, as one might have done with a cassette in the past; but, in my view, you have to purchase enough music to justify your sampling. In the same vein, if you are sampling to create, then you have to create and, in turn, be willing to share what you have created to some extent.'[64]

But how should the law accommodate such considerations? And how far should it deliberately enable us to make virtuous choices, at the risk that we might make vicious ones?[65] Such questions about the nature and purposes of law are unavoidable in the philosophy of IP, as in philosophical debates over freedom of expression and association. Resolving them, in so far as they are resolvable, requires us to compare IPRs with other bodies of law which affect our rights in ideas. Lametti's chapter, therefore, underscores the *comparative* nature of the philosophy of IP, already evident in this collection of chapters. If, on the one hand, these comparative aspects can be disheartening – suggesting that many questions in the philosophy of IP lack a definitive answer – on the other, a comparative approach may help us to make progress on some of the philosophical puzzles which now confront us.

Chief amongst these puzzles, we have seen, is the relationship between control and income rights in the typical bundle of IPRs – a puzzle that does not go away just because one replaces instrumental with deontological justifications of rights. However, another puzzle concerns the implications of recognising that ideas are private, as well as public goods – which means that people may stand to gain or lose a great deal depending on precisely how their provision is secured. We have seen that producer, consumer and entrepreneurial interests in ideas are not alike,[66] and that there are fairly significant conflicts of interest within, as well as across, these groups. The justice of IP arrangements depends on how adequately legal institutions recognise and protect these different

[64] Ibid., p. 301.

[65] For contrasting perspectives on this debate, see Jeremy Waldron's 'A Right to do Wrong', ch. 3 of his *Liberal Rights* (Cambridge University Press, 1993) and Gerhard Overland, 'The Right to do Wrong' *Law and Philosophy* 26 (2007): 377–404.

[66] My hunch is that the specific character and weight of entrepreneurial interests, as opposed to producer and consumer interests, deserve more attention than they have received thus far, as they seem to be elided with producer interests in incentive justifications of IP rights, and ignored or elided with consumer interests in deontological justifications. But this is to miss the specificity of the interests of publishers, theatre producers and pharmaceutical companies, as well as the ways in which the interests of different sets of entrepreneurs may conflict.

interests. Hence, the ways that employment contracts link autonomy and income rights may be a fruitful source of comparison for those concerned with the justification of income rights in ideas, while the nature of democratic elections may provide a point of comparison for the treatment of ideas as both public and private goods.

For example, even those who dislike talk of 'self-ownership', or the reduction of labour relations to property relations, are acutely aware of the financial implications of aspects of employment law which seem primarily concerned with autonomy – such as the legal treatment of the 'closed' or 'union' shop, or of rights to picket and strike.[67] So reflection on rights of associational and occupational choice, and the degree to which they are legally alienable, may help to illuminate the financial dimensions of copyright, patents and trade marks for those seeking an alternative to proprietary approaches to them.

Similarly, debates about the best way to organise and finance democratic politics may help to illuminate the dual character of ideas as public and private goods.[68] Democratic elections, after all, are meant to be a public good, although their competitive aspect means that the stakes can be high in any given election and, therefore, in the choice of rules by which winners and losers are defined. Indeed, if democratic elections suggest that 'winner-takes-all' competitions can be part of a solution to collective action problems, the fact that basic rights and liberties are necessarily excluded from democratic competitions highlights the conditions necessary for ideas simultaneously to be a public and private good. At a minimum, freedom of thought and expression and freedom from arbitrary arrest and imprisonment, equal rights to stand for positions of power and responsibility in one's society and adequate access to education seem necessary if access to ideas is not to be the prerogative of an elite, and their use limited to those who are thought 'deserving' or 'trustworthy'. Conversely, the existence of proportional alternatives to 'winner-takes-all' remind us that it is sometimes better to minimise than to increase the differences between

67 Stuart White, 'Trade Unionism in a Liberal State', in Amy Gutmann (ed.), *Freedom of Association* (Princeton University Press, 1998), pp. 330–56; Joshua Cohen and Joel Rogers, *Associations and Democracy* (London: Verso, 1995); Sheldon Leader, *Freedom of Association: A Study in Labour Law and Political Theory* (New Haven, Conn.: Yale University Press, 1992); Charles Beitz on 'paternalistic' justifications for the inalienability of moral rights in 'The Moral Rights of Creators', 352.

68 See for example, Joshua Cohen, *Philosophy, Politics and Democracy* (Cambridge, Mass.: Harvard University Press, 2009); David Donnelly, Joshua Cohen and Joel Rogers *Money and Politics (The New Democracy Forum)* (Boston: Beacon Press, 1999).

winners and losers in socially useful competitions, out of a sense of respect and solidarity, as well as for instrumental reasons.[69] In other words, open acknowledgement of the private and competitive aspects of ideas may make it easier to decide how best to treat them as public goods.[70]

The new frontiers in the philosophy of IP, then, invite us to stray into new and unexpected areas of law, philosophy and social science. If this collection is any guide, that journey will be stimulating and enjoyably disputatious.

[69] For the differences between proportional and consociational electoral systems, see Arend Lijphart, *Thinking About Democracy: Power Sharing and Majority Rule in Theory and Practice* (New York: Routledge, 2007); George Bingham Powell, *Elections as Instruments of Democracy: Majoritarian and Proportional Visions* (New Haven, Conn.: Yale University Press, 2000).

[70] See, for example, the discussion about the economic repercussions of corporatism in Jukka Pekkarinen, Matti Pohjolat and Bob Rowthorn (eds.), *Social Corporatism: A Superior Economic System (Wider Studies in Developmental Economics)* (Oxford: Clarendon Press, 1992) and Cohen and Rogers, *Associations and Democracy*.

1 Autonomy, social selves and intellectual property claims

*John Christman**

Providing a full normative framework for evaluating intellectual property claims, let alone one that attempts to make sense of existing national and international laws, is a daunting task. No such general attempt at doing so will be made here,[1] so my reflections in this chapter are provisional and piecemeal. But my intention is to trace out, in some detail, the meaning and implications of what I view as a powerful normative lens through which to view and evaluate intellectual property (IP) claims – that of individual autonomy.

Clearly, until recently the dominant mode of analysis of IP has been the study of incentives, utilizing as a background framework either broadly utilitarian thinking or more specifically a wealth-maximization standard.[2] However, other commentators have advanced considerations that deviate from these strict instrumentalist justifications, including Lockean (labour-based) arguments, claims based on personality theory and self-expression, connections to democracy and participation and consideration of broader social goals.

One consideration that has received relatively less attention, but which criss-crosses a number of those just mentioned, is the evaluation of IP based on considerations of autonomy. Although hardly unexamined in this literature, attention to the value of autonomy, as I will unpack it here,

* This chapter is a revised version of a talk given as part of the Philosophy and Intellectual Property Workshop, London School of Economics, 29–30 May 2009. I am grateful to the participants for helpful comments and, in particular, Abraham Drassinower and Annabelle Lever.

1 In discussing 'intellectual property' (IP) I am referring mainly to copyright and patent laws (along with licensing and fair-use regulations that come with them), although that category also applies to trade secrets, so-called 'rights of publicity', and trade marks. I will also make mention below of rights to 'geographical indicators' (GI) which is sometimes treated under this rubric.

2 For an overview, see W. Fisher, 'Theories of Intellectual Property', in S. Munzer (ed.), *New Essays in the Legal and Political Theory of Property* (Cambridge University Press, 2001), pp. 168–200; for critical discussion, see, e.g., M. Sunder, 'IP3' *Stanford Law Review* 59(2) (2006): 257–322.

may help tie together some of the core elements of various approaches and may well avoid some of their most glaring difficulties, though, as I will suggest, its power to justify strong IP protection in some areas may be limited.

In order to illuminate this question, I want to focus on cases where indigenous groups attempt to claim IP protection for various home-grown arts and technologies, generally grouped under the term 'traditional knowledge'. Specifically, I want to examine the claim that the autonomy of the group members is in peril unless IP protections are afforded. I will conclude by suggesting that considerations of autonomy alone, no matter how powerful in capturing the normative core of other arguments and approaches, provide relatively weak support for most clusters of rights and privileges allowed under many IP provisions, both nationally and internationally.

I will only sketch the argument for this last point. My procedure here will be to examine the key concepts involved: first, 'autonomy' where I will suggest a straightforward understanding of that idea which ties it to values central to many arguments about property. In this section I will also discuss the value of autonomy, as I understand it, and propose a close connection between valuing autonomy and supporting democratic procedures; I will next spell out how the protection and promotion of autonomy for individuals is nevertheless consistent with seeing *selves* – the 'self' of self-government – as fundamentally *social*, and in this way attention to individual autonomy can motivate our focus on the survival and integrity of cultural forms of particular sorts. This point will connect with claims made by some groups for IP protections concerning intellectual products and traditional knowledge that are claimed to be central to cultural identity. In order to help build a connection between the value of autonomy and IP claims, it will be necessary to unpack the components of ownership in order to make as clear as possible the general links between property ownership in general and the protection of autonomy. I do this in Section III. I will then return, in closing, to arguments defending IP claims by culturally defined groups based on the value of autonomy; in that discussion, I hope to show how considerations of autonomy might illuminate discussion of IP in some sectors, but would provide less support than some have alleged for IP claims as they are traditionally conceptualized.

I. Autonomy and autonomy-related interests

The conception of the autonomous person plays a variety of roles in various constructions of liberal political theory. Principally, it serves as the model of the person whose perspective is used to formulate and justify political principles, as in social contract models of principles of justice. Also (and correspondingly) it serves as the model of the *citizen* whose basic interests are reflected in those principles, such as in the claim that basic liberties, opportunities and other primary goods are fundamental to flourishing lives, no matter what moral commitments, life plans, or other particulars of the person might obtain.[3] It underwrites the fundamental interests of the participants in democratic regimes that secure the basic rights of such participation and, as I will discuss below, helps establish the validity of the outcomes of those deliberations.

That is to say, one of the cornerstones of liberal democratic theory is the fundamental value placed on individuals' capacities to be self-governing, to be free in the sense of being both independent of coercion and manipulation, as well as having the ability to follow a conception of the good which is 'self-authenticating', that reflects a person's ability to fashion or accept a framework of value that is truly her own.[4] However, while phrases such as 'self-determination' and 'individual sovereignty' are used as synonyms, nothing in the idea of autonomy as I will understand it here carries the implication that people create themselves or their values out of whole cloth (or even are always able to alter them or choose other than what they direct), nor does it imply that such individual capacities are exercised individually or in the service only of rational self-interest.

I will discuss this last point shortly. For now, let us understand 'autonomy' as self-government, specifically as the individual capacity to reflectively accept the fundamental value framework that guides one's life. In this way, autonomy can be seen as roughly equivalent to what Rawls calls 'rational autonomy' of the sort assumed in (political) liberalism, specifically the moral power of having the capacity to form and revise a conception of the good.[5] As I will discuss presently, a more detailed conception of autonomy would include reference to an ability to reflectively accept such a conception in light of one's history and social surroundings, though not all who use this term mention this connection.

[3] See W. Kymlicka, *Liberalism, Community and Culture* (Oxford University Press, 1989), pp. 10–19, and J. Waldron, *The Right to Private Property* (Oxford University Press, 1993), pp. 155–6. Although he does not couch his conception of liberalism in terms of autonomy, Dworkin's view can be understood as in this category: see R. Dworkin, *Sovereign Virtue: The Theory and Practice of Equality* (Cambridge, Mass.: Harvard University Press, 2000), pp. 237–84.

[4] The phrase 'self-authenticating' comes from Rawls (see J. Rawls, *Justice as Fairness: A Restatement* (Cambridge, Mass.: Belknap Press, 2001), p. 23.

[5] See J. Rawls, *Political Liberalism* (New York: Columbia University Press, 1993), pp. 72–81. What Rawls calls 'rational autonomy', however, is what is assumed about representatives in the original position, and it is contrasted with 'full autonomy' of citizens of a well-ordered society governed by principles of justice.

It sometimes makes some sense to ask about the autonomy of particular aspects of the person – what is usually called 'local' autonomy. Indeed, many ways of characterizing that trait make it readily applicable to specific factors.[6] But often it will not be possible to determine whether conditions defining autonomy are met for particular choices, or it will not be important to measure whether specific ranges of acts are autonomous separately from the agent in her entirety. For if we view autonomy as the status marker for entrance into collective deliberations in general, and the interests of gaining, maintaining and exercising autonomy as the interests represented in designing procedures for such processes, then it will be the autonomy of the person as such that is at issue.

So what matters for the social role that autonomy plays in the contexts just outlined is that the person is autonomous relative to her basic, orienting values and motivations, factors that pervasively and fundamentally motivate and guide action. The fundamental structure of normative commitments and patterns of judgment must be 'one's own' in order for the person to be autonomous in the sense that matters here. This refers to those commitments and frameworks of judgment that ground a broad range of decisions, tastes and actions for the agent. So while autonomy in the sense being considered here is, in a way, local, it relates to those basic elements of our personality that are the most pervasive in guiding our deliberation, choices and actions over time. It will therefore not be untoward to call a *person* heteronomous when she lacks autonomy relative to her basic value orientation.

Attention is given to personal history in this model in ways not often emphasized in discussions of the concept.[7] I cannot say much to defend that element here, though it rests on a conception of the self that sees both memory and considerations of one's past (as well as reference to the future) as crucial to one's practical identity. Models of the self that are meant to function in political principles must make room for the way in

[6] For discussion, see G. Dworkin, *The Theory and Practice of Autonomy* (Cambridge University Press, 1990), pp. 13–17. Diana Meyers discusses a similar point under the guise of 'episodic' versus 'programmatic' autonomy. See D. Meyers, *Self, Society and Personal Choice* (New York: Columbia University Press, 1990), pp. 48–9. For a view similar to the position I take in the text, see M. Friedman, *Autonomy, Gender, Politics* (Oxford University Press, 2003), ch. 1. For a general discussion of the concept of autonomy, see J. Christman, 'Autonomy in Moral and Political Philosophy', in E. Zalta (ed.), *The Stanford Encyclopedia of Philosophy* (http://plato.stanford.edu/contents.html).

[7] My own version of the historical approach is worked out in J. Christman, *The Politics of Persons: Individual Autonomy and Socio-historical Selves* (Cambridge University Press, 2009); others who take an historical approach include A. R. Mele, *Autonomous Agents: From Self-control to Autonomy* (New York: Oxford University Press, 1995) and J. M. Fischer and M. Ravizza, *Responsibility and Control: A Theory of Moral Responsibility* (New York: Cambridge University Press, 1998).

which the diachronic nature of agency figures centrally in the meaning and import of our practical identities. Being committed to certain cultural values, for example, cannot be understood without seeing that commitment as tied to an understanding of the history of that culture, or at least to *one's own* understanding of that history. Such considerations relate also to religious values, as well as personal commitments and relations.

What I claim, then, is that autonomy as I conceive it involves the capacity to reflectively accept one's fundamental value commitments as part of a temporally extended personal narrative in light of one's social and material conditions. This last phrase – 'in light of one's social and material conditions' – refers to the fact that while autonomy is often contrasted with negative conceptions of freedom, and so involves internal capacities to think and judge rather than merely opportunities to *act*, one can nevertheless lose one's autonomy because of ongoing social conditions that prevent the full acceptance of one's value commitments. In fact, some theorists have argued that autonomy should contain specific *social* or *relational* conditions which pick out this requirement. My claim here, in contrast, is not that particular social relations are conceptually required for autonomy to obtain, but that insofar as individual persons define themselves and their projects in social terms, then certain social conditions will *contingently* be needed for autonomy to develop and be maintained. I return to this issue below.[8]

Autonomy-related *interests*, then, range over those conditions that allow for the development and maintenance of autonomy so conceived. Of course, basic necessities such as health, housing, education and so on will be required for the normal development of autonomy.[9] Interests connected with the ability to reflect upon and judge one's values and alternatives to them will be similarly underwritten. Some theorists add that a minimal array of valuable *options* are required for autonomy as well, so that one has choices of life plans against which one can embrace a plan as one's own. I agree with this view, but I reject the implication in some views that an array of open options can be objectively determined theoretically, rather than simply be a function of what will be needed by an individual, given her other values and commitments.[10]

[8] For discussion, see M. Oshana, *Personal Autonomy in Society* (Aldershot: Ashgate Publishing Ltd., 2006) and Christman, *The Politics of Persons*, ch. 7.

[9] These interests can be mapped onto Amartya Sen's conception of basic capabilities, in particular those connected with what he calls agency freedom. See A. Sen, *Inequality Reexamined* (Cambridge University Press, 1992).

[10] Raz's view appears to have this implication (see J. Raz, *The Morality of Freedom* (Oxford University Press, 1986), pp. 373–8), though he denies it (ibid., 410–11). See also Oshana, *Personal Autonomy*, pp. 84–6.

That is not to say, of course, that in order to be autonomous one must be *successful* in carrying out the life narrative directed by one's core values. Rather, one loses one's autonomy when sustained alienation from the conditions of one's life over a continuous period, given one's fundamental value commitments, is experienced. When the social and material conditions of one's existence are such that one is not seen as a self-authenticating source of valid claims (to repeat Rawls' phrase), then one's autonomy is denied.

This is also not to say that autonomy-based claims to any particular rights are absolute, or even generally overriding. Many life pursuits inherently involve harm or risk, and so restriction or prohibition may well be justified, even if restrictions on autonomy are involved.[11] Restrictions or prohibitions that make basic autonomy impossible, or which severely restrict the range of autonomous judgment and choice, should have to meet a high bar of justificatory scrutiny; for when basic autonomy is impossible for an agent or agents, they will not enjoy the status of equal participant (actually or potentially) in democratic structures. But this is also to say that respect for individual autonomy is not, by itself, definitive of basic justice; principles such as equality of status (or equal concern and respect) will also be fundamental in liberal democratic regimes.[12] But if oppressive social conditions systematically denigrate or suppress any expression of values by which a person defines herself and practical identity, then autonomy is being denied.

In order to see further how legal rules might facilitate or restrict the enjoyment of autonomy so conceived, including autonomy vis-à-vis membership in cultural groups, we must say more about the factors that explain the value of autonomy.

The value of autonomy

Some theorists see autonomy or freedom as a universal value applicable across cultural lines, an objectively determined ideal that grounds liberal theory. Writers such as Kymlicka and Raz, among others, have been read this way.[13]

[11] At this point it becomes obvious that the conception of autonomy at work here is one that attempts to be 'value neutral', in that it does not require, as part of its defining conditions, that one's basic value commitments be morally acceptable. For discussion of this issue, see Christman, *The Politics of Persons*, ch. 1.

[12] Rawls, for example, lists a sense of justice as the second moral power assumed in the model of the citizen living under liberal principles. See Rawls, *Justice as Fairness*.

[13] Though Kymlicka talks more of 'freedom' than autonomy, it is clear he refers to the concept we are discussing here – see Kymlicka, *Liberalism, Community and Culture*. Cf. also D. A. J. Richards, 'Rights and Autonomy' in J. Christman (ed.), *The Inner Citadel: Essays on Individual Autonomy* (New York: Oxford University Press, 1989), pp. 203–33.

Many see the basic capabilities associated with autonomy as universally required for a decent life, along with other basic needs.[14]

Now many have baulked at the idea that autonomy, as it is conceived in the context of liberal democratic theory, is a value across cultural horizons.[15] An alternative approach, however, is to hold at bay the question of whether self-government, so conceived, is valuable for all persons in all cultures (or, to put it differently, an essential constituent in any flourishing life),[16] and to claim that autonomy must be posited as a *political* value for regimes of a particular type, namely, liberal democracies. That is, autonomy of citizens is claimed to be a fundamental value commitment in democratic structures and inherits the overall value that those structures represent.[17]

The view of democratic justice I envision here, then, rests on an argumentative structure along the following lines: selves are, in variable ways that will be discussed below, socially constituted; this means that values are defined in terms of interaction with others, that our abilities to pursue valued ends are both defined and constrained by the social dynamics in which we engage in those pursuits. Political structures and other institutions of power shape and codify those dynamics in broad and robust ways. That power is justified only if it can be seen as harmonizing with our own judgments, our perspectives about what is valuable to pursue given the fact that we live among people with contrasting values and who (like us) are products of the contingencies of history, both their own and society's.[18] The legitimacy of these social processes must rest, then, on the way they are controlled and produced, and only if citizens' perspectives and interests are properly represented in those processes will that legitimacy be attained.[19]

So only if the principles that guide and shape (and justify) those power structures that shape our social existence rest on the value of autonomous

[14] See M. Nussbaum, *Women and Human Development: The Capabilities Approach* (Cambridge University Press, 2001), pp. 4–14.

[15] See, e.g., C. Larmore, *The Morals of Modernity* (New York: Cambridge University Press, 1996) and J. Gray, *Post-Liberalism: Studies in Political Thought* (London: Routledge, 1993).

[16] For discussion, see L. Haworth, *Autonomy* (New Haven, Conn.: Yale University Press, 1986).

[17] This approach to the value of autonomy is defended in Christman, *The Politics of Persons*, ch. 10.

[18] This claim can be understood to be supported by Rawls' observations about what he called 'the burdens of judgment'. See Rawls, *Political Liberalism*, pp. 54–8. This overview of an argument connecting autonomy with collective decision making and social determination of value is inspired by Rousseau, but finds contemporary resonance in work by Joshua Cohen (see 'Procedure and Substance in Deliberative Democracy', in S. Benhabib (ed.), *Democracy and Difference* (Princeton University Press, 1996), pp. 95–119).

[19] For discussion of the terms of legitimacy in this context, see Rawls, *Political Liberalism*, Lecture IV, and J. Habermas, *Between Facts and Norms* (Cambridge, Mass.: MIT Press, 1996).

citizens will they gain the legitimacy that just institutions require. For these reasons, people's autonomy should be promoted and protected in the operations of legitimate democratic institutions.

This kind of protection then, will require a mode of collective deliberation that allows citizen input into the processes that yield social conditions that shape those citizens' prospects. Even if actual participation and deliberation are not required, practices of these institutions must include elements that effectively represent those citizens' interests and judgments and, as an extension of this, the power to object when policies conflict with their deepest self-understandings. Democratic deliberation, then, also requires participants' abilities reflectively to endorse, indeed publicly defend, the points of view, values, interests and opinions that are the inputs to such deliberative processes (the 'outputs' of which are social principles and policies). This provides further reason for the presupposition that the autonomous person is able reflectively to grasp and present her values and perspective. This accords them the kind of representational authority over those points of view, but also necessitates their capacity to reflect on their values as part of the dynamic of social interchange that produces collectively justified principles. So autonomy as competent, reflective self-acceptance is central to this understanding of justice and politics.

Such an approach to the value of autonomy is clearly posited against the backdrop of a closed and singular political regime. Below I will discuss its applicability in global, transnational contexts (in which discussions of the kinds of IP in question here take place). For now, I merely lay out the foundation for the value of autonomy as a presupposition in the collective determination of the values and opportunities of social life, a determination which, in stable democracies, is or ought to be governed by formal systems of popular sovereignty.[20]

In general, then, the value of autonomy can be acknowledged as a cornerstone of basic rights and freedoms fundamental to the dignity and respect we owe to each other, either on the scale of human rights (and so carrying a universalist cast) or rights and freedoms operative in democratic structures. Although the value of autonomy as described here relies on its connection to democratic practices, there need not be a functioning democracy in a particular locale for autonomy to have value; autonomy is valuable as a necessary prerequisite for democratic institutions, whether they are currently operating or merely possible in the future.

[20] For a discussion of how IP rules can contribute directly to democratic practices, see N. W. Netanel, 'Copyright and a Democratic Civil Society' *Yale Law Journal* 106 (1996): 283–387.

However, to build connections between autonomy considerations, so conceived, and questions of what rights protections should be afforded for groups and communities of the sort we will discuss relative to IP, we must look further at the nature of the 'self' at work in the model of autonomy and self-government.

II. Individual autonomy and the social self

In traditional liberal theory, autonomy has been seen as a value for individuals *as such*, in that it has been understood to be important for the person in developing and exercising her conception of value apart from social ties and any particular communal membership. This implication, however, is now famously rejected by both critics and defenders of liberal theory, and approaches to autonomy have been expanded to take into account the communal and social nature of many value endeavours and practical identities.[21]

Of course, seeing autonomy as an individual capacity – and hence seeing the rights and protections required by it as attaching to individuals – is perfectly compatible with acknowledging that agents themselves must be seen as *socially constituted*. In fact, I will argue below that support for certain social structures and relations will be necessary to support autonomy in ways that have implications for property law, but that will be based on the contingent claim that such relations are necessary for certain *selves* to maintain their own autonomy, *as individuals*. In order to see this, we must look more closely at the idea that the 'self' of self-government is fundamentally relational in its identifying conditions.[22]

As I mentioned, the 'self' in this discussion represents the model of the person whose perspective serves as the ground for legitimacy of political institutions under the broad assumptions of popular sovereignty, and whose projected interests determine the general content of social good that provides the *telos* for the principles that guide such institutions (for

[21] For the claim that standard liberal conceptions of justice detach the autonomous person from communal ties, see M. Sandel, *Liberalism and the Limits of Justice* (Cambridge University Press, 1982). For a response, see Kymlicka, *Liberalism, Community and Culture*; cf. also C. Taylor, *The Ethics of Authenticity* (Cambridge, Mass.: Harvard University Press, 1991).

[22] For overviews of these issues, see L. Barclay, 'Autonomy and the Social Self', in C. Mackenzie and N. Stoljar (eds.), *Relational Autonomy: Feminist Perspectives on Autonomy, Agency and the Social Self* (New York: Oxford University Press, 2000), pp. 52–71; G. Sher, 'Three Grades of Social Involvement' *Philosophy and Public Affairs* 18(2) (1989): 133–57; D. B. Wong, 'On Flourishing and Finding One's Identity in Community' *Midwest Studies in Philosophy Volume XIII. Ethical Theory: Character and Virtue* 13(1) (1988): 324–41; and J. Crittenden, *Beyond Individualism: Reconstituting the Liberal Self* (New York: Oxford University Press, 1992).

example, as in a constitution). To say that such a self is 'socially constituted' is to refer to ways in which relations to other persons, traditions, institutions, practices and so on are an ineliminable part of the defining conditions of such a subject.[23] In some cases, models of the social self have been developed by way of a philosophy of language, according to which the discursive structure of thought generally, and self-conception in particular, is both the product of and shaped by past and present social relations. This approach has been expressed recently by Charles Taylor:

> The general feature of human life that I want to evoke is its fundamentally *dialogical* character. We become full human agents, capable of understanding ourselves, and hence of defining an identity through our acquisition of rich human languages of expression. [This is to] take 'language' in the broad sense, covering not only the words we speak but also other modes of expression whereby we define ourselves, including the 'languages' of art, of gesture, of love, and the like. But we are inducted into these exchanges with others. No one acquires the languages needed for self-definition on their own. We are introduced to them through exchanges with others who matter to us – what George Herbert Mead called 'significant others'.[24]

The social element here is clear, though the dynamic by which the language of the self is internalized can vary, and need not mirror the naturalistic social psychology of Mead. Dynamics of recognition, the structure of communication, the dialectics of self-realization, all describe alternative understandings of *how* socially structured meanings become constructive elements of the self-concept.[25]

An important issue in such models of the self concerns the level of *generality* at which the elements of the self – the social elements that are claimed to be internalized in our self-conceptions – are seen to operate. For example, Taylor refers to 'languages' in a broad sense of including natural languages like French or English, but also larger semiotic matrices, including artistic, cultural and habitual conveyors of meaning. What matters here is whether those systems of meaning referred to are so broad that there is no conceivable standpoint outside of them (for example, language of any sort *per se*), or a more specific, organized system which interacts with competing matrices in cultural encounters, carrying with it specific value perspectives.

[23] See C. Taylor, *Hegel and Modern Society* (Cambridge University Press, 1979), p. 157; for discussion of this issue, see Kymlicka, *Liberalism, Community and Culture*, p. 51.

[24] Taylor, *The Ethics of Authenticity*, pp. 32–3, emphasis in original.

[25] These alternative views are reflected in the work of A. Honneth, *The Struggle for Recognition: The Moral Grammar of Social Conflicts* (Cambridge, Mass.: MIT Press, 1996), Habermas, *Between Facts and Norms*, and W. F. Hegel, *The Phenomenology of Spirit* (trans. A. V. Miller) (Oxford University Press, 1977) respectively. And, of course, there is overlap among them as well.

Also, models of the social self that refer to the internalization of symbolic forms such as languages, allow for the possibility that the meanings attached to the components of those forms are subject to public determination and revision. Insofar as linguistic elements are internalized to form a social self-concept, as these models imply, and linguistic systems bear meaning as a function of public consideration (patterns of speech acts, official dictionaries, public discussion of meaning and connotation), then social selves will be constituted by revisable and publicly discussed elements.

In seeing the languages that constitute our self-concepts as more than merely natural languages but the broad array of semiotic expressions of meaning, we can note the close connection between such a 'dialogic' conception of the self and cultural practices, symbols and rituals. Self-understanding, on this view, establishes itself in terms defined by value systems that, in turn, gain their meaning by way of shared practices, memory, tradition and horizons of value. Cultural forms in particular, in most cases, will be the prominent mode by which such symbol systems find their meaning.[26]

We must also keep in mind synchronic versus diachronic contrasts here. Clearly, it is one thing to point out how relations with significant others, mediated by language, causally produce (adult) selves, but it is quite another to say that we, here and now, are who we are (essentially) by virtue of current and ongoing external relations. This latter point is the crucial one, because it raises another (and indeed, also separate) question about what, and how, social structures must be maintained, in order for selves to continue to exist, act, flourish, and so on. Language is a clear and much-discussed example, where having significant numbers of co-speakers of a language is essential to a person's maintaining her identity and sense of herself.[27]

A fuller survey of the varieties of the social-self thesis would include other dimensions along which this social structuring takes place. Some examples include: what object-relations theory tells us about subconscious

[26] For an anthropological analysis of this issue, see D. Holland *et al.*, *Identity and Agency in Cultural Worlds* (Cambridge, Mass.: Harvard University Press, 1998), ch. 8.

[27] It bears mentioning that approaches to the social constitution of the self often downplay the body as a site of interpersonal self-structure. Many have argued, in fact, that conceptions of self and autonomy, especially those arising from the Cartesian tradition of locating the essence of the self in the thinking 'I', have systematically downplayed our embodied identities and the ways that bodily comportment, expression and identity ground the self as much as, if not more than, our cognitive and reflective functioning. See, e.g., D. Meyers, 'Decentering Autonomy: Five Faces of Selfhood', in J. Christman and J. Anderson (eds.), *Autonomy and the Challenges to Liberalism: New Essays* (Cambridge University Press, 2005), pp. 27–55. This, of course, echoes concerns by feminists and other theorists who emphasize bodily identity in conceptualizing the subject. See, e.g., J. Butler, *Gender Trouble: Feminism and the Subversion of Identity* (New York: Routledge, 1990).

internalization of the source of care in processes of psychological self-development; the way that emotions reflect both interpersonal relations of care and vulnerability, as well as publicly structured expectations; the manner in which values and commitments that define the self depend on social meanings, roles, traditions and other structures; and so on. It should be clear, though, how this understanding of the social self relates to the model of autonomy set out above. Insofar as social practices, rituals, public expressions and shared beliefs are constitutively related to the person's conception of herself, then to be self-governing is for those practices, etc., to be allowed to flourish (or at least survive). A person lacks autonomy if she is unable reflectively to accept her core value orientation in the midst of social conditions that do not reflect its meaningfulness, or at least social conditions that allow for the acknowledgement of the value it has for her.[28]

We will return to this idea when discussing IP claims for cultural groups. To set the stage for such a discussion, however, it will be necessary to make clear the nature of property claims in general and their relation to autonomy interests in particular, a task to which we turn next.

III. Autonomy and the complexity of ownership

It will not be necessary to reiterate the ways that any property claim includes some subset of the standard Hohfeldian bundle of rights, liberties, powers, and so on, associated with what has been called 'full liberal ownership'.[29] Such incidents include rights to use, possess, manage, alienate and rights to income from transfers. IP rules, of course, include limited monopoly rights to use, alienate, sell the idea or expression

[28] A poignant case of such a loss can be seen in a recent study by Jonathan Lear, who discusses the case of the last great chief of the Crow Indian tribe in the United States, one Plenty Coups, who said of the (by then past) way of life of his tribe: 'when the buffalo went away the hearts of my people fell to the ground ... After this nothing happened.' Lear interprets this as expressing a complete loss of moral orientation, a loss of meaningfulness in the core terms of evaluation and value in Plenty Coups' practical identity, so that his sense of history and progress came to an end ('After this nothing happened') (J. Lear, *Radical Hope: Ethics in the Face of Cultural Devastation* (Cambridge, Mass.: Harvard University Press, 2006). What the story implies is that when social practices central to one's sense of moral value, and the ritualistic, religious and cultural expressions of the values inherent in those practices have been eradicated, then one cannot, as an individual, continue to find and follow a conception of the good as one's own. Protecting a collective sense of shared value and social practice, then, will often be required for the ongoing enjoyment of individual autonomy for members of such social groups.

[29] For analysis, see A. M. A. Honoré, 'Ownership', in A. Guest (ed.), *Oxford Essays in Jurisprudence* (Oxford: Clarendon Press, 1961), pp. 107–47; L. Becker, *Property Rights: Philosophical Foundations* (New York: Routledge, 1981); Waldron, *The Right to Private Property*; S. Munzer, *A Theory of Property* (Cambridge University Press, 1990); and Christman, *The Myth of Property*.

(or trade mark, etc.) in question. In all such cases, there is a variable array of legal rights, liberties, powers, liabilities and immunities that attach to ownership claims.

In earlier work I analysed the concept of ownership in terms of the interests the different elements of the typical property rights package tend to protect.[30] I suggested that some rights in the cluster that typically defines ownership are particularly closely tied to the ability of persons to guide their lives in predictable ways and to maintain levels of control and reasonable expectations needed to make plans, pursue values and independently coordinate with others (associated with what I labelled 'autonomy interests'). Rights to possess, use, modify, alienate and destroy one's holdings cluster together to express an owner's ability to manage her life independently, the value of which, I claimed, connects directly to individual autonomy. I called such rights *control rights*.

On the other hand, the rights to transfer and retain goods received in that transfer, at rates set by the voluntary actions of the traders given constraints of the market, I labelled *income rights*. I claimed that such rights are not directly tied to one's autonomy except instrumentally, in that income simply allows one further choice about future use and purchases. But the interests in question are strictly competitive, in that for any given flow of income, one's interest is the same as any other person's, for income generally is in the form of currency or capital. This is not to say that interests in income are negligible or should be ignored, but only that there is no autonomy-related interest to any *particular* bit of income more than any other. Subject to diminishing marginal returns, one simply has an interest in more of it, rather than less.

Of course, distinguishing control rights from income rights will be difficult in many cases and for many aspects of ownership: for example, managing a property (as with real estate) will involve both control and income interests. The fundamental claim being defended here is that in the bundle of rights, liberties, powers, liabilities, and so on, associated with ownership in various social settings, some elements tend much more closely and directly to enable the person to exercise autonomy and self-direction than others. The latter include rights to transfer and receive income from trades subject to surrounding regulation, market conditions and a variety of other factors. These rights protect general welfare interests

[30] Ibid., Part III; for development and clarification of this view, see J. Christman, 'Distributive Justice and the Complex Structure of Ownership' *Philosophy and Public Affairs* 23(3) (1994): 225–50. Criticisms of it can be found in D. Attas, 'Fragmenting Property' *Law and Philosophy* 25 (2006): 119–49.

that at best instrumentally promote autonomy, but only insofar as they increase holdings overall.

Control rights, by contrast, connect the person or persons to *particular* goods, space and resources.[31] The possession and exercise of such rights have been shown to have psychological effects tied to senses of self-efficacy, self-definition and self-expression. In addition to affording persons control over their environment and hence enabling them to coordinate plans and pursue goals, control rights over certain kinds of goods also can serve an expressive and symbolic function for persons. Some social psychological research has attempted to establish a systematic connection between possession and one's sense of self.[32] Others have argued that certain kinds of possessions express and constitute a person's concept of herself, her memories and her values, while other sorts of goods are purely fungible and are valued solely for their market value. As Margaret Jane Radin has put this point: this 'perspective generates a hierarchy of entitlements: The more closely connected with personhood, the stronger the entitlement.'[33]

While Radin makes this distinction in terms of different kinds of things one can own, here I am stressing the different interests protected by separate clusters of property rights for any particular object of ownership.[34] What I am suggesting is that the control rights one enjoys over goods, especially certain types of goods that are closely connected to the exercise and enjoyment of one's basic values, tends to correlate strongly with interests in self-definition, self-control and the other conditions central to the idea of autonomy. We can put the idea this way: when it comes to controlling an asset, it will often make sense to claim 'I need to control this asset to maintain my autonomy', while it will not make sense to claim 'I need income from *this* asset to maintain my autonomy.' In the latter case, one may well need income *per se*, although not from any

[31] It should be noted that one has control rights over one's money, though the interests protected in that case are also purely instrumental in the way just described (except for coin collectors).

[32] See, e.g., L. Furby, 'Understanding the Psychology of Possession and Ownership: A Personal Memoir and an Appraisal of our Progress', in F.W. Rudmin (ed.), *To Have Possessions: A Handbook on Ownership and Property*, Special Issue, *Journal of Social Behavior and Personality* 6(6) (1991): 457–69. It should be noted that this relation is not unwavering, and indeed may vary with such things as gender and age: see H. Dittmar, 'Meanings of Material Possessions as Reflections of Identity: Gender and Social-Material Position in Society' in Rudmin (ed.), *To Have Possessions* 165–86.

[33] M. J. Radin, 'Property and Personhood' *Stanford Law Review* 34(5) (1982): 957–1015, at 986, and Radin, *Reinterpreting Property* (University of Chicago Press, 1993).

[34] For discussion of Radin's views, see Munzer, *A Theory of Property*, and 'The Special Case of Property Rights in Umbilical Cord Blood for Transplantation' *Rutgers Law Review* 51 (1999): 493–568.

particular holding, but in many cases controlling a particular good or asset will be crucial for developing and/or maintaining autonomy.

The upshot of this analysis is, generally, to shift the burden of justification for income rights – which in large part involves setting policy concerning market regulations, taxation, wage and price controls, and so on – to questions concerning overall consequences and distributive effects. I make no defence of any particular approach to those issues, except to say that concern for autonomy does not reach them, except indirectly, by way of ownership claims. We will see that this has interesting implications for the evaluation of IP claims in some cases, a topic to which we should now turn.

IV. Autonomy and IP

Understanding IP claims through the lens of the value of autonomy cuts across two traditional approaches to the justification of IP: Lockean natural rights arguments and Hegelian claims based on positive freedom and self-expression.[35] The connection between Lockean rights and autonomy may not be so obvious, and I can only gesture at it here, but it rests in the view that what makes the particular rights typically listed in natural rights views *cohere* is that they are needed to protect the individual integrity of the person and her ability to lead an independent and worthwhile life. Nozick puts the point this way: in answering the question of why the particular view of rights as absolute side constraints he favours should be adopted, he answers:

> I conjecture that the answer is connected with that elusive and difficult notion: the meaning of life. A person's shaping his life in accordance with some overall plan is his way of giving meaning to his life; only a being with a capacity to so shape his life can have or strive for meaningful life.[36]

This capacity to shape a life in accordance with an overall plan is strikingly similar to the idea of autonomy I describe here, though there is no requirement in my view that the acceptance of one's basic value commitments

[35] For an overview of approaches to IP, see W. Fisher, 'Theories of Intellectual Property', in Munzer (ed.), *New Essays*, pp. 168–200; discussion of Lockean justifications for property generally can be found in Munzer, *A Theory of Property*; Becker, *Property Rights*; Christman, *The Myth of Property*, ch. 3; and Waldron, *The Right to Private Property*. For critical discussions of Lockean approaches to IP, see W. Gordon, 'An Inquiry into the Merits of Copyright: The Challenges of Consistency, Consent and Encouragement Theory' *Stanford Law Review* 41 (1989): 1343–69, D. Attas, 'Lockean Justifications of Intellectual Property', in Gosseries *et al.* (eds), *Intellectual Property and Theories of Justice* (New York and Basingstoke: Palgrave Macmillan, 2008), pp. 29–56, and S. V. Shiffrin, 'Lockean Arguments for Private Intellectual Property' in Munzer (ed.), *New Essays*, pp. 138–67.

[36] R. Nozick, *Anarchy, State, and Utopia* (New York: Basic Books, 1974), p. 50.

underwrite an 'overall *plan*' or that they are seen by the person as shaped *by her*: they may merely be accepted gladly as objectively right, or given by God, or the like.

In a Hegelian register, theorists have argued that the fundamental interest we have in making our will effective in the world involves the expansion of our subjectivity to encompass what is external to us, the ability to make objects our own in a manner guided by reason. The relation between Hegel's notion of *Geist* (positive freedom) and autonomy will have to remain impressionistic here, but I think it can safely be suggested that the capacity reflectively to accept one's value framework as a guide to one's choices and judgments – one's movement through the world – is a very close cousin of Hegelian freedom.[37]

In both cases, it is relevant to ask how the interests connected with individual autonomy could be used to evaluate certain IP rules. The question becomes, then, are IP rights required for persons to continue reflectively to accept the fundamental values that guide their lives without alienation, given the social condition in which those values are pursued?

One clear manner in which claims such as copyright protection and other forms of IP might be necessary to guard autonomy interests are when monopoly rights over use and dissemination are necessary to protect the author's or artist's *identification with the product* when, in turn, such identification is central to the value of the creative enterprise for the author.[38] Often when the life project and guiding values of a person's life are intertwined with certain forms of expression – Picasso's paintings, Wagner's operas, Joni Mitchell's music – simple requirements of source acknowledgement may not be enough. Unless the artist maintains control over the form of expression, the person's life-work ceases to have the form he or she invested in it.

[37] The difference, of course, lies in the relative formality or social specificity in the principles one adopts for oneself (marking the line between Kantian and Hegelian approaches to self-government, respectively). See Waldron, *The Right to Private Property*. For discussion of the general notion of positive freedom, see, e.g., Christman, 'Saving Positive Freedom' *Political Theory* 33(1) (2005): 79–88.

[38] As Rubenfeld puts it regarding free expression, 'art is protected because it is the apogee of self-expression and self-determination. Expressing oneself in "writing, pictures and music" can be central to "a mature person's" "autonomous self-determination."' (J. Rubenfeld, 'The Freedom of Imagination: Copyright's Constitutionality' *Yale Law Journal* 112 (2002): 3–60, at 33–4, quoting David A. J. Richards, 'Free Speech and Obscenity Law: Toward a Moral Theory of the First Amendment' *University of Pennsylvania Law Review* 123 (1974) 45, at 62.) For further discussion of the connection between IP and communication, see A. Drassinower, 'Authorship as Public Address: On the Specificity of Copyright vis-à-vis Patent and Trade-Mark' *Michigan State Law Review* 1 (2008): 199–233.

I will not pursue avenues of this sort here. Rather, I will now turn to arguments for IP that are parallel to these considerations, namely, ones that locate the autonomy interests that motivate calls for such legal claims in the cultural practices of communities.

IP claims for cultural products

In order to give some further flesh to the normative skeleton sketched here linking autonomy interests with IP claims, I will now consider one attempt to follow this very path, concerning indigenous groups' claims to IP over traditional knowledge and artistry. In this way, we can see in broad terms both the promise and the limitations of such normative strategies.

The phenomenon of expropriation of locally developed technological and artistic knowledge is both widespread and controversial. Indigenous communities in particular have often been the target of such allegedly exploitative extraction of intellectual and artistic products, from plant strains used by pharmaceutical companies, to musical and artistic forms, to DNA sequences.[39] For example, Tsosie discusses claims by Native American groups to use legal remedies to control the use and dissemination of traditional tribal symbols, rituals, artefacts and stories. As she points out, 'amendments to the Indian Arts and Crafts Act attempt to prevent non-Indians [in the US] from marketing copies of Native art forms (such as Navajo rugs or 'squash blossom' necklaces) as "Indian art".'[40]

A variety of harms can be delineated that ensue from external appropriation of indigenous art and knowledge, but it is relevant here to specify the connection that must be drawn between claims for IP protections and autonomy interests. As I have argued, it must be claimed that without the establishment of the rights package in question, the ongoing ability of members of communities of this sort reflectively to accept (without alienation) the value framework that guides their lives and meaningfully pursue those values in the current social setting will be substantially denied. The reference to culture, then, relates to the claim that without the legal protections, the cultural practices that allow the meaningful pursuit of basic values would be eradicated or severely denigrated, in turn, making the reflective acceptance of the life narrative defined by those basic values severely curtailed.

[39] For general discussion, see, e.g., T. Greaves, 'The Intellectual Property of Sovereign Tribes' *Science Communication* 17 (1995): 203, and T. Pogge, *World Poverty and Human Rights* (Cambridge: Polity Press, 2002), ch. 9.

[40] See R. Tsosie, 'Reclaiming Native Stories: An Essay on Cultural Appropriation and Cultural Rights' *Arizona State Law Journal* 34 (Spring, 2002): 299–358, at 299.

To trace out the import of such an approach, let us look at one sustained attempt to follow it. Stenson and Gray have developed what they call an 'autonomy-based justification' for IP claims on the part of indigenous communities over traditional knowledge, technologies, art forms and geographical indicators. They describe how such resources have, notoriously, been systematically expropriated by richer and more powerful corporate and state actors in cases where originating communities have been left poorly compensated and where the identification of the community with the products they produced is often removed or completely decimated of its cultural meaning.[41]

Now Stenson and Gray reject Lockean 'entitlement' arguments for IP over traditional knowledge by indigenous groups on the grounds that, among other things, product designs and artefacts and traditional knowledge generally, are not the product of single individuals labouring on previously unowned material, a requirement of Lockean justifications. Rather, they are communal products developed incrementally and cooperatively over generations.

They turn, then, to autonomy, and make use of Kymlicka's claim that respect for autonomy requires provisions that help maintain cultural practices. As Kymlicka argues:

> Liberals should be concerned with the fate of cultural structures, not because they have some moral status of their own, but because it's only through having a rich and secure cultural structure that people can become aware, in a vivid way, of the options available to them, and intelligently examine their value.[42]

Respect for the ability of individuals who define their values with reference to cultural identity, they argue, requires legal provisions that allow for the continued flourishing of cultural practices.

Before turning to the connection they make between this argument and IP, let me comment on the difference between Kymlicka's approach to cultural protection and the one drawn out in this chapter. In his argument, Kymlicka describes what he calls a 'societal culture' which is meant to exemplify the connection between group practices and individuals' self-concept. A 'societal culture', says Kymlicka, is 'synonymous with "a nation" or "a people" – that is, as an intergenerational community,

[41] See, e.g., Greaves, 'Sovereign Tribes'. Stenson and Gray quote Greaves: 'When a Hopi man or woman walks down a Tucson street and sees the mythic symbol, handed down from the elders, adorning a tourist's jogging shorts, culture dies a little' (p. 185). See also K. Raustiala and S. Munzer, 'The Global Struggle over Geographic Indications' *The European Journal of International Law* 18(2) (2007): 337–65.

[42] W. Kymlicka, *Multicultural Citizenship: A Liberal Theory of Minority Rights* (Oxford: Clarendon Press, 1995), p. 165.

more or less institutionally complete, occupying a given territory or homeland, sharing a distinct language and history'.[43] Such cultures, Kymlicka argues, give meaning to the choices and goods the pursuit of which autonomous agency (freedom) is worth protecting. On this view, freedom is valuable because it is a component of the person's pursuit of the good. Insofar as one's societal culture forms a community that defines and gives meaning to such goods, then protecting the social forms that comprise the value of those pursuits is therefore intertwined with valuing autonomy.

Now others have claimed that the strategy pursued by Kymlicka cannot support the devotion of resources to any *particular* culture, since on his analysis autonomy requires merely that one have a choice among goods in general. Insofar as freedom means being able to step back from any particular commitment and revise it in the face of social possibilities, and there are several cultural avenues and traditions I could choose in my society other than the one I grew up with (let us imagine), there is no autonomy-based argument for the survival of *my* culture in particular.[44]

The difference is subtle but, I think, important. On the view of autonomy sketched earlier, the requirement that steps be taken to protect cultures is tied to the social nature of the *self*, not to the context of valuable choices that such selves make and, on the liberal view, should be allowed to make. As I spelled out in Section III, the connection between autonomy and culture does not rest on the ways that culture enriches the particular goods that people might pursue. Rather, it defines the very self that engages in those pursuits themselves. The locus of agency by which we conceive and pursue our conception of the good is itself, on this view, constructed in cultural and social terms. Conditions that deny cultural forms in ways that do not allow adaptation and evolution of our self-concept do not merely rob us of a particularly weighty good that we might pursue, it rather robs us of our ability autonomously to pursue values at all.[45]

[43] Ibid., 18.

[44] For discussion, see C. Taylor, *The Ethics of Authenticity* (Cambridge, Mass.: Harvard University Press, 1991); K. A. Appiah, *The Ethics of Identity* (Princeton University Press, 2005), p. 123. For an attempt to spell out criteria of social identity based on self-esteem, see D. Copp, 'Social Unity and the Identity of Persons' *The Journal of Political Philosophy* 10(4) (2002): 365–91.

[45] This is to describe the extreme case of the oppressive eradication of cultural forms when people's social identities are firmly fixed within them. This is not, in general, the case even with culturally homogeneous groups, as the effects of global communication as well as internal heterogeneity of cultures themselves allow for wide latitude within which individuals can find and interpret their own culturally shaped self-understanding. For discussion of this point, see Appiah, *The Ethics of Identity*.

Returning to Stenson and Gray, they claim that concern for the protection of culture as a way of respecting autonomy supports the granting of IP rights by virtue of a three-step argument: first, cultural creations (it is claimed) are an integral part of a community's identity, and IP protections over such goods are 'essential to protect individual members' capacities to lead meaningful lives'.[46] Second, the kinds of traditional knowledge in question – plant varieties, genetic resources, botanical knowledge, and so on – are themselves cultural creations. Third, IP rights that are needed to protect the cultural identities of such communities include rights 'to possession (exclusion of non-members), use and management: the right (in some circumstances) to receive an income (that is, to rent or sell rights of usage to non-members); and the absence of term (the rights are in perpetuity)'. But they do not include the right to alienate (sell off altogether) or the 'right to destroy'.[47] This last provision is based, among other things, on the community's obligation to future generations to sustain the culture itself and to maintain control over the knowledge that helps define it.

My response to this approach is to endorse the (potential) connection made between control over design and expression and other forms of intellectual products and the survival of culture that allows for the meaningful existence of individual members. Indeed, I would support this step by way of the claims about autonomy and the social self made earlier. However, it is unclear why the elements of ownership Stenson and Gray mention are specifically justified under an autonomy-based approach. It must at least be shown that IP rights are the only or best means to provide the control over practices and materials that are central to the survival of the communities in question. But as I have argued, the rights to *income* generated from markets are not generally supported by concern for autonomy, so it is unclear how that is true in this case.

Stenson and Gray argue that sale of licences and other income-generating uses of IP rights are needed to secure the material supports that many impoverished indigenous cultures need to survive. No doubt this is the case. But that is an argument for the redistribution of income due to the (presumably) unfair economic deprivation experienced by such groups. This is an argument from *distributive justice*, not autonomy. In other words, claims that certain disadvantaged groups should be afforded favourable terms in the regulatory schemes that govern the flow of

[46] A. Stenson, and T. Gray, 'An Autonomy-Based Justification for Intellectual Property Rights of Indigenous Communities' *Environmental Ethics* 21 (Summer, 1999): 177–90, at 186.

[47] Ibid., 186–7.

resources could be validly made on grounds of distributive justice without making any use of IP arguments at all.[48]

Stenson and Gray focus specifically on patents over plant varieties and botanical knowledge, and other writers have looked at geographical indicators, copyrights over locally created art and music, and other property-like protections of culturally connected resources.[49] Often such cases consider relatively impoverished local communities claiming protections against expropriating outsiders. The condition of such communities brings to bear considerations of global maldistribution of wealth, and with it, the differential power in evidence in bargaining agreements involving international organizations and the treaty negotiations that fix the terms of such deals. This raises important questions about inequality and global distributive justice that IP rules could possibly be an effective instrument to facilitate. However, for the particular IP claims to find support in *autonomy* considerations, in particular ones which tie individual autonomy to cultural membership and practices in the ways I have outlined, then the argument comes up short, I claim.

More generally, the following suggest themselves as requirements for making an autonomy-based claim for IP rights on the part of communities:

(1) The items (designs, expressions, geographical indicators, and so on) that are the subject of IP claims must be strongly and centrally expressive of the identity and practices of cultural communities.
(2) Individual members of such communities must see such practices in ways that define their own sense of self.[50]
(3) Invocation of IP rights is required for the practices to continue in ways that allow members to avoid being alienated from the fundamental value orientations that guide their lives (to maintain their individual autonomy).

[48] This suggests, but does not strictly imply, that the argument I make here entails that IP rules should not be seen as a species of property law at all, in the end, but rather as a branch of regulatory policy more generally. For defence of this view of IP, see S. Ghosh, 'When Property is Something Else: Understanding Intellectual Property through the Lens of Regulatory Justice' in Gosseries *et al.* (eds.), *Intellectual Property*, pp. 106–21. I remain non-committal on this point, however.

[49] See, e.g., Sunder, 'IP3' and Raustiala and Munzer, 'Global Struggle'.

[50] An issue that is glossed over here, but which this provision speaks to, is whether cultural practices must be seen as sedimented and homogeneous (or not), as well as whether community leaders fairly represent the broad cultural interests of their members. The requirement stated here, that members' identities must be tied to the cultural practices in question, puts tremendous weight on leaders adequately to represent their constituents. For discussion, see Sunder, 'IP3', 323 ff.; I discuss this issue in general in Christman, *The Politics of Persons*, ch. 9.

In my comments about material property, in particular the distinction between control and income interests, I cast some doubt on the direct connection between autonomy and income rights, in that claims to income flows, while generally beneficial in ways that raise questions of distributive fairness, are not directly required by the exercise of autonomy in general. For IP claims, the question is whether provisions for the possession, exclusive use and alienation rights must be tied to claims over incomes (from licensing agreements, etc.) that typically come with IP rights packages. My suggestion is that income levels in agreements over licensing fees should be determined by consideration of overall social effects, including distributive effects, rather than the autonomy-based claims of their creators. The basis of this claim is the view that market-determined prices and bargaining position in competing in such markets are not simple extensions of the autonomous actions of creators or possessors, but depend on numerous factors external to their control, such as barriers to entry faced by others, transaction costs, externalities and other market imperfections.

A brief intuitive argument may help to motivate this last point. Imagine that a small indigenous tribe in a developing country claimed and was awarded patents on medically valuable plants, say, and such plants became crucial to the development of a life-saving treatment much in demand in the rest of the world. Consider next that the licensing agreements negotiated by the tribe's leaders led to enormous wealth concentration for the tribe over a period of years. If a proposal were then raised that the licensing agreements should be renegotiated so that income flows from the plants should be redirected to, say, other still more impoverished indigenous tribes in nearby areas, could an argument then be made that the *culture* and culturally-related autonomy of the members of the enriched tribe would really be in peril if the income were reduced or redirected? I doubt that claims of injustice would get much of a hearing in such a case, at least not one based on the autonomy interests of the first group.

Of course, claims to the income from trade or licensing of IP may well be inseparable from the value of holding the IP rights themselves. Enjoying monopoly rights on use, for example, may just *mean* controlling, through licensing contracts, the distribution of copies or other instantiations of the protected intellectual product. However, the claim to *market-generated income*, I am arguing, is not grounded in the autonomy interests in question. Such a claim must take directly into account the larger distributive effects of its protection and exercise (and indeed, in the end, be derived from consideration of such effects). Therefore, restrictions on licensing fees in various forms and degrees in many cases will leave untouched the autonomy of the holders of the IP, as long as the use and publication of the product can be controlled by the creator in ways that are consistent with continued autonomy.

But this certainly does not show that IP claims and other agreements favourable to (still) impoverished and vulnerable communities are *not* required to redress historical and ongoing injustices. It is merely to say that such claims and agreements are justified by virtue of broader distributive issues rather than claims of culturally defined autonomy of the originators. Exploitation of indigenous groups is clearly unjust, and granting either IP protections or (in the other direction) compulsory licensing rights may well be the best remedy for such injustice. But the remedy is not, I submit, based on autonomy *per se*.

V. Conclusion

It is true that various writers have mentioned autonomy in their discussions of IP claims (though to my knowledge none have explicated that notion in exactly the manner presented here). For example, Sunder conducts a detailed analysis of what could be called a 'socio-cultural' account of IP arguments, where attention is paid to the need to protect the integrity of cultural production and to guard against vulnerability to various forms of exploitation. In that analysis, Sunder acknowledges that 'we develop our autonomous selves through and within a cultural discourse'.[51] It is further recognized that that cultural misrepresentation is a form of dispossession with grave consequences for individual and communal well-being.[52]

This has much in common with the approach taken here (though I note, in passing, that in the list of values that should be promoted by IP law, Sunder lists 'autonomy' *separately* from 'culture'). In my view, social considerations concerning cultural integrity and community identity will often be inseparable from questions of self-government.[53]

One potential limitation to my approach needs to be mentioned: insofar as respect for autonomy functions as a value framework with which IP claims are evaluated, and controversies over such claims are often transnational in nature (that is, one is referring not merely to domestic statutes, but international law), then the framework applies only if autonomy is seen as a transnational, if not universal, value. I cast some doubt on that

[51] Sunder, 'IP3', 320. [52] Ibid., 322.

[53] Putting things this way illustrates how this approach has much in common with what is called the 'social relations' approach to the justification of property (a framework also embraced by Sunder). For discussion, see Munzer, 'Property as Social Relations', in Munzer (ed.), *New Essays*, pp. 36–47.

position earlier, or at least I contrasted it with the democracy-based (or, in Rawls' language 'political') argument for the value of autonomy. If the scepticism about the universal value of autonomy is widely shared, it might appear that this mode of analysis applied to these areas is wrong-headed from the start.

My only comment is that transnational negotiation over IP and other trade policies can (and I would claim, ought to) take the form of collective deliberation among associations representing affected parties with systems of fair representation in operation. Although such negotiations are often piecemeal and partial, cultural groups can be represented in ways similar to citizen groups in domestic settings. Establishing and maintaining the autonomy of such groups, then, would be called for by way of establishing the legitimacy of such collective decisions and the validity of their outcomes. Therefore, protecting the autonomy of community members will be valuable for reasons analogous to the context of domestic democratic institutions.

I have not shown, of course, merely because an action leaves one vulnerable regarding one's autonomy, that this shows that an IP claim would in fact be justified.[54] Not all threats to autonomy are best shielded by IP. My aim here is to show the limits of autonomy-based arguments for IP, but my view may well be construed as assuming insofar as autonomy is under threat in some situation, that that offers *prima facie* grounds for resisting that threat through an IP claim. But such an assumption is clearly unwarranted and I do not mean to make it here. One must show, in any given case, that not only will autonomy be at risk were an action to take place, but that IP is an adequate tool to respond to that risk.

What I have attempted here is to offer a relatively detailed explication of the concept of autonomy so that claims linking IP to that value might be fleshed out and further defended. In order for legal claims to gain support for considerations of autonomy by way of concern for cultural values, it must be shown both how individual autonomy connects with those cultural forms and, further, how the legal provisions in questions are necessary to meet those cultural concerns in ways that directly impact autonomy. I tried to argue, specifically, that such defence of IP claims must meet the rather high bar of showing that denial of those kinds of rights would lead to the erosion of cultural practices to an extent threatening to autonomy. However, moreover I tried to suggest that autonomy concerns do not reach what for many is the central component of such rights packages, namely, monopoly rights to income flows from market

[54] What follows is an attempt to reply to questions raised by Abraham Drassinower on an earlier version of this chapter.

transactions. Rather, I argued that attempts to allow impoverished groups to secure rights to resources necessary for their survival raised broader questions of distributive justice, ones which bear on issues other than the autonomy of the group members themselves. And while I underscored the weakness of autonomy arguments used for this purpose, in no way do I want to imply that using autonomy to measure the strength of IP claims generally is not useful, as it may very well be, nor that claims of redress by exploited communities of the sort we alluded to here are not without merit, as they surely are in many cases. But sorting out which argumentative box a particular set of claims belongs in is often a valuable lesson to be learned in social and legal theory.

This is clearly a work of political philosophy, not legal analysis. I have made no attempt at analysing or evaluating in any detail current law, nor have I framed the analysis in a way that provides direct recommendations to courts or grounds for critique of past legal decisions. However, I have attempted to provide (at least a prolegomenon for) a framework that may help guide normative debate about legal decisions, in particular by arguing that concern for at least one fundamental democratic value – individual autonomy – has implications for property law that may lead in some surprising directions. What I hope to have accomplished, at least, is to carve out a path for the analysis of IP claims based on what for many theorists of liberal democratic thought is a fundamental value. And while that path may get us some way down the road to justifying claims such as IP rights for indigenous peoples in some form, it does not, by itself, get us all the way to traditional rights of patent or copyright (for example) that would carry with them unlimited rights to market income. To support such claims, we must look elsewhere, specifically to considerations of global distributive justice.

2 Corrective justice and intellectual property rights in traditional knowledge

Stephen R. Munzer[*]

I construct a philosophical and legal corrective justice argument that can better the position of indigenous peoples regarding their traditional knowledge (TK). Indigenous peoples have frequently suffered great wrongs – murder, enslavement, rape, torture, theft, forced relocation – at the hands of outsiders. They have autonomy-based reasons for seeking intellectual property (IP) rights in their TK. There is ample warrant for recognizing these rights as a matter of corrective justice. Even if my argument is not decisive, it is very likely the most parsimonious, and perhaps the strongest argument for IP rights in TK.

I. Laying the groundwork

TK is understanding or skill, which is typically possessed by indigenous peoples and whose existence in some form typically pre-dates colonial contact, that relates to medical remedies, plant and animal products, technologies and cultural expressions. The term 'cultural expressions' includes religious rituals, rites of passage, works of art, songs, dances, myths, stories and folklore generally.[1] These forms of knowledge and cultural expressions are rarely frozen in time. Usually they evolve over decades and centuries. Few deny that indigenous peoples possess TK, sometimes called descriptive traditional knowledge; yet there is much

* For help with this chapter I thank my colleagues and seminar students, and in particular Daniel Bussel, Michael Cholbi, John K. Davis, Graham Dutfield, Oliver Gold, Wendy Gordon, Barbara Rose Johnston, Jerry Kang, H. A. Kelly, Annabelle Lever, Christine Littleton, Hiroshi Motomura, Chris Naticchia, James Nickel, Angela R. Riley, Jennifer Rothman, Dustin Szakalski, Mark Woodhead, Katrina Wyman and Stephen C. Yeazell. The suggestions of gracious audiences at the George Mason University School of Law Colloquium on Property Theory, Loyola Law School in Los Angeles and the Southern California Law and Philosophy Discussion Group led to improvements in the chapter. I am grateful to the UCLA Academic Senate and the Dean's Fund for material support.

1 This definition of TK follows S. R. Munzer and K. Raustiala, 'The Uneasy Case for Intellectual Property Rights in Traditional Knowledge' *Cardozo Arts & Entertainment Law Journal* 27 (2009) 37–97, at 48–50, 84–5.

dispute over whether domestic and international law do, or should, protect TK against outsiders who wish to commercialize it or use it for noncommercial purposes.

One may call any TK that is or should be protected by law normative traditional knowledge. TK thus protected would not lie centrally in the class of what lawyers call personal property – that is, physical objects such as plants, animals, religious articles or shamanistic totems. Rather, it would be a form of IP – akin to, but rarely the same as, copyrights, patents, trademarks, trade secrets or some existing *sui generis* IP rights. Thus, normative TK is not a set of rivalrous physical objects which are incapable of being possessed simultaneously by multiple persons in the same way. It is instead the non-rivalrous knowledge – the understanding, skill or cultural expressions – that can be possessed and used by many people at the same time and in the same way. One should separate (1) the non-rivalrousness of TK vis-à-vis outsiders from the perspective of the group and (2) disagreements within the group over control of its TK from the perspective of dissenting members.[2]

A major current dispute over TK is which arguments, if any, justify IP rights in the knowledge of indigenous peoples. The available arguments are of different kinds. Some arguments adapt the usual justifications for property rights and especially for IP rights. Very different are arguments that sound in human rights, distributive or corrective justice. I consider only the last of these. Corrective justice arguments subdivide into arguments of compensatory justice and arguments of restorative justice. The potential benefits of compensatory justice arguments to indigenous peoples are the moral analogues of money damages at law. The potential benefits of restorative justice arguments to them are the moral analogues of injunctions, restitution and other relief in equity.[3]

Reparations are another form of corrective justice, although they sometimes have punitive aspects as well. If reparations are solely corrective, they can be either compensatory or restorative or both. Reparations, as understood here, are corrective payments in the form of money, materials or intangible assistance that attempt to make amends for and rectify past

[2] This distinction recognizes the possibility that an indigenous people could use its norms to make a group decision that its TK is not to be used outside the group. This decision could then override the preferences of some members to commercialize some or all of the TK. The distinction turns on the difference between group autonomy and individual autonomy, which section VI discusses.

[3] My use of 'corrective', 'compensatory' and 'restorative' suits my aim in this chapter. Other writers sometimes use these terms differently.

wrongs. Historically some reparations, such as those required of Germany by the Treaty of Versailles,[4] have had a punitive dimension. That dimension is absent here, for I understand reparations as being wholly a matter of corrective justice. So understood, the justifications for reparations are mainly backward-looking. They appeal to past wrongs and seek to remedy them by present and future actions. There is at least one respect, however, in which reparations are forward-looking: the remedial payments should be effective and reasonably efficient. If reparations are justified, we want to have reparations that work. Whereas courts grant legal and equitable relief, reparations usually come from treaties, legislation or other means.

Of the four kinds of argument – property, human rights, distributive justice and corrective justice – the last might seem the least promising to some thinkers. So why do I confine this chapter to it? Part of the answer is straightforward. The available property arguments are wanting.[5] Many people know more about human rights and distributive justice than I ever will. With corrective justice, I have a better chance of making a contribution. Another part of the answer is less straightforward: like many, I welcome a challenge. The premises underlying most property, human rights and distributive justice arguments will appear to some, perhaps to many, to rest on strong assumptions that might well favor IP rights in TK. By comparison, the premises underlying corrective justice arguments are weaker and sparer. It is a more bracing task to see whether a philosophically cogent and legally significant conclusion – that in principle indigenous peoples should have some IP rights in their TK – can be derived from comparatively meager assumptions.

The term 'in principle' underscores that my argument proceeds at a general and, at times, abstract level. Deciding which IP rights in TK, if any, indigenous peoples should have at a particularized level requires judgment and detailed knowledge that lie beyond the scope of this chapter. To illustrate, providing IP rights that have no requirement of 'fixation' for copyright-like protection or no need for publication to establish 'prior art' that thwarts outsiders' obtaining patents would necessitate highly particularized analysis of specific situations. Similar analysis would be needed to show that IP rights in TK ought to be of indefinite duration

[4] [1919] *United Kingdom Treaty Series* 4 (Cmd. 153) (signed 28 June 1919, entered into force 10 January 1920), esp. art. 231, which assigned to Germany alone the duty to pay reparations because of 'the responsibility of Germany and her allies for causing all the loss and damage' suffered by the Allied and Associated Governments and their nationals 'as a consequence of the war imposed upon them by the aggression of Germany and her allies'. Only on 3 October 2010 did Germany make its final reparations payment under the Treaty of Versailles.

[5] Munzer and Raustiala, 'Uneasy Case', so argue.

in a specific context, for indefinite duration imposes costs on others by keeping indigenous works and inventions out of the public domain. Also, weaker IP protection for TK demands that an authority responsible for decreeing a remedy take into account, especially when the wrongs occurred long ago, the settled expectations, autonomy interests and vested legal rights of non-indigenous persons in specific situations. If, moreover, establishing a causal link between ancient wrongs and contemporary harm in a specific context requires counterfactual reasoning, the authority should examine this reasoning with care. Although my general argument contends that indigenous peoples should play a role in crafting a remedy for past wrongs, they do not have a veto. Their position on which remedy is best does not always and everywhere override all other considerations. Thus, even if in a specific case an indigenous people prefers certain IP rights in TK as all or part of the remedy, whichever authority ultimately decrees the remedy may, at a particularized level, use discretion on whether the indigenous-preferred remedy is the best, all things considered.

II. The argument

There may be many arguments of corrective justice for IP rights in TK, but I have only one.[6] It takes the following course.

Four background conditions lay out the initial steps of the argument. For IP rights in TK to be available on grounds of corrective justice: (1) some wrongs must have been committed against an indigenous group, some or all of its members, their successors, or both; (2) the wrongdoers or their successors are identifiable as a group, individual members of a group, some other entity, or some combination of these; (3) the wrongs unjustifiably caused harm to an indigenous people or some of its members, or both; and (4) those harmed are identifiable as an indigenous group or as individual members of an indigenous group, or both.

The foregoing conditions are the initial steps in making a case for some corrective relief. Yet they do not take into account the possibility that the

[6] A second argument, not pursued here, might rest on considerations of fair play and free riding. The core intuition, expressed roughly, is that it is unfair for Western, or Westernized, nations, firms or individuals to ride free on the TK developed by indigenous peoples. This intuition, however, raises tricky questions of whether free riding that benefits outsiders is unfair even if indigenous peoples suffer no harm. In addition, there are many conceptions of both fair play and free riding that require careful discrimination. In a vast literature, see, for example, G. Cullity, 'Moral Free Riding' *Philosophy & Public Affairs* 24 (1995) 3–34; S. D. Parsons, 'Fair-Play Obligations: A Critical Note on Free Riding' *Political Studies* 53 (2005) 641–9.

wrongdoers might have some excuse, or that IP rights in TK are not suitable relief for the wrongs inflicted and harm caused. Thus, it must also be the case that (5) no excuse is available such that the wrongdoers or their successors lack a moral duty to rectify their wrongs and undo the harm caused. Finally, (6) recognizing IP rights in TK in principle would be part of an effective and reasonably efficient means of compensating or restoring justice to the indigenous people or its members who have been harmed. The adverb 'reasonably' indicates that the means do not have to be economically optimal, but they cannot be seriously inefficient.

Some theorists of corrective justice would bridle at step (6). Those heavily influenced by Aristotle's account of corrective justice might well insist on a precise correlativity between the wrongdoer and the victim.[7] In Aristotle's analysis, to correct a wrong done by A to B it is necessary for A to disgorge A's gains, which are equal to B's loss resulting from the wrongdoing to B, in order to put B in the same position B occupied before the wrong was done. In the words of an acute contemporary interpreter, 'The remedy consists in simultaneously taking away the defendant's excess and making good the plaintiff's deficiency. Justice is thereby achieved for both parties through a single operation in which the plaintiff recovers precisely what the defendant is made to surrender.'[8] Corrective justice so understood differs not only from distributive justice, but also from 'contemporary consequentialist and reductionist understandings of law'.[9] There is, Weinrib contends, no room for an appeal to efficiency in thinking about the corrective remedy.

I do not follow this Aristotelian line, because it is too rigid to deal with wrongs done by many sorts of wrongdoers to many sorts of victims. Some, indeed, may doubt whether an Aristotelian account works well even in contract, tort and unjust enrichment cases involving one plaintiff and one defendant. Perhaps even then the defendant's gain is sometimes greater or lesser than the harm suffered by the plaintiff, or the remedy should have some deterrent, distributive or loss-spreading effects.[10] Still, in typical situations involving indigenous groups harmed over many generations in many different ways by multiple individuals, outsiders of various sorts,

[7] Aristotle, *Nicomachean Ethics*, bk. V, chs. 2–5, 1130^{a}14–1133^{b}28.

[8] E. J. Weinrib, 'Corrective Justice in a Nutshell' *University of Toronto Law Journal* 52 (2002), 349–56, at 350.

[9] *Ibid.*, 356.

[10] *Cf.* P. Cane, 'Corrective Justice and Correlativity in Private Law' *Oxford Journal of Legal Studies* 16 (1996) 471–88. Even within the theory of tort law, Weinrib's analysis of corrective justice in terms of correlativity and 'personality' (purposive rational agency) has won over fewer scholars on personality than on correlativity: E. J. Weinrib, 'Correlativity, Personality, and the Emerging Consensus on Corrective Justice' *Theoretical Inquiries in Law* 2 (2001) 107–59.

corporations and nation states, it would be Procrustean to try to make the remedy due indigenous groups exactly equal to the gains of wrongdoers under an idealized correlatively-structured system of corrective justice. Given the remedial problems thrown up by these complicated situations, one must make room for some constraints of efficiency. If this is rough corrective justice, so be it.

Although the boundaries of corrective justice are disputed, my argument is one of corrective justice in a broad way, for it rests fundamentally on reasons for undoing past wrongs. Any distributive effects are incidental to, not an intended goal of, the remedy. Under my broad understanding, corrective justice can in principle ground a baseline entitlement such as IP rights in TK. The essential thing is that the remedy compensate for or otherwise rectify a past wrong.

Accordingly, I hitch my star to the six-step argument stated. In Section IV, I fill out this argument in the *Chixoy Dam Reparations* case. Before that, I must dispose of an objection.

III. A fool's errand thrice over?

Some might object that, for three reasons, it is foolish to recognize IP rights in TK. In the first place, the commercial value of such rights would vary too much across indigenous groups. Relatedly, the overall value of most TK is a function of its uses by indigenous peoples in their local environment, which is often greater than its commercial value to outsiders. Most indigenous groups would receive too little were they to receive only the commercial value of their TK. Second, if one crafted IP rights in TK in accordance with indigenous law or custom, the rights would vary too much in content. This variation would increase the transaction costs, especially the information costs, borne by others who wish to buy the rights or obtain licenses under them from indigenous groups. Third, in almost all cases a mismatch exists between the wrongs done to an indigenous people and any remedy in the form of IP rights in TK.

I disagree. In regard to the first reason given, an indigenous group might not be seeking a financial remedy. Instead, it might want to prevent others from using their TK without attribution, or even with attribution if the group regards the TK as sacred or central to its identity or sense of identity. It might want in particular to prevent outsiders from obtaining patents or copyrights based on the group's TK. For these purposes the group would ask for injunctive or declaratory relief. Even if the indigenous group were seeking a financial remedy, it might regard IP rights in its TK as only partial compensation for or restitution of what is owed them because of past wrongs. Just compensation is not always the same as fair market value. The former, but not the latter, takes into account the value of autonomous choice lost by or denied to the group, the group's possibility of capturing some of the gains from trade, and the subjective premium the group places on its TK.

As to the second reason, different rebuttals apply. Sometimes it is justifiable to put up with a modest amount of inefficiency to promote corrective justice. Plus, one could craft the relief so as to reduce the transaction costs to third parties. For example, instead of using indigenous law or custom, one might try to formulate a uniform international law of IP rights for TK. Or at least one might attempt to do something helpful though less grand, such as adopting regional treaties or unifying the domestic law of each nation that is home to one or more indigenous groups.

The third reason might appear to create the most trouble for a corrective justice argument. Suppose that great wrongs, such as murder, enslavement and forced resettlement, were done by outsiders to members of an indigenous group. Why should the group or its members be able to elect IP rights in their TK as a remedy, especially if the wrongs done only indirectly and only slightly harmed the group's TK? Does it not seem more plausible to give the group or its members land and access to housing, health care and education rather than IP rights in TK? Although questions do not amount to an argument, in my experience a negative answer to the first question and an affirmative answer to the second strike some scholars as intuitively plausible. Surely, I have heard some say, you cannot mean that indigenous peoples, if they are able to establish liability, are entitled to whatever remedy suits their fancy. The mismatch would be even more egregious if the group or its members were to elect as their remedy hate-speech codes, affirmative action in hiring, non-sexual full-body massages, a huge supply of whiskey, or ping pong balls.

This third reason is unpersuasive in so far as it is directed at my general argument. If the wrongs committed against the indigenous group were grievous, and if it is possible to identify the wrongdoers or their successors, then it does not lie in the mouths of either the wrongdoers or their successors to say which remedy the indigenous group and its members are entitled to. A salient part of autonomy for indigenous groups rests on their own decisions about what is in their best interest. If they elect IP rights in TK on the basis of accurate information and with due appreciation of the consequences, then it is not evident that outsiders who committed the wrongs or profited from them have standing to tell the indigenous group and its members which remedy they are to have.

Further, the mismatch argument assumes that a close parallel exists between remedies in ordinary civil litigation and remedies for harm done to indigenous groups and their members, yet the analogy is not nearly as close as might be supposed. In garden-variety civil litigation, it makes sense to fit the remedy carefully to the wrong committed. Yet in claims advanced by indigenous groups we should, in fashioning a remedy, take fittingness into account, but also view the remedy as a way of denouncing and atoning for past wrongs. This way proclaims, erects, underscores and provides a new standard that effectively announces that such behavior by wrongdoers will not be tolerated.[11] This standard protects indigenous groups now and in the future. It also provides a way for wrongdoers and victims to reconcile.

It is, then, important to tease apart what one might call the legal–science remedial element and the political–symbolic element. The former element concerns which remedy best suits the wrongs done to indigenous groups. Here my position is that the fit between wrong and remedy insisted upon in ordinary civil litigation is not apt for the wrongs typically committed against indigenous groups and their members. The latter element concerns why indigenous groups often insist on IP rights in TK. The insistence comes from the fact that their grievances arise from their experience at the hands of outsiders, and from the claim that their culture will be taken seriously only if the TK it engenders is identified as *theirs* and in some sense belongs to them as property. This insistence is also bound up with indigenous perspectives on land. Burned in their memory is the fact that outsiders have almost always regarded the land on which they have lived for countless generations as somehow not held in the 'right' way. Their possession was said to be insufficiently intensive, too nomadic, too impermanent, too unproductive, and above all collective-but-not-corporate to count as ownership. Now deprived of their historical uses of the land, they see outsiders directing similar arguments against ownership of their TK. To recognize IP rights in their TK would not correct all misdeeds, past and present, but along with land reform it would restore something they regard as theirs.

Of course, indigenous groups and their members have no moral entitlement to have whatever remedy suits their fancy. Any entity, such as a court or legislature, that authorizes the remedy should have some control over its nature. It should not authorize remedies that might harm indigenous groups or their members, such as a huge supply of whiskey, or prove largely worthless to them, such as a cache of ping pong balls, or would be frivolous, such as massages. To that extent I would in principle allow some paternalism by the remedial entity. At a particularized level, I would

[11] An unpublished work in progress by Samuel L. Bray helped me to frame the point in this way.

not rule out hate-speech codes or affirmative action in hiring without knowing a good deal more about the context. If the harm inflicted on an indigenous group was transgenerational, the remedial entity should make sure that the benefits of the remedy are prospectively transgenerational as well.[12]

IV. Easy cases

One sort of easy case from the very start involves IP rights in TK that are both justifiable and already legally recognized, together with existing identifiable wrongdoers and victims. The IP might be TK that satisfies the usual conditions for a valid copyright, trademark, trade secret, *sui generis* right or, less frequently, patent. To illustrate, in *Milpurrurru* v. *Indofurn Party Ltd*,[13] living aboriginal artists produced images of their traditional creation myths. A Vietnamese rug manufacturer reproduced these images on its carpets and exported the carpets to Australia. The aboriginal artists had given no permission for either the use of the images or the importation of the carpets. They sued for copyright infringement and violation of the Australian Trade Practices Act 1974. The court ruled in the artists' favor and awarded them pecuniary damages, with the stipulation that the money was to be distributed to the owners recognized by aboriginal law. This case is easy because one has wrongs, an identifiable wrongdoer, financial harm unjustifiably caused by an identifiable firm, identifiable indigenous persons who suffered the harm, a moral duty to compensate because the wrongdoer had no excuse for its actions, and the remedy was effective and reasonably efficient.

This sort of case is too easy to be terribly helpful. Because it begins with IP rights in TK that are already justifiable and legally recognized, it cannot by itself justify IP rights in TK in situations where the very justifiability of such rights is at stake. The standard philosophical arguments for property rights in general and IP rights in particular do not support a robust package of IP rights in TK.[14] At best, they support only a modest set of IP rights. Their modesty stems from the fact that they are of limited duration, depend mainly on the fringes of current IP protection for patents, copyrights, trademarks and trade secrets, and shelter only bits of *sui generis* IP rights created for indigenous peoples by various statutes and treaties. These rights are worth something. In particular they support 'defensive' uses of TK – e.g. invalidating or blocking the enforcement of outsiders'

[12] Section III provisionally rejects the mismatch argument. Section VI provides reasons based on group autonomy and self-governance for permanently rejecting it.

[13] 30 IPR 209 (1995) (Australia). [14] Munzer and Raustiala, 'Uneasy Case'.

putative IP rights, such as a patent, where the outsiders employed TK to come up with the patented invention.[15] These rights, however, are a good deal less powerful than those typically sought by indigenous peoples and TK advocates.

All the same, wrongs can take many forms besides the violation of justifiable existing IP rights in TK. In fact, most harms inflicted on indigenous peoples involve murder, enslavement, forced migration, pushing people off land they have occupied over generations and removing natural resources and artifacts. There are more than enough really serious harms to go around. So now the question becomes whether one can work these harms into an argument for IP rights in TK. Factors that make an argument of corrective justice easier to construct in principle are a relatively short span of time between the harms caused and the relief sought, identifiable wrongdoers, and identifiable victims and heirs of victims. A useful example, which will also flesh out the rather skeletal argument of Section II, is the *Chixoy Dam Reparations* case dating from events in the 1980s in Guatemala.[16]

The modernization of Guatemala required a stable source of electric power. The Rio Negro Valley was an attractive place to build a dam, which would be a prime source of hydroelectric power for the nation. As often happens with power dam projects, people were living in the valley, and their homes and other structures would be inundated once the dam was built and water began to fill up behind it. During this period a repressive military dictatorship ruled Guatemala and wanted the dam. The World Bank and the Inter-American Development Bank (IADB) were willing to fund its construction. The Maya-Achí, an indigenous Mayan group, were the main occupants of the valley. They did not want to leave their ancestral lands. The Guatemalan government began a campaign of terror. It removed 3,000 people by force. It paid little compensation and relocated the Mayan peoples to other parts to the country without an effective resettlement policy. Some 6,000 Maya-Achí villagers lost their lands and livelihoods. Some villagers lost more: in a series of massacres from March 1980 through September 1982, Guatemalan Civil Defense Patrols, known by the Spanish-based acronym PACs, kidnapped,

[15] Effective defensive use often requires steps by indigenous peoples, such as publication of their TK so that it counts as 'prior art' to block or invalidate outsiders' patents, or fixing their TK in a tangible medium of expression to forestall outsiders obtaining copyrights.

[16] See Advocacy Project, 'On the Record – The Rio Negro Campaign' 11 (no. 5, 17 April 2000), available at www.advocacynet.org/resource/441 (last accessed 17 November 2010); B. R. Johnston, *Chixoy Dam Legacies. Social Commitments and Resettlement Obligations: Promises, Actions, Consequential Damages, and Community Needs* (17 March 2005), 5 vols. (report presented to the Government of Guatemala Presidential Commission on Human Rights, the World Bank, and the Inter-American Development Bank), available at www.centerforpoliticalecology.org/chixoy.html (last accessed 17 November 2010).

tortured or killed some hundreds of Maya-Achí, including women and children, especially from the village of Xococ.[17]

Leaving the issue of criminal punishment to one side, and granting that most relief should involve monetary payments and effective resettlement, one can construct a straightforward argument in principle for corrective justice in the form of IP rights in TK. Horrible wrongs were committed. Many of the wrongdoers are identifiable: the Guatemalan government, its senior ministers and the leaders of its PACs, and the World Bank and the IADB for their complicity in allowing the project to go forward without just compensation for landholdings, dwellings, personal property and livelihoods lost in the Rio Negro Valley. The government had justification for building the dam. It had no justification for committing the wrongs – the violence and inadequate compensation – that harmed the Maya-Achí. Both this indigenous Mayan group and often individual Maya-Achí and their heirs can be identified. The actions of the wrongdoers were inexcusable, and they have a moral duty to compensate and restore justice to the Mayan victims.

So far this argument is incomplete. It remains to show that IP rights in TK would, at least in principle, be part of an effective and reasonably efficient means to compensate and restore justice. With equanimity one can grant that money damages, appropriate resettlement of the Maya-Achí in other parts of Guatemala, and confessions and apologies by institutions and individuals for the wrongs they committed or were complicit in are the main forms of corrective relief. The case for including TK in the package is stronger than it would otherwise be for three reasons. First, the regional biodiversity of the Rio Negro Valley was the source of some Maya-Achí TK that it is difficult or impossible to recreate in other parts of Guatemala. Second, a major component of Maya-Achí TK is marimba music, which among other things transmits memories and articulates cultural identity.[18] Massacre and forced relocation pushed this music off its normal course of development and imbued it with the trauma of the 1980s.[19] Third, in

[17] B. R. Johnston, 'Chixoy Dam Legacies: The Struggle to Secure Reparations and the Right to Remedy in Guatemala' *Water Alternatives* 3 (2010) 341–61, gives an excellent brief account.

[18] S. Navarrete Pellicer, *Maya Achí Marimba Music in Guatemala* (Philadelphia: Temple University Press, 2005).

[19] Navarrete Pellicer reports that the *marimbistas*, who were associated with traditional local Catholicism and Catholic Action catechists, suffered under the coup led by General Efraín Rios Montt (an evangelical Protestant) (*ibid.*, pp. 20–4). Indigenous gatherings with marimba music were shut down in 1981. *Marimbistas*, 'the most visible symbol of Catholic custom', were 'vulnerable' and 'targeted by rival musicians'. The 'murder of musicians reinforced the message' (*ibid.*, p. 24). As a result of the violence in Guatemala, the marimba tradition has sometimes been lost and more often regenerated (*ibid.*, p. 167). The 'resurgence of interest in marimba music' after the violence of the mid-1960s and the early 1980s 'can be seen as a statement of identity' (*ibid.*, p. 166). See also pp. 176–213.

Guatemala as in most developing countries, indigenous TK not wiped out or rendered worthless by forced resettlement receives spotty and inadequate legal protection.[20] So even if the Mayan Indians of the Rio Negro Valley receive only a small portion of what is due them as a matter of corrective justice in the form of IP rights in their TK, there is scant ground at the level of my general argument for withholding from them that small portion.[21]

A less easy case involves indigenous groups some of whose member victims are dead. A plausible suggestion is to say that the heirs of dead victims should receive corrective relief. There are some technical legal problems with this suggestion. If heirs are defined by an intestacy statute, bear in mind that such statutes have different provisions depending on the jurisdiction, and some legal systems have no intestacy statute. If heirs are defined by victims' wills, the beneficiaries would be what the common law calls the devisees and legatees named or described in the wills. Variation is possible here, too, because different jurisdictions have different rules about who can be named. For instance, one jurisdiction might allow a man to disinherit his wife and leave his assets to his mistress, and another jurisdiction might prevent or limit his doing so. There are also issues pertaining to what is heritable. Land and personal property are usually heritable, but some causes of action, such as a defamation lawsuit filed by a woman prior to her death but with no final judgment at the time of her death, often are not heritable. In the present situation, the question is whether an indigenous person's claim for relief would be heritable. Pecuniary damages and other remedies will be less effective if such claims are not heritable.

[20] As much is evident in the plight of the San of southern Africa, the value of whose knowledge of uses of plants, such as those of the *Hoodia* genus, has been undercut and inadequately protected because of war, forced migration, resettlement and government indifference: S. R. Munzer and P. Chen Simon, 'Territory, Plants, and Land-Use Rights among the San of Southern Africa: A Case Study of Regional Biodiversity, Traditional Knowledge, and Intellectual Property' *William & Mary Bill of Rights Journal* 17 (2009) 831–94.

[21] 'Breakthrough Accord Could Bring Reparations for Guatemala Massacre Survivors', *NowPublic*, 3 December 2008, available at nowpublic.com/world/breakthrough-accord-could-bring-reparations-guatemala-massacre-survivors (last accessed 17 November 2010), reports progress on reparations but says nothing about IP rights in TK being part of any reparations. Barbara Rose Johnston has advised me that a multimillion dollar reparations plan was almost entirely in place in spring 2010, but as of 14 April 2011 several government ministries had not agreed on the exact wording of a document that would give it legal force as an *acuerdo*. The plan addresses socio-economic and socio-cultural harm from displacement, inadequate compensation and other injuries. It does not address reparations for the massacres themselves.

In short, these are technical legal problems that are now in want of legal solutions. One size does not fit all. A uniform statute detailing whether anyone inherits the deceased victim's claim, and, if so, which person or persons do so, seems attractive on the surface. Yet different cultures have different views about inheritance, and decisions on inheritance should be sensitive to such views. If relief to indigenous groups or their members is provided on an ad hoc basis, the relief plan can specify who, if anyone, inherits the right to compensation or other remedies.

V. Hard cases: transgenerational harms and the non-identity problem

The previous case becomes less easy still if we increase the time and the number of generations between the deceased indigenous victims and their remote descendants. It is problematic to call them 'heirs' in a legal sense after, say, five or ten generations. So many intervening events, including events affected by the original wrongs, have occurred, that identifying a person's heirs is even harder than identifying that person's descendants. Indeed, with time it also becomes harder to identify descendants of the original indigenous victim. That is one reason why trying to pay descendants of the Etruscans for harm inflicted on Etruscan ancestors by the Roman Empire would be such an odd enterprise. Another reason is identifying which Etruscans suffered wrongful injuries inflicted by the Romans. These difficulties are lessened, though not extinguished, if the injuries are more recent, such as the harms visited upon Native Americans and black slaves in what is now the United States. One way of avoiding such difficulties, in the case of indigenous peoples, is to pick out how they suffer *continuing* wrongs that grow out of much older wrongs inflicted on their ancestors.[22]

Related to problems with the temporal and generational distance between deceased victims and their remote descendants are further well-known difficulties with inheritance-based claims because of the non-identity problem. Stephen Kershnar, for example, contends that such claims do not succeed. He offers various reasons to support this contention. Among them are doubts about the existence and amount of the claims, concerns about offsets (sums representing benefits that must be subtracted from compensation), and figuring out who owes compensation. But above all, he worries about the existence and identifiability of those who are supposedly entitled to receive inheritance-based compensation.[23]

[22] See G. Sher, 'Ancient Wrongs and Modern Rights' *Philosophy & Public Affairs* 10 (1980) 3–17.

[23] S. Kershnar, 'The Inheritance-Based Claim to Reparations' *Legal Theory* 8 (2002) 243–67, at 243.

Kershnar's argument based on the non-identity problem is straightforward: to justify compensation one must compare the actual world in which present-day African Americans exist to a relevantly similar possible world in which they also exist, but no enslavement and its harms existed. However, slavery involved many wrongful acts that affected the freedom and mobility of slaves. It also played a role in the occurrence and timing of sexual intercourse between particular male and female slaves and thus the birth of ancestors of current African Americans. On metaphysical, probabilistic and reproductive-biological grounds, there is no relevant possible world in which both black enslavement did not occur and present-day African Americans exist. Therefore, the claims for reparations cannot arise, and even if they did, there would be no way to determine how much compensation is in order for them. Kershnar concludes: 'Slavery itself has probably not resulted in a compensable injury to the descendants of slaves.'[24]

Moreover, according to Kershnar, even if descendants of slaves inherited their ancestors' claims to compensation, each such claim is subject to further division upon passing to the next generation. It is extremely difficult to calculate the amount of the inherited fractionated claims, and it is even more difficult to take offsetting benefits into account. By parity of reasoning, Kershnar would presumably contend that harms done a century or two ago to members of indigenous groups do not give rise to rights for their descendants today. Neither do their current descendants have measurable inherited fractionated claims today.[25]

Kershnar's treatment of the non-identity problem is overly simple. George Sher suggests that the situation is more tractable than the difficulties just discussed would suggest.[26] These difficulties might seem to indicate that transgenerational compensation is incoherent, or nearly so. But Sher explores a two-pronged line of argument which offers a possible

[24] *Ibid.*, 251. D. Parfit, *Reasons and Persons* (Oxford: Clarendon Press, 1984), ch. 16, formulates the non-identity problem and discusses whether the fact of non-identity makes a moral difference. C. W. Morris, 'Existential Limits to the Rectification of Past Wrongs' *American Philosophical Quarterly* 21 (1984) 175–82, and others draw out the difficulties that the problem poses for rectification over generations. D. Butt, *Rectifying International Injustice: Principles of Compensation and Restitution Between Nations* (Oxford University Press, 2009), contains much of interest on these issues. However, it lends itself only indirectly to the specific problems addressed here, because, as his subtitle indicates, it deals with compensation and restitution between *nations*, whereas my concern embraces many other sorts of wrongdoers and victims.

[25] T. Cowen, 'Discounting and Restitution' *Philosophy & Public Affairs* 26 (2006) 168–85, points out further problems in calculating restitutionary payments over generations.

[26] G. Sher, 'Transgenerational Compensation' *Philosophy & Public Affairs* 33 (2005) 181–200. His article does not cite and is not a reply to Kershnar. B. Boxill, 'A Lockean Argument for Black Reparations' *Journal of Ethics* 7 (2003), 63–91, offers an argument somewhat similar to Sher's.

way out: 'that (1) the unrectified wrongs of the previous generations are systematically correlated with certain wrongs done *within* the current generation, and (2) what look like claims to be compensated for the earlier wrongs are in fact claims to be compensated for the associated recent wrongs – wrongs which, having been done within the current generation, do not give rise to the non-identity problem'.[27] He recognizes that the argument he explores is problematic, and even to the extent that it works it is 'a technical [philosophical] solution to a technical [philosophical] problem'.[28]

One problem to which Sher gives insufficient attention is that correlation is not the same as causation, and that one needs proof that unrectified past wrongs are causes of wrongs and harms inflicted on members of the current generations. Another problem is that his argument yields only remedies for current wrongs and thus seems irrelevant to remedies for past wrongs in cases in which who-you-are is the result of those past wrongs. Still, Sher leaves the proponent of reparations or other relief for members of indigenous groups with something to go on.[29]

There is a second way out of Kershnar's treatment of the non-identity problem. He and Sher both concentrate on individual members of groups. One can concentrate instead on groups themselves. The remote-descendant/non-identity critique is faulty or incomplete, because an indigenous people is a unitary group or collectivity over time. Those who are responsible for TK form a group of n generations who have largely the same language and similar, if evolving, moral and social practices and ways of life over centuries. One can think, then, of an indigenous group – not the individuals in the group – as the entity that has a claim of TK and is entitled to a remedy. The identity conditions of transtemporal groups include lineage and cultural continuity, and a particular indigenous group transcends its current membership. It is the identity of the group rather than the non-identity of current individual members of the group, that matters from the standpoint of corrective relief in the form of IP rights for TK. Because the group is a transtemporal entity, the remedies can rectify both past wrongs and current wrongs caused by them. Any remedy passed down from the group to individuals must be to individuals *qua* members of the group.[30] *Pace* Kershnar, a group can have legitimate claims of

[27] Sher, 'Transgenerational Compensation', 191 (emphasis in original). Waldron anticipated Sher's position by linking past to persisting injustices: J. Waldron, 'Superseding Historical Injustice' *Ethics* 103 (1992) 4–28, esp. at 14.

[28] Sher, 'Transgenerational Compensation', 200.

[29] A. I. Cohen, 'Compensation for Historic Injustices: Completing the Boxill and Sher Arguments' *Philosophy and Public Affairs* 37 (2009) 81–102, ties off some of the loose ends.

[30] This argument adapts Munzer and Raustiala, 'Uneasy Case', 64.

corrective justice because things can go better for the group in the sense of having greater capacity to tie its members together as an enduring community and to pursue common goals.[31] For this reason, the second way out is superior to the first.

VI. Hard cases: autonomy, self-governance and remedies for violations of diffuse interests and rights

Interests and rights are diffuse if they are indivisible, collective and belong to indefinite classes of persons. A class of indigenous persons is indefinite if intermarriage and migration make it difficult or impossible to pick out all and only those individuals who belong to the class. The interests of indigenous peoples in their TK, as well as in their cultural identity and their survival as distinct groups, are usually diffuse. Their rights *qua* members of a particular indigenous group are usually diffuse, too. Some countries in Latin America and elsewhere make room for diffuse interests and rights. Brazil is a notable example.[32] Other countries make little, if any, room for such interests and rights.

The relevance of diffuse interests and rights to my analysis is as follows. Suppose that the first five steps in my argument are met. That leaves the final step: that recognizing IP rights in TK would in principle be part of an effective and reasonably efficient means of compensating or restoring justice to an indigenous people. Relief that is wholly untargeted is neither effective nor reasonably efficient for this purpose. For example, the Ghanaian Copyright Act 2005 vests 'rights of folklore … in the President for the people of the Republic', who holds them 'on behalf of and in trust for the people of the Republic'.[33] This way of treating indigenous folklore is a staggeringly bad idea. Even if neither the president nor the government is corrupt, proceeds from folkloric rights will go to all of the people of Ghana rather than just to the various indigenous groups that created the folklore. In most countries, members of indigenous groups are a small fraction of the total population. Hence, the share of indigenous groups in the royalties and other income from their folklore is likely to be miniscule. They are not receiving effective compensation or restorative relief for past harm done to them.

[31] Kershnar, 'The Inheritance-Based Claim', begs the question by confining claims of justice to conscious entities (256).

[32] A. Pellegrini Grinover, 'Brazil' *Annals of the American Academy of Political and Social Science* 622 (2009) 63–7.

[33] Copyright Law, PNDCL No. 690, ss. 4, 17 (17 May 2005) (Ghana).

Pooling together all indigenous groups in a country is not much better, for most countries that have indigenous peoples have many different groups of them. A well-known Peruvian statute governing the collective knowledge of biological resources illustrates the problem.[34] It provides that if 'the collective knowledge has passed into the public domain within the previous 20 years', a percentage of the gross sales of goods developed from this knowledge goes into the Fund for the Development of Indigenous Peoples.[35] Peru has numerous indigenous groups. If a particular group has developed TK from biological diversity native to their area, as often happens in the Andes, then the group will not receive compensation or enjoy restorative relief commensurate with the value of its own TK. There are limited circumstances in which the Peruvian pooling strategy is defensible. If indigenous groups are numerous and the value of the TK of each group is roughly the same, then it will be both fair and cost-effective to pool rather than keep separate accounts for each group. Otherwise, a given Peruvian indigenous group will not receive corrective relief for *its* TK. Or if Peruvian indigenous groups agree to share the financial benefits of their TK – under, say, the flag of pan-Indianism and on either a per capita or some other mutually agreed basis – then pooling would be permissible, for each group has waived the corrective relief for its own TK.

If a pooling strategy is at most a second-best means of corrective relief for past wrongs, it makes sense to explore a more targeted form of relief. One way to do so is through a combination of treaties and domestic legislation that protect the rights of indigenous peoples. The domestic legislation would implement treaty obligations by devising a framework for recognizing and enforcing indigenous rights. The enforcement provisions would allow indigenous groups to bring suit under the treaty once they had exhausted their domestic remedies. They would also empower judges to act creatively in fashioning remedies. Of course, equity already recognizes a range of remedies beyond injunctions, restitution and declaratory judgments: accounting for profits, adjustments of various kinds, agency of necessity, constructive trusts, *culpa in contrahendo*, discharges of various kinds, equitable liens, fiduciary duties, *negotiorum gestio* (management of the affairs of another), *quantum meruit*, rescission, offsets, unconscionability, unjust enrichments of various kinds and the

[34] Law No. 27811, Introducing a Protection Regime for the Collective Knowledge of Indigenous Peoples Derived from Biological Resources, *El Peruano, Diario Oficial* (Peru), 10 August 2002; discussed in Munzer and Raustiala, 'Uneasy Case', 90–4.

[35] Law No. 27811, above, art. 13; A. Taubman and M. Leistner, 'Traditional Knowledge', in S. von Lewinsky (ed.), *Indigenous Heritage and Intellectual Property: Genetic Resources, Traditional Knowledge and Folklore* (2nd edn, The Netherlands: Wolters Kluwer, 2008), pp. 59–179, at p. 147.

unwinding of contracts.[36] As will become apparent, some courts have shown more remedial resourcefulness than even this long list would suggest.

Perhaps the best real-world illustrations rest on various international and regional conventions or treaties pertaining to human rights, such as the American Convention on Human Rights (the 'Convention') and litigation under it.[37] For my purposes, two problems beset these illustrations. One is that these conventions often use some assumptions pertaining to property of which my argument may not partake. For instance, Article 21 of the Convention protects the right of everyone to use and enjoy property. It also provides that no one may be deprived of property except upon payment of 'just compensation'. Article 21 does not define 'property'. Were it defined or interpreted to include IP rights in TK, I could not use the Convention. I cannot use an argument for corrective justice that depends on the very point at issue – namely, whether IP rights in TK are justifiable as a matter of corrective justice.

The other problem is that frequently the best real-world illustrations rest on conventions and treaties pertaining to human rights. Often these agreements do not make clear what is the basis for putative human rights. If the basis is an argument of corrective justice, that's fine. But if it is even in part an argument of some other kind, I cannot employ it without begging the question. Consequently, to give this stretch of my argument practical verisimilitude, I will construct an example that uses a hypothetical treaty and domestic law which do not rest on non-corrective-justice human rights justifications. I will also devise a hypothetical example that shows how language in treaties might lead to judicial remedies that are solely corrective in nature. This trapeze work is not, however, quite as difficult as might first appear, for the constitutions of many nations protect property rights with no explicit inclusion of IP rights in TK.[38]

[36] E. von Caemmerer and P. Schlechtriem (eds), *International Encyclopedia of Comparative Law* (Tübingen: Mohr Siebeck and Leiden and Boston: Martinus Nijhoff: 2007), vol. X (*Restitution/Unjust Enrichment and Negotiorum Gestio*); H. Dagan, *The Law and Ethics of Restitution* (Cambridge University Press, 2004). Equitable remedies vary across jurisdictions. Also, some remedies once classified as equitable might later be considered legal remedies; see, for example, *Dairy Queen, Inc.* v. *Wood*, 369 US 469, 477–79 (1962) (casting the complaint in terms of an 'accounting' does not make the remedy equitable rather than legal for purposes of the availability of a jury trial in the federal courts).

[37] Organization of American States, American Convention on Human Rights, 22 November 1969, available at www.cidh.oas.org/Basicos/English/Basic3.American%20Convention.htm (last accessed 17 November 2010).

[38] See, for example, Constitution of Angola, art. 10; Constitution of Botswana, s. 8(1); Constitution of the Republic of Namibia, art. 16; South African Constitution, s. 25; US Constitution, amendments V, XIV s. 1.

Imagine, then, that there exists a Global Treaty on the Rights of Indigenous Peoples (the 'Treaty') which all members of the United Nations have signed. The Treaty includes the following provisions among many others:

1. All signatories have an obligation to respect the rights of indigenous peoples and individuals *qua* members of an indigenous people.
2. Indigenous peoples and their members have property rights to their ancestral lands. These rights are commensurate with their past and evolving uses of the land, including but not limited to: (a) seasonal and non-seasonal wandering and migration; (b) obtaining water; (c) hunting and fishing; (d) harvesting wild plants for food, animal feed, building materials, clothing, dyes and medicines; (e) building temporary and permanent dwellings and other structures; (f) constructing temporary and permanent villages, towns and cities; (g) establishing pastoral, agricultural, aquacultural and animal husbandry operations; and (h) setting up and maintaining graves and burial grounds.
3. Indigenous peoples and their members have property rights to the possession, use and enjoyment of things obtained or removed from their ancestral lands or raised on them, including but not limited to water, fish, game, plants, soil, minerals, timber, crops and domesticated animals, together with products made from these things.
4. Indigenous peoples and their members have property rights to the tangible cultural embodiments made on their ancestral lands or from the things and products in provision 3, including but not limited to petroglyphs, wood carvings, dyed and woven fabrics, earthenware, statues, shamanistic totems and religious artifacts.
5. All signatories shall implement the Treaty through their national constitutions, statutes, administrative rules and judicial systems. Under them administrative agencies and courts shall have the power and the obligation to enforce provisions of the Treaty domestically. Unreasonable delay in enforcement shall be a violation of the Treaty.
6. If an indigenous people or a member or members thereof have exhausted their domestic remedies and regard any relief granted to be insufficient under the Treaty, they may appeal to the Global Court on the Rights of Indigenous Peoples (the 'Court') established by the Treaty.
7. The Court shall have the power and the obligation to investigate, make findings of fact and determine the rights of an indigenous people and its members in the particular dispute with the signatory State which is the subject of the appeal.
8. If the Court determines that the signatory State has denied or failed to enforce certain rights of an indigenous people or its members under the Treaty, the Court shall have broad legal and equitable powers to enforce these rights as corrective justice requires.

Before analyzing a hypothetical case under this imagined Treaty, I offer several comments. The Treaty draws inspiration from some human rights documents but is narrower because, as set forth here, it deals only with property rights. None of the property rights listed is an IP right in TK. Even the tangible cultural property rights in Section 4 are not IP rights in TK, because the various cultural objects are rivalrous, whereas IP rights in TK are non-rivalrous. Furthermore, the Treaty does not use the term 'human rights' and partakes of no theory of human rights. It explicitly invokes only corrective justice and enunciates some property rights. However, it implicitly assumes that murder, torture, enslavement, involuntary servitude, wrongful imprisonment and forced migration without adequate resettlement are independent wrongs for which corrective justice might provide partial relief in the form of property rights. In this implicit respect the Treaty is no different in principle from the laws of some countries that, for example, award monetary compensation to persons wrongfully imprisoned as a result of police or prosecutorial misconduct. Nonetheless, some enforcement provisions of the Treaty – the obligation of signatory States to enforce the Treaty domestically, possible appeals to the Court and the broad enforcement powers of the Court – echo the Convention and the Inter-American Court of Human Rights.

One can illustrate how my Treaty would work at ground level by modifying the facts of a well-known recent case. I modify *Mayagna (Sumo) Awas Tingni Community* v. *Nicaragua*,[39] as follows. The Mayagna Awas Tingni Community (the 'Community') is an indigenous group of approximately 630 individuals who once lived on the Wawa River in the Nicaraguan municipality of Waspan. The Community claimed that the Nicaraguan government had interfered with and failed to protect its traditional lands and its right to fell trees on those lands. They obtained no relief from the government and appealed to the Global Court. The Court investigated and found that Nicaragua had breached its obligations under the Treaty. Specifically, it had breached provisions 1, 2 (c)–(f), 3, 4 and 5. Because of the breaches, about thirty years ago the Community had to relocate some 100 miles away from the Wawa River to an uninhabited area of the country. This area had no trees. In addition,

[39] Inter-American Court of Human Rights, Series C, No. 79 [2001] IACHR 9 (31 August 2001) (holding that Nicaragua had not protected rights of the Mayagna (Sumo) Awas Tingni Community to its ancestral lands and accompanying timber rights and decreeing remedies in favor of the Community), available at www.worldlii.org/int/cases/IACHR/2001/9.html (last accessed 17 November 2010).

there was no nearby river, and the members of the Community had no practical access to the fish of the Wawa, which made up a significant part of their diet. The folklore of the Mayagna Awas Tingni once centered on the many varieties of fish in the Wawa: songs praised them as a gift from the gods, and pottery made from the multicolored clayey banks of the Wawa artfully depicted the assorted fish. After three decades, only a few older members of the Community remembered the songs and knew how to paint the fish on the pottery, and they were so dispirited by life in their new location that they all but ceased to sing and make the traditional pottery.[40]

In the substantive part of the Court's opinion, the only tricky point concerns the grounds for saying that Nicaragua breached provision 4 of the Treaty. Plainly, pottery counts as 'earthenware'. Yet no evidence exists that the government or anyone else stole or destroyed pottery made by the Community. The argument, then, has to be that the displacement of the Community to a remote location with no similar river or clayey soil effectively prevented its potters from making the kind of earthenware that they had done before. This argument might seem broken-backed, for provision 4 seems to address earthenware that already exists, not earthenware that might be made in the future. However, the present/future distinction does not destroy the argument. It shows only that the argument has to be counterfactual: if Nicaragua had not breached provisions 1, 2(c)–(f), 3 and 5, then the Community would have created additional earthenware pots, and hence it would subvert the intended effect of provision 4 if Nicaragua were allowed to limit its liability to such pottery as existed thirty years ago. Consequently, Nicaragua violated provision 4 of the Treaty, too.

In the remedial part of the actual case, the Inter-American Court of Human Rights held that Nicaragua must invest US$50,000 for the benefit of the Community, pay US$30,000 to reimburse the Community for its expenses, and set up a legislative and administrative infrastructure that can demarcate the Community's traditional lands and give it title to these lands.[41] Until the demarcation and titling are complete, Nicaragua, its agents, and third parties acting with Nicaragua's acquiescence or tolerance must not interfere with the Community's use and enjoyment of its lands or compromise the value of them.[42] Moreover, Nicaragua must

[40] The actual case involved only land and timber rights. My modifications include the distant relocation, the plenitude of fish in the Wawa, the tangible cultural objects and the folklore.

[41] *Ibid.*, para. 173(3), (6) and (7) (awarding dollar amounts 'in equity').

[42] *Ibid.*, para. 173(4).

submit reports of its progress on compliance with the decision to the Inter-American Court every six months until the State has fully carried out its responsibilities under the judgment.[43] From a continent away, it is impossible to assess the reasonableness of the monetary amounts ordered by the Inter-American Court even for the ancestral land and timber claims. One could, of course, always modify the facts so that these dollar amounts would be in order.

In my hypothetical case, though, it would appear that the money damages would have to be greater. They would also have to cover the lost value of the fishing rights under provision 2(c), the rights to fish caught and clay extracted under provision 3 and the tangible cultural property rights under provision 4 of the Treaty. For present purposes, however, the main point of interest is whether my hypothetical Court, under my imagined Treaty, could justify protecting any IP rights in TK. Here I see two possibilities for an affirmative answer: a straightforward possibility and a subtle, theoretically interesting one.

The straightforward possibility would be that if the eventual dollar amounts are just compensatory and restorative relief for all violations of the Treaty, in principle Nicaragua could pay a lower amount in monetary damages and make up the difference by recognizing IP rights in the Community's TK. The legal and philosophical underpinning for this result is the right of an indigenous group, elaborated in Section III of this chapter, to have some say in electing a remedy for the wrongs done to it and its members. One could then recraft the Court's order to embrace judicial protection of IP rights in TK and the administrative infrastructure to back them up. Although the actual *Mayagna (Sumo) Awas Tingni* case was decided under a treaty, similar results are available under the legislation of many Latin American countries. Brazil, Costa Rica, Colombia, Guatemala and Paraguay, among others, have kindred provisions for enforcing the diffuse interests and rights of indigenous peoples and consumer groups.[44] This possibility is boring, because group autonomy enters the picture only in the election of remedy by the Community.

The subtle, theoretically interesting possibility would be to construct an argument, based on my imagined Treaty, for IP rights in TK. The argument turns on the impact of Nicaragua's manifold breaches of the Treaty. These breaches were responsible for the Mayagna (Sumo) Awas Tingni relocating to a different area of the country one hundred miles away that had no nearby river, fish or clayey soil. This relocation was in turn responsible for the loss of the ability and interest in singing traditional

[43] *Ibid.*, para. 173(8) and (9). [44] Pellegrini Grinover, 'Brazil', 64–5, 67.

songs on the part of virtually all members of the Community. Suppose that we now supplement the hypothetical case with the further facts that during the last thirty years Western interest in Central American folklore has increased substantially and that Westerners have typically been willing to pay for access to this folklore. Had the Community remained in Waspan on the Wawa River, its members would have been in a position to exploit financially this increased interest. The Community and its members could, for example, have earned money from permitting others to record their traditional songs. The governmental breaches of the Treaty and the consequences of the relocation made it extremely difficult, if not impossible, for the Community and its members to profit financially from their traditional songs. The deprivation of this opportunity could in principle warrant relief in the form of property rights, including IP rights in TK. Corrective justice requires that Nicaragua compensate the Community for its economic loss or provide it with other appropriate relief. This possibility is interesting because, as I will show, the loss of autonomy is central to the harm and the restoration of autonomy is central to the remedy.

Exploring the supplemented hypothetical case helps to show why IP rights in TK are in principle a plausible component of a remedy based on corrective justice. Prior to Nicaragua's breaches of the Treaty, the Mayagna (Sumo) Awas Tingni had only descriptive, not normative, TK. Hence these breaches were not violations of any IP rights in TK *ex ante*. Still, the eventual diminution or loss of the Community's TK was a harm *(damnum)*, even if it was not at the beginning a legally cognizable injury *(injuria)*. The lost or diminished TK was generated by members of the Community.

Also, the TK partly constituted their identity or sense of identity, and it was an expression of their group autonomy. By 'autonomy' I mean, in the case of individual human beings, the psychological capacity to be self-governing. To be self-governing is to determine, guide and control one's behavior and character over time based on reasons.[45] In my view, the autonomy of an indigenous group depends on the autonomy of the individuals, past and present, who comprise it. For two reasons the possession of autonomy does not entail the possession of self-governance. First, an individual or group might have the capacity to be self-governing,

[45] This definition does not commit one to any particular theory in the philosophy of action. I am, though, broadly sympathetic to the (different) views of M. Bratman, *Structures of Agency: Essays* (New York: Oxford University Press, 2007), chs. 1, 8, 10 and 11; J. Christman, *The Politics of Persons: Individual Autonomy and Socio-historical Selves* (Cambridge University Press, 2009).

but neglect to exercise that capacity. Second, an individual or a group might desire to exercise autonomy, and struggle to do so, but might not succeed owing to external factors beyond his, her or its control.

Group autonomy, then, involves the self-governing behavior and character of members of an indigenous group over time. My account does not suppose that all members behave in the same way. Their behavior is often complementary, distinctive or sometimes even conflicting. For instance, their descriptive TK might involve different artistic styles and include parodies of works made by other members of the group. Because human beings are embodied entities, not spirits, they require the use of material resources to express their culture. Wrongs done by outsiders can hinder – and sometimes diminish or even extinguish – their group autonomy and self-governance.

In my hypothetical example, the Nicaraguan breaches were ultimately responsible for the loss of the ability and interest of almost all members of the Mayagna (Sumo) Awas Tingni Community in singing their traditional songs. This loss is a diminution of the group's autonomy and self-governance. A remedy that restores or enhances its autonomy and self-governance *ex post* is a normatively appropriate response to that loss. To give the Community some IP rights in their TK is not merely autonomy-restoring or autonomy-enhancing: It is part of what Nicaragua owes to the Community, because the earlier harm ultimately resulted in an ongoing present autonomy-inhibiting disadvantage to the Community. The same point holds *mutatis mutandis* for self-governance.

We can now see more clearly why the mismatch argument considered and provisionally rejected in Section III ought to be permanently rejected at the level of principle. Massages, whiskey and ping-pong balls are frivolous remedies that have no relation to the harm suffered by the Community. By contrast, IP rights in TK belong on the menu of possible remedies precisely because they are tied to the diminished or lost autonomy and self-governance suffered by the Community as a result of Nicaragua's breaches of the Treaty.

Granting IP rights in TK might seem most appropriate in cases where members of an indigenous group would have commercialized, or continued to commercialize their TK, but for the harm inflicted on the group and its members that impaired their autonomy and self-governance. Yet it does not follow that absent commercialization, IP rights in TK are inappropriate. It follows only that, at the level of the particularized crafting of relief, these rights might seem less appropriate than in cases where commercialization occurred or would have occurred but for the harm done. After all, part of the basis for IP rights in TK is to denounce the behavior of wrongdoers and establish a new standard for dealing with the wrongs they inflicted, not merely to come up with the most fitting remedy under the rules for ordinary civil litigation.

A minor objection to the foregoing argument rests on offsetting. By moving from the Wawa River to a different area of Nicaragua, the Mayagna (Sumo) Awas Tingni gained an opportunity to create different TK. In place of songs about fish, members of the Community could make up new songs about the animals and terrain in their new location. Thus, it is contended, the value of the new songs should offset the value of the traditional songs that would have continued to be sung but for the relocation.

I answer that this objection is largely beside the point. The point of my argument is to give a corrective justice foundation for IP rights in TK at the level of principle, not to supply a practical mechanism for valuing those rights. Furthermore, the objection is callous. I recognize that legal remedies for breach of contract take into account costs saved by the non-breaching party, or require the non-breaching party to mitigate economic loss in order to recover damages. But the wrongs done to indigenous groups and their members go far beyond run-of-the-mill breaches of contract. It is counterintuitive to say that present-day African Americans descended from slaves must offset whatever value their long-dead ancestors had in descriptive TK, shortly before or just after the Middle Passage, by the value of black contributions to jazz. It is almost as counterintuitive to say that present-day members of the Community should have the strength of their IP rights in TK reduced by the proportionate value of new TK they have created, or could have created, as a result of their relocation.

I have heard some object that my argument proves too much. This more serious objection rests on examples such as the following.

(1) A US-based pharmaceutical company has a large plant located in Indonesia. As a result of anti-American political protest in Indonesia, a mob utterly destroys the plant. The economic loss is $500 million. The Indonesian government refuses to compensate the company. Because the company is on the verge of bankruptcy, Congress enacts a law that extends for ten years patent rights that the company holds on its most successful drugs. The value of the patent-term extension is $500 million. But, the objection runs, it is ridiculous to extend patent terms to make up for extraterritorial losses suffered by the company. And yet, the objector concludes, my argument would seem to endorse the extension, because IP rights are made the basis of corrective relief.

(2) A tribe in Venezuela ranges over a large area, including a swampy coastal plain which members of the tribe use for fishing and trapping. No TK results from this use. A Dutch firm, with permission from the

Venezuelan government, discovers oil in a coastal area abutting the coastal plain used by the tribe. In extracting the oil and loading it into a tanker, the Dutch firm negligently causes a serious oil spill that contaminates the tribe's coastal plain. The tribe suffers an economic loss of $40 million ($10 million for lost fish and game and $30 million needed to clean up the oil spill and remediate the coastal plain). The firm offers to pay the tribe $40 million, but the tribe seeks $35 million in cash and certain IP rights in its TK that, to the tribe, are worth $5 million. My objector contends that monetary damages should be the tribe's sole form of relief; no IP rights in TK are appropriate. Nevertheless, the objection concludes, my argument would seem to allow the tribe to select IP rights in its TK as part of the remedy.

(3) An indigenous group in Botswana lives in a part of the country that contains a species of snail found only in that small part of the globe. Members of the group ignore the snail. They do not eat it, draw pictures of it, sing songs about it, or use it for medicinal or any other purposes. Westerners on a government-approved trek through this part of Botswana come upon the snail. One of their company is a researcher in anaesthesiology. He notices that the snails, when disturbed, secrete a clear liquid, and he takes samples of the liquid back to his native France. He isolates from the liquid a molecule that causes skeletal muscles to go limp far more effectively than curare or any other natural or synthetic drug in the French pharmacopeia. He obtains patents on the molecule from the US, Japanese and European patent offices. When the indigenous group in Botswana learns of the patents, its members are furious, and they sue for IP rights in the molecule. Now, the objection continues, it is perfectly ridiculous for the group to have any IP rights in the molecule. The group neither isolated the molecule, nor discovered a use for it, nor even paid any attention to this species of snail. And yet, my objector says, my argument would favor recognizing IP rights in the snail and the active ingredient in the secreted liquid.

At root, this second objection, invoking as it does the three hypothetical cases, is an effort to construct a *reductio ad absurdum*: if one accepts my argument, the objection runs, then one should favor IP rights in TK in cases (1) through (3). Yet it would be the height of folly to do so. Therefore, the objection concludes, one should reject my argument.

I disagree. Case (1) is readily distinguishable. Suppose that 'par' is the average level of protection, across all legal systems, accorded to IP. Descriptive TK receives no IP protection. Normative TK generally receives rather weak and qualified IP protection.[46] Indigenous groups,

[46] Munzer and Raustiala, 'Uneasy Case', 80–95.

then, receive IP protection that is below par. By contrast, pharmaceutical companies receive IP protection that is above par. It makes little sense for Congress to give the company in case (1) ad hoc patent extensions on its most profitable drugs. Monetary damages suffice to remedy the company's loss of its destroyed Indonesian plant. The below-par/par/above-par rebuttal demonstrates that my argument does not lead to the conclusion that the objector claims. Also, I am aware that, for some, this example would not qualify as an illustration of corrective justice at all, For the wrongdoers were the violent mob that destroyed the plant and maybe, at a stretch, the Indonesian government, if it was complicit in the mob's action. Neither supplied a remedy. Congress provided the remedy, but it was not the wrongdoer. One need not accept this reasoning, for it seems an open question whether corrective justice includes a remedy crafted by a third party.

Case (2) is also distinguishable. The Venezuelan tribe has a tradition of using the swampy coastal plain for fishing and trapping. Yet *ex hypothesi* no understanding, skill or folklore that would qualify as 'knowledge' in the relevant sense results from this use. Here we have 'T' but no 'K'. Consequently, no relevant TK exists for which IP rights are an appropriate remedy. The argument I laid out raised the possibility of IP rights in TK as a way to reverse an earlier diminution or loss of autonomy and self-governance so that we come as close as possible to restoring what the tribe lost. A remedy that restores or enhances autonomy and self-governance is the nearest equivalent that might make the tribe whole. Case (2) is not a parallel, because what will come nearest to making the Venezuelan tribe whole are damages to cover the fish and game it would have caught but now cannot, plus damages to pay for the clean-up and remediation of the land. The objector is correct to say that IP rights in TK are inappropriate, but wrong to say that my argument would justify any such rights for the tribe.

Case (3) is likewise distinguishable. The indigenous group in Botswana might well have some descriptive and normative TK. With respect to the relevant species of snail, however, it has no tradition and no knowledge in any relevant sense. Here we have neither 'T' nor 'K'. The Westerners who took note of the snails were on an approved trek. The laws of some countries forbid the removal of plants and animals from the host country. The anaesthesiologist did not do so; he took only samples of the liquid secreted by the snails. Furthermore, he was the one to isolate the active ingredient, discover a use for it, file patent applications and eventually obtain patents on the molecule. None of his actions or those of his fellow trekkers interfered with the autonomy or self-governance of the indigenous group. Once again, the objector is correct to say that IP rights in TK are not appropriate for the group, but wrong to say that my argument would justify any such rights for the group.

A third and final objection appeals to cases in which no gross harms – murder, enslavement, etc. – exist, but outsiders make use of descriptive TK without the informed consent or even the knowledge of the indigenous group. In these cases, the objection claims, there is no interference with the autonomy or self-governance of the group or any of its members.

This claim is false and the objection fails. Here the interference with autonomy and self-governance lies in the inability of the group and its members to control the disclosure and representation of their TK. Research shows that indigenous peoples are keenly interested in marking out their cultural identity and controlling representations of their TK.[47] Impinging on their control thus limits the autonomy and self-governance of groups and their members. Now, it would be a lame defense for a peeping tom who photographed a woman emerging naked from the shower in her hotel room and posted the pictures on the internet to plead that, because she was unaware of the photographing and posting, she suffered no harm. The harm is the interference with the woman's autonomy and self-governance to decide whether she wishes to be photographed nude and to have the pictures put on the web. By parity of reasoning, the indigenous group and its members were unable to exercise control over their TK. Although the harm done them is much less grave than murdering or enslaving them, it is a harm nonetheless and justifies *pro tanto* IP rights in TK.

The law has a phrase – *damnum absque injuria* – which translates as 'harm without injury' – that is, harm to a person or group that does not amount to a legally cognizable injury for which damages or other relief may be granted. A central argument of this chapter is more nearly *in damno aliquando injuria inferri potest* – or, 'sometimes one can infer an injury from a harm'. More precisely, sometimes one can construct an argument that takes us from a harm to a legally cognizable injury for which compensation or restorative relief is due as a matter of corrective justice. No doubt the argument has an implicit premise that a reason exists as to why relief is fitting in principle: namely, that the harm interferes with autonomy and self-governance, and compensatory or restorative relief in the form of IP rights in TK counteracts and atones for this harm. This premise is weaker and sparer than the assumptions that underlie property, human rights and distributive justice arguments for IP rights in TK.

[47] See, e.g., J. Hendry, *Reclaiming Culture: Indigenous People and Self-Representation* (New York: Palgrave Macmillan, 2005).

VII. Prospect

My argument for IP rights in TK based on corrective justice, despite its philosophical and legal merits, might not be decisive on a practical level. At some point, one has to think about what indigenous peoples *need* and *want*. Their needs are not always and everywhere the same, and neither are their wants. Nevertheless, to paint with a broad brush, they generally need land, health care, education and access to natural resources more than they need IP rights to their TK. If I put myself in an imaginary conversation with an indigenous leader who has just seen his or her group conferred, as a matter of corrective justice, with IP rights in TK, he or she might say, 'I have huge problems involving a place for my people to live, access to timber and water, and the prevention of disease – and you have brought me some "rights" which I don't quite understand and seem to me of modest worth!' To some my argument of corrective justice might seem puny in its attempt to support IP rights in TK when indigenous peoples have so many other problems demanding their attention.

And yet hope lies in two quite different practical considerations. The first rests on the possibility of a mutual trade-off. As a practical matter, both indigenous peoples and outsiders must make trade-offs regarding IP rights in TK if these rights are to be of significant help in rectifying past wrongs. Indigenous peoples must choose whether to live traditional lives by making only traditional uses of their TK, or to exploit the commercial potential of their TK so as to gain income that will enable them to live partly traditional and partly non-traditional lives. Outsiders, by contrast, must choose whether to use their economic and political power to maximize their own interests (and advance the interests of indigenous peoples if, and only if, doing so adventitiously maximizes the outsiders' interests), or to make some concessions regarding IP rights in TK to the modest detriment of their own interests. If indigenous peoples and outsiders both make the respective first choices described, IP rights in TK will be worth little. Yet if they both make the respective second choices described, these IP rights will be more valuable.

The second consideration pertains to the strength of the available package of IP rights. Were one confined to property arguments for IP rights in TK, the package would be of modest strength. But under a sound corrective justice argument, the package could be robust, and the compensatory and restorative relief could be substantial. One cannot actualize this possibility if an indigenous people takes all or most of its relief in the form of land, natural resources, health care, education and monetary damages. Still, one could make this possibility a reality if an indigenous people also seeks and obtains a remedy that aggressively advances the strength of its IP rights in TK. Now the package of rights could be robust. It might even include, for example, indefinite duration, no requirement of fixation for copyright, and no need for publication of prior art to block outsiders' patents. Whether an authority should decree such a robust package of rights at a particularized level would require intensive fact-finding and sound judgment. Nonetheless, this package of rights is, I think, the powerful set of IP rights that many TK advocates seek.

3 Designing a successor to the patent as second best solution to the problem of optimum provision of good ideas

Alex Rosenberg★

This chapter reviews welfarist[1] arguments for government intervention to optimize the provision of good ideas that arise from their nature. It shows that, paradoxically, these same considerations provide reasons to think that, as a solution to the good idea–optimization problem, the patent will increasingly fail to be effective. This ineffectiveness is accelerated by technological developments as well. The problem that welfarism thus faces is to provide a new institution or regime that encourages the optimum provision and utilization of good ideas that will avoid the difficulties which the patent must inevitably impose and which technological developments are hastening. An examination of the reward system of pure science, however, suggests such a solution, and the chapter goes on to sketch ways in which this solution pure science uses can be implemented more broadly.

1. The near-public goods character of good ideas and argument for intellectual property rights

The welfarist argument for intellectual property rights is based on the near-public goods properties of good ideas. In a competitive market among economically rational agents that lacks property rights in good

★ I am indebted to Jorn Sonderholm for extremely useful comments on this chapter. No agreement with my claims, however, can be attributed to Sonderholm. See his important contribution to the examination of alternatives to the patent system in pharmacology: J. Sonderholm, 'Intellectual Property Rights and the TRIPS Agreement: An Overview of Ethical Problems and some Proposed Solutions' *Policy Research Working Papers*, (Washington DC: World Bank, 2010).

[1] Welfarism is the thesis that policy evaluation or institution design should be driven by the assessment of consequences for human welfare or well-being. It is not committed to any single maximization requirement (total, average, equal levels of welfare), nor even to the existence of overall measures of welfare. It thus avoids many objections to other consequentialist theses at the cost of its indeterminacy. This problem should not affect the treatment of good ideas here.

ideas, there must inevitably be an undersupply of good ideas: discovering and testing good ideas is costly and risky. Consider the obvious example of crop rotation. Establishing its enhancement of agricultural yields takes several growing seasons, during which some fields are removed from production altogether. No one has an incentive to undertake the experiment, but everyone has an incentive to watch others undertake it and copy the early adopters should the innovation work. But if no one has the appropriate incentive, there are no early adopters and crop rotation is unlikely ever to be invented. Ergo, the absence of property rights in good ideas leads to underinvestment in and undersupply of them.

But what if a good idea is hit upon by accident without investment and risk? To pursue an agricultural example, suppose as must have been the case, that one farmer discovers the effectiveness of animal waste as fertilizer. In a competitive market such an idea will provide an advantage, and so it is in the interest of the discoverer to keep the idea a trade secret. It is obvious in the present example that keeping the idea secret will be difficult, costly and will introduce suboptimal outcomes for the discoverer and for the economy as a whole. Fertilizing only fields distant from others' sights or doing so at night may preserve the secret, but fields in the sight of competitors will have to forgo treatment, and many parts of the fields manured in the dark will be missed, the fertilizer will not be evenly spread, and periods of full moon will interfere; one might build a high fence around one's field, but this will impose a heavy cost of secrecy keeping. So, the discoverer will have to incur significant costs to keep the secret and accept significant opportunity costs of keeping the idea secret. Moreover, the whole farming economy could profit from the good idea, owing to the increase in every farmer's yield if the idea were not kept secret. Whence the conclusion that in the absence of intellectual property rights there is undersupply of good ideas and overinvestment in keeping secret those which are discovered by accident!

The two features of good ideas that produce this result make them very similar to public goods: they are non-rivalrous in consumption: my using crop rotation in no way reduces the amount of crop rotation available to you to use, and yours has no impact on the amount available to a third farmer. So far, good ideas are just like public goods: the street light that makes my evening stroll safe makes yours just as safe whether I take my walk or not. Good ideas differ from public goods in that the latter are not excludable – I can't prevent you from consuming my street light except by making it impossible for me to benefit from it too. As our example shows, ideas are excludable, at least to the extent that you can keep them secret. But as our example also showed, keeping them secret imposes costs, even when it is feasible at all. So good ideas differ from public goods insofar as they are excludable, and in fact it will often be difficult effectively to make them excludable.

The close similarity of good ideas to public goods suggests that the means employed to approach optimum provision of public goods among large numbers of anonymous persons might be employed to do the same for good ideas: governmental central planning and coercion. The only thing that ensures the optimum provision of a good – public or private – is presumably free exchange on a competitive market. This is not possible for a public good – non-rivalrousness and non-excludability breed deceptive demand revelation and free-riders. So we must leave it to the government to estimate how much to provide and permit the government to exact from consumers the amount necessary to pay for the public good. In the case of a good idea, we cannot expect free exchange on a competitive market to work, either. Non-rivalrousness means that anyone who buys the use of a good idea can sell it to others without any reduction in their use of it. If copy costs are low enough, the original owner will reap few market-exchange rewards from her good idea. And the high costs of excludability will depress even resellers' returns. The solution most widely hit upon is governmental coercion and limited monopoly: the inventor/discoverer is forced by the government to disclose the idea to all, so that all can decide whether it will enhance their production (of market goods or household goods), but the government requires all to pay a license to the discoverer/inventor, thus according her a time-limited monopolistic property right. As with other second-best solutions, this solution does not attain an optimal level of good new ideas, but it approaches it more closely than other institutional arrangements. Optima here are, of course, understood in welfarist terms. The competitive market is a Pareto optimum, and second-best approaches to it, such as those provided by intellectual property rights, are supposed to be welfare improvements.[2]

[2] It is worth noting that owing to technological change over the last fifty years and the increased economic importance of good ideas about information technology, and pharmaceutical technology in particular, the argument for governmental coercion to ensure an optimal provision of good new ideas is easily extended to an equally strong argument for a transnational authority with the power to abridge national sovereignty. For without such a strong world government that can override national authorities, the nation states' enforcement of intellectual property rights will be unable to mitigate the problem of optimal supply of good ideas.

The absence of an internationally enforceable patent right is close to the same as no patent right at all. This consequence follows from the difficulty of effective excludability in consumption of good ideas. When the cost of copying a piece of software became only slightly more than the price of a floppy disk, excluding non-purchasers from access to the good rests on the willingness of purchasers or their agents to refrain from reselling or giving away a non-rivalrous good. It is well known that no such willingness can be relied on and

To the standard welfarist 'second-best' arguments for intellectual property rights another one may be added.[3] It is well known that among the three standard factors of production – land, labor and capital – each suffers from diminishing marginal productivity. Holding the other two constant, increases in any one of them will eventually cease to result in increases in output proportional to the increase in the input. And the proportionate increase is widely supposed to move towards zero as the amount of the single factor added is increased. Insofar as welfare is contingent on the total amount of output – the size of the pie, holding shares in it constant – increases in welfare will be subject to diminishing marginal productivity. In particular, as increases in labor supply impose welfare costs – assuming most people are better off if they work less, and increases in capital impose postponement of consumption and so some immediate opportunity cost in welfare consumption – diminishing marginal productivity will have an impact on human welfare.

The only inputs to production that do not seem to suffer from diminishing marginal productivity are good new ideas. Holding land, labor and capital constant, the provision of good new ideas appears to have been subject to large and persistent gains in productivity, and in many cases increasing marginal productivity. As is well known, the main factor in economic growth has always been technological change,[4] and in general

that consequently the protection afforded by nationally enforceable patents is quite inadequate. When the ease and undetectability of copying good ideas dropped further, owing to the availability of high bandwidth to transmit digital copies of information, these protections become non-existent.

In the case of pharmaceuticals, the marginal cost of a single dose may be less than the price of a packet of refined sugar, while the average cost may be thousands of dollars. When, owing to the ability to reverse-engineer a drug and synthesize it cheaply, the good idea that a drug realizes can be implemented almost anywhere at very low cost, the absence of internationally enforced intellectual property rights may make those nationally enforced actually welfare reducing in their home economies. (Consider the impact of Indian or Brazilian pharmaceutical purchases by US residents.) It is no surprise that TRIPS – trade related intellectual property rights – are at the top of the agenda of the World Trade Organization: for the issue of international enforcement has become tantamount to the existence of intellectual property rights altogether.

Notice that owing to the near public goods character of good ideas, they may make more pressing the recent controversy for and against cosmopolitanism in distributive justice (see T. Nagel, 'The Problem of Global Justice' *Philosophy and Public Affairs* 33 (2007): 113–47; A. Sen, 'What do we Want from a Theory of Justice?' *The Journal of Philosophy* 103(5) (2006): 215–38). For if the moral foundations of intellectual property rights, like chattel property rights, can only be provided on a national basis, those rights will not do their intended work, once technology reaches the point where it permits costless duplication.

3 Alexander Rosenberg, 'On the Priority of Intellectual Property Rights, Especially in Biotechnology' *Politics, Philosophy & Economics* 3(1) (2004): 77–95.

4 Technological change is here broadly construed to include good new ideas that bear on the way in which land, labor and capital broadly construed, are combined. New ideas that have such effects will include ideas about changes in social and political arrangements and other institutional incentives to the efficient use of productive inputs.

what has stood between mankind and a Malthusian fate has been the ever-increasing productivity of the other factors of production owing to the persistent provision of good new ideas. What is more, good ideas do not appear to be decreasing in number or in productive effect. Consider Moore's law, according to which the amount of information storable on a microchip doubles every eighteen months. There are few such well-established empirical generalizations in the arena of technological change, but there are also few areas in which deceleration in the provision of productive new ideas appears to be declining.

Suppose, as seems reasonable that, holding proportions constant, each individual's total welfare increases as production of goods and services increases. Then the provision of good ideas will always increase individual welfare; it will continue to do so at higher rates than increases in land, labor and capital; when increases in the amounts of these inputs are not available, it will continue to be available to increase output and thus welfare; finally, insofar as good ideas enable an economy persistently to produce new goods and services with the same physical inputs of land, labor and capital, the continual provision of good new ideas may even produce welfare increases without significant declines in marginal utility! For consider, a constant flow of new goods and services, as opposed to a constant flow of the same goods and services, will not be subject to the psychological and physiological processes that lead to satiation. Thus, as an input to production, good new ideas seem to have some important welfare-relevant advantages over all other factors of production.

This conclusion provides a further welfarist argument for any institutions that will accelerate the provision of good new ideas, including, but not limited to, the establishment of property rights in such ideas. It might be argued that from a welfarist point of view, intellectual property rights should be entrenched, never trumped, established as side constraints on other rights, institutions and policies that might interfere with the protection of property rights in good ideas. For example, in so far as taxing any activity is a disincentive to investing in it, some may argue that gains from intellectual property should be untaxed. The reasoning is straightforward: if good new ideas are the best and sometimes the only reliable sources of welfare improvements in production of goods and services, then every effort should be made to maximize their provision, no obstacle to their provision should be erected – including disincentives to investment in good ideas, such as taxes. In a regime that taxes in order to provide welfare-increasing goods and services which the market might under-produce, such as public goods, taxation of income and wealth generated by intellectual property should never be taxed, nor should such property ever be expropriated, owing to the chilling effect of such state-takings on the future provision of good new ideas. Of course, this argument was subject to qualifications – immediate emergencies of various sources may warrant abrogation of property rights in good ideas in order to avoid catastrophic outcomes: for example, preventing or ending epidemics may require expropriation of pharmaceutical patents. But in the long run, the welfarist case for making ownership of good ideas a right untrumpable by considerations of welfare may appear attractive.

We can make this sort of consideration more concrete by considering the array of problems on the agenda of governments throughout the world and the apparent practical infeasibility of policies that might solve them, or the political obstacles to their implementation. Global warming is an obvious example. The production of greenhouse gasses continues to grow, and the political will to enact policies to reduce them, or even to reduce their rate of growth, appears to be weak. Nothing short of a revolution in private ownership, tax policy and administered prices can deal with the problem, and even these may already be too late. What might not be too late is some sort of 'technological fix'.

This prospect is held out especially by those overwhelmed by the magnitude of any policy that could work to address the problem, combined with great anxiety about its costs in living standards and other sacrifices. These opponents of environmental regulation point to the threat, evident at the end of the nineteenth century, that the continued increase in the demand for horses would result in an insoluble waste-disposal problem by 1920. At that time, petroleum was selling for almost nothing, as many cities in the developed world had switched their lighting from natural gas and kerosene to electricity, and the advent of the mass-produced inexpensive automobile was some years off. The problem disappeared owing to technical change. A horse manure catastrophe is not the only such threat to civilization so dissipated. Exponents of the do nothing response to the problem of global warming may well point to this history, arguing that what we require to solve the problem is a technical change, one that we can neither predict nor call into existence, but which we can incentivize: a change in energy production, or in nuclear waste storage, or a change in consumption efficiencies such as co-generation, or some other innovation as yet undreamed of (cold-fusion?) may yet prevent, abate or mitigate the consequences of global warming and, the argument goes, we need to do everything in our power to make sure such good ideas are produced and implemented. How can we do this? By removing obstacles to inventiveness and disincentives to it. One such disincentive is the ever-present threat to abrogate intellectual property rights; another is to subject them to taxation of any kind. If good ideas are the only thing that can save the modern world from destruction, it would be foolish to take steps that might slow, or stop, the emergence of such innovations. Even those not so pessimistic about the power of social policy to limit the human impact on the human environment will appreciate the attractions of a technological fix if it can be secured in time. This is another argument for untrumpable intellectual property rights.

There is another quite different argument for intellectual property rights that begins not from a welfarist perspective, but from a natural rights starting point. Welfarists and other consequentialists will not generally be sympathetic to such arguments, but the natural rights argument for ownership of intellectual property begins with such minimum assumptions and avoids the most obvious objections so deftly that it must have considerable appeal even to those who hold that such rights are generally 'nonsense on stilts'.[5]

Start with Locke's argument for the natural right of real and chattel property rights. This theory holds that chattel property and real property are morally permissible if they have been acquired in morally permissible ways, and that these include exchange, gift and 'original acquisition'. The Lockean argument begins with a natural right of self-ownership in an otherwise unowned world. This is perhaps the least controversial among the unqualified rights that natural rights theorists have advanced. Property is acquired by original acquisition when the acquirer 'mixes his labor [already his own by right of self-ownership] with nature'. But Locke subjected this right to chattel or real property to the well-known proviso that 'he leave as much and as good for others'. The evident problem is that this proviso can strictly speaking never be satisfied in a well-populated world, since the earth and the fullness thereof are finite! Accordingly, there is no permissible original acquisition, and all subsequent acquisition by exchange or gift is tainted by the impermissibility of any actual original acquisition.

Locke's attempt to circumvent this problem for his proviso was fatuous, and subsequent theorists have not improved matters. For example, Nozick's version of the principle substitutes for the Lockean proviso the much different one that the initial taking and mixing did not produce a Pareto-inferior outcome, one in which at least one person is left worse off than prior to the original acquisition. According to Nozick's interpretation, an acquisition is just if, and only if the position of others after the acquisition is no worse than their position was when the acquisition was unowned or 'held in common'. The requirement that original acquisition satisfies about the weakest requirement known to welfare economics, without even considering its well-known alternatives, is evidently unsatisfactory.

[5] J. Bentham, *Rights, Representation, and Reform – Nonsense upon Stilts and Other Writings on the French Revolution*, P. Schofield, C. Pease-Watkin and C. Blamires (eds) (Oxford: Clarendon Press, 2002), p. 330.

However, the problem of leaving as good and as much does not daunt a similar Lockean argument for intellectual property. After all, when it comes to good new ideas, there seems to be no trouble satisfying the Lockean proviso: good ideas are the result of mixing one's labor with nature: what you do is think about nature – its concrete aspects and its abstract ones, to come up with good ideas, ones that enhance the production of goods and services. And when you come up with a good idea, you have left as good and as much for others. For the number of good ideas is indenumerable. If ideas can be property, then you have satisfied the Lockean proviso. You may give or trade these ideas as you like, confident that you have created property that will satisfy a high moral standard. The only potentially controversial assumption one needs to establish a natural right in the ownership of a good idea is the natural right of self-ownership.[6] Many persons are loath to account chattel and real property a natural, imprescriptive, inalienable or otherwise unqualified right along with life and liberty (for this reason the US Declaration of Independence is said to have substituted the pursuit of happiness for Locke's right to property). But an unqualified property right in good ideas that requires nothing more than an unconditional right of self-ownership is not likely to be as objectionable as other unqualified rights.

Owing to these features, Locke's approach to original acquisition of ownership in good ideas may strongly recommend itself to welfarists as a matter of institution design. One of the institution-design problems facing welfarism is how to deal with various indivisibility and scarcity

[6] What is more, the Lockean may even be able to erect on this relatively uncontroversial basis an equally secure foundation for the moral permissibility of chattel property and real property. Suppose that chattel, real and intellectual property are all treated as just three different types of exchangeable property. Just because the two former are concrete, and therefore relatively easy to make excludable, while good ideas are abstract and so difficult to make excludable, is no basis for a moral distinction between them. If this assimilation of the three types of property is reasonable, intellectual property can lend its cover, so to speak, to the other classes of property. If the number of good ideas is indefinitely, if not infinitely large, then the total number of items – abstract and concrete – with which labor can be mixed is also indefinite, and this 'amount' can only be increased if we add chattel and real property to intellectual property. When we do so, the whole class of items open to permissible private property creation will satisfy the Lockean proviso: when you include good ideas as part of nature, enclosing a field or throwing a pot on a potter's wheel does leave as good and as much for others – not always as good a field or as much clay, but enough other things that will result in property of equal or greater value when they are the result of mixing labor and nature. Since land and things can be exchanged for ownership rights in originally acquired intellectual property that satisfies the Lockean proviso, the halo of moral permissibility that hovers over good ideas will spread to other kinds of property, too. In fact, it will turn out that chattel and real property have always been acquired in a way that satisfies the Lockean proviso. It's just that no one ever noticed, until they realized that besides things and land, there are indefinitely many good ideas to privatize!

problems that arise when we set out to distribute property in a welfare-enhancing or optimizing way. Some items are not easy to divide up for equal distribution, other properties cannot be divided up without destroying their welfare-enhancing potential, and of course, any scheme of distribution will have substantial incentive effects with knock-on consequences for the subsequent welfare of recipients and others. The Lockean proviso sets an implicit distributional standard that has attractive incentive effects: it encourages activities – the mixing of labor with nature – that have socially beneficial consequences, and by apportioning outcomes in accordance with effort, reconciles those who expend less effort to their less favorable outcomes. But a private property regime based on a Lockean account of original acquisition will only have these happy features if it can unarguably be satisfied by original acquirers. This seems much easier to do in the case of good ideas than in regard to any other production or consumption good. So it makes a Lockean rule for assigning private property rights in good ideas one that welfarists should be in sympathy with, even when they reject it as grounds for an unqualified natural right.

2. How the productivity argument and technological change weaken the case for intellectual property rights

These, then, are powerful considerations in favor of a regime of intellectual property rights, which straddle competing political philosophies. There are, however, in these very arguments the seeds of a set of perhaps equally strong counter-arguments that start from a welfarist commitment and conclude that no such intellectual property rights be established.

The argument against a property right in good new ideas begins with the alleged solution to the under-provision/over-investment problem raised by the near-public good character of good ideas. This is the patent right – a time-limited monopoly given to the inventor/discoverer of a good new idea in exchange for full disclosure of the idea to all potential users. The package of a temporary monopoly plus full disclosure is supposed to enable a competitive market to establish a price for the good idea that will do two things. First, it will compensate the inventor/discoverer for risk, investment and production costs; second, the price will be low enough that the idea's implementation by purchasers will enhance their productivity, their income and the welfare of others that results from productivity's increased supply and consequently lower price.

But monopolies are always market failures, ones in which the market-cannot set a market clearing Pareto-optimal price, or at least cannot be known to do so, and in which there are incentives to the supplier not to offer goods at a market-clearing price. In the case of the patent, there is a further want of information about how many years the monopoly should be enforced in the interests of the inventor/discoverer. This should vary as the kind of activity the good idea is to be put to, the difficulty of inventing around the good idea, the costs of discovery/invention, the risks to the inventor/discoverer, the benefits to potential buyers of the license to employ the good idea, etc. It is unlikely that these variables will be very similar in magnitude over ideas and times. At the same time, it is difficult to implement a regime that allows monopoly time to vary in a way that is sensitive to these factors and so ensures optimal provision of good new ideas in the many different areas of innovation. It is no surprise that estimates of the time required for a monopoly to repay the innovator's costs are pretty close to the number of years at present granted to patent rights. Altogether too convenient.

But this proposal does not solve another potentially more serious problem; indeed, it may exacerbate it. If an intellectual property regime modeled on copyright collectives were actually effective, it would thereby increase the likelihood of market failure through increasing concentrations of economic power resulting from increasing returns to scale. This is a feature such a proposal shares with the patent right. We may well be prepared to adopt a scheme that rewards innovators if we have reason to suppose that it more nearly approaches a Pareto optimum that might otherwise be achieved. However, there is reason to think that any privatization of good ideas results in a market failure, one more serious and more cumulative even than that produced by the temporary monopoly of the patent. Recall the argument that good ideas are the only inputs to production which do not suffer from diminishing marginal productivity. This is part of an argument for not placing any barriers to their emergence. But the way in which good ideas always increase productivity is crucial in the present connection. They do so almost always by increasing the returns to scale of the other components of production, either individually or as a package. We know from the proofs of the existence, uniqueness and stability of general equilibrium that markets do not generally clear at Pareto-optimal prices when returns to scale are not constant. Less formally, it is well known that when a small number of producers can effect economies of scale in production, they cease to be price-takers. They can cut prices and drive competitors out of the market, effect market failures of monopolistic competition, and sometimes even complete monopoly with substantial barriers to entry for potential competitors owing to the high returns to scale of their production.

Here we have a phenomenon related to, but much more serious than the 'anticommons effect' that commentators on the patent right in scientific research have noticed.[7] The anticommons effect is the problem generated for researchers in pure science by the intellectual property rights granted to others which obstruct their access to further new ideas. For instance, the patenting of certain reagents, techniques and machines required for basic scientific research in certain fields means that anyone pursuing research in these fields, even without a pecuniary interest in the research's outcome, may have to spend substantial sums to acquire licenses to make use of these tools of basic research.[8] Sometimes the licenses are available only on the condition that the licensor can secure some portion of the stream of income, if any, from the new research. In effect, the established patent rights erect a barrier to entry to the good idea commons, that region of thought and experimentation free to all, in which the innovator seeks to mix his labor with nature. Much has been made of the prospect of this anticommons effect and a certain amount of research has been devoted to determining whether it exists or not.

In fact, the barrier to entry that patent rights create may turn out to be much more extensive if, as seems unarguable, they generally make for increasing returns to scale in whatever productive process they have a role. The owner of a good idea is either in a position to exploit it immediately in production of some good or service directly or indirectly consumed, or in a position to sell it to someone so positioned. The resulting increase in returns to scale enables the owner of the idea to cease being a price-taker and to begin securing the 'rents' associated with increased returns, monopolistic competition and the resulting market failure. When the costs of creating new ideas and putting them to use are so high that only firms already very large are in a position to pay them by employing the creators of these ideas, the resulting impact increasing Pareto-inferior market outcomes is evident and ever increasing. Starting with the slightest enhancement in production and the advantage in rents it secures, canny and fortunate businesses can secure ownership of a continuing stream of good ideas, each built on the last, and all tending to the same suboptimal market outcome.

The impact of good ideas on increasing returns to scale is the 'flip side' of the impact of good ideas on decreasing marginal productivity. After a certain point the potential benefit to welfare which good ideas confer, at least in principle, will be swamped by the potential costs to welfare which they confer. And the trouble is, it is very difficult to see how the benefit can

[7] M. Heller, and R. Eisenberg, 'Can Patents Deter Innovation? The Anticommons in Biomedical Research' *Science* 280(5364) (1998): 698–701.

[8] Cf. the Wisconsin Alumni Research Foundation patents on stem cell creation methods at www.wicell.org/.

be secured without the cost, for they are inextricably linked. It is most often because they produce increased returns to scale that good ideas do not suffer from decreasing marginal productivity. At any rate, it is hard to see how we can arrange matters to have the benefit of good new ideas without the cost, so long as we operate within a market economy.

It may be debated whether at present the interconnected markets of the world are significantly deformed from free-market optima by monopolistic competition, cartels, coalitions, oligopolies and competitors so large that they are no longer price-takers, but successful rent-seekers. What cannot be denied is that to the degree good ideas avoid the problem of diminishing marginal productivity, they increase the opportunities for those who monopolize them, even temporarily, to become price-setters. As their impact becomes economically more and more important from the point of view of productivity, the impact of a patent system on departures from the welfare optima a market system can provide must also increase. If good ideas are so beneficial to general welfare that they merit the conferring of a monopoly, restrictions on their use must be proportionately as harmful to it that the restriction should be minimized.

Technological change has had an obvious and undeniably significant impact on the effectiveness of the limited monopoly patent right as a 'second-best' solution to the problem of optimizing the supply of good new ideas. Good ideas are arguably abstract objects, which need to be stored as inscriptions in a written language powerful enough to include a good deal of mathematics and a variety of conventions for illustrating, diagramming and modeling. The cost of accurate copying of such inscriptions has dropped by many orders of magnitude over the last half-century. Similarly, the cost of transmitting copies of them has dropped, as has the reliability, while the cost of preventing such transmission has also become prohibitive. Additionally, the technological resources available for reverse engineering the actual concrete products made by the implementation of the good ideas has increased, thereby also increasing the ability and reducing the cost of extracting a good idea from its physical realization. The significance of these two trends is evident in the importance that technologically developed nations have attached to TRIPS – trade-related intellectual property – and its protection by the World Trade Organization. The problems and costs of international enforcement of patent rights are just a magnification of the increasingly international ineffectiveness of the patent right as a second-best solution to the problem of optimizing the provision of good ideas.[9]

[9] See n. 2 above.

Creating an international policing agency with the power to investigate, prevent and punish violations of intellectual property rights requires a degree of sovereignty violation that would be unprecedented and is quite unrealistic. But even if nation-states were to waive sovereignty, the cost and the ease of copying and transmission of good ideas that technology now permits means that effective enforcement requires a degree of intrusiveness offensive to most civil liberties and likely to have significant social, as well as administrative costs. Moreover, the cost of misconduct by enforcement agents would also have to be factored into any evaluation of whether patent rights continued to be an efficient second-best solution to the problem of optimal supply of good ideas.

Of course, the problem of international enforcement in an environment of cheap copying and transmission, along with increasingly effective and cheap reverse engineering, is only a more severe case of the problem now facing the enforcement agencies of national governments in their home markets. At least in the United States, enforcement has always been effected by lawsuits against individuals and corporations with deep enough pockets to make the risks of patent infringement significant. As the population engaging in such infringement broadens to include more and more individuals who require fewer and fewer infrastructural resources to pirate patented ideas, or to reimport their concrete instantiations from abroad, and can effectively hide their use, the effectiveness of patent rights as a basis for rewarding invention and discovery will continue to decline until it no longer works at all in certain areas. As these areas become the most important domains of economic activity, the problem of a more effective institutional design solution to the problem of optimal provision of good ideas becomes severe.

Is there an institutional scheme that on the one hand continues to provide large gains to individual inventors or discoverers while reducing or even eliminating the cost of implementing a good idea that everyone can take advantage of freely? If all sellers in a market can take equal advantage of good new ideas, the ideas will not have differential effects on returns to scale that can be parlayed into market failure-producing inequalities. If individuals are adequately rewarded for good ideas, they will invest in their provision up to the level of the expected value of the gain. Is there such a scheme, or mixture of schemes, that can square this circle of free use combined with adequate compensation? The answer may be yes. Indeed, such a system, or at least one that can be adapted to attain these two goals, may already have been operating in pure science for several centuries.

3. The non-property reward regime of pure science

The non-governmental institutions that have emerged since the scientific revolution provide a structure in which innovation has been fostered by the incentives of fame, indeed immortality, of one's achievements, opportunities to engage in more innovation, and shaping the future direction of research, in return for complete public 'ownership' of good new ideas – something easy to accomplish in light of their quasi-public goods character.

The question may arise whether the institutional system of science does as good, a worse or a better job of producing good ideas than the system of patent rights in a competitive market. No answer to this question is available, owing to the nature of scientific innovation. Indeed, its nature is the most serious obstacle to any attempt to explain or predict the direction of economic change over timescales longer than a business cycle. This means that comparisons of the effectiveness of a system without intellectual property rights, like science versus a market rights system, cannot turn on such issues.

Good ideas are quintessentially unpredictable. There is no logic of discovery, nor a psychology or sociology of innovation, still less an economic theory that identifies the conditions that maximize the appearance of good ideas. Economists recognize that growth depends largely on good ideas, a.k.a. technological change, but they are compelled to treat it as the exogenous, 'residual' component of economic growth which they cannot explain.[10] Endogenous growth theory introduces forces familiar to economists (e.g. imperfect competition, human capital, levels of R & D investment by government and firms, international trade barriers, von Neumann/Morgenstern uncertainty) that treat good ideas as a desired outcome – a component of the 'objective function'.[11]

Karl Popper appreciated that good ideas are unpredictable, and used this fact to argue that a predictively powerful social science is impossible. Besides Popper's ('logical' and controversial) argument for the unpredictability of an innovation,[12] there is the fact that good ideas interact 'strategically', not parametrically, and there is no stable equilibrium towards which the production of such ideas moves. Like a move in a strategic game without a Nash equilibrium, one good idea generates a cascade of

[10] R. Solow, 'Technical Change and the Aggregate Production Function' *Review of Economic Statistics* 30 (1957): 214–31.

[11] P. Romer, 'Endogenous Technical Change' *Journal of Political Economy* 98 (1998): 55–79. Rosenberg, n. 3 above.

[12] K. Popper, *The Poverty of Historicism* (London: Routledge, 1957), pp. vii–viii.

interacting improvements that, if anything, increase the unpredictability of subsequent good ideas.

We do not need a proof that no predictively powerful social science is possible to appreciate that identifying conditions sufficient, or even interestingly necessary for the optimal provision of good ideas, is fraught with difficulties, and that in many cases good ideas have arisen in the complete absence of property rights – indeed, in a context in which claims to such rights or to secrecy about them are treated as morally wrong. What we do know about the institutional arrangements of pure science provides some reason to think that the actual system of awarding fame/immortality/scientific influence is the optimal one for resource allocation in the provision of good ideas in pure science. What is more, it provides for a permanent monopoly on credit without any control over other material rewards, and so no market failure consequences.

As we have seen, good ideas are not easily excludable and are non-rivalrous in consumption. Because of this, the first hard copy of a good idea is almost all that is needed to confer its benefit on society. Cheap copying makes another hard copy very easy to provide, and so the price that it fetches will be low. In pure science this means that if two or more individuals or groups are seeking a new idea, once one of them has secured it and made a hard copy of the good idea, the second individual or group to have secured it adds almost nothing to the good idea's social benefit. The success of the first innovator makes the investment of the second-place innovator a sunk cost though, of course, this can only be known retrospectively. Thus, for example A. R. Wallace's years of discomfort in collecting the data to formulate the theory of natural selection turned out to be an almost total waste, since Darwin had already hit upon the idea. In spite of his best efforts to share the credit for independent discovery, Darwin got almost all of it. We call it Darwinian theory, not the Darwinian/Wallacian theory, and the reason is not just euphony. Why? Because in science the norm is that almost all the fame and influence, distinction and merit accrues to the first innovator or innovating group, no matter how close in time the runners-up achieve the same result.

As Michael Strevens has shown, the fact that in science the first discovery confers all the social benefit and that the first discovery gets all the scientific credit is no accident.[13] Strevens shows how, from a rational choice perspective, the uniqueness of the social benefit makes the norm of awarding sole credit to first discoverer a resource-optimizing rule. He writes:

[13] M. Strevens, 'The Role of the Priority Rule in Science' *Journal of Philosophy* 100(2) (2003): 55–79.

A scientific reward scheme such as the priority rule acts as a system of incentives, encouraging researchers to devote their time and energy to some research programs in preference to others. Different reward schemes, then, may result in different allocations of resources among competing research programs. Society has an interest in adopting a reward scheme that promotes an allocation with a relatively high expected payoff.

. . .

The priority system [to the first discoverer goes all the credit] promotes an especially efficient allocation of resources in winner-confers-all situations, that is, in situations where almost all benefit is extracted from a goal the very first time it is reached.[14]

Like other rational choice models, Strevens' makes some assumptions, including the following, plus the stipulation that individuals are risk averse:

(1) Every research program has a single goal. There are only two possible outcomes of the program's endeavors: total success, if it realizes the goal, or total failure, if it does not.
(2) Different research programs have different intrinsic potentials.
(3) A program's chance of success – that is, the probability that it will achieve its goal – depends on two things, its intrinsic potential and the resources invested in the program.

Strevens shows that on these conditions, the rule that all credit for a discovery attends the first discoverer results in individual scientists choosing to devote themselves to the research program with the highest potential of success. Which, of course, is just what is wanted by way of institution design.[15]

What is the relevance of Strevens' modeling here, besides providing an attractive explanation of the actual institutions of scientific credit as they

[14] Ibid., 56.

[15] It is worth sketching some aspects of Strevens' argument in order both to show its plausibility as an explanation cum justification of the priority rule. To begin with, Strevens shows that the symmetry between the fact that the first discoverer confers all the benefit of the discovery to the society and that the society confers all the reward of discovery to the first discoverer, is derivable from a more general system of rewards that confers them in proportion with the benefits individuals confer on society that most people will recognize as fair, coupled with the special features of scientific discovery – that the second discoverer adds no value additional to that conferred on society by the first discoverer.

Strevens' argument compares three principles of reward to individuals – each of which reflects the individual's marginal contribution to some productive outcome, and each of which is preferable, from the point of view of allocative efficiency in the distribution of investment of a scientist's time and effort, depending as to whether the research programs are independent in their goal and equally likely to succeed or fail, or one of the two research programs with independent goals is much more likely to succeed than the other, or finally the two programs have the same goal and one is much more likely to succeed than the other. Under the last of these conditions, Strevens shows, a winner-take-all rule

emerged over the last 400 years, is that it suggests that the institution is rational or optimal from a social point of view. First, it underwrites according discoverers of good ideas in science at least a permanent monopoly, not on sale of their ideas, but on the fame, influence, admiration, respect, kudos, etc. acquired as a result of the benefits to society of their ideas. Second, insofar as this scheme has worked well to provide a constant flow of good ideas over the last half-millennium, it has done so without the need for a market failure-producing second best.

There are significant differences between pure and applied scientific discoveries and practical inventions that will lead some to the conclusion that the scientific model has little of relevance to the problem of institution design that patent rights attempt to solve. In particular, the schedule of practical invention is driven by perceived immediate direct or indirect benefit that consumers will pay for, while the agenda of scientific discovery is driven by curiosity and perhaps the desire for fame, instead of material gain. But these differences should lead us to contemplate how the reward system of science, which avoids the market failures of patent rights, might be adapted to provide an alternative to them that is closer to a welfare optimum.

4. Adapting the regime of scientific discovery to the domain of invention

Let us consider introducing a modified version of the reward system of pure science to the applied arts of practical invention. If it works, we will have no need of an institution of private property in good ideas in order to produce and optimally exploit them. Recall the reward structure of science: all credit to the first discoverer, none to any other, no matter how close on the heels they follow, along with full early disclosure and completely free exploitation of the discovery by anyone else. Remember also Strevens' argument that this system optimizes the resource allocation of science and scientists to the problems that most combine solubility and importance. The following multi-component scheme will enable us to adapt these attractive features from pure scientific discovery to practical applied innovation and invention. The central feature of this scheme is that it makes intellectual property rights unnecessary.

1. *Government-sponsored prizes.* The establishment by national government science agencies boards, modeled on peer-review panels, of single

will provide rational agents with strong incentives to devote themselves to what they judge to be the most promising research program, which is just what from the point of view of social benefit we should wish.

winner prizes for specific inventions and the selection of winners. The National Science Foundation (NSF), National Institutes of Health (NIH), Department of Energy (DOE) in the United States, the Medical Research Council in the UK, the Centre national de la recherche scientifique in France, the Ministry of International Trade and Industry in Japan and the German Science Ministry currently distribute funding on a fairly impartial and largely objective basis, without significant 'rent-seeking' by any party to their policies. The success of these agencies suggests that they can be trusted with the quasi-political task of identifying targets of applied science and calculating the size of prizes that will elicit investments in solutions that will then be made freely available to all. To some extent such decisions will be political, and thus may become matters of democratic electoral debate, a desirable outcome in the opinion of many. This practice exploits a device long ago put in place and effective in the invention of reliable chronometers and the calculation of longitude at sea. Different countries can be expected to identify a range of prize targets depending on their national needs – industrial, agricultural, environmental, medical, even cultural. It is safe to assume that the details of any invention that wins a national prize will be difficult to keep secret even by nations eager to do so.

This system will also require the enforcement of free dissemination of relevant information – data and theories – that has long been a characteristic of pure science. Relevant information that all potential entrants in a prize competition can equally access will be required if they are to estimate their likelihood of success and make rational investment decisions. In the recent past, changes in practices demanded by the USNIH and the increasing attractiveness of free publication on the internet (e.g. *PLOS, the Public Library of Science*) suggest that this problem is a tractable one in the long run (though the present level of trade secrecy in the pharmaceutical industry is much too great to allow for an effective prize system).

2. *Privately sponsored prizes.* Individuals and groups will be allowed and encouraged to pool funds for publicly announced single-winner prizes for specific inventions of their choice. Notice that this practice has already been put in place to encourage the building of private reusable space vehicles, for example. If the prizes were considered untaxable charitable contributions, national tax authorities would have an incentive to monitor these competitions for openness, and to enforce public disclosure of the inventions where there is any reluctance to do so. The availability of the internet makes it feasible easily and cheaply to put together large coalitions of small contributors to establish prizes for particular inventions. The low barriers to entry into this arena and the low transaction costs of

establishing prizes should result in a proliferation of them across a wide range of needs, interests and desires. The feasibility of this proposal turns on the willingness of large numbers of people to provide others with a quasi-public good, even when these others free-ride on the costs of the good. Evidence from experiments in game theory suggests that when the amounts individuals pay are low, the number of cooperating individuals is very large, and the benefit is great and non-rivalrous, the participants are prepared to tolerate free-riders even when exclusion is feasible. When as in these cases it will not be possible, the willingness to participate in these prize-establishing collectives should be considerable.

3. *Celebrity*. Popular culture has made celebrities of many scientists, engineers and inventors, from Einstein and Hawkins to Bill Gates and Steve Jobs. The celebrity itself has been a reward to these innovators and it has been exploited by some of them for income and wealth. The Andy Warhol '15 minutes of fame' effect is well known, and public relations agencies are adept at making it pay for those subject to it. Thus the contemporary ability to capitalize on celebrity can be exploited to provide no- or low-cost incentives to inventors to invest in the creation of good new ideas that immediately become public property. Indeed, their celebrity and the opportunity to turn it to material advantage will be an incentive to make their inventions known and adopted.

4. *First-mover advantages*. These are increasingly important in an information-technology economy. By making a discovery that sets a standard, provides a head start in satisfying it while imposing engineering constraints on competitors, inventors can reap substantial rewards not only in the absence of property rights in the invention, but because they have waived them through free disclosure. When we add to these first-mover advantages those associated with brand name, celebrity, fashion and other non-monetary advantages of first movers in an environment with cheap, fast and international communication to potential customers who seek more than just a product, but alas also an image, the incentives to inventors even in the absence of prizes will be considerable.

5. Conclusion: rent-seeking and the problem of information

The argument against the patent right's effectiveness as a device or institution for providing an optimal level of good new ideas turns on the opportunities that it provides for successful rent-seeking. As an admission that even under perfect competition there is a market failure that can only approximately be rectified by a limited-term monopoly, advocates of the patent must reconcile themselves to such rent-seeking. Indeed, they must reconcile themselves to a persistent increase in opportunities for rent-seeking, with ever-increasing success as good new ideas enhance returns to scale, and the ability to be a price-setter, instead of a price-taker.

As noted above, this is not a problem from which the alternatives of prizes – publicly financed and privately financed – are immune. Moreover, the market inefficiencies that the role of celebrity and first-mover status provides are ones that a prize system will share with a patent system. But the prize system is not likely to incur anywhere as serious a degree of rent-seeking as the monopolistic and oligopolistic results of patent protection. To begin with, there is a good deal of evidence in the conduct of scientific review panels at the US NSF, NIH, DOE, and at the Medical Research Council of Great Britain, that such panels are relatively immune from the deformation of their scientific judgments by bribery and other forms of corrupt practice. As models for the administrative apparatus which would identify research goals, set prizes and adjudicate winners, this experience gives us some confidence that the prize system can be free from serious corruption. Too much confidence in this happy outcome would be misplaced. More important, however, is the trade-off that the prize system offers between a small number of very powerful and effective rent-seekers and a potentially larger number of relatively less effective rent-seekers. In general, the sort of rent-seeking characteristic of large-scale businesses operating in an unregulated 'free market' produces substantial profits (i.e. real rents) while imposing a reduction in consumer surplus and generating a dead weight loss to the economy as well. A large number of relatively weak bureaucrats will each have the opportunity to secure a small rent as the price of their participation in the governmental process. Suppose that in a prize system many of them take this opportunity.

The question then becomes, is the total loss through rent-seeking imposed by a large number of small rent-seekers (1) greater, (2) smaller, or (3) the same in size as the total loss to the economy imposed by a small number of very powerful rent-seekers? There are good reasons to think that (2) is the case. Rent-seeking by relatively weak agents is a 'frictional' phenomenon in all institutions (as public choice economics emphasizes); in the government's scientific institutions it is rather lower than in other parts of the government. Owing to the relative weakness of the rent-seekers in a bureaucracy, it is easier to suppress and sanction than in the cases of powerful rent-seekers (elected officials and corporate executives acting for large corporations). All in all, the dimensions of the market failure imposed by a prize system may be significantly smaller than those already imposed by a patent system.

The real problem for a prize system is an informational one, a problem that, as Hayek emphasized so long ago,[16] has hitherto only been solved by the competitive market. The great achievement of the price mechanism in competitive markets is that it provides an efficient information-processing mechanism that elicits people's real wants and their real willingness to pay for the provision of these wants. No other information-processing device has ever been designed that has these features, and Hayek argued that none could be. The calculation problems alone are so huge that they make state central planning impossible, even in the absence of rent-seeking and strategic behavior by consumers and producers.

Setting prize targets and amounts for good new ideas is something the decentralized decision-making apparatus of the market is very good at, when it is harnessed to do so by the patent system. The price mechanism of a free market does this well, by sending signals about what people really want – the prize targets, and what people are really prepared to pay for them – the prize amounts. The award of a patent allows individuals to secure such information by putting their product on the market. It is the temporary monopoly that produces some market failure, of course, even as it provides the needed information about prize targets and prize awards in terms of the success of the innovation and the returns to the patent holder.

By contrast, setting prize targets and amounts is something a committee of wise persons may not be so good at. Yet this is the task assigned to such a committee by the scheme proposed here. The closest we have come to an institution that can identify prize targets and amounts prospectively, as the scheme requires, are the scientific review boards which vet grant applications and award grants. But here, too, as in the case of the patent cum market-price system, the source of prize goal is the person who proposes to undertake the research, and that person is also the source of information about the cost which is proposed to reward the investment to attain the goal. We require a system in which the prize panel originates the targets and the awards, and providing this is the sort of problem which Hayek has given us good reason to believe can never be solved by central planning.

This problem is the most serious one facing a prize system. The only hope for solving it is to be found in some of the same technological developments that threaten the patent system with failure to elicit optimum investment in new ideas. And there may be such hope after all. The

[16] F. Hayek, 'The Use of Knowledge in Society' *American Economic Review* 35 (1945): 519–30.

low cost of communication and the ease of establishing networks of individual informants that are hard to manipulate, make it increasingly possible to construct an electronic network of information collection, storage and transmission of information about what products and services are wanted and how much people are willing to pay for them that could rival the price system for speed and incentive compatibility in the reliable transmission of people's wants and their willingness to pay. As much recent work in the environment of free-ware, wikipedia, voluntary consumer-satisfaction sites and rating services, open-source program development and other internet-related enterprises suggest, people are increasingly willing to provide reliable information about their preferences, and otherwise to add value to various projects without remuneration. Policing has also arisen spontaneously and has been effective in uncovering attempts to manipulate the information transmission role of the internet. All this suggests that as information-processing costs decline, and the number of persons connected on-line increase, it may be possible to design a variety of bodies that formally and informally advise, or at least provide data that can be used by a body or bodies charged with identifying prize goals and prize amounts. So informed, the prize system will elicit good new ideas without imposing on the economy any of the costs that might arise from their freedom of diminishing marginal productivity and increasing returns to scale.

Two practical problems face the prize system, especially in pharmaceuticals. First, stipulating a minimal target to be secured by an innovation to gain a prize deprives innovators of incentives to exceed the target. Second, once a target is attained and a prize awarded, it may be difficult to incentivize improvements in the winning idea. These two objections have vexed a practical proposal for prizes, such as Pogge's[17] to increase the provision of pharmaceuticals that will alleviate illness in developing nations that cannot otherwise expect commercial interest in the health problems of their populations.[18] How serious such problems are can be gauged from the frequency with which parallel problems arise in the peer-review process of pure science.

[17] T. Pogge, *World Poverty and Human Rights: Cosmopolitan Responsibilities and Reforms* (2nd edn, Cambridge: Polity Press, 2008).

[18] J. Sonderholm, 'Intellectual Property Rights and the TRIPs Agreement: An Overview of Ethical Problems and some Proposed Solutions' Policy Research Working Papers. (Washington DC: World Bank, 2010).

4 Ethical issues surrounding intellectual property rights

Jorn Sonderholm[*,**]

1. Introduction

The Agreement on Trade-Related Aspects of Intellectual Property Rights (TRIPS) negotiated in the 1986 Uruguay Round under the auspices of the General Agreement on Tariffs and Trade (GATT) incorporated substantial and uniform protections of Intellectual Property Rights (IPRs) into the international trade system. A large body of contemporary philosophical and interdisciplinary literature suggests that IPRs as implemented in the TRIPS Agreement, and various other trade agreements, give rise to a number of ethical problems. This chapter seeks to (i) give an overview of what these problems are, (ii) offer an outline of proposals as to how these problems might be alleviated and (iii) briefly explain the two classical defences of the ethical permissibility of IPRs.

The ethical problems raised by IPRs are most pertinent when it is socially valuable goods such as life-saving medicines and genetically modified seeds that are given intellectual property (IP) protection. The discussions in this chapter will revolve around just one product type in order to bring out the broader ethical issues caused by the implementation of IPRs. In line with much contemporary literature on the ethical dimensions of IPRs, the product type in question is life-saving medicines.

2. IPRs and the problems of access and availability

Thomas Pogge offers a good overview of how pharmaceutical innovation is incentivized under an IPR-driven regime and how such a regime might

[*] Cambridge University Press gives Jorn Sonderholm credit as the original author of this chapter. It also acknowledges that this chapter was originally published as 'Ethical Issues Surrounding Intellectual Property Rights' in *Philosophy Compass* 5(12) (2011): 1107–15. Reproduced by kind permission of Blackwell Publishing. The version of the chapter published in this volume, compared to the original version, has one additional paragraph in section 3.

[**] I would like to thank Anthony Laden and an anonymous referee from *Philosophy Compass* for helpful comments on an earlier version of this chapter.

lead to ethically problematical outcomes.[1] It is an expensive, time-consuming and financially risky endeavour to produce new and safe drugs for the market. Given that pharmaceutical companies must bear all the costs of the development process, it is no surprise that such companies are reluctant to undertake research and development (R&D) of new drugs unless the financial prospects of doing so are bright. Without IPRs on pharmaceutical innovations, such prospects would be anything but bright. The reason for this is that as soon as an inventor firm introduces a new innovation on the market, other companies will copy it, and given that these other companies have had no costs in terms of R&D, they will be able to charge a price for the product that is much lower than that charged by the inventor firm. The market price for the product will therefore very likely be driven down to just above marginal costs of production, and the inventor firm will be unable to recoup its R&D costs. A macroeconomic set-up for the buying and selling of drugs that does not offer innovators IPRs to their innovations is therefore likely to lead to a market failure or undersupply of pharmaceutical innovations.

IPRs are a socio-economic tool that creates a temporary monopoly for inventor firms and enables such firms to charge prices for their innovations that are many times higher than their marginal cost of production of the innovations. This allows the inventor firms to salvage their research costs and secure a profit on their innovations. So by virtue of increasing the financial attractiveness of engaging in the process of producing pharmaceutical innovations, IPRs can be, and often are, instrumental in correcting the market failure of undersupply of pharmaceutical innovations.

However, the introduction of IPRs for pharmaceutical innovations often creates another market failure that consists of the fact that a number of mutually beneficial transactions between seller and buyer do not take place. The relatively high price of an IP-protected drug squeezes certain potential buyers out of the market: namely, those who are able and willing to buy the product if it was priced somewhat above its marginal costs of production, but cannot afford the product when it is priced at the profit-maximizing level that obtains during the period in which the product is IP protected. The feature of IPRs that they squeeze out certain potential buyers from the market, creates what might be labelled the 'exclusion problem' or 'access problem'.[2] According to some, the exclusion/access problem is morally troubling when it is life-saving medicines and not

[1] See T. Pogge, 'Human Rights and Global Health: A Research Program' *Metaphilosophy* 36 (1–2) (2005): 182–209.

[2] See M. Selgelid, 'A Full-Pull Program for the Provision of Pharmaceuticals: Practical Issues' *Public Health Ethics* 1(2) (2008): 134–45.

merely computer software, music CDs or movie disks that a group of people is excluded from having access to.[3]

The exclusion/access problem is not the only thing that follows in the wake of strong IPRs. A different problem is the 'availability problem'.[4] This problem is fruitfully introduced in the context of R&D of drugs for diseases that mainly affect people in low-income countries where R&D of drugs for such diseases is very limited. The primary reason for this is that many poor people simply do not have sufficient money to pay for drugs for their ailments. For-profit pharmaceutical companies therefore have little economic incentive for investing resources into the R&D of drugs for these diseases.

The availability problem is a consequence of the fact that the incentivizing mechanism for innovation constituted by IPRs establishes a direct link between the incentive to innovate and the price of the innovative product. Under an IPR-driven regime, profits are generated exclusively from sales. This means that the higher the price a product can command on the market, the higher is the incentive to invest resources into the R&D process of it. An IPR-driven regime is therefore not one that is conducive to the investment in R&D of products that are socially valuable to predominantly poor populations or populations that are small. Socially valuable goods to such populations are simply not being made available at the same rate as goods that are socially valuable to relatively rich populations of a significant size.

3. Two standard solutions to the access problem

As emphasized by Pogge,[5] there are two standard solutions to the access problem. One commonly goes under the name of 'differential pricing', and is the idea that an IP-protected product is sold at different prices in different geographical regions. In high-income countries, the product is sold at one price, whereas it is sold at a lower price in low-income countries. By pricing the product in this way, an inventor firm, at least in theory, is able to have the best of both worlds. High profits on the product are secured in markets with a high buying power without sacrificing the medium to low profits that come from selling the product in markets with a relatively low buying power. In addition to this, the diminished price of the product in low-income countries means that the

[3] See Pogge, 'Human Rights and Global Health', 187.

[4] See Selgelid, 'A Full-Pull Program' and J. Love and T. Hubbard, *The Big Idea: Prizes to Stimulate R&D for New Medicines*. KEI Research Paper, 2007, 1.

[5] See Pogge, 'Human Rights and Global Health'.

inhabitants of these countries have easier access to the product than they would if the product was priced at the level of high-income countries. For someone who sees the access problem as morally problematic when it comes to life-saving medicines, this latter feature of differential pricing makes differential pricing a prima facie attractive pricing scheme for life-saving medicines.

The other standard solution to the access problem goes under the name 'compulsory licensing'. This mechanism bestows a right on governments to issue production licences for IP-protected innovations that are needed to respond to public emergencies. For example, on the assumption that the HIV/AIDS pandemic currently existing in sub-Saharan Africa counts as a public emergency for a number of countries in this region, the governments of those countries can authorize the production of cheaper generic versions of IP-protected HIV/AIDS drugs on the condition that the authorized companies pay a small licence fee to the IP holders. The market entry of companies producing generic versions of HIV/AIDS drugs will very likely drive down the price of these drugs to just above their marginal cost of production, and this in turn will ease access to the drugs.

Both of the standard solutions to the access problem are problematic. Michael Ravvin gives an illustrative overview of some of the problems that pertain to these solutions.[6] With respect to differential pricing, the primary concern is that of the seepage of cheaply sold drugs from poor countries to rich ones through parallel trade and smuggling. This point is also emphasized by other commentators.[7] Furthermore, there is an issue of social justice in the sense that rich people in low-income countries will have access to a given medicine at a relatively low cost, whereas poor people in high-income countries will have to pay a high price for the same medicine. Fifty million consumers in India today have incomes comparable to those of Europeans,[8] and it is by no means ethically uncontroversial that this segment of people should have access to a given drug at a low price whereas poor, uninsured people in, say, the United States should have to pay a high price for the same drug.

When it comes to compulsory licensing, the main problem from a philosophical perspective is that it has social costs that may negate the short-term benefits that such licensing has by virtue of improving access to

[6] See M. Ravvin, 'Incentivizing Access and Innovation for Essential Medicines: A Survey of the Problems and Proposed Solutions' *Public Health Ethics* 1(2) (2008): 110–23, at 114.

[7] See T. Pogge, *World Poverty and Human Rights: Cosmopolitan Responsibilities and Reforms* (2nd edn, Cambridge: Polity Press, 2008), p. 239.

[8] See Love and Hubbard, *The Big Idea*.

life-saving medicines.[9] Chief among these social costs are: (i) a risk of diminished direct investment in countries that resort to compulsory licensing because owners of IP-protected products will seek out more business-friendly legal environments; (ii) a risk that the company which obtains a compulsory licence will 'shadow price' the original high price of the IP-protected product and thereby generate dead weight loss of its own in pursuit of profits; (iii) a risk that compulsory licensing will reduce the research-driven pharmaceutical sector's incentives to innovate; and (iv) a risk that the governments of countries that house companies whose products have been subject to a compulsory licence by a foreign government will retaliate with trade sanctions that could seriously harm the economy of the nation that has issued the compulsory licence.

A line of thought that draws attention to the long-term social costs of compulsory licensing is, in my opinion, worthy of serious attention. Point (iii) made by Bird is especially strong. Pogge also makes this point by arguing that if compulsory licences are widely used, then pharmaceutical companies are likely to be deterred from investing in R&D of drugs that are likely to be subjected to compulsory licensing. For-profit pharmaceutical companies are therefore likely to eschew this type of R&D entirely. In turn, compulsory licensing will constitute a further barrier to R&D of drugs for diseases that primarily exist in a developing world setting.[10]

If neither differential pricing nor compulsory licensing constitutes an attractive way of alleviating the access problem created by IPRs, what other options are available to those who search for a solution to this problem? Currently, a significant amount of interdisciplinary research is being done on a whole host of incentivizing mechanisms that aim at alleviating the access and availability problem. Prominent examples of such incentivizing mechanisms include a Simple Prize Scheme,[11] the

[9] See R. C. Bird, 'Developing Nations and the Compulsory License: Maximizing Access to Essential Medicines while Minimizing Investment Side-effects' *Journal of Law, Medicine and Ethics* 37(2) (2009): 209.

[10] T. Pogge, 'The Health Impact Fund: Better Pharmaceutical Innovations at Much Lower Prices' in T. Pogge, M. Rimmer and K. Rubenstein (eds), *Incentives for Better Global Public Health: Patent Law and Access to Medicines* (Cambridge University Press, 2010), p. 188.

[11] See J. E. Stiglitz, 'Scrooge and Intellectual Property Rights' *British Medical Journal* 333 (2006): 1279 and J. Crager and M. Price, 'Prizes and Parasites: Incentive Models for Addressing Chagas Disease' *Journal of Law, Medicine and Ethics* 37(2) (2009): 292–304.

Advance Market Commitment idea,[12] the Health Impact Fund,[13] Wild-Card Patent Extensions[14] and Priority Review Vouchers.[15]

It lies outside the scope of this chapter to give an overview of all of these incentivizing mechanisms. Pogge and Hollis's Health Impact Fund (HIF) is perhaps philosophically the most interesting one, and it is worthwhile here to give a brief outline of how it works. At the heart of the proposal is the idea that any firm receiving marketing approval for a new medicine would be offered a choice between exercising its usual patent rights through high prices or registering its product with the HIF. Registration would require the firm to sell its product worldwide at an administered price near the average cost of production and distribution. This would radically minimize the access problem. In exchange for selling its product at a low price, the firm would receive from the HIF a stream of payments based on the assessed global health impact of its drug. The HIF, in other words, is an optional pay-for-performance scheme for new pharmaceuticals.[16] Moreover, it is a scheme that promises to reduce the scope of the availability problem by virtue of offering large monetary rewards to firms that develop drugs for diseases that mainly wreak havoc among poor populations in developing countries. The fund is envisaged to be financed largely by contributions made by national governments.

A key feature of the HIF is that when a firm registers its product, the 'traditional' link between a high selling price of the product and a substantive profit for the firm producing the product is severed. A firm that produces an effective drug against, say, malaria, registers the drug with the HIF and sells the drug cheaply is likely to make a substantive profit on it, given that the drug will significantly reduce the global disease burden.

The HIF is not unproblematic. A number of practical and conceptual barriers to its successful implementation have been suggested.[17] With respect to practical matters, there is an issue of how the HIF can secure accurate information about the impact that various pharmaceutical

[12] See M. Kremer and J. Glennerster, *Strong Medicine: Creating Incentives for Pharmaceutical Research on Neglected Diseases* (Princeton University Press, 2004) and O. Barder, M. Kremer, R. Levine and A. Albright, *Making Markets for Vaccines: From Ideas to Action* (Washington DC: Center for Global Development, 2005).

[13] See A. Hollis and T. Pogge, *The Health Impact Fund: Making New Medicines Accessible for All* (Incentives for Global Health, 2008).

[14] See B. Spellberg, L. G. Miller, M. N. Kuo, J. Bradley, W. M. Schild and J. E. Edwards, 'Societal Costs versus Savings' *Infection* 35(3) (2007): 167–74.

[15] See D. B. Ridley, H. G. Grabowski and J. L. Moe, 'Developing Drugs for Developing Countries' *Health Affairs* 25(2) (2006): 313–24.

[16] Hollis and Pogge, *The Health Impact Fund*, p. 1.

[17] See J. Sonderholm, 'A Reform Proposal in Need of Reform: A Critique of Thomas Pogge's Proposal for How to Incentivize Research and Development of Essential Drugs' *Public Health Ethics* 3(2) (2010): 167–77.

products have on the global disease burden. The problem is not only one of devising a plausible metric that can be used to determine a product's impact on the global disease burden. Assuming that this can be done, there is a practical problem of applying the metric and doing the field work of visiting huge, poor and often geographically isolated populations and obtaining an accurate overview of what the disease burden is in the area and how various pharmaceutical products are contributing to its reduction. With respect to conceptual matters, there is an issue of how the HIF should reward producers of ingredients in 'drug cocktails'. One idea is that the HIF begin by determining what overall impact a given drug cocktail has on the global disease burden. Then it allocates a reward to the drug cocktail and splits that reward between all of the producers that have contributed an ingredient to the cocktail. Such an approach however, is under-specified, in the sense that it leaves open whether the reward should be split evenly among all of the producers who have contributed to the cocktail or according to some formula that takes into account, for example, the costs of the individual ingredients.

These two criticisms have been addressed, and work is ongoing on a number of details of the HIF.[18]

It is a characteristic of all of the incentivizing mechanisms mentioned above that they do not advocate the abolition of IPRs. Each of the mechanisms constitutes merely a change or amendment to the IPR regime as established by the TRIPS Agreement. The underlying sentiment seems to be that though IPRs do lead to some unfortunate outcomes in terms of access and availability, at least to some extent they are defensible as an incentivizing mechanism for innovation of some types of products. How can such a sentiment be justified? Put differently, what are the arguments in favour of IPRs?

4. Two defences of the ethical legitimacy of IPRs

Traditionally, two distinct lines of thought have been fielded for the suggestion that IPRs are ethically justifiable. One appeals to the natural right of an inventor to control the use of her innovation. This is the libertarian defence of IPRs which has its historical roots in the writings of John Locke.[19] In more modern times Robert Nozick has been an

[18] M. Peterson, A. Hollis and T. Pogge, 'A Critique in Need of Critique' *Public Health Ethics* 3(2) (2010): 178–85.

[19] J. Locke, (2008). *Two Treatises of Government* (Cambridge University Press, 2008).

advocate for this line of thought.[20] The libertarian view endows individuals with a natural right of appropriation. This is the idea that any innovator/ worker who mixes her labour with a previously unowned object or natural resource comes to own this object or resource in full and can legitimately deny other people use/appropriation of this object or resource.

The natural right of appropriation central to libertarianism has an important proviso (famously formulated by Locke) which is an 'enough and as good' clause on original appropriation. This proviso states that one can only appropriate unowned resources if one leaves enough and as good for others. Where resources are scarce, one cannot legitimately stake a claim to something by annexing one's labour to it. Neither can one come to own the scarce resource by enhancing its value. If the resource is necessary for the continued well-being of others, then the fact that *x* was the one who developed or improved the resource does not give *x* exclusive rights over it. *x*'s entitlement to reward for her labour is overridden by the entitlement of others to that which is necessary for their survival.

On the libertarian view, there is no morally relevant difference between, say, a farmer who mixes her labour with the land and thereby comes to own the results of this interaction (the timber, the harvest, the fruits, etc.) and a medical researcher who mixes her labour with certain chemicals and thereby comes to own the results of the interaction (physical objects *and* an intellectual idea/formula for a useful drug). Provided that the farmer and the medical researcher pay heed to the Lockean proviso, they both come to enjoy a strong property right in the objects that result from their mixing of their labour with unowned natural resources. This natural property right, moreover, is to be written into the legal framework and enforced by the proper authorities (police and courts of law). Libertarians can therefore see trade agreements such as TRIPS as a legitimate legal enforcement of a pre-existing natural/moral right.

The libertarian defence of IPRs has recently come under attack.[21] The objection is that libertarianism, with its strong emphasis on rights to individual freedom and private property, is inconsistent with IPRs. What such rights do is to enable individuals (innovators) unilaterally to place limits on the personal freedom of others and on what they may do with property they have legitimately acquired. IPRs on a particular medicine, for example, are a de facto legal limitation on what other people may do with their legitimately acquired possessions (chemicals), and this is not something that libertarianism can consistently sanction. At its best, what the libertarian argument can yield is only that medical innovators have

[20] R. Nozick, *Anarchy, State, and Utopia* (New York: Basic Books, 1974).
[21] See Hollis and Pogge, *The Health Impact Fund*, p. 23.

strong property rights on the concrete, physical *tokens* of their innovation (pills, powders, liquids, etc.). The argument cannot yield the conclusion that innovators also have property rights on the innovation *type* (the idea/formula for the medicine).[22]

Whether or not this objection to the libertarian defence for IPRs succeeds is a complicated question. In my view, defenders of IPRs need not, however, preoccupy themselves onerously with finding an answer to it. The reason for this is that such defenders are not best advised to try to back up their view with the libertarian argument. To my mind, a better defence for IPRs is likely to be found by exploring a consequentialist line of thought that appeals to the social utility of IPRs. The general idea here is that IPRs are ethically justifiable because they incentivize innovative R&D, which in turn increases overall human welfare.

Alex Rosenberg has presented an argument that is based on this line of thought.[23] Ian Maitland has also pushed this line of thought.[24] Let us focus here on Rosenberg's argument. The argument is broad in scope, in the sense that it defends the ethical permissibility of IPRs on all innovations. However, the argument does entail that there are some very basic scientific discoveries that should not be allowed to be IP protected. Two important premises of Rosenberg's argument are that good ideas are the only factor of production that does not suffer from diminishing marginal productivity[25] and that welfarism should be employed as the normative basis for institutional design.[26] Welfarism is a form of consequentialism which states that morally the best course of action, policy or institution is the one that maximizes future human welfare. One might think that welfarism must be opposed to the ethical legitimacy of IPRs due to the access problem caused by such rights. However, as Rosenberg observes, welfarism only mandates an abrogation of IPRs if the time frame within which human welfare is calculated is narrowed arbitrarily.[27] It is correct that in the immediate and near term, human welfare is best served by abrogating IPRs, but once the horizon is lengthened, it is not at all obvious that human welfare is best served by such a legislative step.

The source of the complication is threefold: (i) once the IPR on a given product is abrogated in order to meet the needs of those who cannot pay monopoly prices for it, disincentive effects on investment in innovation set

[22] See ibid., p. 65.

[23] A. Rosenberg, 'On the Priority of Intellectual Property Rights, Especially in Biotechnology' *Politics, Philosophy and Economics* 3(1) (2004): 77–95.

[24] I. Maitland, 'Priceless Goods: How should Life-saving Drugs be Priced?' *Business Ethics Quarterly* 12(4) (2002): 451–80.

[25] Rosenberg, 'On the Priority of Intellectual Property Rights', 79.

[26] Ibid., 78.

[27] Ibid., 85.

in; (ii) such effects will be long lasting or even permanent; and (iii) scientific innovations are essentially completely unpredictable and more consequential in their welfare-enhancing effects than any other human activity. These features of scientific innovation result in making the medium-and long-term cost of abrogating IPRs impossible to quantify or measure in detail. There is, however, reason to believe that the cost is huge and that it will exceed the immediate and short-term benefits of abrogating IPRs.

Rosenberg offers a semi-technical argument for this claim. Assume that the population of the world will reach a fixed upper limit within the next half-century and remain there. Assume also that the total quantity of arable land, refinable mineral and non-mineral reserves, and so on, will remain fixed thereafter. Now attach a number to the total level of welfare that exists at this generation: 100 units of welfare (distributed unequally among, say, ten billion people). Assume that the unequal proportions remain constant, while the total welfare increases in each subsequent (20-year) generation by 10 per cent as a result of the continued emergence and implementation of patented innovations. At generation two, the index number for welfare is 110, at generation six it is 161.05, and at generation twelve it is 285.3.

Suppose, however, that there is an outbreak of a serious disease in generation one, and that some IP-protected drug is necessary in order to bring the epidemic under control. Society cancels the IPR on the drug in question, and as a result of this, there is a 20 per cent increase in welfare in generation two and a decline from 10 per cent to 9 per cent in per generation welfare increases thereafter (this decline is due to the chilling effect on innovation that the abrogation of the IPR in generation one brought about). Now, at generation two the welfare index is 120. At generation six it is 169.39, but at generation twelve, the index is 284.08. So if one calculates human welfare over a twelve-generation, or any longer time span, it transpires that welfarism cannot sanction the abrogation of the IPR in question.

At least two objections can be raised against this consequentialist argument. The first is that since we cannot predict what will happen in the future, it makes no sense to suggest that one course of action is preferable to another because the medium- and long-term consequences of the former are better in a particular dimension than those of the latter in the same dimension. The second objection is that the argument is expressive of a cynical and/or heartless standpoint that is not troubled by the large-scale and immense suffering that is occurring in developing countries due to a lack of access to expensive IP-protected drugs.

The first objection is hardly convincing, given that the process of weighing immediate benefits with respect to human welfare against medium- to long- term benefits along the same dimension is one we engage in all the time. Consider, for example, our attempts to safely store nuclear waste, to cut emission of greenhouse gases and to recycle waste. If we find that these attempts are not senseless, we do so exactly on the assumption that it is reasonable to compare the immediate benefits in terms of human welfare that arise from not attempting these things with the medium- to long-term benefits in terms of human welfare that arise from attempting them. Moreover, most of us are willing to forgo the immediate benefits that stem from not attempting to do any of these things in order to reduce or eliminate medium- to long-term costs.[28]

The second objection is misguided, and ironic, given that the very core of the welfarist position is the idea that the morally right course of action, institution or policy is the one that maximizes future human welfare. The consistent welfarist is moved by the scale of human suffering in low-income countries due to the combination of disease, the access and availability problems and a multitude of other social, economic and cultural factors. But she is also moved by future human suffering caused by existing and new diseases, and it is because she is not prepared to prioritize the alleviation of current human suffering over the alleviation of greater, future human suffering that she is opposed to the abrogation of IPRs for drugs.[29]

The second objection, moreover, assumes that the only way of making drugs available to those low-income populations that need them is by abrogating IPRs for such drugs. This assumption, however, is false. It is a fallacy of false alternatives to suggest either that IPRs for such drugs are abrogated or that such drugs cannot be made available to those who need them. There are alternative ways of making such drugs available to those who need them and thereby ease the access problem and the suffering that accompanies it. Trade barriers that make it impossible for developing countries to sell their products in the developed world could be eradicated. Such a move would most likely lead to a dramatic increase in the earnings of developing countries, and given that these countries are prepared to spend some, if not all, of these earnings on the welfare of their citizens, there would be a significant amount of resources available for the

[28] J. Sonderholm, 'Paying a High Price for Low Costs: Why there should be no Legal Constraints on the Profits that can be made on Drugs for Tropical Diseases' *Journal of Medical Ethics* 35(5) (2009): 309–13.

[29] Ibid.

purchase of relevant drugs. It is worthwhile noting that writers in both the libertarian[30] and the cosmopolitan tradition[31] are in agreement about the need for eradicating international trade barriers. The unifying thought here is that such barriers pose a serious and unfair obstacle to the earning power of many developing nations.

5. Where to go from here?

It is perhaps useful now to glance ahead and try to identify a few topics for further research. As has hopefully become evident, IPRs raise empirical as well as conceptual issues. Starting with an issue of the former kind, it would be useful to have additional work done on the question of what the correlation is between strong IPRs and the volume of innovation. Some work has already been done on the overall correlation issue,[32] but further work would be welcome. As mentioned earlier, it is a crucial premise of the consequentialist argument in favour of IPRs that weak IPRs lead to a decline in the volume of innovation. This premise is an empirical one, and the consequentialist defence of IPRs gains significantly in strength if this premise can be further reinforced by empirical findings. Conversely, if the premise cannot be underpinned in such a manner, the consequentialist argument loses credibility, and the defender of IPRs must look elsewhere for argumentation supporting her view. As previously discussed, a libertarian defence of IPRs here is a possibility, but this argument has its own controversial premises.

Moving on to a conceptual issue, it would be appropriate to put Pogge's argument against the libertarian defence of IPRs under more scrutiny. On the face of it, this argument licenses the conclusion that one cannot be a libertarian and at the same time believe that plagiarism is morally wrong. If Pogge is right that the libertarian argument in favour of IPRs can only yield the conclusion that innovators have property rights to the physical token of their innovation, then libertarians seem to be committed to the view that an author only has a property right to the physical token of the book she is writing, and not any copies of it. Such a view would, I suspect, be hard to accept for libertarians. So they have an obvious reason here to sharpen their pens and look for a refutation of Pogge's argument.

30 J. Narverson, 'Welfare and Wealth: Provision and Justice in Today's World' *Journal of Ethics* 8(4) (2005): 305–48.

31 Pogge, *World Poverty and Human Rights*.

32 J. Lanjouw, 'Patents, Price Controls and Access to New Drugs: How Policy affects Global Market Entry', Center for Global Development, Working Papers, No. 61.

5 On the value of the intellectual commons

James Wilson

1. Introduction

When we talk about intellectual property, it is often implicitly assumed that we are talking about *private* intellectual property. However, private property and the idea of private ownership do not exhaust the possibilities for accounts of ownership and of property. There are other ways that ownership can operate, such as common property. A resource is common property if its use is 'governed by rules whose point is to make them available for use by all or any members of the society'.[1]

As the economic importance of intellectual property (IP) has increased, the appropriate direction of IP policy has received extensive attention in the law and economics literature: much of this debate has focused on the relative merits of open versus closed approaches to innovation, and of commons-based versus private property approaches. Common ownership of physical resources such as fields and lakes has long been thought problematic. In Hardin's classic example of the tragedy of the commons, people will tend to overgraze a field which is held in common, for it is in the interest of each shepherd to ensure that they have as many sheep as possible, and that each of their sheep is well-grazed; however, if all (or most) shepherds behave in this way, then the commons will become overgrazed, and its ability to support sheep will soon be destroyed.[2] However, the considerations which make common

[1] J. Waldron, 'Property and Ownership', *The Stanford Encyclopedia of Philosophy* (Winter 2010 edn), E.N. Zalta (ed.), available at http://plato.stanford.edu/archives/win2010/entries/property/. Or, in Lawrence Lessig's words, 'The essence [of the commons] is that no one exercises the core of a property right with respect to these resources – the exclusive right to choose whether the resource is made available to others.' L. Lessig, *The Future of Ideas: The Fate of the Commons in a Connected World* (New York: Vintage, 2002), p. 19.

[2] See G. Hardin, 'The Tragedy of the Commons' *Science* 162(3859) (1968): 1243–8. It is worth pointing out – as Ostrom and others have argued – that even where rival goods are held in common, the tendency towards a tragedy of the commons is by no means inevitable; rather, there are various ways of regulating the commons which can successfully protect and sustain it. See further E. Ostrom, *Governing the Commons: The Evolution of Institutions for Collective Action* (Cambridge University Press, 1990).

ownership problematic in the case of real property do not apply in the case of ownership of ideas. Ideas, unlike physical objects, are non-rival: one person's use of them does not interfere with anyone else's. For this reason, and for others we shall explore later, it is much more uncertain whether, and if so, when private property solutions are to be preferred to common property solutions in the case of IP.

Philosophers have so far contributed little to these debates on the optimal regulation of ownership of IP. This chapter analyses what contribution philosophy can expect to make. I begin in section 2 by distinguishing two tasks that philosophy can attempt when it comes to the optimal regulation of IP: first, philosophers can devise a high-level regulatory model for IP, explaining how, for example the ontology of ideas makes a difference to how we should regulate them, and what are the overall goals that we should have in an IP policy. Second, philosophers can attempt to make cogent and concrete policy suggestions on the basis of such a high-level regulatory model. I argue that it is often extremely difficult to draw cogent and concrete policy proposals from even extremely good moral and political philosophy; and given the paucity of philosophical theorising so far about IP, it would be especially ambitious to expect philosophers now to construct theories which will have concrete and cogent policy implications. Hence, this chapter focuses mostly on the first task.

Section 3 examines IP from the perspective of moral rights.[3] I argue that one significant contribution that philosophy can make is to show that there are no moral rights to own IP; and that there are at least some cases where it is plausible to think that private IP could violate the rights of those who are excluded by it.

Section 4 sets out some of the main goals that an optimal regulatory system for IP should encompass. I argue that there is no intrinsic value in restricting access to ideas: the sole reason in favour of having private IP restrictions is that such restrictions create incentives which will speed the production of intellectually creative work. However there are a number of important values – in particular, liberty, efficient use of resources and equality – which will tend to conflict with IP restrictions. The net result of these value conflicts is that private ownership of IP should be thought of as a necessary evil; something that we should support only where the incentives thus provided are necessary for the supply of future ideas, and where using such incentives is a better way of juggling our various value commitments than other alternatives.

[3] Moral rights are used here in the philosopher's sense of rights claims which are justifiable on moral rather than legal grounds, rather than as relating to the *droit d'auteur*.

Section 5 examines what should follow from these claims about rights and goals for concrete IP policies. The answer is frustratingly little, owing to the complexity of the terrain, and the lack of data on the effectiveness of different models of incentivisation.

2. Is philosophy useful for thinking about problems of regulation?

Philosophical thinking gains much of its power from its abstraction: philosophers typically argue that they get to the heart of issues by stripping away contingent and irrelevant details, and focusing on schematic but clearly described scenarios – scenarios which are often very different from those we encounter in real life.

Even when we have a superb piece of moral or political philosophy which is widely believed to make great strides in solving the schematically described problems on which it focuses, it is often far from clear what implications the work has for what we should do, given our current circumstances.[4] To give just one example of a very general problem, Rawls makes various abstractions and simplifications in *A Theory of Justice*, such as that he is concerned with a society in which everyone is a fully contributing member over the full course of their life; that there is no emigration or immigration; that everyone complies with the rules set out by the theory of justice; and that the account of justice only applies to the basic structure of society.[5] In virtue of these simplifications and counter-to-fact stipulations, it is far from clear what implications Rawls' theory has for specific policy areas such as disability or intellectual property. Even if we could confidently derive such a policy implication, it is unclear if it would be a policy that we had good reason to adopt, all things considered.[6]

[4] For two influential takes on this problem, see G. Brennan and P. Pettit, 'The Feasibility Issue' in F. Jackson and M. Smith (eds), *The Oxford Handbook of Contemporary Philosophy* (Oxford University Press, 2005), pp. 258–79; A. Sen, 'What do we Want from a Theory of Justice?' *Journal of Philosophy* 103(5) (2006): 215–38.

[5] J. Rawls, *A Theory of Justice*, rev. edn (Oxford University Press, 1999).

[6] Rawls himself was famously reluctant to draw specific policy conclusions from his theory of justice. In one of the very few interviews he gave, he answered the question 'When you look at current events, in general, do you think of them with the *A Theory of Justice* framework in mind?' as follows: 'I'm sure that my view must affect in some manner how I see them, but I don't just ask what justice as fairness would say. That would be limiting. I don't see a political conception of justice as something that will tell me what to think. It's a great mistake to think of it as a device that will give you answers, that will deliver the answers to all sorts of questions when you want them. That is one reason I am reluctant to answer questions about specific political topics. It suggests the wrong idea: that we could have some theoretical way of doing that, which is usually not so at all. I think of justice as fairness

We can distinguish between two projects for philosophy in the regulation of IP: a less and a more ambitious. The first would be to provide a systematic theoretical account of the normative terrain, and the second to provide cogent and concrete policy recommendations on the basis of this theoretical account. This chapter aims to undertake the first task, and to examine the prospects for completing the second. I undertake the first task by examining IP from the fundamental orientation of moral rights, and from the perspective of what goals government policy should aim at when it comes to IP. However, as I shall argue in section 4, it is not entirely clear what the implications of this theoretical account are for concrete policy decisions: the regulatory problems are sufficiently complex, and the empirical data so unreliable, that it is unclear how best to pursue our values. In part this is only to be expected: doing good applied philosophical work has proven difficult, even in areas such as bioethics, where a large amount of applied work has been done over a long period of time.[7]

3. Private IP and moral rights

One key contribution that philosophers can make to thinking about regulation is the simple distinction between rights and goals. If each citizen has a right to a particular resource or freedom, then the duty holder of the right must secure that particular freedom or resource *for each individual to whom the right applies*. Rights are highly resistant to aggregation: the fact that many people have their rights fulfilled does nothing to reduce the claims of those who do not. Goals give governments general directions for policy, but they do not require a government to guarantee *to each individual* any particular freedom or resource. So long as a government is pursuing a goal diligently and fairly, no citizen has a legitimate individualised complaint about not being supplied with the good at which the policy aims.[8]

as trying to answer certain specific though basic questions. Its scope is limited.' (S. Aybar, J. Harlan and W. Lee, 'John Rawls: For The Record' *Harvard Review of Philosophy* 1 (1991): 38–48, at 45. Online at www.hcs.harvard.edu/~hrp/issues/1991/Rawls.pdf.

[7] I provide an analysis of why policy-oriented bioethics is so difficult in J. Wilson, 'Towards a Normative Framework for Public Health Ethics and Policy' *Public Health Ethics* 2(2) (2009): 184–94. There I argue that philosophers and bioethicists have tended to underestimate the complexity of social systems, and the difficulties involved in reforming them. Once we understand this, then we see that the problems involved in reforming complex institutions are orders of magnitude more complex than is implied or presupposed by simplistic attempts to go from, for example, Mill's harm principle plus a few facts, to a claim about how we should regulate a new technology.

[8] For this way of drawing the distinction between rights and goals, see, for example, T. M. Scanlon, 'Rights, Goals, and Fairness' *Erkenntnis* 11(1) (1977): 81–95. I write more on the concept of rights in J. Wilson, 'Rights' in R. Ashcroft, A. Dawson, H. Draper and J. McMillan (eds.), *Principles of Healthcare Ethics* (London: John Wiley & Sons, Ltd, 2007).

Rights in the sense I am using them are moral rather than legal rights: legal rights are those rights that exist under a given legal system, whilst moral rights are those rights that morality requires us to recognise.[9] We are interested in this section in whether there is a *moral* right to own IP (clearly there is a *legal* right to hold a copyright on a book, or to hold a patent); and we are also interested in whether legal rights to own IP might violate moral rights such as the right to healthcare or the right to life.[10]

Making this distinction between rights and goals does not yet commit us to the claim that there are any rights. Rather, it points up how two different types of consideration can play different roles in the justification of public policy. Some kinds of reasons act as exclusionary: even if a goal were otherwise worth pursuing, it would be wrong to pursue the goal if it involved violating a consideration which was highly resistant to aggregation. Obviously, given this conception of rights, we should start by ensuring that – in whatever policy we adopt – we are not violating anyone's rights. We should select our policies only from the set of those ways of regulating that *do not* violate rights.

There are four different permutations with regard to the rights of those who create IP, and those who would make use of it. (I shall use 'the inventor' to refer to the person who creates a piece of IP, and 'the user' to refer to the person who wants to make use of it.)

If case (1) obtained, we would have to think about IP policy through the lens of the philosophical discussion of conflicts of rights.[11] If case (2) obtained, we would expect the inventor's right-based claims to take precedence over the claims made by the users of the IP: the inventor's claims would be claims of *rights*, whilst those of the users would be of something less than rights. If case (3) correctly described the situation

[9] In the context of IP, the term 'moral rights' is potentially ambiguous, as it is also used for legal rights which accrue particularly to authors, such as the right of attribution and the right not to have one's work bowdlerised. In this chapter I shall reserve the term 'moral rights' solely for rights with a moral as opposed to a legal justification.

[10] As I shall be using the concept of moral rights, they commit us to the claim that they enjoy some sort of (possibly defeasible) priority over non-rights-based claims. Of course, this is not the only way we can coherently think about rights. Whilst this 'rights as trumps' view can be disputed, in as much as many of the legal rights we do recognise are not particularly morally weighty, I shall not enter into the murky waters of the conceptual analysis of rights here. This is because the basic normative claims could be made without reference to rights: those who are worried by the idea of rights as trumps should be able to replace references to rights without loss with the phrase *morally important claims of individuals which ground at least reasonably stringent duties to those individuals*. I use the term rights simply because it is rather less unwieldy than this construction.

[11] See, for example, J. J. Thomson, *The Realm of Rights* (Cambridge, Mass.: Harvard University Press, 1990); F. M. Kamm, *Intricate Ethics: Rights, Responsibilities, and Permissible Harm* (Oxford University Press, 2007), ch. 9.

Table 5.1 *Analysis of rights in IP policy*

Rights in IP policy	
(1) **Both have moral rights** The inventor has a moral right to own IP, and the user also has some moral right or moral rights that would be infringed if we allow extensive private ownership of IP.	(2) **Only inventor has a moral right** The inventor has a moral right to own IP, and the user does not have any moral rights that would be infringed if we allow extensive private ownership of IP.
(3) **Only users have moral rights** The inventor does not have a moral right to own IP, and the user has some moral right or moral rights that would be infringed if we allow extensive private ownership of IP.	(4) **Neither users nor inventors have moral rights** The inventor does not have a moral right to own IP, and the user does not have any moral rights that would be infringed if we allow extensive private ownership of IP.

Source: J. Wilson.

with regard to IP, then we should expect users' needs to constrain what would otherwise be reasonable systems of incentives. If case (4) correctly described the situation with regard to IP, then we should see IP policy as a way of trying to reach toward certain yet to be specified socially valuable goals, without having to negotiate major side constraints.

I argue that neither of the first two options correctly describe the normative situation, because there cannot be any intrinsic moral rights to own IP. Hence the normative situation we face is either one where no one has any relevant rights, or one where only users do. I shall then argue that it is possible for private ownership of IP to wrong people. The upshot is that case (3) describes the normative situation: whilst private ownership of IP is never required in order to respect moral rights, stringent private IP regimes may wrong people if they prevent them from gaining access to goods that they have a right to.

3.1 Ruling out options (1) and (2): there cannot be a moral right to own IP

It is sometimes argued that, just as labouring on unowned physical property can give the labourer a moral right to own the object laboured on, so labouring on ideas which were previously part of the intellectual commons can give rise to a moral right to own the resulting ideas.[12] For instance, it

[12] By the intellectual commons I mean the set of all the ideas, theories and mental constructs which are open to all to use. The intellectual commons excludes all ideas which are subject to private IP. It includes (a) any ideas which are currently deemed inadmissible for IP

might be thought that in writing a novel someone transforms elements which are part of the stock of the intellectual commons – such as archetypal plots and characters – and in transforming these materials creates something new which she has a moral right to exclude others from. If this thought were correct, then it would be wrongful to treat such a work as part of the commons without the author's permission: doing so would breach her rights.

I have argued at length elsewhere that arguments of this kind for moral rights to own IP are unconvincing; and that there cannot be any pre-legislative moral entitlements to own IP.[13] The essence of this argument is that we cannot simply multiply moral rights ad infinitum: we cannot claim that there is a moral right to X without providing a moral explanation or justification of *why* we should recognise such a right. All attempts to justify moral rights must be subjected to what I call the *Rights Justification Principle*. Any justification of an intrinsic moral right must show that violating the right would typically result in either a wrongful harm or other significant wrong to the holder of the right, which is independent of the existence of the moral right we are trying to justify.

The problem for any putative moral right to own IP is that we do not seem to be able to explain how the inventor would be wrongfully harmed or otherwise wronged by unauthorised copying of her work unless we *already presuppose the existence of the very right we are trying to justify*. For there are only three plausible ways in which someone might be wronged by the unauthorised copying of her published work in a way that meets the criteria set down by the Rights Justification Principle:

(1) The creator is wronged by being excluded from the use of what she has created.
(2) The creator is wronged by being prevented from excluding others from what she has created.
(3) The creator is wronged by others benefiting unfairly from her creative effort.

However, none of these putative justifications could plausibly ground a right to own IP, for the following reasons.

(1) is unconvincing because usage of a non-rival good cannot deplete it or stop anyone else from using it. And so *a fortiori* unauthorised use of a

protection (such as mathematical algorithms, scientific theories, natural languages); (b) those ideas which are potentially admissible for IP protection, but which have not yet been claimed as private property; and (c) ideas which were subject to IP protection but which are no longer, because the maximum term of IP protection for them has expired (such as Dickens' novels).

13 See J. Wilson, 'Could There be a Right to Own Intellectual Property?' *Law and Philosophy* 28(4) (2009): 393–427; J. Wilson, 'Ontology and the Regulation of Intellectual Property' *The Monist* 93 (2010): 450–63.

non-rival good cannot prevent the author from using it. Therefore, merely making unauthorised use cannot prevent her from using the work, and thus cannot be the basis for a claim that the inventor's intrinsic moral rights have been violated.

(2) is unconvincing because being prevented from making money by excluding others from access to one's work does not constitute a wrongful harm or other significant wrong which is independent of the (putative) intrinsic moral right to exclude others from access to one's work. It is only if we presuppose the right whose existence we are trying to justify that it seems plausible to claim that being prevented from charging others for access to one's creation is a wrong to the inventor.

(3) is unconvincing because – assuming there are no pre-existing agreements in place – benefiting from another's effort is unfair only where so benefiting imposes a cost on the person providing the benefit. Making use of an inventor's idea does not impose a cost on her, and so is not unfair.

I conclude that none of (1)–(3) provide any justification for thinking that there is an intrinsic right to own IP. Nor are there any other plausible wrongful harms or other wrongs caused merely by unauthorised copying which are independent of the existence of the (putative) intrinsic moral right to exclude others from copying and use of one's creations.[14] It follows that the legal right to make money by excluding others from access to one's work cannot be an intrinsic moral right. As Jefferson put it, 'Inventions then cannot, in nature, be a subject of property. Society may give an exclusive right to the profits arising from them, as an encouragement to men to pursue ideas which may produce utility, but this may or may not be done, according to the will and convenience of the society, without claim or complaint from anybody.'[15]

3.2 The 'no hardship' argument

It is sometimes argued that it is impossible to wrong anyone by asserting private ownership of ideas which would not have existed but for the inventor. On this view, where someone has created something new out of goods which were part of the intellectual commons (say by writing a

[14] I allow that there may be reasons stemming from the importance of privacy to allow authors to prevent the publication of works that they do not want released to public scrutiny. But once an author has made a work public, she does not have a moral right to exclude others from the use of this idea.

[15] T. Jefferson, 'Letter to Isaac McPherson (13 August 1813)' in A. E. Bergh (ed.), *The Writings of Thomas Jefferson* (Washington DC: The Thomas Jefferson Memorial Association of the United States, 1907), vol. XIII, pp. 333–5. Also available at http://etext.lib.virginia.edu/toc/modeng/public/JefLett.html.

novel, or creating a new drug), no one can claim to be wronged if the person keeps the new idea private and charges money for access to it. The basic thought is that in so doing the author leaves those excluded no worse off than they would otherwise have been, and so cannot wrong them. As Mill puts it, 'It is no hardship to any one, to be excluded from what others have produced: they were not bound to produce it for his use, and he loses nothing by not sharing in what otherwise would not have existed at all.'[16] Call this, following Waldron, the *no hardship* argument.[17] I shall argue (in agreement with Waldron) that this argument is not sound.

The no hardship argument makes the assumption that if someone is left no worse off than she otherwise would have been, she cannot have been wronged. However, it does appear to be possible to wrong someone even if one does not leave her worse off than she would otherwise have been. Suppose that Jill is drowning in an isolated location. Fred notices her as he's zooming past in his speedboat. He does not turn around, reasoning that as she's no worse off than she would have been if he hadn't stopped, *he* can't have wronged her. This seems monstrous. It is an open question whether we should say that Fred *harms* Jill in this circumstance; but it seems overwhelmingly plausible to say that he wrongs her. So he either wrongs her without harming her, or wrongfully harms her despite the fact that she ends up no worse off than she would have been had he not been passing.[18]

When a drug comes onto the market which provides the only treatment for a painful and debilitating condition, and the company which holds the patent on the drug uses its monopoly power to charge very high prices and thereby excludes nearly everyone in developing countries from gaining access to the drug, the situation may be relevantly similar to the speedboat case. We might think that if there is a moral right to access essential medicines, then the fact that someone would be no worse off than if the

[16] J. S. Mill, *Principles of Political Economy: With Some of Their Applications to Social Philosophy* (5th edn, London: Parker, Son, and Bourn, 1862), II.2.26.

[17] J. Waldron, 'From Authors to Copiers: Individual Rights and Social Values in Intellectual Property' *Chicago-Kent Law Review* 68 (1993): 841–87, at 862–8.

[18] The concept of harm is surprisingly slippery. Intuitively, A harms B if A makes B worse off than B would otherwise have been. But it is difficult to spell out what the standard is against which we should judge 'would otherwise have been'. There seem to be two basic kinds of answer: either we specify it in terms of a non-normative baseline, or we specify it in terms of a normative baseline. Both can cause problems, and it is far from clear that a single baseline (whether normative or non-normative) can capture all of our intuitive judgements about when one person harms another. For further discussion, see Wilson, 'Could There be a Right to Own Intellectual Property?'; J. Feinberg, *Harmless Wrongdoing (The Moral Limits of the Criminal Law)* (Oxford University Press, 1990); S. Wilkinson, *Bodies for Sale: Ethics and Exploitation in the Human Body Trade* (London: Routledge, 2003), pp. 56–71.

company had not invented the drug is not enough to show that he is not wronged.

Whilst it seems plausible to say that IP restrictions can violate rights, it is much less plausible to think that any and every restriction will do so: if the good which is protected by IP rights does not serve a serious need (like a new type of coffee grinder), or if an existing item in the intellectual commons could perform substantially the same task, then the case for rights violation is weak.[19] It is only where the good from which the person will be excluded is of substantial importance, and where the good cannot be substituted for one from the commons that it seems plausible to think that IP regulation will violate rights.

4. The appropriate goals of intellectual property regulation

Restricting access to ideas that it would be legitimate for people to know is not good in itself.[20] Where it is pursued, it must be for the sake of some other goal.[21] The standard answer – and in fact the only answer with any currency, once we rule out intrinsic moral rights to own IP – is that the goal of IP regulation is to promote the beneficial effects of human creativity.

I understand the 'beneficial effects of human creativity' in a broad sense, to include both the beneficial effects for consumers of having more products on the market that will meet their needs and preferences, and the beneficial effects for current and future creators who will be able

[19] For example, many new drugs are 'me-too' drugs, designed to be substantially similar to existing drugs in action and effect. If the patent has lapsed on the original drug, it seems much less plausible to say that anyone's rights are violated if they are priced out of gaining access to the me-too drug.

[20] There are some bodies of knowledge (for example, about how to make dirty bombs) whose wide circulation it would probably be beneficial to prevent. But these bodies of knowledge would in any case be problematic to publish, whether or not someone had IP rights on the work published. The morality clause of the European Patent Convention, namely that 'inventions the commercial exploitation of which would be contrary to "ordre public" or morality' are excluded from patentability (Art. 53(a)), displays the impotence of IP law here. This clause is not a very effective way of regulating genuinely immoral activity, as refusing a patent is not sufficient to make an activity illegal: if cloning human beings was legal, but we refused to grant patents on such processes, people would still be free to clone human beings. The only thing we would be denying them by denying patentability would be the right to exclude others from so doing.

[21] As Penner puts it, 'The right to property is grounded by the interest we have in using things in the broader sense. No one has any interest in merely excluding others from things, for any reason or no reason at all.' James Penner, *The Idea of Property in Law*, (Oxford University Press, 2000), p. 70.

to draw on the results of more human creativity.[22] Human creativity in this broad sense encompasses new scientific ideas, new inventions, new films, computer programs, plant varieties and so on.

Human creativity is clearly extremely important for the future of human society: it is through such creativity that we have raised living standards over time; and it will be through such human creativity that we will attempt to improve our living conditions in the future. Whilst human creativity has also had substantial negative effects, I shall leave these on one side here. My interest is in a different question: how can attempts to incentivise creativity impact negatively on other goals that societies should have; and when they do, which should take precedence? If the benefits of human creativity are more equivocal than might at first be thought, this would strengthen rather than undermine the reasons for being cautious about incentives to creativity which undermine other important goods. So, for the purposes of my argument, I shall grant the claim that human creativity is an important force for good which there are pro tanto reasons to encourage.

There are a number of important goals which can be threatened by restricting access to human creativity. I shall consider three: liberty, making best use of resources and equality.

Liberty

Ideas are by nature non-excludable.[23] If we wish to prevent sharing of ideas, we need to take positive steps, such as erecting digital fences like Digital Rights Management (DRM), or legislating to allow for private ownership of IP. Such steps involve impositions on liberty: they prevent people from being able to do things that they were previously able to do. Such incursions

[22] IP regulation may not so obviously benefit future producers. But this is part of its rationale: patents, for instance, require the patentor to publish a description of how the invention works. The granting of the temporary monopoly is the quid pro quo for making this knowledge public. If there were no patents, then inventors would have a much greater recourse to trade secrets. Trade secrecy has the drawback that people continually have to duplicate effort, as they attempt to solve problems that have already been solved. In the past there have been some quite significant cases of the withholding of information which could have saved lives: for example, the Chamberlen family kept the discovery of the obstetrics forceps secret for more than 100 years, in order to protect their midwifery business. See W. Moore, 'Keeping Mum' *British Medical Journal* 334 (7595) (2007): 698–a.

[23] As Jefferson put it, waxing poetical, 'That ideas should freely spread from one to another over the globe, for the moral and mutual instruction of man, and improvement of his condition, seems to have been peculiarly and benevolently designed by nature, when she made them, like fire, expansible over all space, without lessening their density in any point, and like the air in which we breathe, move, and have our physical being, incapable of confinement or exclusive appropriation' ('Letter to Isaac McPherson').

into liberty are problematic for two reasons: first, if we think that liberty is a good thing, then reductions of liberty are prima facie bad. Second, it requires us to use the coercive force of the law to criminalise activities which are not wrong in themselves. So whilst liberty is by no means so important that it trumps all considerations,[24] incursions into liberty do have to be justified: we need to be able to show that allowing people the liberty to perform the proscribed action will be bad in some way.

Making best use of resources

Ideas are by their nature non-rival in consumption. If one person has a good idea, everyone can benefit from that idea and build on it, without the original idea being destroyed or degraded.[25] If we allow someone a monopoly on the supply of a non-rival good, the monopoly holder is able to extract an economic rent from those who buy the product. In a competitive market, prices are kept down by competition: companies will seek to differentiate themselves in the market by offering goods either at a higher quality, or a lower price, with the net result that (in an efficient market) profit margins are low. Where we have a monopoly, there is no reason to think that the price charged for a good will bear any relationship to the marginal cost of production. Governments in general have an obligation to make the best use of their resources, and to prevent monopolies from occurring; both obligations are challenged by allowing private ownership of IP.[26]

Equality

Non-rival goods are not capable of scarcity, and are hence capable of being supplied to everyone who desires them. If there is a scarcity in the supply of a given non-rival good, it is because we have elected to create an artificial scarcity. This is different from the case of rival goods where we

[24] I have written about this in the context of health: J. Wilson and A. Dawson, 'Giving Liberty its Due, But no More: Trans Fats, Liberty, and Public Health' *The American Journal of Bioethics* 10(3) (2010): 34–6.

[25] As noted earlier, this is quite unlike a commons such as a village green, or fishing the sea. In the cases of these exhaustible commons, there is reason to restrict access, or to have some kind of governance norms to ensure that the resource is not overused.

[26] The European Regulation on Orphan Medicinal Products provides a good example of this (Regulation (EC) No. 141/2000). When BioMarin was awarded a European orphan licence for amifampridine (Firdapse), 'a slightly modified version of 3,4-diaminopyridine, which is unlicensed but has been used for more than 20 years to treat two rare diseases, Lambert Eaton myasthenic syndrome (LEMS) and congenital myasthenic syndrome', price rises were enormous. Treatment for a patient with diaminopyridine cost £800–£1,000 per year, but BioMarin charged £40,000–£70,000 for amifampridine. N. Hawkes and D. Cohen, 'What Makes an Orphan Drug?' *British Medical Journal* 341 (2010): c6459.

frequently see 'natural' scarcities. Because of this, ideas as goods have a particular resonance from the perspective of equality. A society of equals is one in which each citizen can look each other in the eye, and think of herself as of equal status to the other person. The goal of a society of equals is undermined where there are goods which have a large effect on the way in which social status is negotiated, and which are differentially spread (particularly when this reinforces existing patterns of advantage and disadvantage). Conversely, such a society is promoted where there are goods and freedoms important for social status which are available to each on conditions of equality. Because ideas matter for human life, and because ideas can be made available to all at only a marginal extra cost, the goal of a society of equals will push us towards open access to ideas.

So in sum, approaching IP regulation from an abstract philosophical perspective should lead us to affirm the following claims:

(1) There are no moral rights to privately own IP. We can either grant or not grant such legal rights without wronging inventors.
(2) Granting private IP rights may sometimes violate other rights, such as the right to life.
(3) Denying access to ideas is not good in itself. Denying access to ideas is good only when it serves some further purpose: namely, promoting the beneficial effects of human creativity.
(4) Restricting access to ideas is in tension with other important goals such as protection of liberty, making the best use of our resources, and equality.
(5) Therefore, private IP, where we adopt it as a way of incentivising creativity, should be viewed as a necessary evil.[27]

The next question is what implications these thoughts should have for concrete IP policy decisions.

5. Balancing rights and goals in IP regulation

Going from the more abstract theories to concrete and workable policy proposals is something that is difficult even in those fields of applied philosophy such as bioethics where most work has been done. So what

[27] The position is not so dissimilar from that put forward by Macaulay a while ago: 'Thus, then, stands the case. It is good that authors should be remunerated; and the least exceptionable way of remunerating them is by a monopoly. Yet monopoly is an evil. For the sake of the good we must submit to the evil; but the evil ought not to last a day longer than is necessary for the purpose of securing the good.' Thomas Babington Macaulay, speech delivered in the House of Commons (5 February 1841), in *The Life and Works of Lord Macaulay: Complete in Ten Volumes* (Edinburgh edn, Longmans, 1897), vol. VIII, p. 198.

I shall be doing in this section will be quite programmatic, and will also be relatively cautious about what the implications of the analysis so far should be for public policy.

We can separate two questions to which we would need to know the answer before we could make helpful IP policy recommendations: an empirical question and a normative one. The empirical question is: what kinds of environments and regulatory regimes foster creativity most effectively? The normative question is: how are the goods of creativity to be weighed against other goods such as liberty and equality? I shall discuss each in turn.

5.1 Prospects for answering the empirical question

When we test the safety and efficacy of a new drug, we control the clinical trial through procedures such as random assignment of participants to the different trial arms, double blinding (so that neither the trial participants nor the researchers know who is receiving which treatment), power calculations (estimating how large a sample size is required to show a statistically significant effect) and placebo controls. A well-designed clinical trial thus gives us a high degree of confidence that perceived differences in effects between the two trial arms are caused by differences between the interventions trialled and not some other factor.

It is impossible to perform similarly rigorous tests of the effectiveness of different options for the regulation of IP – to consider, say, the effects of 20-year patent terms against 25 years. First, it would not be feasible to run a randomised trial which allocated some inventors to longer or some to shorter patent terms. Those who were randomised to the shorter patent life would inevitably argue that they were not being treated equally under the law. Even leaving this on one side, such a trial would lack a large number of the other features which allow us to control clinical trials.

The closest we can come to a rigorous empirical test is a natural experiment: we can investigate past changes in IP regulation, and then see the effects that followed in their wake. However, such experiments are so uncontrolled that it is difficult to draw reliable conclusions from them. It is clear that we would not be able to attribute all of any changes of rates of innovation to changes in the regulation of private IP, given that there are many factors which affect how much people are willing to invest in research and development, such as tax breaks, the overall state of the economy, what they think their competitors are likely to be doing and how copyable products are without IP protection. How much of any improvements in innovation rates are caused by the change in IP legislation will be deeply contestable. There will be two further deep problems we would need to solve before taking such natural experiments seriously: first, there is the problem of measuring creativity. Should we adopt an objective metric such as numbers of patents filed, or number of films released; or should we also focus on the quality of innovations? Second, even if we were to know that an intervention such as extending the length of the patent term from 20 years to 25 years had a beneficial effect on creativity in one country, it would not follow from this that increasing the length of the patent term would have similarly beneficial effects for our society now. Public policy does not work in such a straightforward and linear way.[28]

What all this means is that what empirical evidence we do have of the effects of different systems of IP regulation lacks rigour – and is certainly not the kind of evidence on the basis of which anyone should feel comfortable about making wide-ranging choices about the future of societies. We also have economic models of how creativity is best incentivised. Obviously, for the reasons we have just mentioned, it is extremely difficult to test these models empirically, and perhaps unsurprisingly, these economic models have wildly different implications, depending on the value orientations of their proponents. Burk and Lemley identify five main economic models in the literature on patents: prospect theory, competitive innovation, cumulative innovation, the anticommons and patent thickets. Each of these incorporates different assumptions about the kinds of infrastructure and incentives system needed for optimal innovation. Prospect theory assumes that patents should operate like prospects in mining: having IP rights gives companies an incentive to invest more in research and development in the area of their patent in order to reap the benefits of this. This way of looking at innovation implies that 'only strong rights to preclude competition will effectively encourage innovation', and that hence, 'patents should be granted early in the invention process, and should have broad scope and few exceptions'.[29] Competitive innovation theory argues that innovation comes mostly from competition between firms, and that because of this we should ensure that 'patent rights should be narrow and should give less than perfect monopoly control'.[30] Cumulative innovation theorists argue that most useful creativity is additional to already existing inventions, and that we need to ensure that we do not have a winner-takes-all approach such as the prospect theory approach

[28] On the relevant disanalogies between the clinical trial context and the public policy context, see Trisha Greenhalgh and Jill Russell. 'Evidence-Based Policymaking: A Critique' *Perspectives in Biology and Medicine* 52(2) (2009): 304–18.

[29] D. L. Burk and M. A. Lemley, 'Policy Levers in Patent Law' *Virginia Law Review* 89(7) (2003): 1575–696 at 1604.

[30] Ibid., 1607.

incorporates, but rather, one that allows people to make incremental improvements to products that others have produced. Anticommons theorists focus on the transaction costs involved in licensing multiple patents, and use this as a way of arguing that fundamental innovation platforms should be available freely for innovation.[31] Theorists of patent thickets focus on the problems of overlapping patent claims, and argue that patent claims should be narrower, or the non-obviousness requirement should be made more stringent.[32]

There is no reason to think that one of these models will be optimal for the incentivisation of all inventions. Variables which are relevant to the shape of optimal systems of incentivisation include the cost of bringing a new product to market; the cost of copying versus the cost of invention; and the extent of first mover advantage in a particular market. These costs will vary systematically between industries, and it may well be that an industry such as pharmaceuticals (where it is extremely costly to bring a drug to market, and relatively cheap to copy), would have an optimal system of incentivisation significantly different from that of saucepans.

One apparent solution to this might be to have a more highly differentiated system of IP protection: tailoring the incentives provided to what is required for best innovation in each particular industry. However, there are also problems in having highly differentiated systems of incentivisation: we will face problems of categorisation (with incentives to game the system); and challenges from emerging technologies (do we need to be continually inventing new schemes of incentivisation?). Finally, we should not forget that:

> each new amendment to the patent statute represents an opportunity for counterproductive special interest lobbying – Patent law has some balance today in part because different industries have different interests, making it difficult for one interest group to push through changes to the statute. Industry-specific legislation is much more vulnerable to industry capture.[33]

So it is also unclear that providing a highly differentiated system of patents would be a net gain.

[31] For more on anticommons approaches, see M. A. Heller and R. S. Eisenberg, 'Can Patents Deter Innovation? The Anticommons in Biomedical Research' *Science* 280 (5364) (1998): 698–701; M. A. Heller, 'The Tragedy of the Anticommons: Property in the Transition from Marx to Markets' *Harvard Law Review* 111(3) (1998): 621–88.

[32] For patent thicket approaches, see C. Shapiro, 'Navigating the Patent Thicket: Cross Licenses, Patent Pools, and Standard Setting' *Innovation Policy and the Economy* 1 (2000): 119–50.

[33] Burk and Lemley, 'Policy Levers in Patent Law', 1637.

5.2 *Prospects of answering the normative question*

The normative question is how we should weigh the goods of human creativity against other goods such as liberty and equality. Clearly, IP regulation must respect moral rights. We have seen how patents on essential pharmaceuticals might violate moral rights in some cases. To the extent that we are dealing with moral rights, the link between abstract theorising and policy is clear. However, we earlier argued that not much of IP policy will in fact come down to judgements about when moral rights are violated. The great majority of policy decisions will come down to decisions about how to rank different potential policies, in the light of the different values embodied by each policy.

We can approach the task of ranking different policies in the light of the values embodied by each policy in a more or a less ambitious way. On the more ambitious approach, we would attempt to work out a once-and-for-all ranking of all the values in play, and then use this to deduce the answer in the particular case. On the less ambitious approach, we find a way of ranking these values in the particular situation we face, even if that does not amount to a solution for all cases.

It is far from clear that the more ambitious approach is possible: in order for it to be possible, what Henry Richardson calls strong deliberative commensurability would have to be the case: there would have to be 'some single norm (or good) such that all the considerations for and against any option in any situation may be adequately arrayed prior to the choice (for purposes of deliberation) simply in terms of the greater or lesser satisfaction of that norm (or instantiation of that good)'.[34] Strong commensurability is difficult to combine with value pluralism: if the ways in which equality and liberty are valuable are different from the way that human creativity is valuable, then it is difficult to see how strong commensurability could be true.

The implausibility of strong deliberative commensurability does not entail that it is impossible for philosophers (or anyone else) to make correct judgments about individual policies which involve trade-offs between different goods. It follows only that there cannot be a single standard in virtue of which we do this. It is unclear that making trade-offs between competing values in particular contexts and given other constraints is something in which philosophers *qua* philosophers have particular expertise. Rather, I think we do better to consider these to be fit subjects for deliberative democracy: decidable on the basis of rigorous

[34] H. Richardson, *Practical Reasoning about Final Ends* (Cambridge University Press, 1994), p. 104.

arguments by all in the community, not just those with specialist philosophical knowledge.

6. Conclusion

Private ownership of IP is not required by respect for moral rights. But given the public goods problem in the production of new ideas, it is plausible to think that suboptimal amounts of innovation will occur unless incentives are provided. Adopting private property approaches to incentivising production of ideas is in a certain amount of tension with the values of liberty, making best use of resources and equality; and so, if it were possible to attain similar amounts of innovation with a common ownership approach as a private ownership approach, there would be reason to prefer the common ownership approach. It is less clear what the policy implications of these normative claims should be, given the paucity and the unreliability of the evidence we have on the effects of different regulatory regimes.

6 Immorality and patents: The exclusion of inventions contrary to *ordre public* and morality

*Kathleen Liddell**

I. Introduction

Ethical issues implicitly permeate all aspects of patent doctrine, including definitions of invention, novelty, inventive step, utility, disclosure and so forth.[1] Interestingly, and in addition, many patent systems allow explicit ethical objections.[2] This is most notable in the European Patent Convention (EPC) which states at Article 53(a) that:

> European patents shall not be granted in respect of inventions the commercial exploitation of which would be contrary to '*ordre public*' or morality.

In broad terms, this provision means that patent protection is denied to immoral inventions, no matter how novel or inventive the invention may be. Intriguingly, it requires lawyers (including patent examiners and judges) to define morality. Recent cases concerned the morality of commercially exploiting mammals genetically programmed to develop cancer (*HARVARD/Oncomouse*) and stem cells obtained from human embryos (*WARF* and *Brüstle*). These raised difficult questions about genetic engineering, animal experimentation, the moral status of embryos, the morality of patenting animals and parts of the human body. With such troubling ethical issues in the frame, it is not surprising that Article 53(a) itself has proven highly controversial.

The principal difficulty is how to implement such a rule. How does a patent examiner or court assess whether an invention is immoral to the point that, unlike other inventions, it should not be granted patent

* Senior Lecturer, Faculty of Law, University of Cambridge, UK.

[1] See further, Nuffield Council on Bioethics, *The Ethics of Patenting DNA: a Discussion Paper* (NCOB, London, 2002); Rainer Moufang, 'Patenting of Human Genes, Cells and Parts of the Body? – The Ethical Dimensions of Patent Law' (1994) 25(4) IIC 487, 514.

[2] For an international survey, see Lionel Bently, Brad Sherman, Denis Boges Barbosa, Shamnad Basheer, Coenraad Visser and Richard Gold, *Exclusions from Patentability and Exceptions and Limitations to Patentee's Rights – a Study prepared for the World Intellectual Property Organisation* (WIPO, Geneva, 2010), Annex I and IV.

protection? It is a question that runs headlong into the complex intersection of law and morality or, put another way, the intersection of intellectual property and philosophy.

Section III explains some of the contentious issues in the interpretation of Article 53(a). In light of these issues, many authors and patent practitioners have thrown their hands in the air in frustration, suggesting that the problems are insurmountable and that patent law would be better off abandoning the explicit morality exclusion. In the meantime they tend to interpret the provisions in a highly legalistic and usually narrow way, dissecting the words of the statute in fine detail. Often the words might be ascribed more than one meaning, but alternative interpretations are swept away for a legally plausible, but normatively doubtful reason, leaving the decisions mired in controversy and cast adrift in interpretative uncertainty. In contrast, there is very little discussion of what might be the jurisprudential underpinnings of a morality exclusion in the patent system. This is considered briefly in section IV and leads into the main contention of this chapter.

The principal argument is that a better appreciation of the nature and purpose of the immorality exclusion provides some vital clues as to how it should be interpreted (section V). More specifically, it will be argued, building upon Burk and Lemley's seminal paper in 2003,[3] that the explicit morality exclusion is a 'policy lever', similar to the thirteen already identified in their paper, which tailors patent law to its overarching utilitarian objective of promoting socially beneficial inventions in a manner compatible with fair and just social organisation. As such, the explicit morality provision is a valuable opportunity to optimise patent policy, and an advisable inclusion in all national patent systems. Countries like the United States which lack an explicit morality provision, are disadvantaged by its omission. The exclusion calls for policy analysis, which requires more normative input by judges (and patent examiners) than linguistic textual analysis, but considerably less than a search for moral truth. It is thus well within the ordinary duties and capabilities of skilled legal decision makers, who appreciate that law sensibly leaves discretion for judges (and other decision makers) to develop and shape the law in ways that promote desirable goals and behaviour. That is not to say that this is how the immorality exception has been used to date, but rather how it could be used in the future.

Sections V and VI also discuss some of the implications of seeing the explicit morality exception as a policy lever. Section V revisits the debates in the literature, and section VI considers the topical issue of embryo stem cell patents. These comments are necessarily general rather than

[3] Dan L. Burk and Mark A. Lemley, 'Policy Levers in Patent Law' (2003) 89 *Virginia Law Review* 1575.

detailed or prescriptive. More definitive answers require a more fine-grained case-by-case analysis, which the judiciary and examiners would need to tackle in any given case. And although it might be tempting to argue that judges and patent examiners should not be given such an active role in shaping economic and social policy, the fact is that they are doing it at the moment, and it would better that they do it consciously and critically, rather than inadvertently or furtively.

II. Background

Modern debates give the impression that the relationship between patents, morality and public policy is a recent phenomenon, but the link has been recognised since very early days. The English Statute of Monopolies 1624, one of the very earliest patent statutes, generally condemned monopolies, but exceptionally allowed letters patent, provided that 'they be not contrary to the law nor mischievous to the state by raising prices of commodities at home, or hurt of trade, or generally inconvenient'. Clearly the early English Parliament was wary of the anti-competitive economic effects of patents, and also types of scientific progress that might be contrary to the law or 'generally inconvenient'. In the twenty-first century, very few countries use the same phrasing as the Statute of Monopolies. However, the large majority have adopted the same general idea, moulding and modernising it. The main modernising force is Article 27(2) of the Agreement on Trade-Related Aspects of Intellectual Property Rights (TRIPS), which states that:

> [WTO] Members *may* exclude from patentability inventions, the prevention within their territory of the commercial exploitation of which is necessary to protect ordre public or morality, including to protect human, animal or plant life or health or to avoid serious prejudice to the environment (emphasis added).

Professor Shamnad Basheer,[4] in a study led by Professor Lionel Bently for the World Intellectual Property Organisation, surveyed seventy-three World Trade Organization (WTO) member countries in 2010. He found that all the countries, bar six, have taken up the opportunity to include an explicit immorality exclusion. The exceptions include: Australia, Bangladesh, Canada, Guyana, Uganda and the United States.[5]

Amongst the large pool of countries that have included an explicit immorality exclusion in their patent law, European countries are unusual

[4] S. Basheer (with S. Purohit and P. Reddy), 'The *Ordre Public* and Morality Exclusions' in Bently *et al.*, above n. 2, Annex IV.

[5] Ibid. at pp. 56, 58, 62, 71, 73.

in that they agreed, in 1998, a pre-determined (non-exhaustive) list of inventions that trigger the immorality exclusion. The list includes:

- processes for cloning human beings;
- processes for modifying the germ line genetic identity of human beings;
- uses of human embryos for industrial and commercial purposes; and
- processes for modifying the genetic identity of animals which are likely to cause them suffering without any substantial medical benefit to man or animal, and also animals resulting from such processes.[6]

The list was initially agreed in the European Directive 98/44 on the Legal Protection of Biotechnological Inventions, and is thus binding for all EU member governments. However, it was also subsequently adopted by the Administrative Council of the EPC[7] as a list that could be used in the supplementary interpretation of Article 53(a) of the EPC.[8] Accordingly, it also binds countries that are members of the EPC.

The list is in essence a static snapshot of the technologies and activities thought to be too immoral for patent protection at the time of the debates. It appeals to arbitrators (e.g. patent examiners) because it is a (relatively) clear list of exclusions that can be implemented straightforwardly without needing to consider, more deeply, the meaning of 'morality'. However, as a legal matter, the list is not comprehensive and is not meant to replace the general immorality exclusion.[9] This means that where an invention falls outside the four categories, it can still be challenged for being contrary to *ordre public* and morality. When debating the directive's text, some Members of the European Parliament also wanted the list of inventions presumptively stipulated to be immoral to include patents on DNA sequences, parts of the human body, and animals and plants, but these proposals were defeated.[10] These issues can, nevertheless, continue to be raised under the general Article 53(a) exclusion.

[6] Directive 98/44/EC of the European Parliament and of the Council of 6 July 1998 on the legal protection of biotechnological inventions (Biotech Directive), OJ L/213, Art. 6(2).

[7] The EPC is a regional treaty between EU and non-EU members and thus separate and distinct from the EU legal order.

[8] EPC Implementing Regulations to the EPC, Rule 28(a)–(d) (formerly numbered 23d(a)–(d)). The list is thus relevant to national and European patents, irrespective of whether the adjudicator is a national court, a national patent office or the European Patent Office (EPO). The complexity is that no single body is the ultimate legal authority on the meaning of the list. If a party challenges the meaning given by a national court or patent office, the ultimate authority is the European Court of Justice (now known as the Court of Justice of the European Union); but if they challenge the meaning given by the EPO, the ultimate authority is the Enlarged Board of Appeal.

[9] T0315/03 *HARVARD/Transgenic Animals* [2005] EPOR 31, Reasons 6.1.

[10] Instead it was decided that patents would be allowed when the DNA sequences or body part had been isolated, and if the invention applied to different types of animals and plants (not merely a single animal or plant variety): Directive 98/44/EC, above n. 6, Arts 4 and 5.

EPC countries and a number of WTO members also exclude some methods of medical treatment and diagnosis from patentability. Increasingly this is said to be due to ethical and public policy concerns (although some countries link it to doubts about whether such things are 'inventions' in the ordinary patent law sense).[11] A small handful of *ad hoc* exclusions based on ethical or public policy concerns can also be found. For example, the Australians exclude 'human beings, and the biological processes for their generation'.[12] In Thailand, Brazil and the United Arab Emirates, patents are prohibited on animal, plant and naturally occurring microorganisms, but allowed for modified microorganisms. In China and Brazil, concerns about nuclear arms have led to exclusions for products based on atomic nuclear transformation.[13] In India, machines and devices for committing burglary, counterfeiting currency notes and gambling are excluded, as are terminator gene technologies.[14] Several countries have considered adopting an exclusion specifically against DNA sequence patents, but to date, none has enacted such a rule. Proposals along these lines were rejected in Australia in 1990 and 1996, and in Canada in 2001.[15] Prior to TRIPS, many countries also excluded patents on pharmaceuticals and foodstuffs for ethical reasons.

The US patent system differs substantially. It provides:

> Whoever invents or discovers any new and useful process, machine, manufacture, or composition of matter, or any new and useful improvement thereof, may obtain a patent therefor, *subject to the conditions and requirements of this title.*[16] (emphasis added)

None of the subsequent conditions explicitly refer to morality or public policy. Accordingly, there is very little opportunity to raise explicit moral objections. On one occasion it was suggested that a patent application for a human–animal chimera[17] might be rejected for breaching the 13th Amendment to the US Constitution (the prohibition

[11] Some legislation states that such inventions shall not be considered to be capable of industrial application. This was the case in Europe until the EPC was amended in 2000.

[12] Patents Act 1990 (Cth) s. 18(2). The precise scope of this provision is unclear, particularly in relation to inventions involving human stem cells and stem cell technologies: see ALRC, below n. 15, paras 7.5, 7.6.

[13] Patent Law of the People's Republic of China (2008), Art. 25(5); Law No. 9. 279 of 14 May 1996 (Industrial Property), provision 18 (II).

[14] Basheer *et al.*, above n. 4, p. 63.

[15] Australian Law Reform Commission (ALRC), *Genes and Ingenuity: Gene Patenting and Human Health (Report 99)* (2004) paras 7.13–7.15.

[16] US Patent Code: 35 USC §101.

[17] A human–animal chimera is an organism composed partly of human and partly of animal biological material.

on slavery).[18] It has also been suggested that inventions contrary to morality might be dealt with under the US 'moral utility' doctrine.[19] This doctrine, first articulated in *Lovell* v. *Lewis*[20] by Storey J and subsequently cited many times in US jurisprudence, states that an immoral invention is not 'useful' and therefore falls foul of paragraphs 101 and 112 of the US Patents Code. At root, the doctrine is based on a special interpretation of the word 'useful' – more specifically, an interpretation that holds that something is useful only if it serves a beneficial purpose; since immoral developments are not beneficial, an immoral invention is not useful.[21] The doctrine was the basis for rejecting patents claiming gambling machines and deceptive products (e.g. seamless 'seamed' stockings, and unnaturally spotted tobacco leaves) but was thought to have been overturned by the Supreme Court's expansive interpretation of paragraph 101 of the US Patents Code in *Diamond* v. *Chakrabarty*,[22] and the Federal Court's dismissal of a moral utility argument in *Juicy Whip*.[23] There has been little enthusiasm for reviving it.[24]

III. Issues in the interpretation of an explicit immorality exclusion

As noted in section I, the explicit immorality exclusion found in Article 53(a) has been highly controversial.[25] This is because lawyers find it

[18] Margo Bagley, 'Patent First, Ask Questions Later: Morality and Biotechnology in Patent Law' (2003) 45 *William and Mary Law Review* 469, at 502.

[19] Ibid., 490. [20] *Lovell* v. *Lewis* 15 F.Cas. 1018 (CCD Mass. 1817).

[21] A narrower understanding of the word 'useful' is simply that something can be 'put to use'.

[22] *Diamond* v. *Chakrabarty*, 447 US 303 (1980).

[23] *Juicy Whip Inc.* v. *Orange Bang Inc.*, 185 F.3d 1364 (Fed. Cir. 1999). For background, see Bagley, above n. 18.

[24] Although the US Patents and Trademarks Office has not abandoned it completely: Basheer *et al.*, above n. 4, p. 72.

[25] Prior literature includes (in chronological order): Deryck Beyleveld and Roger Brownsword, *Mice, Morality and Patents* (CLIIP, London, 1993) (a foundational issue-raising book discussing Art. 53(a) and the EPO's examination of the *Harvard/Oncomouse* patent); Moufang, above n. 1 (a foundational issue-raising article calling for clarification of the relationship between patent law and ethics); Stephen Crespi, 'Biotechnology Patenting: The Wicked Animal Must Defend Itself' (1995) 17(9) *European Intellectual Property Review* 431 (arguing that objections to biotech patents purportedly based on ethical principles are unconvincing); Sigrid Sterckx (ed.), *Biotechnology, Patents and Morality* (Ashgate, Aldershot, 2000) (collected edition of short papers presented at a conference in 1996 shortly after the first draft of the EU Biotech Directive was rejected by the European Parliament); Donna Gitter, 'Led Astray by the Moral Compass: Incorporating Morality into European Union Biotechnology Patent Law' (2001) 19 *Berkeley Journal of International Law* 1 (an examination of interpretative difficulties surrounding the morality provisions in the EU Biotech Directive, arguing that the United

devilishly difficult to apply. As a result, some have argued that it is unworkable and should not be adopted in the United States and that, in Europe, it should be applied narrowly or cautiously.[26] Some have also tried to avoid the uncertainty and difficulty of deciding what is 'immoral' within the meaning of Article 53(a) by appealing to legalistic techniques mostly divorced of explicit moral content, for example, appeals to earlier EPO or WTO decisions, parallel concepts in

States should not follow the European approach); Nuffield Council of Bioethics, above n. 1 (recommendations to improve the ethical legitimacy of patent law in the field of biotechnology based on a series of case studies); David Resnik, *Owning the Genome: A Moral Analysis of DNA Patenting* (State University of New York, Albany, 2004) (a thorough examination of the ethical arguments for and against the patenting of DNA sequences); Oliver Mills, *Biotechnological Inventions: Moral Restraints and Patent Law* (Ashgate, Aldershot, 2005) (a description of European and US laws relevant to the patenting of biotechnological inventions, including the European morality exclusion); Matthew Rimmer, *Intellectual Property and Biotechnology: Biological Inventions* (Edward Elgar, Cheltenham, 2008) (several in-depth, descriptive case studies highlighting controversial aspects of patenting biotechnological invention); Mark J. Hanson, 'Religious Voices in Biotechnology: The Case of Gene Patenting' (1997) *Hastings Center Report Special Supplement* (a clear and helpful explanation of religious objections to biotech patents for secular readers); Annabelle Lever, 'Is it Ethical to Patent Genes?' in A. Gosseries, A. Marciano and A. Strowel (eds), *Intellectual Property and Theories of Justice* (Palgrave Macmillan, New York and London, 2008) (a clear explanation of ethical arguments swiftly dismissed by the patent profession); Amanda Warren-Jones, 'Finding a "Common Morality Codex" for Biotech – A Question of Substance' (2008) 39(6) *IIC* 638 (an argument for a three-step analysis of the European morality exclusion, namely (1) identifying the focus of the moral assessment; (2) a definition of the terms '*ordre public*' and morality; and (3) understanding what is meant by 'the proviso' in the second half-sentence of Art. 53(a); A. Warren-Jones, 'Morally Regulating Innovation: what is "Commercial Exploitation"?' (2008) 2 *Intellectual Property Quarterly* 193 (an argument that the legally-significant phrase 'commercial exploitation' found in the European morality exclusion is unclear, but would appear to have been, and should continue to be, read narrowly by the EPO); Sigrid Sterckx, 'The European Patent Convention and the (Non)Patentability of Human Embryonic Stem Cells – the *WARF* Case' (2008) 4 *Intellectual Property Quarterly* 478 (summarising the oral proceedings before the EPO Enlarged Board of Appeal in the *WARF* patent proceedings and arguing that the patent should be rejected); Aurora Plomer and Paul Torremans (eds), *Embryonic Stem Cell Patents: European Law and Ethics* (Oxford University Press, 2009) (edited collection of chapters considering the application of the explicit morality exclusion to embryo stem cell patents with a particular focus on the overlapping systems of the EPC, EU, international and national law), Basheer *et al.*, above n. 4 (international survey of explicit morality exceptions in the patent legislation of WTO countries).

26 See, e.g., Crespi, above n. 25; Bagley, above n. 25; A. M. Viens, 'Morality Provisions in Law Concerning the Commercialization of Human Embryos and Stem Cells' in Plomer and Torremans (eds), above n. 25, ch. 4; A. Plomer, 'Towards Systemic Legal Conflict: Article 6(2)(c) of the EU Directive on Biotechnological Inventions' in ibid., ch. 7; A. Plomer, 'Human Dignity, Human Rights, and Article 6(1) of the EU Directive on Biotechnological Inventions' in ibid., ch. 8; Antonina B. Engelbrekt, 'Institutional and Jurisdictional Aspects of Stem Cell Patenting in Europe (EC and EPO): Tensions and Prospects' in ibid., ch. 9.

European law, or general principles of statutory construction (such as the avoidance of textual redundancy).[27]

The purpose of this section is to explain as clearly as possible the nature of the debates so that the confusion is less overwhelming. Section V will also return to the issues identified here and see how they might be more readily resolved if judges and examiners focused more steadfastly on the purpose of the explicit morality exclusion and understood it to be a policy lever rather than a linguistic puzzle.

Most of the legal debate centres on two subjects:

(a) the focus of the moral inquiry; and
(b) the standard of immorality required to trigger the exclusion.[28]

The second subject – the standard of immorality – sub-divides into further debates, including over:

(i) the definition of immorality to be used in the context of patents;
(ii) the evidence that can be led to establish immorality (e.g. public opinion surveys, moral philosophy, religious teachings, human rights declarations, ethics committee opinions);[29]
(iii) whether the concepts of *ordre public* and 'morality' are one and the same, or separate and distinct;[30]
(iv) whether the subject of an invention must be illegal (i.e. prohibited) before it triggers the patent exclusion;[31]
(v) the timing of the immorality inquiry in patent law, given that more than twenty years may have passed from the time at which the

[27] See, e.g., Crespi, above n. 25; G0002/06 *Wisconsin Alumni Research Foundation (WARF)/ Stem Cells* [2009] EPOR 15; Edinburgh Patent EP 06953351 (Opposition Division) 21 March 2003.

[28] See, e.g., Warren-Jones, above n. 25. While this chapter agrees with Warren-Jones that it is important, first, to clarify the focus of the moral assessment and second, to define the benchmark of morality, it takes a different view of the answers that should be given to those questions.

[29] See, e.g., Amanda Warren-Jones, 'Identifying European Moral Consensus: Why are the Patent Courts Reticent to Accept Empirical Evidence in Resolving Biotechnological Cases?' (2006) 29 *European Intellectual Property Review* 26; Elodie Petit, 'An Ethics Committee for Patent Offices?' in Plomer and Torremans (eds), above n. 25, ch. 11.

[30] In T0356/93 *PLANT GENETIC SYSTEMS*, the EPO Technical Board of Appeal treated the two issues as distinct concepts: the reference to *ordre public* excludes inventions that are likely to breach public peace or social order (e.g. inventions related to terrorism), whereas the reference to morality excludes inventions which are not in conformity with conventionally accepted standards of conduct (see Reasons 5 and 6). But in other cases the EPO has indicated that there is a lot of overlap between the two concepts: T0315/03 *HARVARD/Transgenic Animals* Reason 10.5. See also Amanda Warren-Jones, 'Vital Parameters for Patent Morality – A Question of Form' (2007) 2 *Journal of Intellectual Property Law & Practice* 832, at 834.

[31] See, e.g., Gerard Porter, 'Human Embryos, Patents and Global Trade: Assessing the Scope and Contents of the TRIPS Morality Exception' in Plomer and Torremans (eds), above n. 25, pp. 343, 345, 359–63.

invention was conceived and when the patent finally expires. More concretely, the question is what should happen if an invention declared patentable in 2000 comes to be regarded as immoral in 2010, and an opponent requests that the patent be revoked – does one apply the morality of 2000 or 2010 in the revocation proceedings? Likewise, what should happen if an invention ceases to be morally troubling (for example, because it no longer necessitates the destruction of embryos)?;[32] and

(vi) whether an invention that has moral as well as immoral applications should be excluded from patentability. (By way of an example, suppose a chemical composition could be used for the humane mercy killing of animals, but also involuntary human euthanasia – should it be patentable?)[33]

At first blush philosophers might find some of the above questions familiar – in particular the first four (a, b, b(i), b(ii)). But the other questions are less familiar, and even the familiar-looking questions are discussed in ways quite different from what philosophers might imagine.

(a) The focus of the moral inquiry

When one looks more closely at what lawyers think should be the target of the question – is it immoral? – it turns out that they are not debating whether morality is a question about actions or values, or rules or consequences, as philosophers might. Rather, they are concerned with the awkward phrasing of Article 53(a) and what it means. To appreciate this, it is necessary to recall that Article 53(a) states: 'European patents shall not be granted in respect of inventions *the commercial exploitation of which* would be contrary to *ordre public* or morality' (emphasis added). Lawyers' attention has been focused on the italicised words. What do they mean? Why didn't the drafters simply write 'European patents shall not be granted in respect of inventions contrary to *ordre public* or morality?' Is the judge supposed to assess the morality of utilising the invention (i.e. exploitation in the sense of utilisation), or the morality of owning and profiting from the invention (i.e. exploitation in the sense of financial benefit)? Or perhaps something else altogether; for example, immorality in the preceding research or lack of desert? These alternatives can be presented in the following typology.

[32] See, e.g., T0315/03 *HARVARD/Transgenic Animals*, Reasons 9.5, 9.6, 14.3.

[33] See, e.g., T0866/01 *Euthanasia Compositions* 11 May 2005; P. Grubb and P. Thomsen, *Patents for Chemicals, Pharmaceuticals and Biotechnology* (5th edn, Oxford University Press, 2010).

Objections to the technology and its use: exploitation in the sense of utilisation According to this view, the focus should be the immorality of utilising the thing invented. This includes complaints about the immorality of the invention's intended use (e.g. animal research, burglary, contraception, euthanasia). It also includes complaints about the immorality of the steps which must be carried out in order to manufacture or perform the invention (e.g. destruction of embryos, crossing the species barrier).

Objections to the consequences of patenting (property rights, exclusivity, financial gain): exploitation in the sense of commercial use and benefiting financially On this view, the focus is not so much whether the thing invented is good or bad, but whether it would be immoral to grant *a patent* over the thing. It might be ethically concerning that the product or process will thereby become a piece of private property (commodification), or that it will be owned by a single legal person who can prevent other people from using it without permission, or who can request high licence fees which only the wealthy can afford (exclusivity).

Objections to the preceding research: exploitation in the sense of taking commercial advantage of 'poisoned fruit' On this view, the focus is neither the thing invented, nor the impact of patenting it, but the morality of the preceding research activities. For example, did the researchers treat animals cruelly during the development of the invention? Did they obtain valid consent from human research participants? Did they ask them for permission to patent cell lines or other inventions resulting from their tissue? Did they kill human embryos to make the invention?

Objections that the technology does not deserve a patent: exploitation in the sense of taking advantage of an unmeritorious situation On this view, the allegation is that it would be immoral to grant a patent over the 'invention' because it is not really new, or inventive, or properly explained.

The complexity is compounded because the possible foci are not mutually exclusive. It is arguable that one, two, three or all four are relevant issues for the judge adjudicating Article 53(a). So, for example, in the proceedings surrounding the *HARVARD/Transgenic Animals* patent, opponents raised arguments that fell in all four categories. They believed the technology at the heart of the invention to be morally wrong because it caused painful tumours in animals like mice and rats. They were also concerned that the patenting of transgenic mammals was an inappropriate commodification of animals because it gave an individual person (legal or natural) exclusive rights to buy, sell, keep and even create an entire population of animals. They were further concerned that the research preceding the realisation of transgenic oncomice was immoral because it was unnatural and posed a risk to the environment if mice escaped from the laboratory. And finally, they were of the view that the innovation at the heart of the patent was not an invention, lacked an inventive step and was insufficiently disclosed.

To date, the European Patent Office (EPO) openly considers the first type of objection. But despite the fact that critics of patents on DNA sequences, body parts, animals and plants frequently raise other sorts of objections, the EPO is unreceptive to these arguments. In its view, the words 'commercial exploitation of the invention' is a clear indication that the focus of the immorality enquiry must be on the morality of utilising/ performing the invention, and not the socio-economic implication of granting a patent. Thus it has emphatically rejected objections of the second kind.[34] This is despite the discussion above which demonstrates that there are several different ways of understanding the words 'commercial exploitation of the invention'. Generally the EPO also rejects objections of the third kind,[35] although it entertained the idea on one occasion that a patent should be refused on immorality grounds if researchers failed to obtain the free and informed consent of research subjects.[36] A recent

[34] In G0001/98 *NOVARTIS/Transgenic Plant* the Enlarged Board asserted that 'the EPO has not been vested with the task of taking into account the economic effects of the grant of patents in specific areas and of restricting the field of patentable subject matter accordingly' (Reason 3.9). See, e.g., T0866/01 *Euthanasia Compositions*, above n. 33 Reasons 5.6; T0315/03 *HARVARD/Transgenic Animals*, Reason 4.2. The EPO refuses even to consider the morality of the invention itself – e.g. an allegation that the invention (namely, a transgenic oncoanimal) is immoral because it is unnatural. However, such considerations might be considered if they are rephrased – e.g. an allegation that the use of the invention is immoral because the use of a transgenic oncoanimal involves an unnatural crossing of the species barrier.

[35] In T0866/01 *Euthanasia Compositions*, above n. 33, the EPO said that Art. 53(a) does not concern 'whether or not the making of the present invention as such *or the inventor's activities during making or development of his invention* or the development of the present invention as such *might be regarded as breach of the principles of* ordre public *or morality*' (Reason 5.6(c), emphasis added). A similar outlook is also evident in cases concerning embryos and cells isolated from embryos. The EPO has rejected patents where it thinks that anybody exploiting the technology in the future would need to kill embryos, but has not been troubled by the fact that embryos might have been killed during the research phase. Contrast the CJEU's decision in *Brüstle*. See below, section VI and Post Script.

[36] On the facts of this particular case, the EPO's Opposition Division held that no immoral research conduct had taken place because the women who donated tissue had, in fact, been asked for their consent: T0272/95 *HOWARD FLOREY/Relaxin*, Reasons 6.3.1. For discussion, see Graeme Laurie, 'Patents, Patients and Consent: Exploring the Interface between Regulation and Innovation Regimes' in Han Somsen (ed.), *The Regulatory Challenge of Biotechnology: Human Genetics, Food and Patents* (Edward Elgar, Cheltenham, 2007).

case suggests that the Court of Justice of the European Union (CJEU) might consider arguments of this kind, however it is far from certain as the case focused on the wording of the stipulative exclusion for uses of human embryos (but see now Post Script). The fourth type of objection is generally rejected as an inappropriate attempt to question whether the invention meets the standard criteria of patentability. The EPO would rather these issues were dealt with comprehensively under other provisions of patent law (e.g. the concept of 'invention' (Art. 52), novelty (Arts 54–5), inventive step (Art. 56), sufficient disclosure and fair basis (Arts 83–4)), than cursorily under Article 53(a).

Even with the first type of objection, the EPO and commentators tie themselves in knots. It is not clear whether the EPO should focus on the invention *as claimed*, [37] or the performance of the invention. The invention as claimed may be narrower than the activities involved in performing the invention because the patent attorney may have worded the claim such that it does not refer to certain controversial steps. This was a crucial issue in the *WARF* patent litigation.[38] The invention *as claimed* was a stem cell culture, which few consider immoral *per se*. However, the inventor had only explained one way to perform the invention and this necessarily involved the use and destruction of human embryos. To commentators' annoyance, the EPO's Enlarged Board of Appeal focused its analysis on one of the predetermined categories of immorality rather than the general immorality exclusion. The stipulated exclusion disallows a patent when the invention involves 'uses of human embryos for industrial and commercial purposes'.[39] Since it could be assumed that such uses were immoral (given the stipulative drafting of rule 28(c)), the EPO approached the question as an exercise in linguistic analysis to ascertain whether 'the invention' 'used' 'human embryos' for 'industrial and commercial purposes'. The complexity was that the patent *claims* did not refer to the use of human embryos *per se*. Nevertheless, the Enlarged Board held that the performance of the invention (i.e. the making of stem cells)

[37] A patent document is comprised of a description of the invention followed by claims. Assuming the patent is valid, the claims define the 'scope of protection' or in other words, the patent owner's exclusive property (EPC Art. 69). In the description, the invention is explained and the inventor must 'disclose the invention in a manner sufficiently clear and complete for it to be carried out by a person skilled in the art' (EPC Art. 83). The patent description therefore must describe at least one way to perform the invention, unless this is clear from the claims or is a matter of common general knowledge.

[38] G0002/06 *WARF/Stem Cells* [2009] EPOR 15.

[39] Ibid., [31]. Commentators saw this as a cowardly attempt to avoid the legal debates surrounding the general morality exclusion in Art. 53(a): see, e.g., Paul Torremans, 'The Construction of the Directive's Moral Exclusions under the EPC' in Plomer and Torremans (eds), above n. 25.

necessarily required the use of human embryos, and this was enough to trigger the rule 28(c) exclusion. If the patentee had explained in the patent description how the claimed invention could be performed without killing embryos (e.g. how to request a sample of the cell line from a Stem Cell registry), the Enlarged Board hinted that the Patentee would have escaped the exclusion.[40] This is because the performance of the invention would no longer have necessitated 'the use of human embryos'.

(b) *The standard of immorality required to trigger the exclusion*

Lawyers have also disagreed about how the courts and patent offices should delineate moral and immoral ways of exploiting an invention. The EPO has toyed with several possible definitions. In 1990, in T19/90 *HARVARD/Oncomouse*, the Technical Board of Appeal held that, at least in animal genetic manipulation cases, the decision whether or not Article 53(a) EPC is a bar to patenting:

> would seem to depend mainly on a careful weighing up of the suffering of animals and possible risks to the environment on the one hand, and the invention's usefulness to mankind on the other.[41]

This is a characteristically utilitarian standard of morality, or in the words of the EPO, 'a balancing approach'.

Four years later, however, the EPO was emphasising another approach, at least for inventions other than genetically-modified animals. A key example was the Opposition Division's decision in T0272/95 *HOWARD FLOREY/Relaxin*. In this case, it was called upon to consider whether Article 53(a) was a bar to the patenting of an isolated human DNA sequence coding for the human protein H2-relaxin that was developed from tissue samples obtained from pregnant women. Quoting the EPO Guidelines current at that time, the Opposition Division said:

> A fair test to apply is to consider whether it is probable that the public in general would regard the invention as so abhorrent that the grant of patent rights would be inconceivable. If it is clear that this is the case, objection should be raised under Article 53(a); otherwise not.[42]

Unlike the utilitarian definition offered in T19/90 *HARVARD/Oncomouse*, this definition did not suggest weighing up detriments and benefits. Rather, it suggested that whether an invention is immoral for the purposes of patent law depends on two points: the invention being

[40] G0002/06 *WARF/Stem Cells*, above n. 38, [35].
[41] T19/90 *HARVARD/Oncomouse* (Examination), Reasons 5.
[42] T0272/95 *HOWARD FLOREY/Relaxin* (Opposition), Reasons 6.2.1.

particularly heinous and the public in general sharing this view. The Opposition Division, however, was somewhat uncertain how it wanted to define the public in general. In subsequent paragraphs it referred to a need for the view to be shared by 'the overwhelming *majority* of the public',[43] then an 'overwhelming *consensus* among Contracting States' and in its concluding paragraphs it said that what was needed was 'an overwhelming consensus'[44] and 'a clear consensus among members of the public'.[45]

In subsequent decisions by Technical Boards of Appeal, the EPO has shown little enthusiasm for the test applied in *HOWARD FLOREY/Relaxin*, perhaps because public consensus is an impossibly demanding standard in a pluralist society like Europe. In 1995, the EPO introduced a third approach in T0356/93 *PLANT GENETIC SYSTEMS*. It stated:

> the concept of morality is related to the belief that some behaviour is right and acceptable whereas other behaviour is wrong, this belief being founded on the totality of the accepted norms which are deeply rooted in a particular culture. For the purposes of the EPC, the culture in question is the culture inherent in European society and civilisation. *Accordingly, under Article 53(a) EPC, inventions the exploitation of which is not in conformity with the conventionally-accepted standards of conduct pertaining to this culture are to be excluded from patentability as being contrary to morality.*[46]

Thus, it seems the Board of Appeal in this case agreed in part with the *HOWARD FLOREY/Relaxin* test. It agreed that the definition of immorality calls for some reflection on 'conventionally-accepted standards of conduct', but unlike *HOWARD FLOREY/Relaxin*, the *PLANT GENETIC SYSTEMS* definition calls for the beliefs to be 'deeply rooted' and 'conventionally-accepted', rather than for a clear public consensus.[47]

[43] Ibid., Reasons 6.3. [44] Ibid., Reasons 6.5. [45] Ibid., Reasons 6.6.

[46] T0356/93 *PLANT GENETIC SYSTEMS*, Reasons 6 (emphasis added).

[47] This led to further discussion about the sort of evidence that can be advanced to demonstrate that a norm is deeply rooted or conventionally accepted. Clearly, a public referendum is impractical. The Board also took a dim view of opinion polls. It pointed out that there are many issues to consider including, for example, whether the type and the number of questions posed within a single poll were appropriate, whether the sample of people surveyed was sufficiently large and representative, whether the respondents were given adequate information and time to provide a considered response, whether the questions were appropriately open-ended, whether respondents were paid, whether trained professional pollsters were engaged and whether there was sufficient consideration given to the interpretation of the results obtained. It is also necessary to make a judgement as to the number of people who must share a view in order for it to be 'conventionally accepted'. To date, there have been very few opinion polls that satisfactorily addressed these issues, and even fewer on the specific issue of patents and biotechnology. Media analyses are an unsatisfactory substitute, as it is well known that the media will distort stories simply in order to increase circulation.

With several different definitions of morality on offer, the EPO was soon faced with the question whether the various tests set out in *HARVARD/Oncomouse*, *HOWARD FLOREY/Relaxin* and *PLANT GENETIC SYSTEMS* could be reconciled or, if not, which was the most authoritative. The EPO had the opportunity to address this question in T0315/03 *HARVARD/Transgenic Animals* (Opposition Proceedings). The Board said, rather unclearly, that T0356/93 *PLANT GENETIC SYSTEMS* supplied the definition of morality, but given the lack of reliable public opinion evidence, the balancing approach in T19/90 *HARVARD/Oncomouse* was the appropriate approach in animal manipulation cases.[48] While this indicated that at least two of the tests were legally valid, it failed to explain whether the tests were optional alternatives (which could be problematic if they led to different conclusions), or if they applied in different case scenarios. The Enlarged Board of Appeal was invited to rule on the issue in *WARF*, but (to the disappointment of the parties and commentators) it declined to do so on the grounds that it was not necessary in order to decide the case.

IV. Deeper issues

Despite copious literature about how to apply the morality exclusion and a number of relevant cases, there has been very limited discussion of the deeper issues that the explicit morality exclusion raises or the underlying purpose that the exclusion might be intended to serve. At a superficial level it is appreciated that it is meant to exclude immoral inventions of some kind or another. But without delving deeper, adjudicators launch into decisions about immoral inventions concentrating on intricate verbal analysis and appeals to precedents (few of them binding). Commentators similarly rush headlong into a discussion whether a rule excluding immoral inventions is practical. Many argue that patent offices lack expertise in morality, meaning the patent system is ill-equipped to apply a morality provision. Others argue that the principle is redundant (because other government agencies police immoral inventions, prohibiting their use where appropriate) or self-defeating (if an immoral invention is denied patent protection, it becomes *more* widely available because there is no requirement to seek a patent owner's permission to use it). Practicalities and textual appraisal are certainly significant, but they should be secondary rather than primary considerations.

48 T0315/03 *HARVARD/Transgenic Animals*, above n. 9, Reasons 10.10.

First, one needs to step back from the legal and institutional details to consider what really is at stake, what we might hope to achieve with the exclusion, and then how it might be operationalised. The immorality exclusion of Article 53(a) is in fact a situation where law and morality come head to head. Accordingly, it raises deeper uncertainties about how law and morality relate to each other. Shamnad Basheer is one of the few who has drawn attention to this point.[49] In a report for the World Intellectual Property Organisation he simplifies the situation, explaining the issue in terms of the law and morality debate that has dogged scholars of jurisprudence for several centuries. He notes that the positivist school of law tends to argue that law has to be divorced from morality and instead based on the rules of textual logic and reason. The school of natural law, on the other hand, tends to argue that the law necessarily reflects the morals of society and that it cannot therefore be divorced from morality and based solely on textual logic and reason. Thus, in the context of patent law, the positivist would argue that an invention should be granted a patent so long as it is novel, inventive and displays an industrial application and that morality, unless well defined in terms of the law, should have no role to play in the decision to grant or withhold a patent. In contrast, the school of natural law would argue that an invention that offends the morality of society cannot possibly be given a legal character. With this in mind, it is possible that the debates over Article 53(a) are fuelled by positivist leanings and a worry that the general morality exclusion has not been sufficiently well defined, except in the few instances where it has been given a predetermined meaning (e.g. Art. 6(2) of the Biotech Directive). This would not be a surprising state of affairs, as there is considerable evidence of positivist and formalist leanings in other areas of patent law.[50]

While Professor Basheer's comments help us to understand some of the essence of the debate around Article 53(a), they do not offer any kind of solution for moving forward. The debate between positivists and natural law scholars has been long-running and shows little sign of resolution. Plus, it tends to be built upon overly-stylised accounts of law and morality. To a large extent modern-day law and morality are epistemological systems that have a variety of similarities and differences, making it difficult and unfruitful to suggest they are distinct or co-terminous.

A bioethicist, familiar with the patents and morality debate, who apparently agrees with this, is Elodie Petit. In a chapter debating whether ethics

[49] Basheer *et al.*, above n. 4, p. 43.

[50] See, e.g., Justine Pila, *The Requirement for an Invention in Patent Law* (Oxford University Press, 2010); Justine Pila, 'Bound Futures: Patent Law and Modern Biotechnology' (2003) 9(2) *Boston University Journal of Science and Technology Law* 326.

committees should be set up to assist Patent Offices in their interpretation of Article 53(a),[51] she rejects the idea that there is either a firm distinction or identicality between modern-day law and ethics. Instead she notes a mix of similarities and differences between legal and ethical reasoning[52] when one considers their respective goals, the finality of ethical and legal decisions, and the methods of decision making. Ultimately, though, she concludes that the differences between the epistemologies of law and ethics are such that it would be better *not* to involve ethics committees in Article 53(a) debates. She worries that they will either give answers too vague or too divorced from legal authorities to be useful, or that they will be forced to adopt a style of reasoning that overly legalises and juridifies bioethical reasoning.

Petit's chapter is an interesting (albeit very cautious) account of the social implications that can follow when ethical and legal systems of thought and decision making run up against each other as they do in the European morality exclusion. It is also one of the few pieces to focus on the unusual *direct* juxtaposition of law and ethics in Article 53(a). However, her analysis does not resolve the interpretative question – which inventions should be excluded from patentability for being contrary to morality? It simply advises that we not muddy the waters further by inviting ethics committees to help solve the questions.

V. Article 53(a) as a policy lever for judges and patent examiners

It is useful at this stage to recap the argument so far. Although many countries have seen fit to include an explicit morality exclusion in their patent laws (section II), there is a great deal of uncertainty about how this

[51] Sweden and Norway have already instituted such a system. Some of the difficulties are discussed by Åsa Hellstadius, 'A Comparative Analysis of the National Implementation of the Directive's Morality Clause' in Plomer and Torremans (eds), above n. 25, pp. 129–32.

[52] Elodie Petit, 'An Ethics Committee for Patent Offices' in ibid., pp. 306–9. In her view, ethics and law both strive to improve well-being, but whereas ethical analysis is primarily concerned with the individual's well-being within society, the law seeks to balance this with social stability. She also argues that ethical analysis is a dynamic process with fairly vague parameters of reference making it an uncertain field, but also a field suitable for addressing uncertain directions in science and technology. In contrast, the law must aim for a reasonable degree of foreseeability, giving it a more staid and inflexible character. Third, Petit argues that while law and ethics are both concerned with justificatory reasons, ethical analysis is based on a consensual, dialectic approach that tries to forge a compromise out of pluralist opinions through a search for shared values (albeit not necessarily complete agreement on underlying ethical principles). In contrast, law is prone to making decisions based on political power, particularly in the legislature, or hierarchical adjudication (albeit with accompanying reasons to explain why the decision should be perceived as an acceptable balance of interests for the population).

provision should be applied (section III). Some deeper understanding can be gleaned from acknowledging the epistemological tensions between law and ethics (section IV), but ultimately the law and morality debates (modern day and traditional) are descriptive of the difficulties rather than prescriptive of solutions. In this section and the next, I want to suggest that some of the dilemmas can be mitigated if we perceive Article 53(a) as a 'policy lever' as described by Dan Burk and Mark Lemley.[53]

Burk and Lemley's seminal article in 2003 encouraged the patents community to think about patent legislation not as a legalistic set of principles and rules, but rather as a sophisticated set of policy levers designed to achieve the primary goal of patent law, which they defined as the promotion of new technologies. More specifically, they took issue with the way that US courts, particularly the Federal Circuit (a specialised patent court), was developing legal precedents uncritically and with little reference to empirical data or relevant scholarship. The resultant problem, they observed, was a patent system poorly adapted to different technological industries, which was often hindering rather than promoting new innovations. In contrast, they argued that courts should utilise the inherent flexibility in patent law and tailor it to industry differences.[54] In other words, patent principles – such as the exclusion of abstract ideas, the requirement of utility, the perspective of the person skilled in the art – should be interpreted with sensitivity to the primary goal of patent law and industry-specific issues. Burk and Lemley discuss nine principles of patent law which could currently be considered policy levers and four additional principles that might be developed or resurrected as policy levers. The *ordre public* and morality exception was not on their list, but this reflects the US context of their writing and audience. In fact, it seems a prime example of a policy lever through which patent law can be consciously optimised.

A crucial part of Burk and Lemley's thesis about patent policy levers is to identify the overarching policy goal. As they point out, this is easier in patent law than other areas of intellectual property. It is widely agreed that the overarching purpose of patent law is utilitarian;[55] patents are granted

[53] Burk and Lemley, above n. 3, 1638–41.

[54] Burk and Lemley also consider possible counter-arguments: ibid., 1668–74. They leave open the suggestion that patent agencies also have a role to play. They have some niggling doubts about whether the United States Patent Trademark Office institutional configuration and authority is compatible with their approach: ibid., 1696.

[55] Alternative explanations have been offered, but these bear little resemblance to the patent system as currently conceived. For example, Lockean labour theory fails to account for the fact that only the inventor first-in-time is granted property in the inventions produced

in order to encourage inventions.[56] What is sometimes overlooked is that, stated more accurately, patents should be granted in order to encourage *socially beneficial inventions* in a manner compatible with *fair and just* social organisation. This reflects the fact that patent law should not encourage *any* type of invention at *any* cost. That would be perverse unless we thought that the delivery of socially beneficial inventions was more important than equity and justice. Once this overarching goal is recognised, the purpose of the explicit morality exclusion becomes plain. Its policy-oriented purpose is to exclude inventions that are positively undesirable. Granted, this is just the first step – it is still necessary to articulate more precisely the sorts of inventions that should therefore be excluded. But it is an important first step.

Turning to the next step – the interpretation of the immorality exclusion once it is understood as a policy lever – it is important to keep in mind two general points. First, there are many policy levers in patent law, so it is not necessary or even advisable to reject all disadvantageous inventions on the grounds that they are contrary to *ordre public* or morality. Some are better dealt with by other parts of the patent system, for instance, principles excluding discoveries, principles setting thresholds for protection (such as novelty, inventive step and disclosure), or principles limiting liability (such as the research-use exemption, Crown use or compulsory licensing). I will return to this point below. Second, it should be noted that the character of policy levers is such that they necessarily vest a fair degree of discretion in the judiciary[57] (and patent examiners). Accordingly, determinate answers may be elusive until detailed arguments are considered. But this uncertainty should be applauded, not denigrated, because it allows general principles to be optimised in specific fact contexts.

Despite some residual indeterminacy, seeing the immorality exclusion as a policy lever does cast some light on the legal confusions surrounding Article 53(a). Most significantly, it helps with the confusion surrounding the focus of the moral inquiry. As noted above, the EPO has only been willing to consider:

(1) Objections concerned with the use of the technology itself.

For example, it will entertain arguments that using letter bombs or chemical compositions to euthanise humans would be immoral, or that using methods of genetic engineering or products of genetic engineering would pose a risk to the environment or are immoral for being unnatural,

by his labour. Those who develop the same invention (without copying) do not have any property recognised (and in fact might be served with a notice of infringement) despite the fact that an equal or even greater degree of labour has been expended.

[56] Burk and Lemley, above n. 3, 1597. [57] Ibid., 1638.

but it will not consider other sorts of ethical objections described in the typology above. So, for example, it will not consider:

(2) Objections based on the consequences of patenting, including:
  (i) arguments concerned with the immorality of conferring property – for instance, conferring property over classes of animals; or
  (ii) arguments concerned with the immorality of patent exclusivity – for instance, arguments that it is immoral to grant a patent over a diagnostic association between DNA and breast cancer because the patentee's rights of exclusivity could increase the price of the genetic test to a level which excludes poorer women from checking their risks of breast cancer.

(3) Objections based on the preceding research[58] – for instance, that the researchers cruelly used animals to arrive at their invention.

(4) Objections based on accusations that the invention does not deserve a patent – for instance, accusations that it would be unethical to patent DNA sequences because it would be akin to patenting the moon.

Once the immorality exclusion is understood as a policy lever as described above,[59] it is clear that the EPO is correct to consider the first type of objection (accusations that the technology itself is immoral), but incorrect to ignore some of the other objections. This can be explained as follows.

Since the purpose of the immorality exclusion is to ensure that patents incentivise socially beneficial inventions in a manner compatible with just and fair social organisation, it is obviously important to assess whether the protected technology and its likely uses are immoral. Failing to consider and exclude immoral technology would mean that the patent system was economically encouraging scientists to work on immoral forms of technology and to pressure governments to allow their use.

Second, it is also important to consider whether, by granting a patent, the State is conferring property status on things which should not be handled or even perceived as tradable commodities. This would be contrary to just and fair social organisation. Identifying the things which should not be 'propertised' is difficult in modern capitalist societies, but nevertheless important. Although we are conditioned to see almost everything as a commodity, beliefs about common heritage, human rights, human dignity and non-commodification are important and should not be diluted or threatened by patent law. This is not to say that every

[58] Subject, perhaps, to an *ad hoc* consideration whether human research participants validly consented to research.

[59] That is, a policy lever to exclude clearly undesirable patent applications which do not incentivise socially beneficial inventions in a manner compatible with just and fair organisation.

objection along these lines should result in the exclusion of a patent. Rather, it means that the objection should at least be considered relevant, and the judge (or patent examiner) should go on to consider whether the objection meets the requisite standard of immorality.

Third, the morality exclusion *qua* policy lever should take account of objections about the implications of patent exclusivity in order to avoid patents which are contrary to fair and just social organisation. For instance, patents should be carefully scrutinised if they are likely to make it difficult or impossible for members of the public to access medical care, or difficult or impossible for other researchers to find new uses or improve upon the patented technology. However, there is a proviso. With these sorts of arguments the first general consideration (see above) should be borne in mind. As noted, the *ordre public* exception is one of several patent policy levers which can be deployed to avoid these outcomes. The Crown use exemption,[60] compulsory licensing,[61] and the research use exemption[62] might be better policy levers where the ethical objection is, in essence, against the granting of imbalanced patents or patents that conflict with countervailing public interests, rather than patents *per se*. Some of the respective advantages and disadvantages of using 'exclusions' and 'exemptions from liability' to achieve the same policy goals are neatly summed up by Professor Bently.[63] The key advantage of liability exemptions is that they allow a more balanced or nuanced solution – rather than deny the patent incentive *in toto* (which is the effect of patent exclusions), liability exemptions allow the patent protection to be granted, but with the scope of subsequent rights curtailed or with adequate remuneration guaranteed. For example, a patent might be granted for a new and important drug, thus incentivising its development, but according to principles of

[60] The Crown use exemption is a limited exception that allows the Crown to use and even to authorise others to use patented inventions for specified 'services of the Crown', including the supply of drugs and medicines. One condition is that the Crown must pay compensation on reasonable terms, which can be determined by the parties themselves, or failing that, by a court: Patents Act 1977 (UK) ss. 55–8.

[61] The UK's compulsory licensing scheme (for patent owners based in WTO member countries) allows any party to request a licence from the Patents Comptroller to use (import, keep etc.) a patented invention. As with Crown use, the licensee must pay reasonable compensation, as determined by the Patents Comptroller or courts. Another condition is that the request will only be granted if: the demand for the patented product in the UK is not being met on reasonable terms; the exploitation in the UK of another important invention is being prevented or hindered; or commercial or industrial activities in the UK are being prejudiced. Furthermore, the compulsory licence can be requested at the earliest three years after the patent was granted: Patents Act 1977 (UK) s. 48A.

[62] The research use exemption provides that an act is not an infringing act if it is done for experimental purposes relating to the subject matter of the invention: Patents Act 1977 (UK) s. 60(5).

[63] Bently *et al.*, above n. 2, Annex I, pp. 60–9.

Crown use or compulsory licensing, the patent owner is limited to charging a reasonable royalty. Similarly, a patent might be granted for a new and useful isolated DNA sequence, thus incentivising the discovery of useful DNA sequences, but according to the European-style research use exemption, those who wish to investigate the DNA sequence can do so without paying a fee.

Fourth, objections based on the preceding research should also be considered to avoid a situation where the State is rewarding scientists with a valuable economic benefit for the 'poisoned fruits' of unethical research. Research that is too risky or contravenes important norms should not be rewarded or assisted by the patent system. The explicit morality exclusion is an opportunity to ensure this. There will, of course, be limits to the degree of scrutiny that can be achieved by the patent system, but it should at least consider the direct and immediate ways in which the preceding research might have been tainted. It should also try to avoid policy clashes with policies governing research. For instance, if research has been ethically approved by ethics committees or embryo research guidelines, this might be enough to avoid patent exclusion. Note, though, that there is a distinction between a decision by a regulator or ethics committee that research is morally legitimate, and the grant of a patent which suggests that it is not only acceptable but also socially desirable and something to be incentivised.

Fifth, some objections are more properly dealt with by other policy levers, namely novelty, inventive step, or sufficiency of disclosure. For example, the objection that patenting DNA is akin to patenting the moon is better dealt with by rules of novelty (genomic DNA is not new), inventive step (a claim to 'isolated' DNA may well lack an inventive step), and sufficiency of disclosure (unless it is possible for a skilled person to repeat the invention, the invention is not sufficiently disclosed.)[64]

Understanding the morality exclusion as a policy lever also helps to clarify some of the debates surrounding the standard of immorality that should trigger it. Most significantly, it highlights the fact that courts and patent examiners need not fear that the explicit morality exclusion requires them to define immorality with philosophical rigour. Far from solving the puzzles that have troubled and divided philosophers for centuries, and purporting to have identified the moral truth, they simply have to grapple openly and conscientiously with a lower-order goal of responding reasonably to moral pluralism and the empirical information that is currently available.

[64] For this reason, patenting a DNA sequence (with instructions as to how it can repeatedly be made by skilled scientists) is *not* the same as patenting the moon.

On the questions circulating in the literature (identified in section III), the following comments can be made.

Which test of 'morality'?

As outlined above, the EPO has toyed with various tests of morality, and even suggested in T0315/03 *HARVARD/Transgenic Animals* that more than one test might be appropriate (one consequentialist, another based on publicly accepted norms). This might appear indecisive and unsound to philosophers, but it makes sense if the morality exclusion is understood as a policy lever. The point of the policy lever is to give judges discretion to identify legal tests that distinguish inventions that are not socially beneficial, or that contribute to unfair and unjust social organisation. In some situations, a consequentialist weighing-up of harms and benefits will be appropriate, for instance, if relevant empirical information is available or if the invention falls in a field (e.g animal suffering) which the public typically responds to in consequentialist ways. In other situations, the test of morality might need to be more responsive to non-consequentialist norms, for example, 'human dignity' where inventions are based on human or embryo experimentation. The test outlined in T0356/93 *PLANT GENETIC SYSTEMS* is flexible enough to accommodate a range of normative concerns along these lines (it looks for non-conformity with conventionally accepted standards of conduct). Unlike the test in T0272/95 *HOWARD FLOREY/Relaxin*, it does not call for an overwhelming consensus, which will hardly ever pertain in Europe.

What evidence?

A diverse range of evidence is relevant to the policy inquiry in Article 53(a): public opinion surveys, moral philosophy, legal standards, religious teachings, human rights declarations and ethics committee opinions. They are all sources of information about the undesirability of a particular patent application and one does not need to choose between them or to exclude any pre-emptively. However, none is likely to be determinative, as they all have their limitations.[65] Together, though, it is possible to build up a picture of conventionally accepted standards of conduct.

[65] See, e.g., for instance the EPO's discussion of the limits of public opinion polls: above n. 47.

Are the concepts of 'ordre public' *and 'morality' separate and distinct?*

There is no need to draw a hard and fast distinction between these concepts. Both pertain to the question, is this patent application incentivising a socially beneficial invention in a manner compatible with fair and just social organisation?

Must an invention or activity be illegal before it triggers the patent exclusion?

It should not be necessary to find an invention or research activity is illegal before excluding a patent application. Some activities and inventions may be legal (i.e. not prohibited) but nevertheless socially undesirable and something which the public would not wish to encourage.

What happens if standards of morality change during the twenty-year period following the filing of a patent?

If a patent is granted but, during its lifetime, the exploitation of the invention comes to be regarded as immoral, it should be possible to revoke the patent. As a policy lever, the immorality exclusion should be used to withdraw incentives as and when it is clear that an invention is undesirable. In the reverse scenario, where a patent is refused or in the process of being challenged for immorality but over the next twenty years comes to be regarded as moral, the exclusion under Article 53(a) should cease. This may or may not mean that a patent takes effect. If the original patent application was published without being granted, or if the invention has for other reasons become public knowledge, the rules of novelty will disallow the patent. This may seem harsh on the inventor, but it reflects the fact that there are many policy levers in patent law. Rules on novelty are intended to protect the public domain and define it with a high measure of certainty so that other members of the public can use it secure in the knowledge that they will not subsequently be subject to patent infringement proceedings.

What happens if an invention has different applications, some of which are moral and some of which are immoral?

One approach would be to grant a patent if at least one of the applications is moral. Another approach would be to reject a patent if at least one of the applications is immoral. However, a more nuanced policy response would ignore these two extremes and look for the middle ground. For instance, a patent might be granted provided the applicant disclaims immoral applications. Or a patent might be granted if the seriousness of the immoral applications outweighs the social utility of the moral applications.

VI. Embryo stem cell patents: the current controversy

Given the technical promise of regenerative medicine based on embryo stem cells and public concerns about the ethics of research using human embryos, the current controversy in Europe is the patentability of inventions related to embryo stem cell research. It raises not only the general morality exclusion, but also one of the predetermined, stipulative examples of the explicit moral exclusion. More specifically, the controversy concerns which, if any, inventions related to embryo stem cell research are excluded from the patent system on the grounds that their commercial exploitation is contrary to *ordre public* and morality? And which, if any, of these inventions involves 'the use of human embryos for commercial or industrial purposes' (the stipulative exclusion)?[66] In addition, other provisions state that the human body, at any of the various stages of its development, is not patentable, but parts isolated from the human body may be patentable.[67] Thus, it is also necessary to consider whether, and in what circumstances an embryo-related invention constitutes the human body at any stage of its development. The EPO, and more recently the CJEU, have been asked to answer these questions.

Broadly speaking, the most controversial patents concern:

- human totipotent cells isolated from embryos;
- differentiated or pluripotent human cell-lines isolated from human embryos.

Totipotent cells develop soon after the fusion of gametes, and have the potential to divide and develop into a full human being given the right conditions (currently, a human womb). Based on this, there is wide agreement amongst patent offices that totipotent cells represent the first, early stage of the human body and are thus unpatentable according to the rule that excludes the human body at any stage of its development. In addition, totipotent cells could be classified as 'human embryos' and excluded under the stipulative morality rule that excludes 'commercial and industrial uses of human embryos'.

[66] EU Directive 98/44, above n. 6, Art. 6(2)(c). The EPO's equivalent provision is rule 28(c) of the Implementing Regulations to the European Patent Convention 2000 (formerly rule 23d(c) of the Implementing Regulations to the EPC 1973).

[67] EU Directive 98/44, above n. 6, Art. 5(1) and (2). The EPO's equivalent provision is rule 29 of the Implementing Regulations to the European Patent Convention 2000 (formerly rule 23e of the Implementing Regulations to the EPC 1973).

Human cell lines isolated from human embryos do not have the same capacity to develop into a full human being. They are thus not excluded by the human body rule, but may nevertheless fall foul of the general morality exception or the stipulative morality rule that excludes 'commercial and industrial uses of human embryos'. To minimise the risk of exclusion, patent attorneys have tended to draft patent *claims* such that they omit all reference to embryos, instead claiming isolated cells or cell lines. It is therefore less straightforward for their opponents to argue that the invention involves the commercial, industrial or immoral use of human embryos.[68] Nevertheless, according to rules about disclosure (or 'teaching') in patent law, the patent document must include information that enables other skilled scientists to perform the claimed invention.[69] In some instances, the only way to perform the claimed invention will involve the destruction of embryos. Furthermore, the scientist (or another person creating base materials) might have destroyed human embryos during the preceding research. Therefore, the morality exclusions are not necessarily avoided, and there has been much debate as to their scope in the context of these inventions.

As explained above, the EPO's Enlarged Board of Appeal gave its opinion in G0002/06 *WARF*. Notwithstanding the relevance of the general morality exclusion, it focused its analysis on the stipulative example that disallows a patent when the invention involves 'uses of human embryos for industrial and commercial purposes'.[70] In this way it hoped to avoid the debates surrounding the phrases 'commercial exploitation' and 'contrary to morality', and focus on a wholly legal, mostly morally neutral, interpretation of the text in the stipulative exclusion. One of the disputed claims in the patent claimed 'stem cells' isolated and cultured from human embryos. The Enlarged Board held that the performance of the claimed invention (i.e. the making of the stem cells) necessarily required the use of human embryos, and this was enough to trigger the stipulative exclusion. It did not matter that the use of embryos was not, as such, part of the patentee's claim (his exclusive property); it was enough that the use was essential and unavoidable in order to utilise the things he had claimed. The Enlarged Board also hinted that if the patentee had explained in the patent description how the claimed invention could be performed (at the patent's priority date)

[68] See the discussion above, text at n. 37.

[69] This is known as 'sufficient disclosure' and is a core part of the *quid pro quo* for patent protection and ensures that patents encourage the wide disclosure of technical information (as well as its development).

[70] G0002/06 *WARF/Stem Cells*, above n. 27, [31]. Commentators saw this as a cowardly attempt to avoid the legal debates surrounding the general morality exclusion in Art. 53(a): see, e.g., Torremans, 'The Construction of the Directive's Moral Exclusions under the EPC' in Plomer and Torremans (eds), above n. 25.

without destroying embryos – for example, he might have deposited a sample of the cell line in a Stem Cell registry and explained how to access it – the patent would have escaped the morality exclusion.[71] This is because the performance of the invention would not have necessitated 'the use of human embryos'; it would have been possible to perform the invention in another way. In reaching its conclusion, the Enlarged Board purported simply to be applying the words of the stipulative exclusion and not making any moral or policy decisions itself. However, it is clear that it chose between three possible readings of the text – (i) one where the phrase 'uses of human embryos shall not be patentable' refers to what is claimed as property; (ii) one where the same phrase refers to what is claimed as property *or* necessary for the performance of the claimed property; and (iii) one where the same phrase also refers to a patent which claims the invention that resulted from research using human embryos. Its reason for preferring the second option was legalistic,[72] and ignored the policy issue at stake – namely, which of these three readings would best promote the realisation of socially desirable inventions compatible with just and fair social organisation?

At the time of writing, the decision from the CJEU is pending, but the opinion of the Advocate General, advising the Court, has been published (but now see Post Script).[73] It is a confused and confusing Opinion,[74] which excludes the same sorts of things as the decision by the EPO's Enlarged Board, but could also be read as excluding more. The inventor, Mr Brüstle, obtained a German patent in the late 1990s claiming isolated and purified neural precursor cells, processes for their production from embryonic stem cells, and the use of neural precursor cells for the treatment of neural defects. Essentially, neural precursor cells are immature brain cells which exist in human embryos and which can be transplanted into adults suffering from neurological diseases such as Parkinson's disease. Greenpeace requested that the patent be revoked on the grounds that it contravened German patent law provisions which implemented Article 6(1) and (2) of EU Directive 98/44 (the general morality exclusion and the

[71] G0002/06 *WARF/Stem Cells* above n. 27, [35].

[72] The first option was dismissed because the relevant provision of the EPC refers to 'the invention' and does not mention 'the claims'. Furthermore, since it refers to the invention in the context of its exploitation, the Enlarged Board held that it was necessary to consider the technical teaching, not merely the words of the claims: G0002/06 *WARF/Stem Cells*, above n. 27, [22]. The third option was not even considered. In other cases, the EPO has dismissed such considerations on the grounds that the preceding research does not concern the morality of the 'commercial exploitation' of the invention. See above, n. 35.

[73] Case C-34/10 *Brüstle* v. *Greenpeace*, CJEU, Opinion of the Advocate General, 10 March 2011.

[74] At least, in the English translation.

stipulative example against 'uses of human embryos for industrial and commercial purposes') and Article 5 (which excludes the human body at any stage of its development). The CJEU was asked to clarify the meaning of these provisions so that the German courts could make a final decision.

Like the EPO's Enlarged Board of Appeal, the Advocate General ducked the questions raised by the general morality exclusion. He was also at pains to avoid any suggestion that his opinion reflected a particular moral perspective or would privilege any particular stance, stating 'I do not intend to decide between beliefs or to impose them'[75] and 'the question which the Court is asked ... is exclusively legal in nature'[76] and 'only legal analyses based on objective scientific information can provide a solution which is likely to be accepted by all the Member States'.[77] Of course, his anxious claims to neutral objectivity were futile. Whatever decision he reached, his conclusion (if followed by the CJEU) will significantly affect European social and economic policy for embryo stem cell research. Ultimately, he concluded that the phrase 'human embryo' includes the embryo immediately after fertilisation, totipotent cells and human ova that have been stimulated to develop like an embryo through cell nuclear transfer or other means (e.g. parthenogenesis).[78] These entities were therefore excluded from patentability according to the stipulative exclusion (and also presumably the rule against patenting the human body at any stage of its development). There was no place, in his view, for a distinction between embryos and pre-embryos,[79] although the Advocate General did not explain how he was able to rule out this distinction focusing only on 'scientific information'.

In addition, the Advocate General opined that pluripotent cells were excluded from patenting (according to the stipulative exception) 'where the application of the technical process for which the patent is filed necessitates the prior destruction of human embryos or their use as base material, even if the description of that process does not contain any reference to the use of human embryos'. Unfortunately the latter statement did not clarify whether the patentee could side-step the exclusion (as hinted by the EPO's Enlarged Board) by explaining in the patent description how the claimed invention could be performed (at the patent's priority date) without destroying embryos. His choice of words and examples[80]

[75] Case C-34/10 *Brüstle* v. *Greenpeace*, above n. 73, [40]. [76] Ibid., [45].
[77] Ibid., [47]. [78] Ibid., [115].
[79] A distinction made, for example, in Spain: Ibid., [70].
[80] For instance, the Advocate General said that the issue was akin to developing an invention via research that killed prisoners. In saying this, he might have been suggesting that even if the invention could be replicated without killing more prisoners (he did not say what he had in mind, but perhaps a new drug), the invention was the poisoned fruit of immoral research activities, and should not be patentable: Ibid., [106].

suggested a different opinion – that is, an opinion that the invention would also be excluded if the research *preceding* the realisation of the invention (past facts) involved the destruction of embryos (even if future performance could be achieved without destroying more embryos, for example, using immortal cell lines deposited in a tissue bank).

A striking feature about the decisions by the EPO Enlarged Board and the CJEU's Advocate General is their determined, but vain, attempts to avoid dealing with the 'morality' question. They illustrate all too well the stereotypical 'lawyerly' approach to the explicit morality exclusion – fearing that they cannot reach a convincing answer about 'the moral question', they try to avoid it altogether. But in doing so they are distorting the effects of patent law and ignoring the opportunity to shape it so that it incentivises socially beneficial inventions. Treating the morality exclusion and its stipulative examples as policy levers would help to avoid this outcome.

Putting the morality exclusion *qua* policy lever into effect, decision makers should explain which of several linguistic interpretations, all compatible with the conventions of legal methodology, would best bring about socially desirable inventions compatible with fair and just social organisation. They should also engage in more up-front discussion of the general morality exclusion, rather than a studious focus on provisions that omit the word 'morality'. More specifically, this means that they need to grapple with what they consider to be a socially beneficial invention, and what they consider to be fair and just social organisation.

This may not be easy, but a few examples assist. For instance, the morality exclusions might be seen as an opportunity to avoid a situation where patent law treats embryos as 'property'– in this case claims should be rejected if they include embryos. The morality-exclusion 'lever' might also be tailored so that patent law does not encourage the destructive use of human embryos – in this case, claims should be rejected if their performance necessitates the use of embryos. Or the lever might be tailored so that the patent system does not assist researchers who work destructively with human embryos – in this case, claims should be rejected if the research preceding the invention destroyed human embryos, irrespective of whether the claims or the description of how to perform them refers to embryos.

This is not to say that the decision makers should foist their personal views upon the rest of us. Rather, they should make a concerted effort to discern European values about the use of embryos in medically beneficial research. As Advocate General Bot pointed out, there is no consensus amongst Member States and we cannot be sure which (if any) of the various views put forward is philosophically or religiously true. But he might also have noted that there is no consensus *within* individual Member States – *and* that governments have still managed to formulate policies largely acceptable to their constituents. Patent law must do the same. It must accept that a degree of policy shaping is required after law leaves the legislative assembly, and that the task of a policy shaper, not only in patent law, but in law generally, is to respond reasonably and conscientiously to the fact of moral disagreement and empirical uncertainty. This means finding and explaining a position that is acceptable, albeit not necessarily wholeheartedly endorsed, by those who have their own views but at the same time recognise the fact of reasonable disagreement. Describing this in more detail cannot be the subject of this chapter, but suffice to say that sometimes policy makers achieve this through representative democracy, sometimes sophisticated surveys of public opinion, sometimes by searching for an overlapping consensus, and sometimes reaching a reasonable compromise. The latter three are options for patent judges and examiners.

VII. Conclusion

This chapter has tackled one of the frontiers of intellectual property and philosophy – namely, the explicit morality exclusion that appears in many intellectual property regimes, including patent law. It is, in fact, a consideration with a long history, incorporated as early as 1624 with reference to 'general inconvenience' in the Statute of Monopolies. But it has taken on new significance as legal professionals and members of the public have become more aware of the promise and perils of modern biotechnology and the economic value of patents. The issue has also become more vexed because modern-day patent law is drafted to exclude inventions the exploitation of which is contrary to morality. This intertwines two highly complex epistemological systems, and reopens age-old questions about the relationship between morality and law (which most lawyers hoped they left behind when they graduated!).

To a large extent, this chapter offers a simple suggestion for the complex conundrum – how should patent law define immorality and apply the exclusion? But despite its simplicity, it is an important point which has been largely overlooked by those criticising the explicit morality exclusion. And, as the chapter has hopefully shown, it can provide a useful steer in current debates.

The suggestion is that we should understand the explicit morality exclusion as a policy lever; no more, no less. In other words, the explicit morality exclusion is not a call to identify moral truth-hoods which elude even philosophers, theologians and wise members of the public. But nor is it a cluster of words whose meaning can be properly determined using positivist legal techniques empty of normative content except for the 'framers' intention'. It calls for an exercise in policy shaping that requires a degree of judicial activism. It is similar, I have suggested, to the policy shaping advocated by Burk and Lemley. They invited judges to reflect consciously and conscientiously on interpretations of invention, inventive step etc. and adopt the interpretations that would best shape patent law to achieve its overarching goal. Likewise, I am inviting judges and patent examiners to reflect on the overarching goal of patent law (which I have defined as the promotion of socially beneficial inventions compatible with just and fair social organisation) and use the morality exclusion to help achieve that. Admittedly, this does not give answers 'on a plate'. It is a tailoring device which necessarily vests a substantial degree of discretion in the judiciary. But the reflections in this chapter have indicated some new directions.

One point that emerges is that countries without the morality exclusion are short-changing their society – leaving them with a patent system that promotes any kind of new, inventive invention, even socially harmful ones. I have also criticised the attempts in recent cases concerning embryo-related inventions to read the stipulative examples of morality exclusions in a 'neutral' 'scientific' way ignoring the general morality exclusion. Adopting this approach, the decision makers are simply making policy blindly (or covertly), and probably badly. I have also suggested that when the EPO and national courts are once again faced with cases concerning the general morality exclusion, they should broaden the sorts of morality objections that are considered relevant to it. More specifically, they should consider not only the immorality of utilising the invention, but also the implications of commodification, exclusivity and unfair licensing, and the immorality of preceding research. That said, they will also need to consider the interaction between policy levers. Some challenges (e.g. those concerned with the implications of exclusivity and unfair licensing) might be better dealt with by policy levers in other parts of patent law (e.g. limits on liability for Crown use, compulsory licences or research use exemptions). I have also suggested that the policy perspective sheds some light on debates about the standard of morality – what test, what evidence, the timing of the inquiry and related issues. Here the suggestions differ in less significant ways from the EPO's current approach, but I have offered an additional, and more compelling reason for taking that path.

Post Script

On 18 October 2011, the Grand Chamber of the CJEU ruled on the patentability of embryo stem cells.[81] Unfortunately, but predictably given

[81] Case C-34/10 *Brüstle* v. *Greenpeace*, CJEU, 18 October 2011.

the Enlarged Board of the EPO and the CJEU's Advocate General earlier decisions,[82] it tried to avoid questions of an ethical nature. It did at least admit that when determining the meaning of legal terms, for which no definition is given, it is necessary to consider the context in which the words occur and the purposes of the rules of which they form part.[83] This is not hugely different from the approach recommended in this chapter, but the remaining step – a significant one – is for the Court to have the courage to grapple with the context and purposes of the general rule that inventions are not patentable where their commercial exploitation would be contrary to *ordre public* or morality. Instead, the CJEU focused solely on the stipulative rule that uses of human embryos for industrial or commercial purposes shall be unpatentable. On this it concluded (with very little reasoning) that in order to protect 'human dignity' (which it said was the context and purpose of the stipulative exclusion) patents must not be granted where the subject matter of the patent required the prior destruction of an embryo or their use as a base material, *whatever the stage at which that takes place.*[84] This seems to mean that if an embryo was necessarily destroyed in the research preceding the invention, the invention is unpatentable even if it is not necessary to destroy any additional embryos (for example if the invention could be performed in the future using an immortal stem cell line derived from an embryo as base material). As noted above (section VI), this is a plausible ruling but quite unsatisfactory because CJEU (the most authoritative decision maker in European law) excludes more embryo stem cell-related inventions than the Enlarged Board of Appeal (the most authoritative decision maker in the EPO) with little explanation for the inconsistency. Moreover, the decision completely ignores the important and overarching general rule that inventions are not patentable where their commercial exploitation would be contrary to *ordre public* and morality. So the debates in this chapter and the surrounding literature will have to wait.

[82] See Section VI. [83] *Brüstle* v. *Greeenpeace*, above n. 81, [31].
[84] Ibid., [49], [52], [53] (emphasis added).

7 'The genetic code is 3.6 billion years old: it's time for a rewrite': Questioning the metaphors and analogies of synthetic biology and life science patenting

*Graham Dutfield**

1. Introduction

In 2002, scientists announced that they had synthesised the polio virus out of bits of DNA acquired by mail order.[1] While the initial report of this achievement published in *Science* states that the virus had been '*baked* from scratch',[2] as if it were a cake or a loaf of bread, the researchers had not in fact made a virus in its entirety. Rather, they had synthesised 'a nucleic acid that allows the virus to be produced once it has been inserted into a cell'.[3] In their article describing their still rather impressive achievement, the polio-makers commented as follows: 'if the ability to replicate is an attribute of life, then poliovirus is a chemical [$C_{332,652}H_{492,388}N_{98,245}O_{131,196}P_{7501}S_{2340}$] with a life cycle'.[4] Eight years later, Craig Venter and Hamilton Smith and their team at the J. Craig Venter Institute announced their successful assembly of a synthetic bacterial genome based on digitised

* Early versions of this chapter were presented in a staff seminar at the School of Law, University of Leeds, and at the Summer Institute in Intellectual Property, Biotechnology and Agricultural Sciences, Drake University in Des Moines, Iowa. I am grateful to both audiences for giving my ideas the time of day and for their challenging questions, and to Peter Yu for inviting me to Drake. This is a challenging subject to write on and I must thank Jane Calvert for her enormously helpful comments on certain sections of the text I found especially taxing. Any inaccuracies and errors in logic, interpretation and fact are, of course, my sole responsibility. I am grateful also to Henk van den Belt for kindly sending me a pre-publication draft of his excellent paper on philosophy of biotechnology. Special thanks to Uma Suthersanen for inspiration, as ever.

1 J. Cello, A. V. Paul and E. Wimmer, 'Chemical Synthesis of Poliovirus cDNA: Generation of Infectious Virus in the Absence of Natural Template' *Science* 297 (2002): 1016–18.

2 J. Couzin, 'Active Poliovirus Baked from Scratch' *Science* 297 (2002): 174–5 (emphasis added).

3 M. Morange, *Life Explained* (New Haven, Conn.: Yale University Press, 2008), p. 9.

4 Cello *et al.*, 'Chemical Synthesis', 1018 (citations deleted).

sequence data and its uptake by the cell of a related species.[5] Patent applications on the techniques employed have been filed.

Much of this volume concerns the philosophical and other justifications for patents, copyright and other intellectual property rights. This chapter accepts the existence of patents without question. Instead, it considers how far the patent system should rightly be allowed to go in the life sciences of today. Inventions, if they are more than just discoveries, are artefacts or methods, the 'recipes' (that is, the patent specifications) for which are novel and unobvious descriptions enabling others to achieve the same result. Few proponents of patenting would claim that *all* creative achievements in the life sciences should be recognised as patentable inventions. Many of them are pure discoveries, or else have no clear industrial application. But the fact that so many *are* patentable has much to do with how they are described.

This chapter is about science, patent law and the use of language that supports the extension of patent claims ever deeper into the realms of nature. By language I refer in particular to the use of figures of speech, terminologies and epistemologies that both express and support powerful explanatory and justificatory conceptual systems. Undoubtedly, chemical, informational and mechanistic ways of understanding life have all been enormously helpful to scientists, as are the metaphors and analogies which frame their verbal and written forms of expression. The point of the chapter is not to undermine them, but to examine critically what implications they have for patent law and policy, in particular their consequences for the positioning of boundaries between the patentable and the unpatentable.

From the mid-nineteenth century, patents were regularly being granted on chemical substances in those countries, like the United States, United Kingdom and France, which had no statutory chemical exclusions.[6] In the early twentieth century, patents claiming isolated and purified natural compounds were allowed, or else found by courts to constitute acceptable subject matter. Since the 1970s, an increasing number of jurisdictions have granted patents on microorganisms, cell cultures, seeds, plants, animals and genes. Patenting in the life sciences is often criticised for

[5] D. G. Gibson, J. I. Glass, C. Lartigue, V. N. Noskov, R.-Y. Chuang, M. A. Algire, G. A. Benders, M. G. Montague, L. Ma, M. M. Moodie, C. Merryman, S. Vashee, R. Krishnakumar, N. Assad-Garcia, C. Andrews-Pfannkoch, E. A. Denisova, L. Young, Z.-Q. Qi, T. H. Segall-Shapiro, C. H. Calvey, P. P. Parmar, C. A. Hutchison III, H. O. Smith and J. C. Venter, 'Creation of a Bacterial Cell Controlled by a Chemically Synthesized Genome' *Science* 329 (2010): 52–6.

[6] G. Dutfield, *Intellectual Property Rights and the Life Science Industries: Past, Present and Future* (Singapore: World Scientific, 2009).

inappropriate expansionism. I would argue that some, but not all such criticisms are justified, not least because the application of what philosopher Michael Ruse calls 'root metaphors'[7] have served to erase boundaries (to use a territorial metaphor) that should exist, at least in the context of patent claims. This is especially so when metaphor is put forward not as metaphor, but as literal truth, so that a *like* gets treated as an *is*. (Perhaps we could call this 'the metaphoristic fallacy'.) In other words, a claim that A is like B in certain helpful respects becomes A is B, or is a subset of B. Modern English is replete with examples of this happening, and life science discourse is particularly susceptible to this happening unnoticed. Metaphor and analogy are central to communication and understanding and we are totally reliant upon them. However, they can also mislead, or persist beyond their useful lifespan.

In a previous article, I offered a number of objections to the claiming of patents on whole organisms.[8] These are that life forms are more complex than any truly human artefact; that they are too little understood for us to justify legal dominion over their production and progeny; that the role of natural forces independent of any human intervention is far too great for us to claim that we have made them ourselves; and that as living things they have agency[9] – they are not robots designed purely to serve human

[7] M. Ruse, *Science and Spirituality: Making Room for Faith in the Age of Science* (New York: Cambridge University Press, 2010).

[8] G. Dutfield, 'Who Invents Life – Blind Watchmakers, Intelligent Designers or Genetic Engineers?' *Journal of Intellectual Property Law and Practice* 5(7) (2010): 531–40.

[9] Note Pottage and Sherman's comment (in the US context) that 'whereas traditional utility patents were based on the assumption that the only actor able to exercise agency in relation to the development of a novel invention was the human inventor, the regime of plant patents acknowledged that nature played a key role in the creation of new plant varieties'. What they are saying is that patent law assumes that the inventor is the sole agent in coming up with the invented 'thing'. Any creative contribution of nature independent of humans is disregarded. Consequently, in the United States a parallel intellectual property system (not a conventional patent regime despite its being based on a law called the Plant Patent Act) had to be established for plants that were asexually reproduced from discovered buds, sports or mutations. The only creative contribution from humans was thought to be that of discovering the bud, sport or mutation and then reproducing it asexually, and in this way the breeder was analogised – not entirely accurately – to the inventor. A. Pottage and B. Sherman, *Figures of Invention: A History of Modern Patent Law.* (Oxford University Press, 2010), p. 175. In the United States, from the 1980 *Diamond* v. *Chakrabarty* case, the genetic engineer was analogised to the traditional inventor after initial opposition from the US Patent and Trademark Office. When plants became patentable from 1985, the breeder of sexually reproducing plants also became analogised to the inventor. In the United Kingdom and Germany, patent examiners had less difficulty than those in the United States in analogising genetic engineers to traditional inventors, but Europe has never been able to extend such a 'privilege' to the classical plant breeder, whose innovations continue to be kept outside the patent system – reliant as they are on 'essentially biological processes'. My use of the word 'agency' goes a little further than its

needs, and they cannot yet be made to behave as such. All life forms are recalcitrant from a human perspective. Metaphors and analogies have served to distract our attention from these fundamental problems. However, I also concluded that at some point in the near future, on the basis of advances in the emerging field of synthetic biology, these objections might no longer hold. The question is whether the metaphors and analogies now being deployed by synthetic biologists and patent applicants are sufficient to legitimate the grant of *product* patents in this new field. Or are they still misleading and inadequate? The purpose of this chapter is to address this question.

The rest of the chapter is structured as follows. After a discussion on the basics of synthetic biology, section 3 comprises a critical analysis of metaphor and analogy in the life sciences. It shows how deep rooted some of the metaphors and analogies are in this area, and we will see the extent to which they contribute to explanation and understanding and the reinforcement of conceptual systems and epistemologies. Section 4 is a discussion on the implications of synthetic biology on patent law, focusing on the conceptual and epistemological aspects. It considers whether the language currently being deployed is masking some basic problems in applying patent law in this area, particularly with regard to claims to metabolically enhanced microbes. We also consider the patentability of production methods and the protection of these microbes' functional components; but this matter is given less weight, as such claims are less controversial than those for whole life forms.

2. What is synthetic biology?

Synthetic biology is 'the design and construction of new biological parts, devices and systems, and the re-design of existing, natural biological systems for useful purposes'.[10] More colloquially, it has been referred to as 'genetic engineering on steroids'.[11] Synthetic biology is an emerging area of both tremendous opportunity and consternation. It aims at creating artificial cells and life forms functionally indistinguishable from naturally occurring ones and interoperable with them. At its most extreme it seeks to add completely new functions. But in the shorter term, the aims

application here by Pottage and Sherman, in that I apply it not only to the inventive act, but also to reproduction of the 'invention' plus the full panoply of metabolic activities going on that relate to development, growth, reproduction, resistance and persistence.

[10] Academy of Medical Science and the Royal Academy of Engineering, *Systems Biology: A Vision for Engineering and Medicine* (London: AMS and RAE, 2007), p. 10.

[11] ETC Group, *Extreme Genetic Engineering: A Guide to Synthetic Biology*, 2007, available at www.etcgroup.org.

of most of its practitioners are more modest, albeit still tremendously ambitious as well as broad in scope. A recent European Commission survey of funded research projects in Europe amply demonstrates this, with synthetic biology research activity in such areas as:

- the engineering of bacteria to produce hydrogen as fuel and sugars in high yields;
- biological computing;
- healthcare delivery systems for complex diseases like diabetes;
- improved monoclonal antibody production;
- synthetic cell nuclei analogues;
- artificial DNA sequences designed to detect and possibly correct dysfunctional processes in cancer cells that allow them to proliferate;
- new nucleic acids for safer genetic engineering; and
- the 'stripping down' of bacteria to their most basic genetic elements for use in a potentially vast range of bio-engineering and manufacturing processes.[12]

Currently the following interrelated activities are among the best known.[13]

Creating minimal genomes

That is to say, subtracting genes from a microorganism until it is left with the minimum number to exist and reproduce in an artificial environment. This promises to rapidly increase understanding of cell function. The resulting 'chassis' can then be used as a platform for the introduction of new metabolic pathways, thereby converting these simplified organisms into useful modified microbes. Such organisms are desirable in that: 'every reduction in complexity is likely to yield a biological system that is easier to understand and manipulate, as well as one that has more surplus energy available to devote to making or doing something useful'.[14] Among the leaders in this endeavour are Craig Venter and Hamilton Smith, and their team of researchers working at the J. Craig Venter Institute. Chassis has an automotive ring to it, but the analogy is with computer hardware, DNA forming the 'software'.[15]

[12] European Commission – Directorate-General for Research, 'Synthetic Biology: A NEST Pathfinder Initiative' (Brussels: European Commission, 2007).

[13] Anon., 'Forum on Synthetic Biology' *BioSocieties* 4(2–3) (2008): 273–4.

[14] L. Silver, 'Life 2.0' *Newsweek*, 4 June 2007: 41–5, at 44.

[15] One exponent, Pamela Silver, takes 'chassis' to mean 'a kind of encasing "shell" for the synthetic biological system'. P. A. Silver, 'Making Biology Easier to Engineer' *BioSocieties* 4(2–3) (2009): 283–9, at 287.

The 'standardisation of parts, devices and systems'[16]

This is conveniently analogous to factory or workshop production systems involving the use of interchangeable parts, as pioneered in the nineteenth century by engineers like Eli Whitney, William Sellers, Marc Brunel and Henry Maudslay.[17] Massachusetts Institute Technology has a Registry of Standard Biological Parts. The parts (commonly referred to as BioBricks) include DNA promoters, ribosome binding sites, protein domains, protein coding sequences, translational units, terminators, DNA, plasmid backbones, plasmids, primers and composite parts.[18]

Metabolic engineering

This involves the assembly of metabolic pathways in microorganisms for the enhanced production of valuable natural products that are otherwise produced far less efficiently. A well-known example is Jay Keasling's engineering of *E. coli* to produce a chemical precursor to the anti-malarial drug artemisinin (see below).[19] Yeasts are also being used to mass-produce plant metabolites, as in the Canadian PhytoMetaSyn project.[20]

Synthetic biology is regarded by many of its practitioners as an engineering discipline, a biological counterpart to chemical and mechanical engineering. But if it is engineering, then what is, or should be, the underlying science? Hitherto, biotechnology was dependent on the science of molecular biology, without which we would never have gone further than fermentation and cell culture. Apart from biochemistry, molecular biology and microbiology, all of which are extremely relevant, the key underlying science is systems biology. Systems biology strives to integrate biological knowledge at all levels from the molecular to the cellular to the whole organism.[21,22]

16 Anon., 'Forum on Synthetic Biology'.

17 E. F. Keller, 'What does Synthetic Biology have to do with Biology?' *BioSocieties* 4(2–3) (2009): 291–302, at 297.

18 http://partsregistry.org/Main_Page, last visited 8 January 2011.

19 See J. Keasling, 'Synthetic Biology in Pursuit of Inexpensive, Effective, Anti-malarial Drugs' *BioSocieties* 4(2–3) (2008): 275–82.

20 See the website of PhytoMetaSyn, a project of which the present author serves as a member of its Scientific Advisory Board: www.phytometasyn.ca.

21 'Systems Biology is defined as the quantitative analysis of the dynamic interactions between several components of a biological system and aims to understand the behaviour of the system as a whole, as opposed to the behaviour of its individual constituents. It applies the concepts of systems engineering to the study of complex biological systems through iteration between computational and/or mathematical modelling and experimentation.' AMS and RAE, 'Systems Biology', pp. 9–10.

22 M. Heinemann and S. Panke, 'Synthetic Biology – Putting Engineering into Biology' *Bioinformatics* 22 (2006): 2790–9.

However, it is not self-evident that a full comprehension of these highly complex multilevel relationships will be advantageous to synthetic biologists who, as we will see, are keen on simplification. And yet, they must surely have to face up to the extraordinary complexity of life if they are truly going to fulfil synthetic biology's promise. However, systems biology is a relatively new science. Consequently, we are really scratching the surface and remain, one might say, in the biological Dark Ages. To paraphrase a famous quote from Isaac Newton, the great undiscovered ocean of biological truth still lies before us.

Already, a few genuine achievements seem to be well in progress. For example, several research groups are involved in producing novel antibiotic polyketides through synthetic biology techniques, essentially recombining the DNA in the genes that are involved in their biosynthesis. Polyketides are secondary metabolites produced by a wide range of living things, mainly microorganisms, some of which have antibiotic and other therapeutic properties that have yielded several commercially successful drugs over the years. This is especially important, as antibiotics have been neglected by the pharmaceutical industry in recent years despite the urgent need to deal with the growing problem of drug-resistant bacterial pathogens.[23]

Another important area of activity relates to malaria, which the pharmaceutical industry has tended to overlook in recent decades. In this case, the effort is targeted not to producing new substances, but to a more efficient and economical way of making an existing one. Scientists have constructed from scratch a metabolic pathway towards the production of artemisinic acid, a precursor to artemesinin.[24] As described by Heinemann and Panke, 'this goal essentially requires the design of an entirely new pathway in a suitable production organism. The corresponding pathway elements can be recruited from bacteria (*E. coli*), yeast (*Saccharomyces cerevisiae*) and plant (*Artemisa annua*), redesigned and functionally expressed in bacteria or yeast, effectively paving the road to a low-cost production route to effective malaria treatment.'[25] This sounds almost too good to be true given today's situation whereby diseases that disproportionately affect the poor are normally given little attention.

[23] D. J. Payne, 'Desperately Seeking New Antibiotics' *Science* 321 (2008): 1644–5; Royal Society, 'Innovative Mechanisms for Tackling Antibiotic Resistance' *RS Policy Document 14/08* (London: Royal Society, 2008).

[24] Keasling, 'Synthetic Biology'. [25] Heinemann and Panke, 'Synthetic Biology', 2796.

3. Metaphor and analogy in the life sciences

Metaphors are words used in place of another that are literally unrelated but share some correspondence to the one being substituted for. The replacement words are selected either for practical explanatory purposes or for aesthetic ones (as in poetry). As such, they are figures of speech, other common examples of which include simile and hyperbole. Analogies may include metaphors, but they normally entail much more than the replacement of one word with another. Frequently we explain a phenomenon, such as the way that something works, by reference to something else that is unrelated. The more complicated the phenomenon, the more likely we are to have to resort to analogy for us to make sense of it. Analogies may be contrasted with homologies. Homologies are true relationships. In genetics, homologous genes are ones shared by different species by dint of their having common (albeit perhaps extremely distant) ancestors. Analogies are false relationships that people imagine so as to generate arguments, explanations and decisions that make sense despite a shift in context, the differences being downplayed or ignored. For example, in patent cases life forms may be analogised to chemical compositions or human-made machines despite the fact that they have autonomy, order and the power to metabolise and reproduce without human intervention (see below).

Metaphors and analogies are integral to language and therefore to verbal and written communication.[26] Indeed, they can hardly be avoided: our ability to reason from incomplete evidence or information would be severely impoverished without them. Arguably, metaphorical and analogical thinking are central to all creativity. As historian of technology Thomas Hughes reminds us, for Aristotle 'the greatest thing by far is to be a master of metaphor; it is the one thing that cannot be learnt from others; and it is also a sign of genius, since a good metaphor implies an intuitive perception of the similarity in the dissimilar'.[27] Hughes claims that those famed eureka moments of independent inventors frequently involve metaphor.[28] So it is quite possible that without metaphor and analogy, we would not have gone far beyond the Stone Age.

A classic example of analogy having both biological and mechanistic elements comes from Thomas Hobbes in his introduction to *Leviathan*, in which he treats human bodies as machines, and governments as artificial

[26] G. Lakoff and M. Johnson, *Metaphors We Live By* (Chicago University Press, 1980).

[27] T. P. Hughes, *American Genesis: A Century of Invention and Technological Enthusiasm, 1870–1970* (New York: Viking, 1989), p. 76.

[28] Ibid., pp. 75–83.

people. Accordingly, he asks 'what is the Heart, but a spring; and the Nerves, but so many Strings; and the Joynts, but so many Wheeles, giving motion to the whole Body . . .?'[29] As for the State, Hobbes takes a biological turn: this 'is but an Artificiall Man . . . in which, the Soveraignty is an Artificiall Soul, as giving life and motion to the whole body; The Magistrates, and other Officers of Judicature and Execution, artificiall Joynts; Reward and Punishment (by which fastned to the seat of the Soveraignty, every joynt and member is moved to performe his duty) are the Nerves, that do the same in the Body Naturall'.

Generally, the most effective metaphors and analogies are those that people take literally. Accordingly, one supposes without any reflection that there is a relationship. But whether or not they are taken completely literally, they can still support a robust and widely adopted conceptual system. They may then persist for a very long time. Our language is full of anachronistic metaphors and analogies, many of which we could not get rid of if we wanted to. For example, it is more than 300 years since Robert Hooke identified miniature walled compartments, or 'pores', in the tree bark he was observing through his microscope, and named them after the enclosed spaces inhabited by monks: cells.[30] Now people use the word with no thought as to its appropriateness; neither is there any point in their doing so, since it is indelibly part of the English language. Thus may metaphors become common nouns, as they should, since this is one way that language evolves.

Of course, we have come a long way since Descartes and his conception of living things (except humans) as being nothing but machines without sense or feeling. We imagine science in relation to the most advanced technologies of the time.[31] Thus, William Harvey in the pre-steam era thought in terms of hydraulics when treating the heart as a pump, a metaphor that continues to hold water (or should that be blood!).[32] Analogically, Descartes was closely aligned to Harvey and Hobbes, using very similar language. As Gaukroger observes in the cardiovascular context, 'Descartes'

[29] T. Hobbes, *Leviathan, Or The Matter, Forme, & Power of a Common-Wealth Ecclesiasticall and Civill* (London: Penguin, 1985, 1st pub. 1651), p. 81.

[30] See R. Hooke, *Micrographia: Or some Physiological Descriptions of Minute Bodies Made by Magnifying Glasses with Observations and Enquiries Thereupon* (London: John Martyn and James Allestry 1664). The relevant section of this work is: 'Observ. XVIII. Of the Schematisme or Texture of Cork, and of the Cells and Pores of some other such frothy Bodies'.

[31] S. Rose, *The Making of Memory: From Molecules to Mind* (London: Vintage, 2003), p. 79.

[32] Ibid. This is a good example of a very precise (and durable) analogy: 'after all, hearts can be replaced by artificial pumps, and the mathematics that describes the heart's action in driving blood through the circulatory system is the same as that used to describe the functioning of a water pump in a car engine' p. 33.

mechanistic model is not that of a clock, but one of hydraulic systems, such as those that worked the fountains and moving statues in the gardens of Saint-Germain'.[33] But he also found the workings of a church organ to be a useful analogy for comprehending the cardiovascular system. Intriguingly, Denis Noble, a systems biologist, has likened the operations of the human genome complex not, as is very common, to a 'book of life', but to a church organ.[34]

But some metaphor usage is more controversial. In the present century, Steven Rose comments on 'the power of technological metaphor in biology', one consequence of which is that 'living systems become analogized to machines'.[35] About this, more later. Suffice it to say here that while not self-evidently pernicious (indeed, it has in many ways proved helpful), for patent attorneys and biotechnologists this metaphor is rather convenient since new, unobvious and useful living things can thus more easily be cast as manufactures. Clearly, analogies of the kind indicated by Rose are quite long standing and affect our language and thinking. The point is that they should not be taken for granted and that just as they can helpfully explain and illuminate the complex and obscure, they can also mislead and deceive. J. S. Mill pointed out the deficiency of analogical reasoning in his *System of Logic*:

> In the strictest induction, equally with the faintest analogy, we conclude because A resembles B in one or more properties, that it does so in a certain other property. The difference is, that in the case of a complete induction it has been previously shown, by due comparison of instances, that there is an invariable conjunction between the former property or properties and the latter property; but in what is called analogical reasoning, no such conjunction has been made out.[36]

Accordingly, as Mill goes on to assert 'no competent inquirer into nature will rest satisfied with it when a complete induction is attainable; but will consider the analogy as a mere guidepost, pointing out the direction in which more rigorous investigations should be prosecuted'.[37] One of the difficulties, of course, is that metaphors and analogies have a tendency once widely accepted to be taken literally. Perhaps that is one of the beauties of

[33] S. Gaukroger, 'Introduction', in S. Gaukroger (ed.), *The World and Other Writings* (Cambridge University Press, 1998), p. xxiv.
[34] R. Descartes, 'The Treatise on Man', in ibid., p. 140; D. Noble, *The Music of Life* (Oxford University Press, 2006).
[35] S. Rose, *Lifelines: Life Beyond the Gene* (London: Vintage, 2005), p. 19.
[36] J. S. Mill, *A System of Logic, Ratiocinative and Inductive: Being a Connected View of the Principles of Evidence and the Methods of Scientific Investigation* (1843), p. 365. Quoted in M. Carignan, 'Analogical Reasoning in Victorian Historical Epistemology' *Journal of the History of Ideas* 64(3) (2003): 445–64.
[37] Mill, *A System of Logic*, p. 368.

language: that they do not stay the same forever. But it is sometimes necessary to remind ourselves that we are dealing in metaphor and not in unvarnished and literal truth. In the case of the word cell, it has no power to mislead, since the reason for the word's coinage has mostly been forgotten. But other metaphors and analogies are far less benign. In intellectual property, for example, extending such terms as piracy and theft to cover any cases of commercial imitation and intellectual property infringement needs to be challenged. The point I make is not that we should defend all infringement and counterfeiting, but to underline the point that while metaphors can be beautiful, elegant and illuminating, they can also be deployed for purposes of propaganda.[38]

Explanation in biology: chemistry, mechanism, information and systems engineering

Scientifically, commercially and also in terms of patenting, much hangs on the impression that synthetic biology is an exact science. This was true also for the first generation of genetic modification that started with recombinant DNA techniques. The latter is still commonly assumed to be precise and predictable in ways that conventional techniques like classical plant breeding are not. Choosing the right metaphors, analogies and discourse is very important in creating the right impression.

This leads us to a discussion on chemical, mechanistic and informational ways of explaining life, which thus far have only been alluded to. We will begin with chemistry.

Life as chemistry A number of discoveries in the converging sciences of biology and chemistry, starting from the late eighteenth century, finally refuted some very long-held misconceptions that were holding back these sciences from emulating the amazingly steep learning curves achieved in sixteenth- and seventeenth-century astronomy, mathematics and physics thanks to Copernicus, Descartes, Kepler, Galileo, Newton and Leibniz. Alchemy, which Newton himself practised, was discredited and became mostly a matter for ridicule. The great chain of being concept, whose essential tenets dated back to ancient Greece,[39] was

[38] That the latest edition of the *Concise Oxford English Dictionary* has 'the infringement of copyright' as one of the definitions of 'piracy' shows how the use of metaphor for purposes of propaganda can, if widely adopted and with sufficient time, affect the language. See A. Johns, *Piracy: The Intellectual Property Wars from Gutenberg to Gates* (University of Chicago Press, 2010).

[39] 'The Chain of Being is the idea of the organic constitution of the universe as a series of links or gradations ordered in a hierarchy of creatures, from the lowest and most

eventually replaced by evolution through natural selection. Spontaneous generation began to be disproved by Francesco Redi in the 1660s. Admittedly, disbelief in spontaneous generation was nothing new: to the ancient Roman poet and philosopher Lucretius, 'nothing from nothing ever yet was born' was one of the laws of nature,[40] a notion updated in the 1850s by Rudolf Virchow, who popularised the phrase *Omnis cellula e cellula* ('every cell originates from another existing cell like it').[41] But it was fatally discredited at last in the nineteenth century, by Louis Pasteur. Vitalism[42] in its most extreme form, according to which only living things could produce organic chemicals,[43] was undermined by Antoine Lavoisier, who began to show that the new discipline of chemistry, which he contributed to founding, offered adequate means to describe the key processes taking place in living organisms, such as respiration. Its credibility was further weakened when scientists began to make these substances in the lab. In 1828, Friedrich Wöhler accidentally synthesised, albeit partially, a naturally-occurring biochemical, urea.[44] In time, the chemical constitution of all living things and biological processes became ever more apparent and vitalism withered away, at least among the vast majority of scientists. It turned out that life was made of the same stuff that non-life is made of, nothing more, nothing less. In other words, living organisms were made of, to put it colloquially, bits of non-life. Eventually, as we will see, this allowed for the possibility of making some of these bits in a laboratory, and of using living things in industrial processes for commercial ends.

Life as information The idea that biological molecules and molecular processes can be defined in informational terms is hardly new. When Ernest Starling coined the word 'hormones' in 1905, he immediately

insignificant to the highest, indeed to the *ens perfectissimum* which, uncreated, is yet its culmination and the end to which all creation tends.' L. Formigari, 'Chain of Being', in P. P. Wiener (ed.), *The Dictionary of the History of Ideas: Studies of Selected Pivotal Ideas. Vol. I* (New York: Charles Scribner's Sons, 1973–4), pp. 326–36. For a detailed history and commentary, see A. O. Lovejoy, *The Great Chain of Being: A Study of the History of an Idea* (Cambridge, Mass.: Harvard University Press, 1936). Arguably, the persistence of words like 'higher' and 'lower' to divide complex and relatively less complex forms of life suggest that the great chain of being has not been entirely abandoned as a metaphorical source.

40 From *De Rerum Natura (Of the Nature of Things)* (trans. W. E. Leonard), downloaded from Project Gutenberg website.

41 Wikipedia entry on Rudolf Virchow (last visited 5 January 2011).

42 Vitalism is the doctrine that living things possess some special principle that makes them more than the sum of the chemicals they are composed of and not fully explicable by chemistry or the laws of physics.

43 Hence the artificial distinction we still draw between inorganic and organic chemistry.

44 G. K. Hunter, *Vital Forces: The Discovery of the Molecular Basis of Life* (London and San Diego: Academic Press, 2000), pp. 56–9; J. H. Brooke, 'Wöhler's Urea and the Vital Force – A Verdict from the Chemists' *Ambix* 15 (1968): 84–114.

referred to them as 'chemical messengers'.[45] But life-as-information *technology* goes back to the post-World War Two era, a time when biology became especially susceptible to information and computer science analogies, metaphors and definitions. In the mid-1950s, physicist George Gamow conceptualised the cell as 'a storehouse of information' and also as 'a self-activating transmitter which passes on very precise messages that direct the construction of identical new cells'.[46] This suggested to Gamow that 'the continuity of all life on our planet depends on this information system contained in the tiny cell nucleus'. According to a historical account of molecular biology by Michel Morange, information terminology was hard-wired into the discipline's language from its inception: 'molecular biology is a result of the encounter between genetics and biochemistry, two branches of biology that developed at the beginning of the twentieth century . . . Strictly speaking, *molecular biology is not a new discipline, but rather a new way of looking at organisms as reservoirs and transmitters of information*'.[47] Understanding life in terms of information also became a preoccupation of two of the greatest mid-twentieth-century mathematicians and pioneers of the computer age, Alan Turing and John von Neumann.

The life-as-information idea has obvious contemporary appeal, given the digital nature of so many modern technologies, including those used by molecular biologists (as in the field of bioinformatics), and, of course, the apparent similarity between raw DNA sequence data and computer code. Scientists are thus encouraged to assume that information technology provides the best means for us to understand how life 'works'. Indeed, it hardly seems a stretch to regard molecular biology as a branch of information science with the enormous amount of genetic sequence data now available to be processed and analysed. From this, many are inclined to

[45] E. S. Starling, 'The Croonian Lectures on the Chemical Correlation of the Functions of the Body. Lecture I' *The Lancet* 4275 (1905): 339–41, at 340.

[46] G. Gamow, 'Information Transfer in the Living Cell' *Scientific American* 193 (1955): 70–8, at 70. Quoted in L. E. Kay, *Who Wrote the Book of Life? A History of the Genetic Code.* (Stanford University Press, 2000), p. 154. Arguably, this conception originates with physicist Erwin Schrödinger, whose 1944 book, *What Is Life?*, was extremely influential: E. Schrödinger, *What Is Life?* (Cambridge University Press, 1944). The elevation of the notion that DNA initiates an irreversible flow of information to a fact of life can be attributed to Francis Crick. His Central Dogma posits that 'once "information" has passed into protein it cannot get out again. In more detail, the transfer of information from nucleic acid to nucleic acid, or from nucleic acid to protein may be possible, but transfer from protein to protein, or from protein to nucleic acid is impossible. Information means here the precise determination of sequence, either of bases in the nucleic acid or of amino acid residues in the protein.' The Central Dogma has not gone unchallenged. See R. Olby, *Francis Crick: Hunter of Life's Secrets* (Cold Spring Harbor Laboratory Press, 2010), pp. 308–13.

[47] M. Morange, *A History of Molecular Biology* (Cambridge, Mass.: Harvard University Press, 1998), pp. 1–2 (emphasis added).

take the next step, which is to understand cells and organisms as highly sophisticated information-processing systems which are capable of being harnessed, reconstructed and improved for our benefit. According to one account, 'an organism's physiology and behaviour are dictated largely by its genes. And those genes are merely repositories of information written in a surprisingly similar manner to the one that computer scientists have devised for the storage and transmission of other information.'[48]

Terms like 'genetic code', 'translation', 'transcription' and 'messenger RNA' are well established.[49] A review of the current popular science literature reveals a highly imaginative but sometimes confused use and mixing of the same largely IT-related analogies, metaphors and definitions. Frequently one comes across terms like 'programmers', 'software' and 'hardware'. For Richard Dawkins, 'genes are master programmers, and they are programming for their lives',[50] while humans are just 'lumbering robots'. To Freeman Dyson, 'hardware is mainly protein and software is mainly nucleic acid',[51] though he qualifies this by explaining that RNA can be both hardware and software. Steven Mithen, an archaeologist who studies the evolution of the human mind, characterises the mind as a piece of software. Natural selection is the computer programmer – 'the designer'.[52] Are such writers using them metaphorically, analogously or as definitions? One sometimes wonders if writers, even such clear-minded ones as those just quoted, are sure themselves.

Such language is popular in journalism, too, hence the title of a 2007 *Newsweek* feature on synthetic biology: *Life 2.0.*[53] Presumably, Life 1.0 is the now rather obsolete version comprising DNA that humans did not write! However, this language is based on what the synthetic biologists themselves are saying. Tom Knight of MIT's Artificial Intelligence Laboratory reveals some of the current ambitions in synthetic biology in saying that 'the genetic code is 3.6 billion years old. It's time for a rewrite';[54] as if life is just a set of coded instructions for 'packages' of chemicals to maintain themselves and self-replicate. One computer scientist recently claimed that 'we can now regard cells as "programmable matter"', and that he is aiming to 'program

[48] 'Drowning in Data' *The Economist* 26 June 1999: 97–8.

[49] H. van den Belt, 'Philosophy of Biotechnology', in A. Meijers (ed.), *Philosophy of Technology and Engineering Sciences* (Amsterdam and London: Elsevier, 2009), pp. 1301–40.

[50] Quoted in M. Amos, *Genesis Machines: The New Science of Biocomputing* (London: Atlantic Books, 2006), p. 10.

[51] F. Dyson, *Origins of Life* (2nd edn, Cambridge University Press, 1999), p. 7.

[52] S. Mithen, *The Prehistory of the Mind: A Search for the Origins of Art, Religion and Science* (London: Thames and Hudson, 1996), p. 243.

[53] Silver, 'Life 2.0'. [54] Quoted in ibid.

cell behaviours as easily as we program computers'.[55] One way of rewriting the genetic code is by adding new letters, or bases, an endeavour pioneered more than two decades ago by Steven Benner and Peter Schultz at ETH Zürich. A number have been added to the natural four bases of adenine (A), cytosine (C), guanine (G) and thymine (T). There has also been some success in producing artificial cells with genetic code made not from DNA, but another nucleic acid entirely. In February 2010, it was announced that scientists at Cambridge University have found a way to alter *E. coli* ribosomes and RNAs so that the molecular transcription processes are able to generate completely novel proteins partly out of amino acids that no known cells or organisms ever produce.[56]

Thus humans become authors of life; or so the analogies imply. Is making synthetic life akin to writing a novel, poem or play, in which case perhaps copyright should apply rather than patents?[57] Obviously not. However, reasoning by analogy can be used to make the most absurd logical leaps. A software program is a literary work for the purposes of copyright law. So, some might argue, why shouldn't a synthetic life form, or at least its genome, be one too?

One of the key problems some critics have identified with all this information talk, especially in the context of genetics, is the woolliness and inconsistency in how some scientists use words like 'information' and (genetic) 'code', and a tendency to over-rely on their explicatory power.[58] There are those who talk of information *about* DNA in relation to growth, development, regeneration, reproduction, disease, resistance to disease and general cell functioning, of which vast amounts are being generated and await definitive interpretation. Understood this way, of course, the information one wishes to acquire cannot be acquired simply by looking at the data – that is, the sequence of bases.

Scientists may alternatively think of 'DNA information', by which they refer to the arrangement of the 'letters' of the so-called genetic 'code', which

[55] Ron Weiss of Princeton University, quoted in ibid.

[56] L. Geddes, 'Rewriting Life in Four-letter Words' *New Scientist*, 20 February 2010: 14.

[57] For a discussion on the possible application of copyright law to synthetic biology, see A. W. Torrance, 'Synthesizing Law for Synthetic Biology' *Minnesota Journal of Law, Science and Technology* 11(2) (2010): 629–65, at 640.

[58] Van den Belt, 'Philosophy of Biotechnology'; P. E. Griffiths, 'Genetic Information: A Metaphor in Search of a Theory' *Philosophy of Science* 68 (2001): 394–412. According to one especially critical commentator: 'there is no clear, technical notion of "information" in molecular biology. It is little more than a metaphor that masquerades as a theoretical concept and ... leads to a misleading picture of possible explanations in molecular biology'. S. Sarkar 'Biological Information: A Sceptical Look at some Central Dogmas of Molecular Biology', in S. Sarkar (ed.), *The Philosophy and History of Molecular Biology: New Perspectives* (Dordrecht: Kluwer Academic Publishers, 1996), pp. 187–232, at p. 187, quoted in Griffiths, 'Genetic Information', 395.

is frequently presented in the form of sequences of As, Cs, Gs and Ts. Here 'information' refers to what might more accurately be called 'raw data'. As with the former use of 'information', though, the complex chemistry of the DNA molecule is deemed to be rather less interesting than the possibility of information being presentable in easy, readable form.

The former approach (i.e. 'information about DNA') is surely the correct use of the word 'information' and a more accurate vision of the limits to what DNA sequence data can really tell us by itself. For the scientists, DNA sequence data does contain information, but it is *not* in itself information. This is why we have bioinformatics, whose purpose is to apply information science and digital technology to interpret this data. In so doing, bioinformatics generates information that is intelligible, usable and sharable (albeit potentially proprietary). If not for the scientist, then, for whom DNA sequences are data and not information, are cells able to treat them as information? This is worth considering, because if we accept for a moment that cells are a category of computational information-processing system, it may appear plausible to regard genetic sequences as complete information *for that cell's immediate application.*

But that does not stand up to critical examination either. Genetic sequences are mere data, and partial data at that, which the cell's organisational faculties actively need to extract meaning from and thus find useful in a far less complete and direct manner. Biology is not information technology, and there is no programmer – only natural selection. As Paul Griffiths, a firm critic of 'information talk in biology' explains, just as planets do not 'compute their orbits around the sun', but just blindly go round elliptically according to the laws of physics, cells cannot 'compute' in any kind of intentional way.[59] Furthermore, complicated as genomes are, their informational value is limited. They simply cannot explain everything about such phenomena as growth and development. While a direct relationship can clearly be made between a codon (a three-base sequence) and a specific amino acid, that is about as far as one can go in treating DNA sequences as pure information, and even then that tells the cell little about what protein to assemble and how to do it properly so it folds in the right way.

To use a counter-analogy of my own, to view DNA as information for the cell is akin to claiming that our neolithic ancestors knowing how to use a wheel would have had sufficient information to be able to construct a workable rotary engine (and perhaps even the vehicle containing it). Doubtless there are major holes in my analogy, but it does at least underline the point that there is some considerable conceptual distance between a

[59] Ibid.

lengthy sequence of base pairs and a correctly folded protein; even more between those base letters and a whole functional cell or organism. The sheer complexity, subtlety, context-dependence and informational-incompleteness of DNA does require us to cast a sceptical eye on the view that genes may be treated as four-letter texts comprising all the necessary instructional information for the cell or organism to use. It may be reasonable to say that cellular machinery 'reads off' the DNA 'code', but this does not make the genome an instruction manual for the cell. It is far more complicated than that. The late science historian, Lily Kay, offered an intriguing spin on the life-as-information perspective: 'genetic messages might read less like an instruction manual and more like poetry, in all their exquisite polysemy, ambiguity, and biological nuances'.[60] This may be a replacement of one poor analogy with another, but it does at least discourage our unthinking acceptance that DNA sequences are meaningful in the most parsimonious and literal way as are the recipe, car repair manual, or the flat-pack furniture assembly guide.[61]

From machine to mechanism

Is a living thing a biochemical machine? The idea of organisms being nothing more than soulless self-copying automata goes back at least as far as the materialist philosopher Thomas Hobbes, who held that even the human mind is little more than a calculating machine: 'reason is nothing but reckoning'.[62] To Descartes animals were just automata. Humans were the only exception to this since they had minds, making them machines[63] with souls. Treating living things as machines was one of the consequences, inevitable or otherwise, of Galileo's and Newton's systems of the world.

But it is von Neumann who tried to take organism-as-machine to its logical conclusion by describing a plausible man-made 'automaton' capable of reproducing itself by assembling its parts out of the bits and pieces floating around nearby, and putting these parts together to form another machine. He did not actually make one himself, though a certain Homer

[60] Kay, *Who Wrote the Book of Life?*, pp. xviii–xix.

[61] Indeed, the human genome appears to be far longer than it needs to be, laden with error, repetition and redundancy. In describing this feature, one recent book refers to it as 'baroque design' and 'gratuitous genomic complexity'. J. C. Avise, *Inside the Human Genome: A Case for Non-Intelligent Design* (New York: Oxford University Press, 2010). However, one may also infer that there is a tremendous amount of hidden meaning in the human genome that we are completely ignorant of.

[62] From Hobbes' *Leviathan*, quoted in P. Ball, *Critical Mass: How One Thing Leads to Another* (London: William Heinemann, 2004), p. 17.

[63] Descartes, 'The Treatise on Man', p. 140.

Jacobson of Brooklyn College did build a von Neumann machine, 'producing an intricate trainlike apparatus that generated a kind of primitive self-replication'.[64]

This might now seem a bit outdated. But organism-as-machine language and thinking are still with us, especially in the study of brains and consciousness.[65] Many scientists continue to talk a bit like the eighteenth-century animal breeder Robert Bakewell, who was supposed to have called a sheep 'a machine for turning grass into mutton'. Dawkins is a prime exponent. Physicist and science writer, Paul Davies, has referred to living cells as 'nanomachines'.[66] But in the context of the cellular level, a word more commonly encountered in the scientific literature is not 'machine', but 'mechanism'.

One might suppose the notion of cellular mechanisms to derive directly from Cartesian or Hobbesian organisms-as-machines thinking, or else from Galileo or Newton, whose world was like a clockwork machine obeying universal physical laws. In truth, 'mechanics' had drifted away from its origins in the study of machines as early as the seventeenth century.[67] As to the present context, it is in fact misleading to derive 'mechanism' from 'machine', notwithstanding their common etymological ancestry. As William Bechtel explains in his history of modern cell biology:

> The key to the mechanistic approach was not the analogy of physiological systems to human made machines, but the quest to explain the functioning of whole systems in terms of the operations performed by their component parts .... Increasingly, biology became a science in which phenomena were explained by discovering the organized parts and operations by which a mechanism performed its function.[68]

An inference that one may draw from this differentiation is this: old organism-as-machine analogies fail, in that while human-made machines are designed and produced for a purpose, the higher purpose of life forms is clearly a matter for philosophers and theologians. For biological scientists, postulating a purpose for any type of life form is decidedly tricky. (This is not to say that they have not attempted to do so, as in Dawkins' assertion in *The Selfish Gene*, for example, that 'a monkey is a machine which preserves genes up trees, [and] a fish is a machine which preserves genes in the water'.[69] Even he, though, can find no higher purpose for genes or nature

[64] Kay, *Who Wrote the Book of Life?*, p. 112. [65] Ruse, *Science and Spirituality*, p. 142.
[66] P. Davies, *The Origin of Life* (London: Penguin, 1999), p. 76.
[67] Ruse, *Science and Spirituality*, p. 53.
[68] W. Bechtel, *Discovering Cell Mechanisms: The Creation of Modern Cell Biology* (New York: Cambridge University Press, 2006), p. 4.
[69] R. Dawkins, *The Selfish Gene* (30th ann. edn) (Oxford University Press, 2006), p. 21.

generally.) But with cellular 'mechanisms', identifying them and then figuring out how they work *and what they are for* are absolutely central to what scientists are trying to find out. Again, equating them to human-made machine parts can only go so far. Biological mechanisms are not designed; they just appear to have been designed. Beneficial mechanisms tend to persist, and in some cases have done so for eons. In actual fact, mechanism talk in biology is rather recent, only becoming common in the twentieth century.[70] In part this is because hitherto cell biology was not sufficiently advanced for such language to be of much service. The quality of microscopes has improved rather a lot in the last four centuries!

Of course, to the extent that the meaning of the word mechanism does not require its linkage to a human artefact or connote design, we may have ceased to deal in analogy but in a correct usage of the term.[71] *The New Shorter Oxford English Dictionary*'s 1993 edition is not entirely conclusive in this regard. Of the five definitions given, here are two which, taken together, suggest that the word's meaning has been stretched to some extent to justify biological usage:

(1) The structure or way of working of the parts in a machine or natural system; the mode of operation of a process.
(2) A system of mutually adapted parts working together (as) in a machine; a piece of machinery; a means by which a particular effect is produced.

In addition, 'mechanism' is also defined in the *Dictionary* as 'the doctrine that all natural (esp. biological or mental) phenomena are produced by mechanical forces'. Overall, then, it seems as though calling a functional element of a cell a type of 'mechanism' is no radical semantic stretch, and is indeed a perfectly helpful application of the word and the assumptions behind its use.

Engineering

The legacy of mechanical philosophy combined with the ambitions of synthetic biology encourages the adoption of engineering language.[72] In fact, discourse borrowed from engineering, particularly electrical engineering,[73] is now very common. It affects increasingly how the science is

70 Bechtel, *Discovering Cell Mechanisms*, p. 3.
71 For discussion, see Ruse, *Science and Spirituality*, pp. 57–8.
72 J. H. Brooke, *Science and Religion: Some Historical Perspectives* (Cambridge University Press, 1991), p. 117.
73 For example, see H. Kitano, 'Systems Biology: A Brief Overview' *Science* 295 (2008): 1662–4; L. Lok 'Software for Signaling Networks, Electronic and Cellular' *Science's STKE* 122 (2002): PE11.

described and reported on, how it is carried out, *and of course how patent specifications and patent claims are going to be drawn up*. Since engineering in its various technological guises and electronics are very well-established patenting fields, this is just as well if you are in the business of making money out of the science.

Some leading synthetic biologists, having to mitigate the inherent unpredictability of barely understood complex biological systems, are inspired by semiconductor engineering and applying very similar terminology. Accordingly, 'if individual transistors are the basic components of electronic circuits, then their biological equivalents are genes'.[74] Hitherto, as they claim, applying engineering approaches to molecular biology has not been possible due to lack of standardisation in the genetic 'parts' available and a biology mind-set that tends to stress complexity as opposed to the simplification of biological systems desired by the synthetic biologists. Much of this is inevitable. As historian of science Evelyn Fox Keller explains, in the present context 'the practice of analysis and synthesis in conceptual terms is generally referred to as science; but when it is performed in terms of concrete physical components and involves literal reconstruction of the system in question, it is generally called engineering'.[75] 'Literal' reconstruction of DNA means straight copying of an extant sequence. But with metabolic engineering, the challenge is far greater, involving the reconstruction of whole metabolic pathways from, say, a plant, to a completely different organism like a bacterium or yeast in order to scale-up production of the metabolite. It is not just about reconstructing naturally occurring processes, but also about rebuilding them in different biological 'platforms' so as to make them more efficient; in a sense, to *improve* on nature.

This might appear to be an arrogant notion, but it is hardly without precedent. Europe has had a 'culture of improvement' for about 1,000 years, the idea of improvement being linked to technology and technological change, and also to staking ownership claims to land by cutting down trees, building fences and planting seeds or grazing animals.[76] In the Enlightenment, improving nature became associated with scientific progress and subsequently with incipient conceptions of *intellectual* property rights.[77]

[74] D. Baker, G. Church, J. Collins, D. Endy, J. Jacobson, J. Keasling, P. Modrich, C. Smolke and R. Weiss (The Bio Fab Group), 'Engineering Life: Building a FAB for Biology' *Scientific American* June (2006): 34–9.

[75] Keller, 'What does Synthetic Biology have to do with Biology', 292.

[76] R. Friedel, *A Culture of Improvement: Technology and the Western Millennium* (Cambridge, Mass. and London: MIT Press, 2007).

[77] H. Ritvo, 'Possessing Mother Nature: Genetic Capital in Eighteenth Century Britain', in J. Brewer and S. Staves, *Early Modern Conceptions of Property* (London: Routledge, 1996), pp. 413–26.

In this context, it is noteworthy that scientists have recently devised a new graphical notation for biology diagrams that they hope will become universal, and which likewise adopts this circuit engineering approach. As one of its creators explained in a recent article:

> Once people learn the symbols and grammar they will be able to share biological pathways in the same way musicians share music . . . An American pianist, a European pianist, and a Chinese pianist can all read and interpret the same sheet of Mozart.[78]

Noting that 'the synthetic biology industry . . . takes an engineering approach to designing and assembling biological systems', the article explains that 'SBGN's developers hope that their language will become "the circuit diagrams of biology," meaning that with standardized maps of biological pathways, the industry will be able to operate on a larger scale than ever before'. One critic interviewed for the same article expressed concern that 'when trying to design a language that will advance our understanding of something as complex as a biological system, adhering so closely to any sort of analogy – be it with circuit diagrams or traffic signs – can be unnecessarily limiting'. Time will tell if this notation succeeds in the marketplace for metaphors. Ultimately it depends on how feasible the engineering approach will turn out to be.

Does the analogy work?

Analogies work only to the extent that the similarities are significant and the differences are not. In fact, we cannot be sure that the differences between true engineering systems and modified microbes do not matter. An article in *Scientific American* suggests that the engineering analogy has its limits:

> Electrical and mechanical machines are generally self-contained . . . But synthetic biologists are mainly interested in building genetic devices within living cells, so that the systems can move, reproduce and interact with the real world. From a cell's point of view, the synthetic device inside it is a parasite. The cell provides it with energy, raw materials and the biochemical infrastructure that decodes DNA to messenger RNA and then to protein. The host cell, however, also adds a great deal of complexity.[79]

[78] J. Kloc, 'Scientists Develop a Visual Language for Mapping Biological Systems that They Hope Will Become "The Circuit Diagrams of Biology"' *Seed Magazine*, 28 Sept. 2009 (http://seedmagazine.com/content/article/blueprinting_biology/P1/).

[79] W. W. Gibbs, 'Synthetic Life' *Scientific American* May 2004: 75–81, at 78.

The key issue, of course, is whether the first generation of synthetic biologists are over-confident in their ability to eliminate complexity, or at least complexity's effects. Is their conviction well founded, or is it a matter of faith? Calvert suggests the latter.

For some, this reduction of complexity is not merely an instrumental aim, but is based on a faith that synthetic biology will ultimately lead to 'the elucidation of the underlying simplicity' of nature.[80] The pervasive idea of the simplicity of nature, and its connection to truth, is found throughout the history of biology (often in tension with ideas about its complexity), and perhaps the most striking example of this is the iconic image of the double helix, famously described by Crick and Watson in 1953.[81]

Much of synthetic biology depends on the validity of the concept of modularity, a notion imported from engineering, according to which parts are interchangeable, possessing intrinsic properties, and performing specific functions. Simplification and decontextualisation certainly have their place in science. Treating parts as modular components, and seeking to enhance natural modularity, also encourages collective innovation – hence the advocacy of open source approaches. However, do we yet have the ability to downplay or even eradicate biological complexity? On this matter there is an ongoing debate among scientists, philosophers and science and technology studies practitioners.[82]

To sum up this part of the chapter, biologically-trained mechanical engineers, chemical engineers, geneticists and information scientists are keen for us to envision life according to their chosen languages and epistemologies, and it can all get a bit mind-boggling (see Table 7.1). Be that as it may, experience does show that metaphors and analogies can provide considerable guidance for researchers making very important discoveries they might otherwise never have made.[83] The real issue is not whether they are wrong or misleading *in themselves*, but whether they are still *sufficient* at least (in the present context) for the purpose of claiming patent rights. Life remains mysteriously complex and increasingly seems to require ecological and interdisciplinary approaches for us to understand what it is and what it does. Steven Rose, a biologist who has written extensively on

[80] B. Palsson, 'The Challenges of In Silico Biology' *Nature Biotechnology* 18 (2000): 1147–50, at 1149.

[81] J. Calvert, 'Synthetic Biology: Constructing Nature?' *The Sociological Review* 58(1) (2010): 95–112, at 99; B. Palsson, 'The Challenges of In Silico Biology' (other reference removed from quote).

[82] For detailed discussion, see Calvert, 'Synthetic Biology'.

[83] E. M. Neumann-Held, 'The Genetic Code: Foundation of Life or Heuristic Device' in Max Planck Inst. for the History of Science, *History and Epistemology of Molecular Biology and Beyond: Problems and Perspectives* (Berlin, 2006), pp. 141–9.

Table 7.1 *Conceptual systems in biology with examples of metaphor, analogy and their limitations*

Conceptual system	Metaphor	Analogy	Limitations to the analogy
Life/living processes are chemical and can be adequately described by their chemical composition	'Life is largely chemistry'.[a] 'If the ability to replicate is an attribute of life, then poliovirus is a chemical [$C_{332,652}H_{492,388}N_{98,245}O_{131,196}P_{7501}S_{2340}$] with a life cycle.'[b]	'We see no *legally* significant difference between active chemicals which are classified as "dead" and organisms used for their *chemical* reactions which take place because they are "alive"'.[c] 'Patentable micro-organisms are formed in such large numbers that any measurable quantity will possess uniform properties and characteristics . . .'.[d]	'. . . The same cannot be said for plants and animals. It is far easier to analogize a micro-organism to a chemical compound or another inanimate object than it is to analogize an animal to an inanimate object.'[e]
Biology is a branch of information technology	'Life is information technology writ small'.[f] 'Hardware is mainly protein and software is mainly nucleic acid'.[g]	'An organism's physiology and behaviour are dictated largely by its genes. And those genes are merely repositories of information written in a surprisingly similar manner to the one that computer scientists have devised for the storage and transmission of other information.'[h]	'The claim that biology "is, itself, an information technology" ("Drowning in Data" 1999, 97), is on a par with the claim that the planets compute their orbits around the sun or that the economy computes an efficient distribution of goods and resources.'[i] 'Genetic messages might read less like an instruction manual and more like poetry, in all their exquisite polysemy, ambiguity, and biological nuances.'[j]

Organisms are machines, their functional components are mechanisms.	'What is found in biology is *mechanisms*, mechanisms built with chemical components.'[k] 'Nature's robots': proteins.[l]	'It is not open to doubt that the living body *is* a machine. It is a complex chemical engine that applies the energy of the food-stuffs to the performance of the work of life'.'[m] 'The world is already full of nanomachines: they are called living cells. Each cell is packed with tiny structures that might have come from an engineer's manual. Minuscule tweezers, scissors, pumps, motors, levers, valves, ropes, chains and even vehicles abound . . . . The miracle of life is not that it is made of nanotools, but that these tiny diverse parts are integrated in a highly organized way.'[n]	'The key to the mechanistic approach was not the analogy of physiological systems to human-made machines, but the quest to explain the functioning of whole systems in terms of the operations performed by their component parts.'[o]
Cells can be improved by applying principles of engineering	'Genes are master programmers, and they are programming for their lives'.[p] 'We can now regard cells as "programmable matter"'.[q]	'Just as engineers now design integrated circuits based on the known physical properties of materials and then fabricate functioning circuits and entire processors . . ., synthetic biologists will soon design and build engineered biological systems.'[r]	'The idea from biology of self-replication is a crucial feature and what essentially distinguishes synthetic biology from regular engineering.'[s] '. . . we will see synthetic biology continually eluded in its quest to isolate the properties of living systems. The concern here is that by attempting to eliminate complexity and contingency, synthetic biologists might end up losing sight of the emergent properties that define living

Table 7.1 (*cont.*)

Conceptual system	Metaphor	Analogy	Limitations to the analogy
			systems, which are themselves historical accumulations, being the result of billions of years of evolution.'[t]

Source: Compiled by the author.

[a] Judge Rich, *Application of Malcolm E. Bergy, John H. Coats, and Vedpal S. Malik. Application of Ananda M. Chakrabarty* 596 F.2d 952 (Fed. Cir. 1979), 29 March 1979; as amended 19 April 1979.

[b] Cello, J., Paul, A. V. and Wimmer, E., 'Chemical Synthesis of Poliovirus cDNA: Generation of Infectious Virus in the Absence of Natural Template' *Science* 297 (2002): 1016–18, at 1018 (citations deleted).

[c] Judge Rich, *Application of Malcolm E. Bergy*.

[d] Judge Bastarache, *Harvard College* v. *Canada (Commissioner of Patents)* 2002 SCC 76.

[e] Ibid.

[f] Davies, P., *The Origins of Life* (London: Penguin, 1999), p. 11.

[g] Ibid., p. 7.

[h] 'Drowning in data', *The Economist* 26 June 1999: 97–8.

[i] Griffiths, P. E., 'Genetic Information: A Metaphor in Search of a Theory' *Philosophy of Science* 68 (2001): 394–412, at 395.

[j] Kay, L. E., *Who Wrote the Book of Life? A History of the Genetic Code* (Stanford University Press, 2000), pp. xviii–xix.

[k] Francis Crick, quoted in Bechtel, W., *Discovering Cell Mechanisms: The Creation of Modern Cell Biology* (New York: Cambridge University Press, 2006), p. 3.

[l] Tanford, C. and Reynolds J. *Nature's Robots: A History of Proteins* (New York: Oxford University Press, 2001).

[m] Wilson, E. B., 'Biology'. Lecture delivered at Columbia University in the series Science, Philosophy and Art, 20 Nov. 1907 (New York: Columbia University Press, 1908), pp. 7–8. Quoted in Ruse, M., *Science and Spirituality: Making Room for Faith in the Age of Science* (New York: Cambridge University Press, 2010), p. 72.

[n] Davies, *The Origins of Life*, p. 76.

[o] Bechtel, *Discovering Cell Mechanisms*, p. 4.

[p] Dawkins, R., *The Selfish Gene* (Oxford University Press, 1989), p. 62, quoted in Amos, M., *Genesis Machines: The New Science of Biocomputing* (London: Atlantic Books, 2006), p. 10.

[q] Weiss, quoted in Silver, L., 'Life 2.0'. *Newsweek*, 4 June 2007: 41–5, at 44.

[r] Keasling, J., 'Synthetic Biology in Pursuit of Inexpensive, Effective, Anti-malarial Drugs' *BioSocieties* 4(2–3) (2009): 275–82, at 276.

[s] Silver, P. A., 'Making Biology Easier to Engineer' *BioSocieties* 4(2–3) (2009): 283–9, at 284.

[t] Calvert, J., 'Synthetic Biology: Constructing Nature' *The Sociological Review* 58(1) (2010): 95–112, at 103.

biochemistry, explains that all life forms must have the ability 'to *be* and to *become*',[84] hence the currently popular notion of 'emergence',[85] which in turn requires a biology that encompasses what he calls 'epistemological pluralism'.[86]

4. Intellectual property and synthetic biology

We now turn to the patent system. Does synthetic biology represent a true technological discontinuity that renders obsolete reasonable objections that have been made to the inclusion of life forms as patentable inventions? And if not, are the metaphors and analogies used misleading us into thinking there are genuine inventions when there are not?

Before going further, the purpose of this discussion is not to attack the epistemologies and supporting metaphors and analogies deployed by life scientists; nor is it to demand unrealistically high standards of scientific error avoidance. Hindsight is the best determinant of scientific accuracy. I would not try to usurp hindsight's position as supreme arbiter. Suffice it to say that however confident the likes of Tom Knight may appear, the practice of science in this field unavoidably entails an underlying sense of humility. Biology still requires it. According to the scientifically trained theologian Alister McGrath, 'natural scientists find themselves having to believe some things that they know will later be shown to be wrong – but not being sure *which* of their present beliefs would turn out to be erroneous'.[87]

True or not, patent examination and validity assessment are not tests of proper scientific theory or description, nor should they be. As Lord Justice Jacob has asserted (in a criticism of an earlier work by the present author, as it happens): 'if you devise something new and useful, it does not matter if you explain it all by phlogiston theory or have no explanation at all. All that matters is that it works.'[88] Rather, our aim is to question whether patents will be allowed in this field, not because what is claimed is a true

[84] Rose, *Lifelines*, p. 142, emphasis in original.

[85] See M. Mitchell, *Complexity: A Guided Tour* (New York: Oxford University Press, 2009); S. D. Mitchell, *Unsimple Truths: Science, Complexity and Policy* (Chicago and London: Chicago University Press, 2009).

[86] Ibid., p. 14.

[87] A. McGrath, *Dawkins' God: Genes, Memes, and the Meaning of Life* (Malden: Blackwell, 2005), p. 104, emphasis in original. McGrath attributes this insight to Michael Polanyi. See M. Polanyi, *Personal Knowledge: Towards a Post-Critical Philosophy* (Chicago University Press, 1962).

[88] R. Jacob, 'Foreword', in C. W. Ng, L. Bently and G. D'Agostino (eds), *The Common Law of Intellectual Property: Essays in Honour of Professor David Vaver* (Oxford and Portland, Oreg.: Hart, 2010), p. viii.

invention, but because the metaphors and analogies employed make it seem as if what is described is an invention when it is not. This is a point that the esteemed judge may be overlooking.

Experience tells us that courts facing difficult patentable subject-matter decisions adopt one of at least three approaches. They may decide on the basis of certain tests, the fulfilment of which satisfies the invention criteria. For example, in the United States, the machine-or-transformation test may be used in deciding certain process claims. In Europe, the technical character test is applied, for example, to computer-implemented inventions. Otherwise, they may resort to an analysis of what certain key words and concepts mean: is this subject matter a patentable invention according to the meaning of this word or concept? They may also, or in addition, reason by analogy, especially if the subject matter at issue has not previously commonly been protected.

By illustration, let us look briefly at a couple of important North American cases. These are interesting in that both the United States and Canada require *physical* inventions to be machines, manufactures or compositions of matter, and yet both have accepted that life forms are patentable. What is interesting is that they have done so in quite different ways, despite the very similar statutory language.[89]

The US Supreme Court's famous *Diamond* v. *Chakrabarty* decision in 1979 concerned a bacterium modified to consume oil which was held to be patentable subject matter.[90] Microorganisms, just like any inanimate units of matter, are, of course, made of chemicals. But one does not have to be a vitalist to question the validity of the assumption that a modified bacterium may be just as much an invented composition of matter as, say, a new small molecule pharmaceutical substance, simply because both have a molecular structure that diverges to some degree from any known one. The autonomy, complexity and self-reproducibility of the microbe are in this way being treated as irrelevant: it has become just a chemical.

The Court also affirmed that such an 'invention' could be classed as a 'manufacture'. Over the years, manufacture has escaped from its original meaning as something made by hand to include things produced by machinery. Meanings of words inevitably evolve, as they should when need arises or common sense demands. But to call a living organism an article of manufacture neatly sidesteps the immense differences between inanimate chemical substances, whether or not they are fully characterised, and even the most 'simple' unicellular life-forms.

[89] 35 USC 101; Patent Act, RSC 1985, c. P-4, s. 2.
[90] *Diamond* v. *Chakrabarty*, 447 US 303 (1980).

In 2002, the Canadian Supreme Court decided, in the *Harvard Oncomouse* case, that a line should be drawn.[91] However, this was not between the inanimate and the animate, but between the lower and the higher life form. In the latter case, analogising from the statutory language was deemed to be a stretch too far for the time being. In the words of Judge Bastarache, who delivered the Court's decision, 'it is far easier to analogize a micro-organism to a chemical compound or other inanimate object than it is to analogize a plant or an animal to an inanimate object'. Moreover, 'while a mouse may be analogized to a "manufacture" when it is produced in an industrial setting, the word in its vernacular sense does not include a higher life form'. Such line-drawing based on the perceived limits of conventional analogies, I would argue, makes far less scientific or legal sense than distinguishing between the animate and the inanimate.

It would appear that in the United States and Canada, claiming a metabolically enhanced microorganism in a patent will not present any difficulties, as in any other jurisdiction in which microorganisms are already patentable, including Europe and East Asia. The chemistry analogy certainly helps in this respect, *at least as long as chemicals are deemed as inherently patentable subject matter.*

But how stable really is the view that chemicals are inherently patentable? In the United States and United Kingdom, they have been considered so for most of the time since the late nineteenth century. In the United States, patents claiming chemicals were sometimes rejected for being products of nature, but generally, the principle of chemical substances being patentable was not seriously challenged. From 1919 to 1949, chemical substances were not patentable in the United Kingdom except where made by means of a specific process disclosed in the patent. In 1916, opposition to absolute (by any process) protection for chemicals came from the British Comptroller-General of Patents, no less.[92] Despite this, the historical shift to chemicals as subject matter in the common law world, while problematic in some ways, and controversial at times largely due to the fact such a large proportion of the patents granted tended at first to be held by German and Swiss inventors,[93] did not generally give rise to opposition on the basis that the boundaries of patent law were being expanded into areas that were conceptually incompatible.

[91] *Harvard College* v. *Canada (Commissioner of Patents)* 2002 SCC 76.

[92] J. Pila, *The Requirement for an Invention in Patent Law* (Oxford University Press, 2010), p. 84.

[93] This is mostly why the American Pharmaceutical Association in 1919 advocated changes to the law allowing only chemical processes to be patented. F. C. Stewart, 'Letter to M. H. Coulston, President of the Patent Office Society' *Journal of the Patent Office Society* 2(1) (1919): 73–5.

In many other parts of the world, including the European continent, the inherent patentability of chemicals was confirmed much more recently. Chemical substances were unpatentable in several European countries until just a few decades ago. While public interest considerations and industry demands were often behind the prohibition, it is possible that more conceptual grounds were sometimes applied, such as those proffered by the turn of the twentieth century German legal philosopher, Josef Köhler. Köhler denied chemicals could be inventions 'on the basis of the *theoretical* possibility that one day these synthetically produced chemicals might also be found in nature. He further argued that the tendency of chemical substances to combine with each other reflects an inherent, natural disposition, so that man's contribution consists not so much in the creation of a new compound as in the removal of the obstacles that block its formation.'[94] The fact that Germany did not allow patent claims on chemicals until the late 1960s, almost a century after infant industry protectionist and anti-monopoly arguments against such patenting had ceased to be credible, suggests these arguments would have been convenient and thus may have been influential. It also implies that in much of continental Europe, the chemicals-to-microbes-to-plants-to-animals analogical shifts may have more shaky foundations than some might suppose. However, there does not appear any likelihood of reverting to the ban on chemicals era. Indeed, India, which for a long time resisted the extension of patent law to include chemicals, has recently introduced product patent protection for chemicals in conformity with its obligations as a member of the World Trade Organization (WTO). As is well known, the WTO Agreement on Trade-related Aspects of Intellectual Property Rights obliges member states to provide patents for microorganisms, *but protection for plants and animals is not mandatory*. Expanding patentability from chemicals all the way up to animals is not required under international law.

With respect to method and product claims to transplanted and improved metabolic pathways, these will most likely be deemed acceptable in light of long-established patent law statutory interpretation and jurisprudence. As for genetic sequences, both the United States and Europe have been allowing isolated DNA with disclosed utility or industrial application to be patented for well over two decades. In Europe, for example, the European Patent Office's Technical Board of Appeal affirmed in the mid-1990s that 'DNA is not "life", but a chemical substance which carries

[94] Van den Belt, 'Philosophy of Biotechnology'.

genetic information and can be used as an intermediate in the production of proteins which may be medically useful.'[95]

Notwithstanding recent rule changes in both jurisdictions and a 2010 court decision in the United States making the situation less certain (see below), this remains the practice. However, there is little doubt that objections to the patenting of isolated DNA sequences, according to which they are mere discoveries or products of nature, will not hold if claimed sequences include bases other than A, C, G and T, or if the sequences are made of other nucleic acids than DNA. Indeed, allowing such sequences while denying the patentability of isolated ACGT sequences may be good policy if the objective is to encourage synthetic biology. According to Torrance, rejecting the patentability of isolated DNA sequences, as a court in US District Court recently did,[96] but accepting genuinely new sequences devised by scientists as patentable inventions, would likely encourage research to shift towards the development and application of truly original synthetic genes.[97]

We now move to whole organisms. The reasons for denying the patentability of life forms remain relevant, albeit with some modification. However, product by process claims will be easier to justify. Moreover, product claims over modified cellular mechanisms would appear to be reasonable. But as long as debate continues as to the feasibility of the simplified organism approach, one should continue to be cautious in accepting the patentability of these metabolically enhanced organisms. Indeed, for synthetic biology, the real proof of concept requires the complete construction of a life form in the laboratory:

> SynBio scientists haven't quite proven that a cell is a kind of biochemical machine, and religious biologists like [Leon] Kass and [Francis] Collins hang on tightly to this uncertainty. Proof will come when the first discrete, self-maintaining, stable organic creature – Life 2.0 – is created from scratch in the lab.[98]

Despite the hype coming from certain quarters, we are simply not there yet. When we are, the engineering analogy presumably will finally fit perfectly, thereby ceasing to be an analogy. Synthetic biology *will be* a form of engineering. Life forms will truly become manufactured mechanical devices *at least in the artificial environments in which they will be placed.*

But does it follow that opponents of patents on life forms will have no more technical or conceptual grounds to support their position? Perhaps

[95] TO272/95 *HOWARD FLOREY INSTITUTE/Relaxin*, Decision of Technical Board of Appeal 3.3.4 dated 30 August 1994, [1995] EPOR 357, 373–455, at 400.
[96] *Association for Molecular Pathology* v. *U.S. Patent and Trademark Office*, No. 09 Civ. 4515, 2010 WL 1233416 (SDNY 29 Mar. 2010).
[97] Torrance, 'Synthesizing Law', 640. [98] Silver 'Life 2.0', 45.

not. Even to a materialist like the present author, until such organisms cease to be animate – and how one will determine *that* is going to fascinate future scientists, philosophers and lawyers – the present objections will still carry weight.[99] Life *is* different from non-life, and that is relevant for patent law. As for moral and religious objections to such patenting, that is another issue – and another chapter.

[99] In the absence of an agreed definition on what life is and what its most defining characteristics are, producing scientific criteria for differentiating between life and non-life remains difficult and perhaps always will be. For an intriguing discussion on this matter, which as the authors show has parallels with the challenge in artificial intelligence of determining whether machines can think, a test for which was devised by Alan Turing, see L. Cronin, N. Krasnogor, B. G. Davis, C. Alexander, N. Robertson, J. H. G. Steinke, S. L. M. Schroeder, A. N. Khlobystov, G. Cooper, P. M. Gardner, P. Siepmann, B. J. Whitaker and D. Marsh, 'The Imitation Game – A Computational Chemical Approach to Recognizing Life' *Nature Biotechnology* 24 (2009): 1203–6. Of course, we are likely one day also to face the opposite scenario: that a computer system may become so complex and autonomous that it will claim the right to be treated as a person rather than as a property. A jurisprudential study on this situation has already been carried out. See F. P. Hubbard, (2010), '"Do Androids Dream?" Personhood and intellectual artefacts' http://ssrn.com/abstract=1725983, last visited 15 January 2011.

8 Copyright infringement as compelled speech

Abraham Drassinower[*]

I. Introduction

This chapter offers a rights-based account of copyright law. It argues that copyright infringement is a wrong to an author's autonomy as a speaking being. Copyright infringement is wrongful because it is compelled speech.

By an *account*, I mean a conceptually rather than an empirically oriented understanding. My purpose is not to explore the history or politics of copyright statutes or provisions. It is, rather, to exhibit the fundamentals of copyright law as a coherent whole. By a *rights-based* account, I mean a non-instrumentalist account. That is, an account that interprets copyright law as a juridical recognition of the inherent dignity of authorship, rather than as a policy instrument designed to promote the public interest in works of authorship. By an account of *copyright law*, I mean an account exhibiting salient features of copyright doctrine as emanations of a single concept. This is the concept of authorship. A rights-based account of copyright law

* Earlier versions or aspects of this chapter were presented at the Colloquium on Innovation Policy, New York University School of Law (February 2010); Innovation Law and Theory Workshop, University of Toronto Faculty of Law (February 2010); Intellectual Property Speaker Series, George Washington University School of Law (September 2010); Intellectual Property Group Guest Speaker Lecture, Notre Dame Law School (November 2010); Copyright Theory Seminar, McGill University Faculty of Law (April 2011); IP and Competition Seminar Series, Bocconi University School of Law, Milan, Italy (May 2011); Queen Mary Intellectual Property Research Institute Special Lecture, University of London Faculty of Law (May 2011); and Progressive Property Workshop, McGill University Faculty of Law (May 2011). I want to thank Barton Beebe, Michael Birnhack, Maurizio Borghi, Robert Brauneis, Bruce Chapman, Rochelle Dreyfuss, Chris Essert, Jeanne Frommer, Paul Geller, Wendy Gordon, Megha Jandhyala, Phillip Johnson, Stavroula Karapapa, Ariel Katz, David Lametti, Annabelle Lever, Mark McKenna, Michael Madison, Margaret Radin, Arthur Ripstein, Mark Rose, Katherine Strandburg, Catherine Valcke, Arnold Weinrib and Ernest Weinrib for comments. I also want to thank the students in David Lametti's 2011 Copyright Seminar at the McGill University Faculty of Law, the students in the Authorship and Copyright: Theory and History Seminar that Mark Rose and I co-taught at the University of Toronto Faculty of Law in 2010, Rebecca Rodal and Diana Lee for their research assistance, Borden Ladner and Gervais LLP for a Research Fellowship supporting Diana Lee's assistance, and the Centre for Innovation Law and Policy at the University of Toronto Faculty of Law for ongoing support.

is, in short, an understanding rendering copyright doctrine intelligible as a sustained elaboration of rights inhering in the act of authorship.

The account I have in mind is neither descriptive nor normative. I do claim to provide a description of copyright doctrine, but this description is not an uncritical justification of existing copyright doctrine. It is, rather, an account of fundamental features of copyright doctrine as a coherent whole. Precisely as such, the description is inseparable from the claim that aspects of existing practice at odds with the coherence of copyright are unjustified or unjustifiable. At the same time, the normative import embedded in the account is not rooted in a deployment of normative claims external to copyright. The norms juxtaposed against existing copyright are themselves derived from the requirements of elucidating copyright as a coherent whole. The account is thus a critique of existing copyright in its own terms. It is not merely a critical theory, but a critical theory *of copyright*.

The account makes use of an insight of Immanuel Kant's into the nature of copyright subject matter. Formulated in Kant's brief 1785 essay, 'On the Wrongfulness of Unauthorized Publication of Books', the insight is that, considered as the work of an author, a book is not a thing but a 'speech to the public'.[1] The argument I want to present is that because a 'work' subject to copyright is a speech to the public, infringement of the right attendant on the work is best grasped as a disposal of another's speech in the absence of her authorization. As Kant puts it, '[t]he right of the author is . . . not a right to the thing, namely to the copy (for the owner can burn it before the author's eyes), but an innate right in his own person, namely, to prevent another from having him speak to the public without his consent, which consent certainly cannot be presumed because he has already given it exclusively to someone else'.[2]

Kant's insight into copyright subject matter as a speech to the public thus gives rise to an understanding of copyright infringement as compelled speech. Copyright infringement is ventriloquism practised on an unwilling subject. The infringer speaks not from his mouth but from his belly, making it seem that it is another who speaks. This seeming is the

[1] Kant's thesis is that the nature of authorial entitlement is intelligible only if we let go of the view of the work as a commodity in favour of a view of the work as an act – namely, 'the *speech* of a person'. See Immanuel Kant, 'On the Wrongfulness of Unauthorized Publication of Books', in Mary J. Gregor (trans. and ed.), *The Cambridge Editions of the Works of Immanuel Kant: Practical Philosophy* (Cambridge University Press, 1996), pp. 30, 34. Elsewhere, Kant defines a book as a 'writing . . . which represents a discourse that someone delivers to the public by visible linguistic signs'. See Immanuel Kant, 'The Metaphysics of Morals', in Gregor (trans. and ed.), *Practical Philosophy*, p. 437. Note that, for reasons that need not concern us here, Kant's concept of a 'discourse to the public' – which he offers as a definition specifically of a 'book' – is narrower than our concept of a copyrightable 'work'.

[2] See Kant, 'On the Wrongfulness of Unauthorized Publication', p. 35, note *.

wrong to the other, whose mouth is being moved, so to speak, behind her back. The depth of the wrongfulness of copyright infringement is nothing other than this unauthorized use of another's speech to deny her the very autonomy manifested in and through her speech. It is as if the infringer were using another's speech to prove that the other is not worthy of the respect she is owed as a speaking being.

Because I have formulated essential aspects of a Kantian account of copyright elsewhere,[3] I want to specify at the outset the particular role that the present iteration has in that ongoing project. My concern here arises once a viable construal of copyright doctrine as a coherent whole has been constructed on the basis that copyright subject matter is through and through a matter of speech. Assuming that copyright doctrine does indeed respond to such construal, and that therefore copyright is a right to preclude another from repeating one's own speech, what, if any, would be the justification supporting such a right? The answer I want to develop is that copyright infringement is compelled speech. The right is justified as an affirmation of an author's autonomy as a speaking being.

While Kantian, the argument I offer is not Kant's. By that I mean that I am far less concerned with an exegesis of a philosophical text than I am with an account of copyright doctrine.[4] Accordingly, I set forth the

[3] On the idea/expression dichotomy, see Abraham Drassinower, 'A Rights-Based View of the Idea/Expression Dichotomy in Copyright Law' *Canadian Journal of Law and Jurisprudence* 16 (2003) 3. On originality, see Abraham Drassinower, 'Sweat of the Brow, Creativity, and Authorship: On Originality in Canadian Copyright Law', *University of Ottawa Law & Technology Journal* 1 (2004) 105; Abraham Drassinower, 'Canadian Originality: Notes on a Judgment in Search of an Author', in Ysolde Gendreau (ed.), *An Emerging Intellectual Property Paradigm: Perspectives from Canada* (Cheltenham: Edward Elgar Publishers, 2009), pp. 139–62. On user rights and fair dealing, see Abraham Drassinower, 'Taking User Rights Seriously', in Michael Geist (ed.), *In the Public Interest: The Future of Canadian Copyright Law* (Toronto: Irwin Law, 2005), pp. 462–79. On the specificity of copyright on the basis of authorship as a communicative act, see Abraham Drassinower, 'Authorship as Public Address: On the Specificity of Copyright vis-à-vis Patent and Trade-Mark' *Michigan State Law Review* (2008) 199. On copyright as dialogue rather than distributive balance, see Abraham Drassinower, 'From Distribution to Dialogue: Remarks on the Concept of Balance in Copyright Law' *Journal of Corporation Law* 34 (2009) 991. On copyright exceptions, see Abraham Drassinower, 'Exceptions Properly So-Called', in Ysolde Gendreau and Abraham Drassinower (eds), *Language and Copyright* (Brussels: Yvon Blais/Carswell and Bruylant, 2009), pp. 205–38. On the superiority of rights as opposed to incentives for a theory of the public domain, see Abraham Drassinower, 'A Note on Incentives, Rights and the Public Domain in Copyright Law' *Notre Dame Law Review* 86 (2011) 1869.

[4] On Kant and copyright, see Jonathan Peterson, 'Liberalism and the Public Interest in Art', unpublished Ph.D. thesis, University of Toronto, 2008; Maria Chiara Pievatolo, 'Publicness and Private Intellectual Property in Kant's Political Thought', in Valerio Rohden, Ricardo R. Terra, Guido A. de Almeida and Margit Ruffing (eds), *Law and Peace in Kant's Philosophy* (Berlin: Walter de Gruyter, 2008), pp. 631–42; Kim Treiger-Bar-Am, 'Kant on Copyright: Rights of Transformative Authorship' *Cardozo Arts & Entertainment Law Journal* 25(3) (2008) 1059; Maurizio Borghi, 'Copyright and Truth'

proposition that a work is a communicative act not by appeal to Kant's text, but through a brief deployment of the well-established juridical distinction between inventions subject to patent protection and works subject to copyright protection (section II). Briefly put, my point is that whereas inventions are novel ways in which we do things in and to the world, works of authorship are instances in which we speak to each other as speaking beings. I will argue that it is this speaking, an address to others in one's own words, that animates the doctrine of originality and its corollary, the defence of independent creation specific to copyright as distinct from patent law. I find support for this deployment of the distinction between copyright and patent in the classic case of *Baker* v. *Selden*[5] (section III).

The concept of the work as a 'speaking in one's own words' grounds the proposition that copyright infringement is compelled speech (section IV). My argument here takes off from the intuition that an infringement of the right of first publication[6] is an instance of compelled speech – that is, the defendant publishes the plaintiff's unpublished work without the plaintiff's authorization. The position I set forth is that a unified theory of copyright law must formulate the wrongfulness of pre- and post-publication infringement from a single point of view. On that basis, the thread I follow is that no meaningful normative distinction can be drawn on a copyright basis between unauthorized publication of unpublished work and unauthorized publication of published work. In both instances, the defendant disposes of the plaintiff's speech in the absence of authorization. The intuition as to the wrongfulness involved in infringement of the right of first publication is therefore serviceable for our understanding of the wrong in copyright infringement generally.

The concept of the work as a communicative act also grounds an understanding of the limits of an author's entitlement as a matter of copyright law (section V). Not only the defence of independent creation, but also the idea/expression dichotomy, as well as central aspects of the defence of fair use or fair dealing, among other fundamental copyright concepts, are readily intelligible from the standpoint of the work as a 'speaking in one's own words'. Because the work is a communicative act, rights attendant on it must be consistent with the communicative rights of others, even – or

Theoretical Inquiries in Law 12 (2011) 1; Anne Barron, 'Kant, Copyright and Communicative Freedom' *Law and Philosophy* 31 (2012): 1–48. See also, Rita Risser, 'Determinism, Creative Works and Proprietorship' *The Monist* 93(3) (2010) 353.

5 *Baker* v. *Selden* 101 US 99 (1879).

6 Section 3(1) of the Canadian Copyright Act provides that: 'For the purposes of this Act, "copyright", in relation to a work, means the sole right to produce or reproduce the work or any substantial part thereof in any material form whatever, to perform the work or any substantial part thereof in public or, *if the work is unpublished, to publish the work or any substantial part thereof*, and includes the sole right . . .' (emphasis added).

especially – where such rights require unauthorized reproduction of a work for the purposes of responding to its author's communication. Copyright doctrine protects not an author's absolute rights over her work, but only such rights as are consistent with the structure of the dialogue of which the work is but a part.

I will conclude with some remarks on the implications of this construal of copyright law for our understanding of the public domain in particular and of copyright law generally (section VI). My point is that, as distinct from a policy-driven incentive-based account, a rights-based account can help us broach the deep significance of copyright law as an effort to organize normatively an irreducible aspect of human interaction.

II. Speaking in one's own words

'Originality' and 'novelty' respectively denote cardinal requirements of copyrightability and patentability. An author's work is not subject to copyright protection unless it is *original*.[7] An inventor's invention is not subject to patent protection unless it is *novel*.[8]

This familiar distinction highlights the equally familiar observation that whereas the law of patent – through the novelty requirement – focuses on an inventor's contribution to existing knowledge, the law of copyright – through the originality requirement – focuses not on an author's contribution to existing knowledge, but rather on the form in or through which she communicates her thinking. As the idea/expression dichotomy teaches, expressing an old idea in one's own words is sufficient to give rise to a finding of originality for copyright purposes.[9] If patent law is

[7] Section 5(1) of the Canadian Copyright Act provides that: 'Subject to this Act, copyright shall subsist in Canada, for the term hereinafter mentioned, in every *original* literary, dramatic, musical and artistic work . . .', (emphasis added).

[8] Section 2 of the Canadian Patent Act defines an 'invention' as 'any *new* and useful art, process, machine, manufacture or composition of matter . . .', (emphasis added). I discuss the distinction between originality and novelty in Drassinower, 'Authorship as Public Address', 214–20.

[9] On originality, see *CCH Canadian Ltd.* v. *Law Society of Upper Canada*, [2004] 1 SCR 339, para. 16 ('For a work to be "original" within the meaning of he Copyright Act, it must be more than a mere copy of another work. At the same time, it need not be creative, in the sense of being novel or unique. What is required to attract copyright protection in the expression of an idea is an exercise of skill and judgment.'); *Feist Publications, Inc.* v. *Rural Telephone Service Co.*, 499 US 340, 345–6 (1991) ('Originality does not signify novelty; a work may be original even though it closely resembles other works so long as the familiarity is fortuitous, not the result of copying. To illustrate, assume that two poets, each ignorant of the other, compose identical poems. Neither work is novel yet both are original and, hence, copyrightable.'). On the idea/expression dichotomy, see *Moreau* v. *St. Vincent* [1950] 3 DLR 713, para. 8 ('It is . . . an elementary principle of copyright law that an author has no copyright in ideas but only in his expression of them. The law of copyright

concerned with *what* an inventor contributes, copyright law is concerned with *how* an author says what she says. Not the content of an author's speech, but the *very speaking itself* is at issue in copyright law.

Nowhere is this focus on the 'very speaking itself' clearer than in the defence of independent creation, which provides that a defendant cannot be held liable in copyright where he can show that his work, though identical to the plaintiff's, was independently created. Independent creation of two identical works gives rise not to a finding of infringement, but to a finding that two independent copyrights arise over two distinct works.[10] Thus, whereas the idea/expression dichotomy teaches that copyright law is indifferent to the novelty or lack thereof of the idea expressed in a work, the principle of independent creation teaches that copyright law is equally indifferent to the novelty or lack thereof of the form of expression itself.

Of course, two independently created yet identical works *look* the same. But this does not mean that they *are* the same in the eyes of copyright law. Seeing through the mere appearance of identity is fundamental to understanding copyright. As a copyright matter the works are different, because each of them originates in an independent act of authorship. This is why they are each subject to a radically distinct copyright. To be duped by the appearance of identity is but to misunderstand the fundamentals of originality. Originality is literally about origination. Once we focus on the distinct authorship of each of the works, their so-called identity collapses. It is at best a remarkable coincidence. At no point is it a denial of their juridical difference as independent acts of authorship.

While it is true that copyright protects the form of expression, it is important to observe that this does not mean that copyright protects expression as some kind of proprietary object – whether intangible or otherwise – exclusively held by its author. If that were the case, identical

does not give him any monopoly in the use of the ideas with which he deals or any property in them, even if they are original. His copyright is confined to the literary work in which he has expressed them. The ideas are public property, the literary work is his own. Everyone may freely adopt and use the ideas but no one may copy his literary work without his consent.'); *Nichols* v. *Universal Pictures Corporation*, 45 F.2d 119, 121 (2d Cir. 1930) ('Upon any work, and especially upon a play, a great number of patterns of increasing generality will fit equally well, as more and more of the incident is left out. The last may perhaps be no more than the most general statement of what the play is about, and at times might consist only of its title; but there is a point is this series of abstractions where they are no longer protected, since otherwise the playwright could prevent the use of his "ideas", to which, apart from their expression, his property is never extended.').

10 Judge Learned Hand expressed it memorably in *Sheldon* v. *Metro-Goldwyn Pictures Corp.*, 81 F.2d 49, 54 (2d Cir. 1936): '[I]f by some magic a man who had never known it were to compose anew Keats's Ode on a Grecian Urn, he would be an "author," and, if he copyrighted it, others might not copy that poem, though they might of course copy Keats's.' I discuss the defence of independent creation in Drassinower, 'From Distribution to Dialogue', 1002–4.

expression, even if independently created, would amount to a trespass on the author's exclusive holding of her work as an object of ownership. Thus, the defence of independent creation is intelligible only if we posit the work as an act of authorship rather than as the reified result of an act of authorship. A work is not a thing, but an act: at issue is the 'work' not as a noun, but as a verb. An author does not hold her expression as an object of ownership to the disposition of which she has exclusive rights. Copyright infringement is less a matter of disposing of an object than of repeating or reproducing an act of authorship without authorization. This is why to infringe the work is to repeat it or to reproduce it – i.e. to copy it – but not to create it independently. Either we insist on grasping the work as an act, or we jettison the defence of independent creation from copyright doctrine.

The defence of independent creation, then, entails that the apparent identity between two independently created works is juridically irrelevant, and that, notwithstanding that identity, two copyrights arise over two distinct works. This distinction between the two seemingly identical works is possible only to the extent that we abstract from the works as objects of ownership – as things – and focus on the works as acts of authorship. Viewed as things, the seemingly identical works do indeed look identical. It is only as independent acts of authorship that the two works embodied in identical material form can be construed as radically distinct. What is juridically significant as a matter of copyright law is the 'very speaking itself', regardless of the novelty of either its content or its form. What gives rise to distinct copyrights for independent authors of so-called identical works is that – albeit identically – each speaks in her own words. Originality *is* this 'speaking in one's own words'. To be an author is to speak in one's own voice.

III. *Baker* v. *Selden*

The classic authority of *Baker* v. *Selden* supports this view of a work as a communicative act, and of infringement as its unauthorized repetition.

In *Baker*, the Court dealt with the copyrightability of accounting forms included in a book explaining the operation of a novel accounting system. The peculiarity of the forms from a copyright perspective was that they performed a twofold function. As part of the plaintiff's book, they were part of the explanation of how the accounting system operates. That is, the forms were part of the plaintiff's communication, as an author, of his contribution to the art and science of accounting. In addition to being an aspect of the plaintiff's explanation of the accounting system, the forms were integral to the very operation of the system that, as an inventor, the plaintiff had devised. The forms were thus part and parcel of both book and system, of both work and invention.[11]

Juridically, this twofold significance of the forms amounted to the finding that they were copyrightable as aspects of the book, but not as aspects of the system. The defendant in *Baker* was free from liability because the use of which the plaintiff complained was a use of the accounting system, to which copyright law could not grant exclusivity. The plaintiff's claim as an author could not succeed as a claim to the exclusive use of the system. Yet the Court pointed out that communicative uses (i.e. uses of the forms to explain rather than operate the accounting system[12]) would nonetheless give rise to copyright liability. In short, while the defendant could operate the plaintiff's system free from copyright liability, he could not have reproduced the forms in another book explaining the plaintiff's system.[13]

[11] As the Court puts it,

> The plausibility of the claim put forward by the complainant in this case arises from a confusion of ideas produced by the peculiar nature of the art described in the books which have been made the subject of copyright. In describing the art, the illustrations and diagrams employed happen to correspond more closely than usual with the actual work performed by the operator who uses the art. Those illustrations and diagrams consist of ruled lines and headings of accounts; and it is similar ruled lines and headings of accounts which, in the application of the art, the book-keeper makes with his pen, or the stationer with his press; whilst in most other cases the diagrams and illustrations can only be represented in concrete forms of wood, metal, stone, or some other physical embodiment. But the principle is the same in all. The description of the art in a book, though entitled to the benefit of copyright, lays no foundation for an exclusive claim to the art itself. The object of the one is explanation; the object of the other is use. The former may be secured by copyright. The latter can only be secured, if it can be secured at all, by letters-patent, *Baker*, 104–5.

[12] That is, uses of the forms, to track the Court's own language, as explanatory 'diagrams (which merely stand in the place of words)'. The full passage reads as follows:

> The copyright of a book on perspective, no matter how many drawings and illustrations it may contain, gives no exclusive right to the modes of drawing described, though they may never have been known or used before. By publishing the book, without getting a patent for the art, the latter is given to the public. The fact that the art described in the book by illustrations of lines and figures which are reproduced in practice in the application of the art, makes no difference. Those illustrations are the mere language employed by the author to convey his ideas more clearly. Had he used words of description instead of diagrams (*which merely stand in the place of words*), there could not be the slightest doubt that others, applying the art to practical use, might lawfully draw the lines and diagrams which were in the author's mind, and which he thus described by words in his book (emphasis added), *Baker* 103.

[13] The Court observes:

> the teachings of science and the rules and methods of useful art have their final end in application and use; and this application and use are what the public derive from the publication of a book which teaches them. But as embodied and taught in a literary composition or book, their essence consists only in their statement. This alone is what is secured by the copyright. *The use by another of the same methods of statement, whether in*

Baker yields the proposition that because a work subject to copyright is a communicative act, its infringement must be conceived as an unauthorized communicative use. In *Baker*, the defendant's use was technological rather than communicative. Therefore, it did not give rise to liability. The defendant used the plaintiff's forms as aspects of a novel accounting system, not as aspects of an explanation of the accounting system. He escaped copyright liability because he used the forms as *tools* and not as *works*. To be sure, there can be no doubt that the defendant copied the plaintiff's forms. But he copied the plaintiff's *invention*, not her *work*. Thus, while the plaintiff may have succeeded in a patent infringement action, had she been able to pursue one, she could not succeed in a copyright infringement action.

The analysis of the distinction between patent and copyright in *Baker* is entirely consistent with the doctrine of originality and the defence of independent creation. Had the defendant independently created the accounting forms, the *Baker* Court could have said that the appearance of identity between the plaintiff's forms and the defendant's forms was a mere coincidence that, as such, could not give rise to liability. But in *Baker* the identity between the plaintiff's forms and the forms used by the defendant was no coincidence. The defendant did indeed copy the forms, and did so deliberately. Still, the Court finds no liability. The distinction between patent and copyright, between the forms as invention and the forms as work, permits the Court to see through the mere appearance of identity.

The apparent identity between the plaintiff's invention (which the defendant copied and used without authorization) and the plaintiff's work (which the defendant neither copied nor used) is no more than an identity at the level of material form. It is merely a physical identity of patterns of ink on a page. The legal meaning of these patterns, and of their unauthorized use, varies in accordance with the juridical order from which they are interpreted. In *Baker*, we learn that it is not as a pattern of ink on a page, but only as a communicative act that a work falls within the purview of copyright law. The use of exactly the same pattern of ink for purposes other than communication – e.g. as an accounting tool – is not a use of copyright subject matter. This is because the copyright is not in the pattern of ink as such, but in the communicative act that it embodies. The infringement of

words or illustrations, in a book published for teaching the art, would undoubtedly be an infringement of the copyright(emphasis added), *Baker*, 104.
In the previous paragraph, the Court notes:

> And where the art it teaches cannot be used without employing the methods and diagrams used to illustrate the book, or such as are similar to them, such methods and diagrams are to be considered as necessary incidents to the art, and given therewith to the public; *not given for the purpose of publication in other works explanatory of the art*, but for the purpose of practical application (emphasis added), *Baker*, 103.

the work must therefore arise as an unauthorized communicative use. Not any and all unauthorized copying of a work gives rise to copyright liability: actionable copying is copying of a work *as a work*.[14]

IV. Compelled speech

The distinction between copyright and patent formulated in *Baker* thus confirms the construal of the work not as a thing, but as a communicative act, and of its infringement not as any and all unauthorized use, but rather as its unauthorized repetition. The right attendant on speaking in one's own words – i.e. copyright – is a right to preclude others from repeating one's speech. What is it, then, about the act of speaking in one's own words that entitles the speaker to prevent others from repeating it? What plausible justification could such an entitlement invoke?

Relying on an insight formulated by Immanuel Kant in 1785,[15] I want to argue that unauthorized publication amounts to forcing another to speak. Unauthorized publication is wrongful because it is compelled speech. This view is intuitively available in the case of unauthorized publication of *unpublished* work. Unauthorized publication of unpublished work is publication outside the conditions of the author's consent or voluntariness. Because the author did not consent to the publication, the publication is forcing her to speak. Unauthorized publication can thus be characterized as a wrong to a right to remain silent. Because the right of first publication is a clearly recognized aspect of an author's copyright, this characterization supports the view that, at least in one of its determinations, copyright infringement impinges on the author's autonomy as a speaker.

It is more difficult, however, to characterize the unauthorized republication of *published* work as a matter of compelled speech. If an author has already spoken, and has done so voluntarily, in what way can it be said

[14] I discuss *Baker* briefly along these lines in Drassinower, 'A Note on Incentives, Rights and the Public Domain in Copyright Law', 1882–3. On *Baker*, see Pamela Samuelson, 'The Story of *Baker v. Selden*: Sharpening the Distinction Between Authorship and Invention', in Jane C. Ginsburg and Rochelle C. Dreyfuss (eds.), *Intellectual Property Stories* (New York: Foundation Press, 2006), pp. 159–93; Pamela Samuelson, 'Why Copyright Law Excludes Systems and Processes from the Scope of Its Protection' *Texas Law Review* 85 (2007) 1921. On the concept of works as works, see Drassinower, 'Authorship as Public Address', 199; Abraham Drassinower, 'The Art of Selling Chocolate: Remarks on Copyright's Domain', in Michael Geist (ed.), *From 'Radical Extremism' to 'Balanced Copyright': Canadian Copyright and the Digital Agenda* (Toronto: Irwin Law, 2010), pp. 121–50. On the word 'copy' as a term of art, see *Millar* v. *Taylor*, (1769) 4 Burr. 2302, 2396 (*per* Lord Mansfield, 'I use the word "copy," in the technical sense in which that name or term has been used for ages, to signify an incorporeal right to the sole printing and publishing of somewhat intellectual, communicated by letters').

[15] See Kant, 'On the Wrongfulness of Unauthorized Publication', p. 23.

that her autonomy is impinged upon because another reprints her work without her consent? To wrench unpublished work from an author's hands, so to speak, and to thrust it upon the public in the absence of her authorization, does seem to involve a violation of her autonomy. But it seems more far-fetched to characterize an unauthorized repetition of her published work as an autonomy violation. The repetition of published speech seems less a matter of compelled speech than of disseminating voluntary speech.

It goes without saying that this distinction between pre- and post-publication situations is extremely important. If copyright is anything at all, then it must be a post-publication right. Any and all versions of copyright law must account for an author's claim in respect of *published* work. Thus, the intuition that unauthorized publication is wrongful because it amounts to compelled speech can be helpful in an account of copyright infringement only to the extent that it is applicable also to the post-publication situation. In what way, then, can the intuition that unauthorized publication of unpublished work is wrongful help to account for the wrongfulness of unauthorized publication of published work?

I want to posit the continuity between pre- and post-publication situations. My point is that the wrongfulness of unauthorized publication of unpublished work has nothing to do with the work's unpublished status. The wrong is in the *unauthorized* nature of the publication, not in the fact that it is a publication of unpublished work. Thus an intuition into the wrongfulness of unauthorized publication of unpublished work is also an intuition into the wrongfulness of unauthorized publication of published work. At stake is unauthorized publication, whether of unpublished or published work. Analysing the intuition further, so as to grasp more precisely what it is, and what it is not, will yield that conclusion.

To begin with, it is clear, from a copyright standpoint, that the wrong in unauthorized publication of unpublished work is not that the publication amounts to a violation of privacy. Unauthorized publication amounts to copyright infringement even where the publication reveals nothing previously unavailable to the public. Consider, for example, a celebrity's autobiography containing only material already made public in an earlier biography. The attraction of the autobiography is not that it reveals new material, but that it presents the old material in the celebrity's own words. Unauthorized publication of the autobiography is still copyright infringement. That is, unauthorized publication infringes copyright even in the absence of any breach of privacy. This is because the infringed right is not a right to privacy, but a right of first publication. The author's complaint is not that his privacy has been violated, but that his autonomy as a speaker – his right to speak or not to speak – has been ignored.

Of course, breach of privacy need not be narrowly confined to situations involving unauthorized disclosure of previously undisclosed personal information. Privacy may be conceived as involving not only previously undisclosed personal information, but also the very transmission or use of personal information – regardless of previous disclosure – in varying contexts.[16] In this vein, use of personal information for a purpose other than that for which it was previously disclosed may amount to a breach of privacy. Unauthorized publication of a celebrity's autobiography can thus be characterized as a breach of privacy even if the autobiography contains no previously undisclosed personal information. From that point of view, the unauthorized publication of an unpublished autobiography could involve both breach of privacy and copyright infringement. Still, whereas the privacy analysis would target the defendant's unauthorized dealings with personal information, the copyright analysis would target the defendant's unauthorized dealings with a work of authorship. Interference with the plaintiff's privacy is not the same as interference with her choice to speak or not to speak.

While privacy and copyright could each come to bear over the fact of unauthorized publication of unpublished work, the distinction between 'personal information' and 'work of authorship' would ensure that each regime would construe that fact from its own distinct juridical standpoint. Just as privacy law does not require that the personal information in issue be 'original' in the copyright sense, so copyright law does not require that a work of authorship be 'personal' in the privacy sense. Unauthorized disclosure or use of personal information in an unpublished autobiography would amount to a breach of privacy, even if no part of the actual text of the manuscript were published. This is breach of privacy in the absence of copyright infringement. Similarly, unauthorized publication of substantial parts of the actual text of the manuscript would amount to copyright infringement, even if the published parts involved no personal information. This is copyright infringement in the absence of breach of privacy. That privacy and copyright may overlap over identical facts, especially in the case of unpublished works of authorship, need not obscure the fundamental distinction between the causes of action.

Thus, for example, unauthorized publication by a third party of an unauthorized biography containing undisclosed personal information

[16] For discussion and development of wider views of privacy, see Lisa Austin, 'Privacy and the Question of Technology' *Law & Philosophy* 22 (2003) 119; Michael Birnhack, 'A Quest for a Theory of Privacy: Context and Control' *Jurimetrics: The Journal of Law, Science and Technology* 514 (2011) 447. For a political theorist's view, see Annabelle Lever, *On Privacy* (London: Routledge, 2011).

amounts to an infringement of the *author*'s copyright and to a breach of the *subject*'s privacy. The distinction between the two causes of action in that instance would also arise as a distinction between plaintiffs. Privacy and copyright are distinct juridical regimes addressing categorically distinct interests. This is why the intuition that there is something wrong with unauthorized publication of unpublished work cannot be fully captured as a privacy matter.[17]

Nor is the wrong in unauthorized publication of unpublished work a matter of misrepresentation. Unauthorized publication is wrongful even if entirely faithful to the original. Accurate yet unauthorized publication of our celebrity's unpublished autobiography is still copyright infringement. This is because the infringed right is not a right to accurate representation, but a right of first publication. Once again, the author's complaint is not that he has been misrepresented, but that his autonomy as a speaker has been ignored.

One might be tempted to suggest that the wrong in unauthorized publication of unpublished work has something to do with lack of attribution, as when I publish someone else's work under the pretence that it is mine (what we commonly call plagiarism), or when I publish someone else's work and credit no one, or someone other than the author. But that is clearly not the wrong at issue. The author's right of first publication is infringed even if the author is duly acknowledged. Proper acknowledgement is no defence, because the complaint is not lack of attribution but, rather, infringement of the author's autonomy as a speaker, of her irreducible choice to speak or not to speak.

Much less can it be argued that the wrong in unauthorized publication of unpublished work is somehow a wrong to the author's property. This view could take one of two forms, one focusing on the author's property in the unpublished manuscript conceived as a chattel, and the other focusing on the author's work conceived as a kind of metaphysical chattel. Neither view can account for the wrong in unauthorized publication of unpublished work.

The wrong at stake is certainly not the wrong in using the author's manuscript, in the sense of pages with patterns of ink imprinted on them, without his consent. Copyright infringement is not conversion. If I borrow your pen to write a short story in your notebook, your ownership of ink and pages does not deprive me of my copyright. You can no more copy the poem without infringing my copyright than I can rip the pages out of your notebook without infringing your property right. Similarly, if the author of the work and the owner of the ink and pages happen to be the same person,

[17] Thanks to Michael Birnhack, Phillip Johnson and Annabelle Lever for insisting that I make these remarks about the privacy/copyright relation explicit.

as in the usual case where I write a short story in my notebook with my pen, the distinction between the copyright claim and the proprietary claim nonetheless remains valid. Unauthorized publication of my unpublished short story is wrongful in its own right, so to speak, and not because it may also have involved, as a proprietary matter, conversion of my manuscript. From a copyright perspective, the right infringed is a right of first publication, not a property right in a chattel.

Nor can the wrong in unauthorized publication of unpublished work be captured as a conversion of, or trespass on, the work conceived as a metaphysical chattel. If the work were conceived as a metaphysical chattel, such that any and all uses of the work could be regarded as *prima facie* infringing, then the act of reading the work, for example, would presumptively count as infringement. Of course, there is no known formulation of copyright law that construes reading as infringing, whether presumptively or otherwise.

Conceiving the work as a metaphysical chattel, after all, is inconsistent with the defence of independent creation, which teaches that the work is not an object of ownership, but an act of authorship, and that therefore copyright infringement is less a matter of disposing of an object without authorization than of repeating or reproducing a communicative act without authorization. I suppose that it is true that the concept of the work as a metaphysical chattel would provide an explanation of sorts of unauthorized publication as some kind of conversion, but this so-called explanation would tell us little about the specificity of copyright law. It would subsume copyright as a sub-category of property, and thus bypass the need to account for copyright as such. The basic point is that wronging an author as an author is not the same as wronging an owner as an owner. Everything turns on holding on to this distinction. Insisting that a work is a metaphysical chattel, so as to dissolve the distinction, does nothing to further the analysis, and a great deal to obfuscate it.

By contrast, the view of unauthorized publication of unpublished work as compelled speech is consistent with, and in fact flows from, the fundamentals of copyright doctrine. As noted above, the doctrine of originality and the idea/expression dichotomy provide that copyright protects not the content of what is said, but the very speaking itself. Once a work is properly conceived as speaking in one's own words, in abstraction from the content of one's speech, then the infringement of the work must also be conceived as impinging on the speaking itself, rather than its content.

The reason that the categories of privacy, misrepresentation, attribution and property cannot account for the wrong in copyright infringement is that each of them, albeit in its own way, focuses on the content of the work rather than on the work as a communicative act. Privacy focuses on the content of the work from the standpoint of its previous public availability or personal import, and hence on the entitlements that may or may not obtain in respect of rendering that content publicly available or in respect of the use of personal information. Misrepresentation goes to the accuracy or lack thereof of the content of the unauthorized publication, whereas copyright infringement goes to the very fact of the unauthorized publication, even if faithful to the original content. Attribution targets the author's entitlement to attach (or refuse to attach) her name to her work, treating the work as an external content to which an author chooses (or not) to attach her name. But, once again, copyright infringement goes to the very fact of the unauthorized publication, even if attributed correctly. Finally, the wrong involved in copyright infringement cannot be characterized as a conversion of the work, because the copyright holder does not hold her work as owned content or as an object of ownership.

Perhaps the category of privacy comes closest to capturing the intuition that unauthorized publication of unpublished work is wrongful, but it, too, must fail, because it targets the status of the work as unpublished or as container of personal information, thus focusing on the previous public availability or personal import of its content. What is at stake from a copyright standpoint, however, is the unauthorized nature of the publication, not the unpublished status or the personal content of the work. Publishing another's manuscript without her consent may indeed involve a privacy breach. But this is no reason to confuse the wrong to her privacy with the wrong to her authorship. The wrongfulness of unauthorized publication of unpublished work as a copyright matter is about the absence of authorization for the publication, not about the absence of previous publication, or about the absence of authorization for the use of personal information. The copyright-specific wrong has nothing to do with whether or not it is a first publication, or with whether or not it amounts to unauthorized use of personal information.

This view takes issue with certain aspects of Warren and Brandeis's classic deployment of the copyright law of unpublished works as evidence for the proposition that a recognized legal interest in privacy exists.[18] It may well be true that legal concern over unpublished works evidences legal concern over privacy interests, but this is a far cry from the proposition that privacy interests animate the copyright law of unpublished works. Copyright infringement does not require infringement of privacy interests; nor does infringement of privacy interests require copyright infringement. The copyright law of unpublished works is not an understudy for poorly

[18] See Samuel Warren and Louis D. Brandeis, 'The Right to Privacy' *Harvard Law Review* 4 (1890) 193.

developed privacy law. It is not there to fill gaps left untreated by privacy law. To deploy the copyright law of unpublished works as evidence of legal concern over privacy interests is problematic to the extent that (1) it misunderstands the distinction between the two legal interests, and (2) in so doing, it deprives copyright law of the opportunity to formulate its own view of the wrongfulness of unauthorized publication of unpublished works. The reduction of the law of unpublished works to privacy interests in effect precludes the possibility of grasping the legal issues pertinent to unpublished *and* published works from a single, copyright-specific point of view. That is, it precludes the possibility of grasping the core of the legal issues involved as a matter pertinent to works of authorship, rather than as a matter pertinent to their unpublished or published status.[19]

Thus, grasped from a copyright-specific standpoint, the intuition that unauthorized publication of unpublished works is wrongful is equally applicable to the unauthorized publication of *published* works. What is

[19] This is not to say that copyright law does not or should not draw distinctions between unpublished and published works. It is only to say that the standpoint from which such distinctions are drawn is of crucial importance. For example, copyright law routinely distinguishes in a variety of contexts and for a variety of purposes between works that are closer to, and works that are further from, the 'core' of intended copyright protection. The resulting distinctions thus operationalize a copyright-specific standpoint invoking copyright's core. See *Feist Publications, Inc.* v. *Rural Telephone Service Co.*; *Campbell* v. *Acuff-Rose Music, Inc.*, 510 US 569 (1994). See also Bastarache J's judgment in *Euro-Excellence Inc.* v. *Kraft Canada Inc.*, 2007 SCC 37. Similarly, copyright law routinely considers the unpublished or published status of a work under the rubric of fair use or fair dealing. My point is not that such distinctions should be foreclosed, but that they should be construed as flowing from the diverse ways in which different circumstances, including the circumstance that a work is either unpublished or published, may impinge upon authorship interests. Like the right of reproduction, the right of first publication is an aspect of an author's copyright, not privacy. It should therefore be interpreted as such. For examples of judicial treatments of the unpublished/published distinction, see *Harper & Row* v. *Nation Enterprises*, 471 US 539 (1985); *A.V.* v. *iParadigms, LLC*, 562 F.3d 630 (4th Cir. 2009); *Beloff* v. *Pressdram Ltd.* [1973] 1 All ER 241; *Lion Laboratories Ltd.* v. *Evans* [1984] 3 WLR 539; *Hyde Park Residence Ltd* v. *Yelland* [2000] 3 WLR 215. One can hardly fail to mention in this context a recent remark of the Supreme Court of Canada: 'Although certainly not determinative, if a work has not been published, the dealing may be *more fair* in that its reproduction with acknowledgment could lead to a wider public dissemination of the work – one of the goals of copyright law'. See *CCH Canadian Ltd* v. *Law Society of Upper Canada*, para. 58 (emphasis added). For commentary on unpublished works and fair use seeking to disentangle privacy and copyright, see Kenneth D. Crews, 'Fair Use of Unpublished Works: Burdens of Proof and the Integrity of Copyright' *Arizona State Law Journal* 31 (1999) 1. For commentary on unpublished works and fair dealing, see Robert Burrell and Alison Coleman, *Copyright Exceptions: The Digital Impact* (Cambridge University Press, 2005), pp. 45–8. On aspects of the history of the unpublished/published work distinction, see Sunny Handa, *Copyright Law in Canada* (Markham: Butterworths, 2002), pp. 107–12; Ronan Deazley, *On the Origin of the Right to Copy: Charting the Movement of Copyright Law in Eighteenth-Century Britain (1695–1775)* (Oxford and Portland, Oreg.: Hart Publishing, 2004), pp. 69–74.

wrong with each and both is that they amount to forcing another to speak. Unauthorized publication is compelled speech. The fact than an author has already spoken does not mean that we are thereby entitled to force him to speak again. A ventriloquist is not any less a ventriloquist because he compels me to say what I have already said. That his belly happens to speak through my mouth exactly what I have already spoken – or what I would have spoken – does not make me any less of a puppet. On the contrary, the injury is even greater where he uses my own speech to treat me like one. In short, an author does not relinquish his right to speak or not to speak merely because he has spoken. By no means: the view that an author somehow loses something as a result of publication seems at best in tension, if not radically inconsistent with, the essence of copyright as a right involving enforceable claims over published works of authorship.

V. Dialogue

The perceived difficulty with formulating copyright fundamentals as a matter of voluntary speech, and hence with the correlative proposition that copyright infringement is compelled speech, is that the derivation of the right from voluntariness seems to preclude the limitation of the right, as if the author were now in a position to make all kinds of demands in the name of his or her autonomy. Portrayed as voluntary speakers, authors may now seek to determine unilaterally the scope of their entitlement, alleging that any limitations imposed by law would amount to compelled speech – that is, any and all unauthorized uses of a work would amount to involuntary speech. It is as if the status of the public domain as a necessary, integral and irreducible aspect of copyright law were to dissolve in the solvent of the author's autonomy.

It is the author's own standing as a voluntary speaker, however, that restricts his ability to choose unilaterally the conditions under which he speaks. The author cannot impose conditions on his speech that deny its character as speech. Because the doctrine of originality grants the author rights for speaking in his own words, he cannot derogate from his speech in the same breath in which he claims standing as a speaker. That is, he cannot ask copyright law to grant him rights inconsistent with the grounds upon which copyright law recognizes him as an author. Thus, his irreducible choice to speak or not to speak cannot, as a copyright law matter, translate into an unencumbered autonomy to restrict unilaterally the conditions under which his work is publicly available. The question is not about what the author wants, but about what his autonomy as an author permits him to claim.

Consider, for example, an author alleging that he speaks on condition that others do not discuss or adopt the ideas expressed in his work without his consent. Use of those ideas would thus amount to an infringement of the author's copyright. Of course, it is uncontroversial that an allegation of that sort is inconsistent with the idea/expression dichotomy. This does not mean, however, that we must grasp the idea/expression dichotomy as some kind of doctrinal 'taking', as it were, of aspects of the author's work without his consent. It is not as if copyright doctrine deprives the author of anything that is otherwise rightfully hers. On the contrary, precisely as a communicative act, an author's work is an invitation to talk about the ideas it conveys. It is an invitation to dialogue.[20] By asserting his copyright, the author seeks to be treated as a person, and not a mere puppet, and so insists that he not be compelled to speak. By the same token, his work, as copyright subject matter, is addressed to persons, and not mere puppets, and so contemplates the responses of its audience. By framing ideas as radically available, the idea/expression dichotomy protects and affirms the conditions for the possibility of those responses.[21] It is but the doctrinal manifestation of the ongoing conversation from which an author's work arises and to which it must necessarily address itself. Far from 'taking' from the author, the idea/expression dichotomy affirms the nature of copyright subject matter as speech and of the author as a speaking being engaged in dialogue with others. The author's autonomy does not dissolve, but rather, opens itself up toward the public domain.

The concept of the work as speech also helps to account for the legitimacy of 'transformative' uses of the author's work under the rubric of fair use or fair dealing.[22] Such uses must remain outside the purview of the author's copyright to the extent that they are but responses that the author's work as speech necessarily contemplates. Fair use or fair dealing for the purpose of criticism is a paradigmatic example of the way in which

[20] For elaboration of the dialogic concept of the work from the standpoint of the distinction between copyright and trade mark, see Drassinower, 'Authorship as Public Address', 199.

[21] For discussion of the idea/expression dichotomy in this vein, see Drassinower, 'A Rights-Based View of the Idea/Expression Dichotomy', 3; Maurizio Borghi, 'Owning Form, Sharing Content: Natural-Right Copyright and Digital Environment', in Fiona Macmillan (ed.), *New Directions in Copyright Law*, vol. V (Cheltenham: Edward Elgar Publishing, 2007).

[22] On transformative use, see Laura A. Heymann, 'Everything is Transformative: Fair Use and Reader Response' *Columbia Journal of Law and the Arts* 31 (2008) 445; Treiger-Bar-Am, 'Kant on Copyright: Rights of Transformative Authorship', 1059; Paul Edward Geller, 'A German Approach to Fair Use: Test Cases for TRIPs Criteria for Copyright Limitations' *Journal of the Copyright Society of the U.S.A.* 57 (2010) 553.

copyright law inserts the work into the network of utterances and responses of which it is a part.[23]

Along similar lines, narrowing authorial entitlement to the use of the work as speech and only as speech also flows from the very nature of copyright subject matter. Where the defendant's unauthorized use of the plaintiff's work is not a use of the work as speech, the plaintiff cannot claim that such use amounts to forcing him to speak. Thus, where the author's copyright is grounded in her right to remain silent, the limitations formulated in a case such as *Baker* v. *Selden* are but corollaries of the nature of the claim. The use of accounting forms as accounting forms, of photographic images as thumbnails for internet searches,[24] or of student papers as data for purposes of detecting plagiarism,[25] are not appropriations of an author's voice. They do not amount to unauthorized use of the work *as a work*.

More generally, the point is that the determination made through the originality doctrine that a work is subject to copyright is not a once-and-for-all determination entitling the author to make exclusive claims of right to any and all uses of copyright subject matter. On the contrary, copyright doctrine as a whole is but an insistence that copyright subject matter be treated as speech, and as nothing but speech. The defence of independent creation, the idea/expression dichotomy, along with the fundamental distinctions made in *Baker* v. *Selden*, and the defence of fair dealing or

[23] On fair use as dialogue, see Drassinower, 'Authorship as Public Address', 199; Drassinower, 'From Distribution to Dialogue: Remarks on the Concept of Balance in Copyright Law', 991.

[24] Consider *Kelly* v. *Arriba Soft Corp.*, 336 F.3d 811 (9th Cir. 2003): although Arriba made exact replications of Kelly's images, the thumbnails were much smaller, lower-resolution images that served an entirely different function than Kelly's original images. Kelly's images are artistic works intended to inform and to engage the viewer in an aesthetic experience. His images are used to portray scenes from the American West in an aesthetic manner. Arriba's use of Kelly's images in the thumbnails is unrelated to any aesthetic purpose. Arriba's search engine functions as a tool to help index and improve access to images on the internet and their related web sites. In fact, users are unlikely to enlarge the thumbnails and use them for artistic purposes because the thumbnails are of much lower-resolution than the originals; any enlargement results in a significant loss of clarity of the image, making them inappropriate as display material.

[25] Consider *A.V.* v. *iParadigms, LLC*: 'iParadigms' use of these works was completely unrelated to expressive content and was instead aimed at detecting and discouraging plagiarism ... Rather than ignore it, however, the district court simply concluded that even if the plaintiffs' works were highly creative in nature, iParadigms' use of the plaintiffs' works was not related to the creative core of the works.' I am aware that *Arriba Soft* and *iParadigms* are fair-use, not subject matter cases. Elaboration of the reasons for seeing them as subject matter cases in the spirit of *Baker* is the topic of another chapter. For different views, see Matthew Sag, 'Copyright and Copy-Reliant Technology' *Northwestern University Law Review* 103 (2009) 1607; Maurizio Borghi and Stavroula Karapapa, 'Non-Display Uses of Copyright Works: Google Books and Beyond' *Queen Mary Journal of Intellectual Property* 1 (2011) 21.

fair use ensure, among other aspects of copyright doctrine, that the scope of the author's right correctly tracks the nature of copyright subject matter. It is as speech and only as speech that the work is subject to copyright protection. Copyright doctrine precludes the reification of copyright subject matter as a thing. It preserves the work as a communicative act. Thus, copyright protection neither encompasses uses of the work as something other than speech, nor permits the author to extend the scope of his entitlement in a manner that precludes another's speech responding to his. Viewed in this light, grounding the author's right in his autonomy as a speaking being is already a way of limiting the scope of her entitlement. Not any and all unauthorized uses of a work can be regarded as compelled speech.

VI. Concluding remarks

By way of conclusion, I want to highlight some implications flowing from the rights-based justification of copyright law.

First, the purpose of copyright law is not to provide incentives for creativity, but to affirm the inherent dignity of the author as a speaking being.[26] The distinction between originality and novelty, works and inventions, is enough to indicate as much. Because it must be novel, non-obvious and useful, an invention confers a previously unavailable benefit upon the public. Accordingly, an inventor can appeal to that benefit as a justification for the legal protection she seeks. An author, however, has more difficulty in invoking the authoritative imprimatur of the public interest in innovation as a justification for her copyright. A work need not be novel to merit copyright protection. Even where a work happens to be novel, it is not its novelty, whether of content or of form, but its originality – i.e. the very speaking itself – that copyright enshrines. As a matter of copyright law, a work has no authority but its own. Copyright in this sense is an irreducible affirmation of the autonomy of the human person as a speaking being. To appeal to any external benefits that this affirmation may produce is to divest authorship of its self-constitutive authority.

[26] For a survey of intellectual property theory, including the incentive-based model of copyright law as the dominant approach, see William Fisher, 'Theories of Intellectual Property', in Stephen Munzer (ed.), *New Essays in the Legal and Political Theory of Property* (Cambridge University Press, 2001), pp. 168–200. For critical discussion of the incentive-based approach from varying points of view, see, for example, Seana Shiffrin, 'The Incentives Argument for Intellectual Property Protection', in Axel Gosseries, Alain Marciano and Alain Strowel (eds), *Intellectual Property and Theories of Justice* (London and New York: Palgrave Macmillan, 2008), pp. 94–105; Diane Zimmerman, 'Copyright as Incentives: Did We Just Imagine That?' *Theoretical Inquiries in Law* 12 (2011) 29; Jessica Silbey, 'Harvesting Intellectual Property' *Notre Dame Law Review* 86 (2011) 2091.

Second, the focus on the author's autonomy as a speaking being opens up toward, rather than forecloses, the public domain in copyright law. To appreciate this, we need to compare briefly the rights-based with the incentive-based models of copyright law. On the incentive model, the public domain, like the author's entitlement, is an instrument of the public interest. That is, broadly speaking, the requirements of the public interest in the incentive model are twofold: on the one hand, the public interest requires that incentives for creativity be provided; on the other, it requires that the products of creativity be widely disseminated. The public interest is neither about incentives nor about dissemination, but about the balance between them. The task of copyright law is none other than the achievement of this balance between creators and users, authors and the public domain. Copyright law in this view is a distributive mechanism through which authors and users compete for the value of the products of creative labour, and in which authorship is construed as value-creation and the public domain as value for which no payment is extracted. Even in the most public friendly of its iterations, the incentive model sustains an ironic situation wherein public domain advocacy cannot help but appear as bargain hunting.

By contrast, the focus on the autonomy of the author as a speaking being brings into relief the correlative autonomy of the members of her audience not as consumers of value, but as speaking beings. On this view, copyright law arises not as a distributive balance of intangible commodities, but as a juridical order addressing aspects of the interaction between speaking beings. In so doing, it defines and confines the scope of an author's copyright in light of her place in the ongoing conversation of which she is but a participant. The public domain thus emerges far more forcefully, not as a depository of value for which no payment is extracted, but as a set of conditions for dialogue flowing from the very nature of copyright subject matter as communicative.[27]

Finally, it is worth emphasizing that the construal of the work as a communicative act has implications for copyright limitations arising not only at the level of scope, but also at that of subject matter. Once the image of the work as a metaphysical chattel or intangible object is left behind, so is the recurrent and habitual inclination to regard any and all unauthorized reproduction as some sort of *prima facie* actionable conversion of, or trespass on, a proprietary holding. On the contrary, only communicative uses of a work (i.e. uses of the work *as a work*) can give rise to liability.

[27] I discuss the shortcomings of the incentive-based model as a theory of the public domain in Drassinower, 'From Distribution to Dialogue', 1001–2; Drassinower, 'A Note on Incentives, Rights and the Public Domain in Copyright Law' 1880–2.

The construal of the work as a communicative act thus liberates the concept of infringement from that of reproduction.[28] In so doing, it functions as a welcome propaedeutic for the study of the encounter between copyright law and digital technology. Because the very operation of digital technology is rooted in reproduction, such as, for example, the reproductions involved in Internet browsing, the assumption that any and all unauthorized reproduction is *prima facie* infringing, is no longer serviceable as the core concept in copyright law. The proposition that the wrongfulness of copyright infringement is about compelled speech, rather than about the unauthorized extraction of value through copying, offers a viable alternative, derived from the settled fundamentals of copyright doctrine and jurisprudence, to the concept of reproduction as the axis around which copyright law must function. We might say that a Kantian reading of *Baker* v. *Selden* contains some of the deepest available insights into the encounter between copyright law and digital technology.

[28] On the distinction between reproduction and infringement, see Jessica Litman, 'Revising Copyright Law for the Information Age', in Jessica Litman, *Digital Copyright* (Amherst: Prometheus Books: 2001), pp. 171–91; Ernest Miller and Joan Feigenbaum, 'Taking the Copy Out of Copyright', in Tomas Sander (ed.), *DRM '01 Revised Papers from the ACM CCS-8 Workshop on Security and Privacy in Digital Rights Management* (London: Springer-Verlag 2002), pp. 233–44; Drassinower, 'Taking User Rights Seriously', 462–79; Sarah Stadler, 'Copyright as Trade Regulation' *Pennsylvania Law Review* 155 (2007) 899; Drassinower, 'Authorship as Public Address', 199; Paul Edward Geller, 'Beyond the Copyright Crisis: Principles for Change' *Journal of the Copyright Society of the U.S.A.* 55 (2008) 165; Borghi, 'Copyright and Truth', 1.

9 Public reason, communication and intellectual property

Laura Biron

In light of concerns about the strengthening of intellectual property regimes in recent years,[1] attempts are being made to discuss alternative ways of conceptualising the objects protected by copyright, patent and trade mark law. The most well-known discussion has taken place within copyright law, where it has been suggested that there is an important connection between copyright and freedom of speech, and that highlighting this connection 'may prove a useful counterweight to labelling copyright as "property" . . .'.[2] But how should we understand the connection between copyright and speech? Is it a matter of protecting the 'expressive autonomy' of authors, as some have argued?[3] Or could copyright law incorporate principles of communication besides self-expression, to reach a richer understanding of the sense in which it might protect authorial speech?[4] After discussing these questions in the first part of my chapter, I go on to consider whether an alternative conceptual approach to intellectual property – based on communication rather than property – has application to trade mark and patent law, where similar concerns about expansion and propertisation exist.

My interpretation of the connection between intellectual property and communication is based on a Kantian account of public reason.[5] I accept,

[1] See, e.g., M. Spence, *Intellectual Property* (Oxford University Press, 2007), p. 43.

[2] N. Netanel, 'Why has Copyright Expanded? Analysis and Critique', in F. Macmillan (ed.), *New Directions in Copyright Law* (Cheltenham, UK, Edward Elgar, 2007), vol. VI, p. 33.

[3] See section 1.2.1 below.

[4] Onora O'Neill's recent work on what she has termed 'ethics *for* communication' is one example of this broader approach, and the one that has been most influential to my thinking on this topic (O. O'Neill, 'Ethics for Communication?' *European Journal of Philosophy* 17(2) (2009) 167–80). Barron's work on the communicative dimensions of copyright also incorporates O'Neill's earlier writings on Kantian public reason, drawing on principles of communication such as toleration, maturity and publicity, again to illustrate the sense in which protecting self-expression is just one aspect of a broader approach to developing principles of communication (A. Barron, 'Kant, Copyright and Communicative Freedom' *Law and Philosophy* 31(1) (2012) 1–48).

[5] The connection between Kant's writings on copyright and his theorising about public reason – as well as the fruitfulness of applying Kantian principles of public reason to

of course, that there may be other accounts of public reason suitable for this project, and it will be interesting to see whether alternative approaches to the communicative aspects of intellectual property – drawing on Habermas or Rawls, for example – emerge as scholarly interest in this area grows.[6] For the purposes of this chapter, however, I have chosen to focus on a Kantian account for two reasons. First, since Kant's writings on unauthorised publication have already generated a great deal of attention in recent years, it is interesting to explore the possible connections between these writings and his broader philosophical theorising about public reason and the norms of reasoned communication.[7] Second, Kant's account of public reason explicitly focuses on communicative norms in general, rather than individual acts of self-expression, which makes it easier to appreciate the ways in which it might have application beyond the realm of copyright to other areas of intellectual property law. Since concerns about the strengthening of intellectual property rights are by no means unique to copyright law, this seems to be an attractive feature of the Kantian approach explored here.

Introduction: concerns about propertisation

I shall begin by highlighting some well-known concerns about the expansion and strengthening of intellectual property regimes, often referred to as the 'propertisation' of intellectual objects. In the realm of copyright,

copyright law – was first brought to my attention by an earlier draft of Anne Barron's paper, 'Kant, Copyright and Communicative Freedom', which I responded to at a conference entitled 'Philosophy and Intellectual Property', Institute of Philosophy, London, 29–30 May 2009. The connection has also been made and applied to contemporary copyright law by M. Borghi, 'Copyright and Truth' *Theoretical Inquiries in Law* 12(1) (2011) 1–27; R. Capurro, 'Das Internet und die Grenzen der Ethik', in M. Rath (ed.), *Medienethik und Medienwirkungsforschung* (Weidebaden, Westdeutscher Verlag, 2000), pp. 105–26; M. Chiara Pievatolo, 'Publicness and Private Intellectual Property in Kant's Political Thought', in V. Rohden, R. Terra, G. Almeida and M. Ruffing (eds), *Recht und Frieden in der Philosophie Kants, Akten des X Internationalen Kant-Kongresses* (Berlin/New York, Walter de Gruyter, 2008), pp. 631–42 and A. Johns, 'The Piratical Enlightenment', in C. Siskin and W. Warner (eds.), *This Is Enlightenment* (University of Chicago Press, 2010), pp. 301–20.

6 Or there may even be 'hybrid' approaches that combine insights from different theorists of public reason. Barron, for example, suggests reading Kant's writings on public reason in light of Habermas's account of the 'structural transformation' of the public sphere (Barron, 'Kant, Copyright and Communicative Freedom', p. 43). Capurro also stresses the connections between Habermas and Kant in discussion of the ethics of electronic communication (Capurro, 'Das Internet und die Grenzen der Ethik').

7 This connection has also been highlighted by Barron, Borghi, Cappuro, Chiara Pievatolo and Johns (Barron, 'Kant, Copyright and Communicative Freedom'; Borghi, 'Copyright and Truth', 9–13, Capurro, 'Das Internet und die Grenzen der Ethik'; Chiara Pievatolo, 'Publicness and Private Intellectual Property in Kant's Political Thought'; Johns, 'The Piratical Enlightenment', pp. 316–18).

Netanel describes this as a 'conceptual metamorphosis ... from limited grant to robust property right'.[8] Calling a work of copyright 'property', it is argued, seems to have a powerful connotation of absolute right, emphasising the *prima facie* power of the copyright holder to control various uses of his work and overriding the view that copyright is a privilege whose ultimate purpose is to promote the public interest. This insight is not specific to copyright law. Spence points out that viewing trade marks as 'property' gives trade mark holders a 'presumptive right of control' over uses of their mark, broadening the class of actions that are said to count as infringement.[9] Likewise, Merges has described the proliferation of patents in scientific research as the 'creeping propertisation' of science, and discusses the detrimental impact this has had on scientific innovation.[10] For each area of intellectual property law considered, then, there is a general concern about the expansion and strengthening of intellectual property regimes, and the worry that this phenomenon has something to do with the very idea of intellectual 'property'.

Even if we accept the oft-made points that there is nothing particularly new about the 'intellectual property' label,[11] that property rights come in various shapes and sizes, and that Blackstone's proverbial hyperbole need not be our default conception of intellectual ownership,[12] these often get buried at the level of popular rhetoric. The description of intellectual objects as 'property' may be rhetorically dangerous, then, because it can cause us to lose sight of the various ways in which intellectual objects differ from tangible objects of property. In light of this problem, we might wonder whether there are alternative ways of conceptualising intellectual objects that avoid the rhetorical baggage of the property label. Kant certainly thought there might be, as copyright scholars have recently pointed out. Accordingly, section 1 of this chapter will engage with Kant's writings on intellectual property, and offer an interpretation of Kantian public reason that draws attention to three important norms of communication:

[8] N. Netanel, *Copyright's Paradox* (Oxford University Press, 2008), p. 56.

[9] M. Spence, 'The Mark as Expression/the Mark as Property' *Current Legal Problems* 58 (2005) 492.

[10] R. Merges, 'Property Rights Theory and the Commons: The Case of Scientific Research' *Social Philosophy and Policy* 13 (1996) 164.

[11] See, e.g., J. Hughes 'Copyright and Incomplete Historiographies: Of Piracy, Propertization and Thomas Jefferson' *Southern California Law Review* 79 (2006) 993–1082.

[12] In discussions of strong conceptions of private ownership, many authors cite Blackstone's hyperbole, according to which property is 'that sole and despotic dominium which one man claims and exercises over the external things of the world, in total exclusion of the right of any other individual in the universe' (W. Blackstone (1766) in H. Broom and E. Hadley (eds), *Commentaries on the Laws of England* (London, William Maxwell & Son, Henry Sweet, and Stevens & Son, 1869), vol. II, p. 1).

authority, intelligibility and consistency. After illustrating how these communicative norms shed light on some problems surrounding the expansion of copyright, where Kant's writings are traditionally applied, I go on in sections 2 and 3 to explain their application to similar concerns about the expansion of both trade mark and patent law.[13]

1. Copyright law

This section puts forward an interpretation of Kant's writings on intellectual property which follows on from some recent work in stressing a connection between his discussion of authors' rights and his account of public reason.[14] I begin by describing the problem of copyright expansionism in more depth, before moving on to a brief discussion of Kant's writings which, as interpreters have pointed out, appear to support a communicative approach to copyright as an attractive conceptual alternative to the currently dominant proprietary model. I shall frame my interpretation of Kant's writings using three distinctions that help illustrate some important features of a Kantian approach to communication: first, the distinction between *individual* and *principled* autonomy; second, as an instance of the first distinction, the difference between *self-expression* and *public communication*; third, and finally, the distinction between *public* and *private* reason. Having outlined the fundamental components of a Kantian approach to communication in more detail, I illustrate some ways in which it might be applied to problems associated with copyright law's expansion – in particular, problems about the integrity of the public domain, propertisation and the role of transformative authors.

1.1 Copyright expansionism

Since its inception, copyright law has faced the difficult task of balancing the rights of creators to control uses of their works with those of the public – including so-called transformative authors – who have an interest

[13] Borghi and Drassinower have also applied Kantian arguments about the communicative dimensions of copyright to patent and trade mark law – in both cases, to stress the fundamental 'specificity' or 'uniqueness' of the subject matter of copyright compared to these other areas of intellectual property, even if all are interpreted in communicative terms (Borghi, 'Copyright and Truth' and A. Drassinower, 'Authorship as Public Address: On the Specificity of Copyright vis-à-vis Patent and Trade Mark' *Michigan State Law Review* 199 (2008) 200–29).

[14] See Barron, 'Kant, Copyright and Communicative Freedom', *passim*; Borghi, 'Copyright and Truth', 9–13; Capurro, 'Das Internet und die Grenzender Ethik', *passim*; Chidra Pievatolo, 'Publicness and Private Intellectual Property in Kant's Political Thought', *passim*; Johns, 'The Practical Enlightenment', pp. 316–18.

in access to and use of creative works. This need for balance is reflected in the scope and duration of copyright which has a limited term, subsists in expressions, not ideas, and has fair dealing provisions to ensure that sufficient material remains in the public domain, allowing new generations of authors to build on existing material in creating their own works.[15] However, many commentators have drawn attention to the expansion of copyright in recent years.[16] Today copyright is no longer a limited monopoly of short duration, but rather, is said to have developed into a near-perpetual property right, close to Blackstone's proverbial hyperbole of 'exclusive dominion'.[17] Currently, copyright holders are said to 'enjoy a capacious bundle of rights in controlling many more uses of many more types of published works for a far greater time and with fewer preconditions'.[18] Moreover, it is argued that 'this expansion [of copyright] has not been matched by countervailing relaxations in the scope of user freedoms; rather, these freedoms have, themselves, been limited'.[19]

In consideration of the above points, we might ask whether any of the theoretical justifications for copyright can be appealed to in order to explain its recent expansion (along with the rhetoric used to support it) and, for those opposed to this expansion, provide a theoretical pushback against it. Keeping our focus on traditional property-based rationales, we might follow commentators in reinterpreting the Lockean account of copyright, calling into question 'creator-centred' interpretations of Locke's theory, and suggesting that authors' rights should be limited by the Lockean provisos or Locke's commitment to common ownership.[20] But we might wonder whether a more radical approach is needed, based on a different conceptual framework – the language of speech as opposed to the language of property. Indeed, a speech-based rationale for

[15] For an argument that the metaphor of 'balance' in copyright law is fundamentally misplaced, and should be replaced with a metaphor of 'dialogue', see A. Drassinower, 'From Distribution to Dialogue: Remarks on the Concept of Balance in Copyright Law' *The Journal of Corporation Law* 34(4) (2009) 992–1007.

[16] See, e.g., Barron, 'Kant, Copyright and Communicative Freedom'; L. Lessig, *Free Culture* (New York, Penguin Press, 2004); J. Litman, *Digital Copyright* (New York, Prometheus Books, 2001); M. Lemley, 'Property, Intellectual Property and Free Riding' *Texas Law Review* 83 (2005) 1031–75; Netanel, 'Why has Copyright Expanded?'; Netanel, *Copyright's Paradox*.

[17] See Blackstone, in Broom and Hadley (eds), *Commentaries on the Laws of England*, vol. II, p. 1.

[18] Netanel, *Copyright's Paradox*, p. 55.

[19] C. Waelde, 'Copyright, Corporate Power and Human Rights', in Macmillan (ed.), *New Directions in Copyright Law*, vol. II, p. 293.

[20] See, e.g., W. Gordon, 'A Property Right in Self-expression: Equality and Individualism in the Natural Law' *Yale Law Journal* 102 (1993) 1533–609 and S. Shiffrin, 'Lockean Theories of Intellectual Property', in S. Munzer (ed.), *New Essays in the Legal and Political Theory of Property* (Cambridge University Press, 2001), pp. 138–68.

copyright could draw on the proposition that speech ought to be free, and place the burden of justification on those who think that speech should be restricted by a strengthened copyright regime.[21] In their attempt to put forward speech-based rationales of this sort, some commentators have suggested that a Kantian theoretical framework is most appropriate for the task, and have cited Kant's writings on intellectual property approvingly.[22] As such, I shall now examine the prospects for putting forward a Kantian account of copyright in speech-based terms, beginning with a brief exposition of Kant's own writings on the subject.

1.2 Kant's writings on copyright

Kant wrote two short essays on copyright,[23] both of which are focused on demonstrating the injustice of 'unauthorised publication'. There is not room for me to enter into a detailed discussion of Kant's arguments here; however, I would like to highlight some salient features of his approach which appear to support a speech-based rationale for copyright in the sense outlined above, before moving on to discuss how we might interpret them in light of Kantian theorising about the principles of reasoned communication.

First, it is clear that Kant favours a speech-based conception of the book in both essays, calling it a 'discourse',[24] or 'speech ... (opera)',[25] in which the author speaks to the reader, or the public more generally, via the mediation of the publisher. A book, that is, is not a mere commodity, but an active means of communicating with the public 'in the name of the author'.[26] Second, and connected to this characterisation of the book, Kant suggests that an author's (moral) right to his work is 'not a right in an object', but rather 'an innate right in his own person'.[27] By connecting

[21] See also Spence, 'The Mark as Expression', 492, for a similar argument applied to trade mark law. Spence's argument is discussed in depth in section 2 below.

[22] See, e.g., Barron, 'Kant, Copyright and Communicative Freedom'; Borghi, 'Copyright and Truth'; Drassinower, 'Authorship as Public Address'; Netanel, 'Why has Copyright Expanded?', 30–2; K. Treiger-Bar-Am, 'Kant on Copyright: Rights of Transformative Authorship' *Cardozo Journal of Arts and Entertainment* 25(3) (2008) 1060–103.

[23] I. Kant, 'On the Wrongfulness of Unauthorized Publication of Books' and 'What is a Book?', in M. J. Gregor (ed.), *The Cambridge Edition of the Works of Immanuel Kant: Practical Philosophy* (Cambridge University Press, 1996), pp. 29–35 and pp. 437–9, respectively.

[24] Kant, 'What is a Book?', p. 437.

[25] Kant, 'On the Wrongfulness of Unauthorized Publication', p. 34. Kant uses *opera* in the feminine singular to mean work understood as activity, as opposed to the plural of the neuter *opus*. This seems to make clear the distinction between a book as a thing (*opus*) and a book as a speech or activity (*opera*).

[26] Kant, 'What is a Book?', p. 437.

[27] Kant, 'On the Wrongfulness of Unauthorized Publication', p. 35.

authorship to the realm of innate right in this way, which on Kant's account is importantly bound up with speech,[28] he is once again emphasising the important connection between authorship and communication. Third, Kant's remarks about transformative authorship illustrate that he was acutely aware of the ways in which copiers of literary works could exercise their own communicative abilities: a transformed literary work (such as a translation), he argues, is not the speech of the primary author, but the speech of the transformative or transforming author.[29] Finally, Kant's focus on communication makes him acutely aware of the public dimension of authorship, and he is insistent that the communicative activity involved in writing a book is one that obtains between the author and his audience – the public at large.[30] As such, authorial discourse is not only between two authors, or between the author and some individual reader, but between the author and the public.

With these brief points of exposition made, I shall now outline three important and interrelated distinctions that help clarify the key components of a Kantian approach to communication: individual vs. principled autonomy; self-expression vs. public communication and public vs. private reason. It should become clear from the discussion that Kant's approach is quite distinct from some contemporary approaches to both autonomy and freedom of expression – sometimes grouped together using phrases such as 'expressive autonomy' or 'autonomy of expression'.[31] Rather, the key to the interpretation outlined here is to move away from the attribution of autonomy to *individuals* in any sense, and to apply it instead to *principles* of communication. This, indeed, is the approach we find in Kant's own writings on public reason. Finally, with this analysis in place, I return to the issue of copyright expansionism, outlined in section 1.1, and explain how a Kantian approach to communication has the resources to deal with this problem.

1.2.1 Individual vs. principled autonomy It is important to consider whether the concept of autonomy is relevant to discussions of the

[28] In the introduction to the *Rechtslehre*, Kant states that innate right encompasses innate equality, self-determination and a person's 'being authorised to do to others anything that does not in itself diminish what is theirs – such things as merely communicating his thoughts to them . . .'. As he goes on to add in a footnote, 'when someone merely says what he thinks, the other always remains free to take it as he pleases' (I. Kant, 'The Metaphysics of Morals', in Gregor (ed.), p. 394).

[29] Kant, 'On the Wrongfulness of Unauthorized Publication', p. 35.

[30] As Kant stresses, the publisher 'possesses the manuscript only under the condition that he make use of it for the author's affair with the public' (ibid., p. 34).

[31] These are the phrases used by Netanel and Treiger-Bar-Am, respectively (Netanel, 'Why has Copyright Expanded?', 33 and Treiger-Bar-Am, 'Kant on Copyright', 1075–8).

possible connection between copyright and speech. After all, this is the aspect of Kantian philosophy which is often referred to by copyright scholars, particularly when thinking about the relationship between Kantian autonomy and freedom of expression.[32] But it is important to tread carefully when connecting autonomy to self-expression in this way. In contemporary discussions of the topic, autonomy is often interpreted as a matter of individual independence (from external interference, say), 'which individuals can have in some but not other contexts and to varying degrees'.[33] It is often appropriate to draw attention to the political origins of the term, defining it as a matter of self-governance or self-legislation. But, as O'Neill has persuasively argued, Kant's conception of autonomy does not equate autonomy with self-expression, independence, or even self-governance.[34] As she notes, Kant speaks of the autonomy of reason, ethics, principles and willing, rather than autonomous selves, persons or individuals.[35] A clear way to understand this distinction – between individual and principled autonomy – is to note that 'unlike most recent "Kantian" writers [Kant] views autonomy or *self legislation* not as emphasising a *self* that does the legislating, but rather legislation that is not done by others, that is not derivative'.[36] Thus, O'Neill's interpretation makes it clear that a Kantian approach to autonomy does not view it as a feature of individuals at all, but a quite different ideal of self-legislation; the independence of principles, not individual legislators.

Can the above distinction between individual and principled autonomy help to clarify the application of Kantian autonomy to copyright law? One recent interpretation, linking Kantian autonomy to freedom of expression, is found in the work of Treiger-Bar-Am, who argues that 'the Kantian position on authors' rights and Kant's moral theory of autonomy' should be read as a theory of 'autonomy of expression'.[37] In putting forward this account, Treiger-Bar-Am clearly interprets Kantian autonomy as a form of individual rather than principled autonomy. Even if this goes against the

[32] Treiger-Bar-Am attempts to maintain the lineage between contemporary liberal understandings of autonomy and Kant's own conception, arguing that '[Kantian] autonomy has largely developed into a contemporary concept of autonomy of expression' (ibid., 1075). Netanel also connects contemporary debates about First Amendment restrictions on copyright to Kantian autonomy ('Why has Copyright Expanded?', 29–31).

[33] O. O'Neill, 'Autonomy, Plurality and Public Reason', unpublished manuscript, p. 2. For a sense of the various conceptions of autonomy that theorists appeal to, see G. Dworkin, *The Theory and Practice of Autonomy* (Cambridge University Press, 1988).

[34] See, e.g., O. O'Neill, *Autonomy and Trust in Bioethics* (Cambridge University Press, 2002), ch. 4.

[35] Ibid., p. 83.

[36] O'Neill, 'Kant's Conception of Public Reason', unpublished manuscript, p. 14, emphasis in original.

[37] Treiger-Bar-Am, 'Kant on Copyright', 1065–6.

interpretation of Kantian autonomy favoured here, might it nonetheless have application to copyright law? In my view, there are at least two reasons for thinking that such an application is problematic. The first is that any attempt to conceptualise authors' rights as individual rights of self-expression leaves us with a highly individualistic conception of authorship, stressing the *prima facie* rights of individual authors and saying little about the public dimension of authorship, with the result that authors are venerated at possible cost to the integrity of the public domain. There is little reason to think that such a conception of authorship would be attractive to those who are opposed to copyright expansionism; on this approach, the communicative model leads to exactly the same problem as the proprietary model it is supposed to replace.

In response to this charge, Treiger-Bar-Am argues that copyright should uphold the so-called 'autonomy of expression' of both primary and transformative authors, once autonomy of expression is understood as 'grounding obligations to respect other authors'.[38] There is an important and plausible suggestion, then, that Kantian autonomy – rooted as it is in notions of equality and respect – can provide constraints on the activities of primary authors, leaving room for transformative users of their works to exercise their own 'expressive autonomy'.[39] Indeed, the emphasis on protecting transformative works harmonises well with Kant's own discussion of authors' rights, as we have already noted.[40] But this move leads us straight into the second problem with conceptualising authors' rights as rights of self-expression. The move to protect both primary and transformative authors with a broadly construed conception of individual autonomy leaves us with few resources to decide whether it is the rights of primary or transformative authors that should be given greater weight in copyright rulings; arguments from autonomy, that is, seem to cut both ways.[41] So the challenging task facing those who wish to

38 Ibid., 1091.

39 Drassinower, too, has argued that a Kantian approach to authors' rights would grant equal rights to primary and transformative authors, but proceeds not from any notion of 'expressive autonomy', but instead from a notion of equality derived from Kant's account of property (A. Drassinower, 'A Rights-based View of the Idea/Expression Dichotomy' *Canadian Journal of Law and Jurisprudence* 16 (2003) 3–23). For further discussion of Drassinower's argument, see section 1.3 below.

40 See section 1.2 above.

41 Spence and Waldron both make this point, arguing that if we start protecting the autonomy of both primary and transformative authors, there is no principled way of settling the balance of authors' rights between the two (Spence, *Intellectual Property*, pp. 52–8; J. Waldron, 'From Authors to Copiers: Individual Rights and Social Values in Intellectual Property Law' *Chicago-Kent Law Review* 68 (1993) 841–87). As Waldron puts it, 'once again we have an impasse; invocation of the value of autonomy settles nothing' (ibid., 877).

invoke the value of autonomy in these discussions is to put forward a principled way of settling such deadlocks.

It is difficult to see how deadlocks of this sort can be broken unless we move away entirely from attributing autonomy to individual acts of authorship, and focus instead on the principles or standards that should govern authors' communication.[42] It is in this context that our second distinction can be drawn between *self-expression* and *public communication*. When we focus more broadly on *principles* of communication – such as intelligibility or truthfulness, for example – we begin to appreciate the important point that 'freedom of expression can provide only one part of an adequate ethics of communication',[43] because rights of self-expression can be exercised without meeting other important principles of public communication. As O'Neill makes clear, 'a right of self-expression does not secure a right to communicate';[44] mere self-expression is not autonomous, in Kant's sense, even if seen as a paradigm example of individual autonomy. Viewed in this way, the distinction between self-expression and public communication can be seen as an instance of O'Neill's more general distinction between individual and principled autonomy. Applied to conceptions of authorship, it suggests quite a radical re-thinking of traditional ideals; rather than attributing autonomy to individual authors, it shifts our attention towards the principles that might be said to lie at the heart of authorial communication.

The above distinction between self-expression and public communication is emphasised in Barron's Kantian approach to the communicative dimensions of copyright. After outlining some Kantian principles of communication found in O'Neill's earlier work on Kant's account of reason,[45] Barron goes on to note that '[t]o think and communicate in accordance with these principles is to think and communicate autonomously. It should be clear that this intellectual/communicative autonomy is irreducible to freedom of expression in the standard liberal sense of the term.'[46] As highlighted here, Barron's discussion emphasises 'intellectual' or 'communicative' autonomy which, she argues, is quite distinct from a 'standard liberal model of expressive freedom'[47] that she attributes to a number of copyright scholars, Treiger-Bar-Am included.[48] Surprisingly, perhaps,

42 For a fuller discussion of how principles of communication can be applied to transformative authorship, see section 1.3 below.

43 O'Neill, 'Ethics for Communication', 169. 44 Ibid., 168.

45 O. O'Neill, *Constructions of Reason* (Cambridge University Press, 1989), chs. 2–3.

46 Barron, 'Kant, Copyright and Communicative Freedom', 26. 47 Ibid., 9.

48 According to Barron, Treiger-Bar-Am, Drassinower and Merges, all attribute liberal conceptions of expressive freedom to Kant. As she argues, 'Treiger-Bar-Am's notion of "autonomy of authorial expression" is clearly informed by this liberal conception of autonomy' (Barron, 'Kant, Copyright and Communicative Freedom', 11, n. 34).

Barron does not stress the point emphasised above, that the distinction between self-expression and public communication is an instance of the more general distinction between individual and principled autonomy, also put forward by O'Neill in her later work on Kantian autonomy and communicative ethics. Rather, Barron's approach focuses on so-called 'intellectual autonomy' (which she distinguishes from 'moral autonomy') – importantly connected to values such as maturity and toleration – and not on what O'Neill has termed 'principled autonomy'. The fact that Barron's approach diverges from O'Neill's in this sense is not necessarily a criticism, but in the following discussion of Kantian public reason I shall rely on O'Neill's distinction between individual and principled autonomy, which seems to me to provide a clearer way of appreciating the distinctiveness of a Kantian approach to communication than Barron's distinction between moral and intellectual autonomy.

1.2.2 Public vs. private reason Finally, then, let us turn directly to a discussion of the distinctive Kantian conception of public reason, since it is crucially connected to the project of developing standards for public communication, standards that impose constraints on individual exercises of self-expression in ways that make them truly 'autonomous' in Kant's sense of the term. It is interesting to note that Kant wrote his essay on unauthorised publication one year after he first put forward his famous distinction between public and private reason in the essay 'What is Enlightenment?', written in 1784.[49] Given this chronological closeness – and the fact that these two essays appeared in the same journal, the *Berlinische Monatsschrift* – speculation has arisen regarding the connection between these two discussions.[50] But although Kant's 1784 essay contains his most famous statement of the distinction between public and private reason, the principles that underlie the distinction arise in a number of

However, as I understand her work, Treiger-Bar-Am's characterisation of Kantian autonomy – although undeniably a conception of individual autonomy – is distinct from highly individualistic liberal theories that might see Kant's account of authorship along the lines of personality theorists (see Treiger-Bar-Am, 'Kant on Copyright', 1066–75). This, to my mind, makes her approach quite distinct from that recently put forward by Merges (R. Merges, *Justifying Intellectual Property* (Cambridge, Mass., Harvard University Press, 2011), ch. 3) and no doubt helps to account for Barron's observation that Merges 'is able to reach a diametrically opposed conclusion' to Trieger-Bar-Am regarding the rights of transformative authors (Barron, 'Kant, Copyright and Communicative Freedom', 9, n. 28). For my discussion of Drassinower's approach, see section 1.3 below.

49 I. Kant, 'An Answer to the Question: What is Enlightenment?', in Gregor (ed.), pp. 13–22.

50 As Johns notes, 'shortly after it ['What is Enlightenment?'] was published, Kant took up his pen to write a related argument that addressed similar themes' (Johns, 'The Piratical Enlightenment', 316).

writings; in the following discussion, I shall focus on three principles of communication put forward in the *Critique of Judgement* – principles I term authority, intelligibility and consistency – and elaborate on them by focusing on key passages from 'What is Enlightenment?', 'What is Orientation in Thought?' and the *Conflict of the Faculties*, as well as Kant's two discussions of authors' rights.[51]

Kant's three maxims of the *sensus communis* in the *Critique of Judgement* are often introduced in discussions of Kantian public reason, and in my view provide a comprehensive account of the principles at the heart of a Kantian approach to communication.[52] The maxims are, first, *to think for oneself* or, in the context of authorship, to speak in one's own name (as highlighted by Kant's two discussions of authors' rights which, as we have seen, emphasise strongly the point that an author is someone who speaks to the public 'in his own name').[53] This principle raises the fundamental question of the authority of an individual's communication, which is the question at the heart of 'What is Enlightenment?', where Kant expressly refers to 'calling of each individual to think for himself'.[54] In this essay, Kant draws a distinction between public and private uses of reason which is notably different from contemporary accounts of the distinction.[55] *Private* uses of reason, for Kant, are uses of reason that are limited by their appeal to certain external authorities. As examples, he speaks of the reasoning of civil servants, clergymen and military officers, officials whose communications are carried out under the authority of their 'civil post or office'.[56] In contrast, a *public* use of one's reason is that which someone makes of it 'as a scholar, who by his writings speaks to the public in the strict sense, that is, the world . . . he enjoys an unrestricted freedom to make use of his own reason and to speak *in his own person*'.[57] Public reason, then, is a

[51] I. Kant, 'Critique of the Power of Judgement', in P. Guyer (ed.), *The Cambridge Edition of the Works of Immanuel Kant: Critique of the Power of Judgement* (Cambridge University Press, 2000), p. 173; 'What is Orientation in Thinking?', in H. Reiss (ed.) and H. B. Nisbet (trans.), *Kant: Political Writings* (Cambridge University Press, 1991), pp. 237–49; and 'The Conflict of the Faculties', in M. J. Gregor (ed.), *Immanuel Kant: The Conflict of the Faculties* (University of Nebraska Press, 1979).

[52] I am grateful to Onora O'Neill for helping make this connection explicit, and elaborating on her original exposition of Kant's maxims in her *Constructions of Reason*, chs. 2–3.

[53] Kant, 'What is a Book?', p. 437. See section 1.2 above.

[54] Kant, 'What is Enlightenment?', p. 18

[55] The most instructive comparison is between Kant and Rawls. As O'Neill points out, Rawls' account is 'bounded' insofar as it presupposes a conception of democratic citizenship; as such, Rawlsian uses of public reason would be considered 'private', or at least not fully public, on a Kantian account (O'Neill, 'Kant's Conception of Public Reason', unpublished manuscript, pp. 2–4).

[56] Kant, 'What is Enlightenment?', p. 18. As he states, 'the private use of one's reason is that which one may make of it in a civil post or office with which one is entrusted' (ibid.).

[57] Ibid., p. 19, emphasis added.

non-derivative use of one's reason insofar as it does not appeal to any external authority. By relying on authorities that are 'private' or limited, our communication becomes restricted in both its scope – the reach of our intended audience – and its authority, which rests on arbitrary assumptions.

If public reasoning were solely a matter of thinking for oneself or speaking in one's own voice, it would be tempting to think of it as largely a matter of rejecting arbitrary sources of reason – a mere matter of freedom from restrictions. But Kant makes it clear that additional principles are needed beyond the principle that our communication be non-derivative, and stresses the importance of subjecting our communication to disciplined constraints.[58] This is evident when we consider the second and third maxims of the *sensus communis*. The second maxim is the principle *to think from the standpoint of everyone else*. In the context of authorship, this condition might be read as a necessary condition for writing or speaking that aims at public communication, not just self-expression. The idea that thinking for oneself and communicating publicly are inextricably linked is fundamental to Kant's account since, as he argues, acts of thinking presuppose audiences of some kind, as we endeavour to think 'in community with others to whom we communicate our thoughts and who communicate their thoughts to us'.[59] This point is also emphasised in his two discussions of authors' rights which, as we have seen, clearly stress the public dimensions of individual authorial 'discourse'.[60] Private uses of reason, in his very distinctive use of the phrase, are addressed to restricted audiences; public uses of reason, on the other hand, are addressed to unrestricted audiences. A use of reasoning is fully public, then, when it addresses an audience in a fully inclusive sense – the 'world at large' as he puts it.[61] This need not be seen as presupposing any actual audience or real-time communication, but as the requirement that communication be carried out in a way that makes it accessible by and intelligible in principle to others.[62] As such, I shall refer to this second maxim as the principle of *intelligibility*.

Finally, Kant adds a third maxim, which is the maxim *always to think consistently*. This condition may seem to be elementary to reasoning, but

[58] This is most evident from his discussion in 'What is Orientation in Thinking?'.

[59] Ibid., p. 247. [60] See section 1.2.1 above.

[61] Kant, 'What is Enlightenment?', p. 18.

[62] Thus, O'Neill argues that Kant's account of public reason should not be seen as 'dialogical', because his account is about the necessary conditions for anything to count as reasoned communication, rather than communication as real-time, actual dialogue. To illustrate, she distinguishes *publicisability* (in the sense of the conditions for public debate) from *publicity* (actual public debate). On her interpretation, this is another fundamental difference between Kant's theory and many contemporary accounts of public reason (O'Neill, 'Kant's Conception of Public Reason', 17).

Kant argues that it 'can only be achieved through the combination of the first two and after frequent observance of them has made them automatic'.[63] Consistency depends on a genuine attempt firstly to think for oneself (first maxim) and secondly to expose one's (own) thoughts to public scrutiny (second maxim). Bringing these first two principles of public reason under a third principle of *consistency*, we begin to appreciate the important connection between principled, Kantian autonomy and public communication. As we have seen, what is crucial to the first principle of public reason is the idea that an individual's communication cannot be derived from any external power or authority. But, according to the second principle, public reasoning is not a matter of freedom from restrictions; rather, for a use of reason to be truly public, it must also be disciplined in whatever ways are needed for it to be followable by and intelligible to others. The third principle can then be read as reinforcing the need for individuals to subject themselves to these requirements in a consistent way – adjusting their communications in ways that make them followable by and intelligible to relevant audiences.

To make it clear how the three constraints on public communication outlined above are connected to Kantian, principled autonomy, O'Neill suggests that we consider Kant's own requirement that, for a use of reason to be truly autonomous, it must have a 'non-derivative' and 'lawlike' character.[64] Indeed, as she notes, Kant often characterises thought that is not disciplined in any way as a 'lawless' use of our cognitive powers.[65] This contrast between 'lawless' and 'lawlike' uses of reason is made clear in 'What is orientation in thinking?', when Kant states:

> freedom in thinking signifies the subjection of reason to no laws except those which it gives itself; and its opposite is the maxim of a lawless use of reason.[66]

When public reason is subjected to no laws except those which it gives itself, its authority is 'non-derivative', in the sense outlined by the principle of authority. Moreover, for public reason to have a 'lawlike' rather than a 'lawless' structure, reasoning must be subject to the requirement that it is in principle followable by and intelligible to relevant audiences – as per the principles of intelligibility and consistency – since on Kant's account, 'nothing … can count as reasoned unless it is followable by

[63] Kant, 'Critique of Judgement', p. 175.

[64] O'Neill refers to Kant's claim that reason requires a 'wholly nonderivative and specifically negative law-giving' ('da scheint eine ganz eigene und zwar negative Gesetzgebung erforderlich zu sein', *Critique of Pure Reason* A711/B739, trans. O'Neill).

[65] O'Neill, 'Kant's Conception of Public Reason', pp. 8–16.

[66] Kant, 'What is Orientation in Thinking?', p. 247.

others, that is, unless it is lawlike'.[67] This makes it clear that a public use of reason and an autonomous or lawlike use of reason are one and the same thing; indeed, as Kant expressly states in the *Conflict of the Faculties*: 'the power to judge autonomously – that is, freely (according to principles of thought in general) is called reason'.[68] Taken in this way, the connection between principled autonomy and public reason can be seen as the requirement that authors address their communications in ways that could be assessed by unrestricted audiences, in such a way that the principles they think and act on 'could be principles for all, rather than principles which are fit for limited audiences as defined by some civil or other authority'.[69]

By reflecting further on these three principles of reasoned communication, we can appreciate more fully the connection between principled autonomy, public communication and public reason. Applied to authorial rights, principle (1) is clearly indispensable, since without it an author would be a mere slavish copier. We might explain this further by reminding ourselves of the point that a truly public use of reason has non-derivative authority. The authority of the author's speech must not be derived from another person's speech; rather, their communication must be carried out in their own name. Likewise, principle (2) is indispensable for any author who seeks to have readers, since an author who genuinely wishes to communicate with the public has to go beyond principle (1) and has to act on some version of principle (2) to achieve intelligibility. This means that, through a combination of principles (1) and (2), we reach conditions for authorship that have both non-derivative authority and intelligibility. Finally, principle (3) can be read as a demand that authors adjust their communications to meet the requirements of intelligibility consistently, depending on the interaction with and also the scope of their possible audiences. As Garrath Williams puts it, this condition entails 'regarding oneself, first, as the genuine

[67] O. O'Neill, 'Kant on Reason and Religion', in G. Peterson (ed.), *The Tanner Lectures on Human Values* (University of Utah Press, 1997), p. 276.

[68] Kant, 'The Conflict of the Faculties', p. 43. O'Neill notes how 'startling' it might seem to identify reason with autonomy in this way, because 'contemporary interpretations of autonomy see it largely as a matter of independence rather than of reason' (O'Neill, 'Kant's Conception of Public Reason', p. 14).

[69] Ibid., p. 15. On O'Neill's interpretation, this is the key point of difference between Kant and other theorists of public reason, whose accounts address 'bounded' rather than 'unbounded' pluralities (ibid.). As Kant puts it, 'To employ one's own reason means no more than to ask oneself, whenever one is urged to accept something, whether one finds it possible to transform the reason for accepting it, or the role which follows from what is accepted, into a universal principle governing the use of reason' (Kant, 'What is Orientation in Thinking?', p. 249).

author of one's judgments, and second, as [epistemically] accountable to others'.[70] If principle (3) is in some sense regulative of principles (1) and (2), we can see that public reasoning is not static but, just like all communication, dependent on its audience, its interlocutors and the willingness of authors to reconsider and re-evaluate their communications in light of the testing and mutual questioning of their writings.

Now that we have explained more clearly the lawlikeness of public reason, we have reached a conception of autonomy that is relevant to Kant's discussion of authorship, but is a far cry from 'autonomy of expression'. This is not to go as far as to say that authors must always be conceived of as communicating autonomously, since this would be a rather heavy constraint on authorship, but rather that their communications should aim to meet the conditions for possible communication; conditions that go far beyond self-expression, and towards (1) authority, (2) intelligibility and (3) consistency. Moreover, introducing these Kantian principles of public reason to our discussion of authorship enables us to return to the questions with which this section began – questions about expansionism and propertisation in copyright law – and examine them in light of what this connection tells us about authorship and public communication.

1.3 Copyright law revisited

Can Kant's writings on public reason offer a way of looking critically at copyright's encroachment on the public domain? The most instructive way to do so is to connect together his account of public reason with the public domain. In the course of this discussion, I shall follow Drassinower in drawing a distinction between the public domain and the public interest.[71] The public domain is an internal feature of copyright, negatively defined as materials that are not subject to copyright protection, either because their copyright has expired or because they constitute parts of works that do not warrant copyright protection, such as facts or abstract ideas.[72] The public interest, on the other hand, is a broader set of concerns

[70] G. Williams, 'Kant's Account of Reason', in E. Zalta (ed.), *The Stanford Enyclopedia of Philosophy* (Summer 2009 edn).

[71] Drassinower, 'A Rights-based View of the Idea/Expression Dichotomy', 20–1.

[72] Barron draws attention to some concerns raised by defenders of the public domain when it is viewed negatively in this sense (Barron, 'Kant, Copyright and Communicative Freedom', 3). On her view, a more radical rethinking of the public domain is needed than its defenders may currently imagine, arguing that it is 'what Jürgen Habermas and others have called the public sphere . . . and not the public domain as such, that should serve as the key reference point in any evaluation of copyright law's role in relation to the possibility of a free culture' (ibid., 1).

often said to connect to the public domain, but is not an internal feature of copyright law. I return to this distinction below.

The Kantian account of public reason imposes internal limitations on the scope of authors' rights, because authorship is understood as a process of communicating to others. And once we introduce standards of public reason as constraints on such communication, we see clearly that authors' communicative entitlements, understood in Kantian terms, are subject to limitations. Applied to copyright, such limitations would appear to require a public domain that contains enough material for both primary and transformative authors to draw upon, in order that authors' communications meet these standards. This account of the public domain emerges once we understand the various constraints that authors' communication would be subject to, on a Kantian account. Rather than discussing authors' rights of expression, we would be better talking about their duties to communicate; duties that must be subject to criteria of reasoned communication, showing respect for a broad public domain as a condition of intelligible and inclusive communication.

This interpretation of the public domain is distinct from consequentialist accounts. The consequentialist account views both authors' rights and the public domain as means to the promotion of the public interest, as Drassinower points out.[73] As such, consequentialist accounts of copyright may be premised upon and committed to the public interest, but it does not follow from this that they must be committed to a particular understanding of the public domain. If it were discovered that a broad and inclusive public domain did not promote the public interest, the public domain would shrink accordingly and copyright would expand; indeed, this is what some commentators fear is happening under the influence of consequentialist considerations at the moment.[74] But no such implication follows on the Kantian account. Rather than imposing an external limit or permission on the scope of authors' rights, then, Kant's account of public reason supports an internal one, and this same internal standard requires a broad enough public domain to ensure the conditions for reasoned communication are met.[75]

[73] Drassinower refers to 'instrumentalist' rather than 'consequentialist' accounts, but the implications are the same (Drassinower, 'A Rights-based View of the Idea/Expression Dichotomy', 20).

[74] See, e.g., Lemley, 'Property, Intellectual Property and Free-riding', 1031.

[75] Drassinower also argues that Kantian arguments support internal rather than external limits on the public domain but, interestingly, does so via Kant's theory of property rather than his account of public reason (Drassinower, 'A Rights-based View of the Idea/Expression Dichotomy', 7–8).

The second implication of linking Kant's discussion of copyright to his account of public reason is that, as we have seen, we gain greater understanding of his claim that authors' rights are rights of speech, not property. This illustrates how Kant's analysis could be appealed to by those who support attempts to 'de-propertise' the concept of intellectual property; that is, to play down the significance of the analogy drawn between intellectual property and tangible property and find an alternative model for conceptualising rights over intellectual objects that does not rely on the logic and rhetoric of private property. Stressing the communicative nature of copyright, it is thought, provides a useful counterweight to labelling it as property, with the connotation of open-ended exclusive rights that term has come to imply. And this insight applies not only to copyright law, but also to trade marks and patents, as I shall suggest below.

Although Kant himself rejects a proprietary account of authorship in his writings, it is worth noting that his theory of property appears to support a similar conception of authorship to that supported by his account of public reason – namely, that authorship has a fundamentally public dimension. Drassinower, for example, has argued that 'precisely as a matter of proprietorship rather than authorship, the analysis of copyright is an analysis not of the relation between author and work but of the relation between author and audience'.[76] This is because, on Kant's account, an author's property right would be grasped not as a relation between author and work, but as a relation between persons with respect to the work.[77] So the crucial point to draw from Kant's discussion of property is that his analysis of the author–work relationship would still highlight the public aspect of this relationship, even if construed in proprietary terms. Drassinower's analysis is helpful insofar as it illustrates that not all conceptions of property need contribute to copyright's expansionist tendencies; nonetheless, it seems conceptually clearer to base an account of the public dimensions of authorship more positively and directly on Kant's account of reasoned communication, rather than his conception of ownership. Moreover, such an analysis fits neatly with the spirit of Kant's own account of authors' rights, which Drassinower highlights in his later work on authors' rights as rights of 'public presentation'.[78]

[76] Ibid.

[77] Ibid., drawing on Kant's criticism of attempts to view property relations as though they were purely bilateral (between a person and a thing) as opposed to interpersonal (between persons with respect to a thing).

[78] Drassinower, 'Authorship as Public Address'.

But introducing Kant's communicative conception of authorship to copyright theory also illustrates that the project of developing, maintaining and respecting normative standards for communication is distinct from the project of protecting individuals' rights to self-expression. What is important, as we have seen, is not mere presentation or expression of speech, but the possibility of public communication, guided by norms for reasoned communication. As Onora O'Neill has noted in her recent work on communication, conceptions of freedom of speech that identify it mainly with freedom of individual expression may provide a basis for an adequate ethics of self-expression, but they do not provide a basis for an adequate ethics of communication. She argues that both *accessibility* and *assessability* are needed for genuine communication, and that the various media channelling communication are normatively relevant. Indeed, as she notes, assessing speech-acts is most demanding when they are mediated – assembled, edited, transformed and transmitted by complex processes and institutions, including, of course, publishers.[79] Although copyright is just one way in which speech is mediated, it is highly important precisely because it has the potential to ensure accessibility of the informational content it regulates.

Finally, can the Kantian account of public reason, outlined above, shed any light on the ways in which copyright law should treat transformative works of authorship, such as translations, abridgements and new editions of copyrighted works? As I highlighted in my exposition of his writings, Kant suggests that the creative process can be transformative; authors often use, copy and transform existing materials in order to exercise their own communicative abilities. Moreover, in my discussion of transformative authorship above, I noted that principles of reasoned communication – rather than notions of 'expressive autonomy' – could be drawn upon to help resolve some of the difficult deadlocks that arise in cases in which the rights of both primary and transformative authors are protected. Now that we have a clearer account of the Kantian norms of communication, how might these be applied to resolve such deadlocks?

First, applying the principle of authority, we might ask: to what extent has a transformative author communicated 'in his own name' in his transformative use of a work? If his communication rests merely on the authority of the primary author, and is thereby merely 'derivative', it would fail to meet the principle of authority outlined here. If, on the other hand, he uses the primary author's work as a stimulus or source from which to speak non-derivatively, in his own name, the primary author cannot have any

[79] O'Neill, 'Ethics for Communication', 175

legitimate claim to prevent the transformative author from using her work in this sense, as the transformative author's communication meets this important standard of public reason. Moreover, if a primary author attempted to prevent a transformative author from speaking non-derivatively – simply because she was concerned that her work might be misunderstood or applied in a way she did not agree with, or even if she decided for some reason to withhold her writings from public scrutiny after having made them available – such an attempt would be contrary to the standards of 'intelligibility' and 'consistency', which require not only that authors communicate publicly, in ways that make their communications accessible and intelligible to others, but also that they are willing to subject their writings to revision, scrutiny and criticism, illustrated clearly when transformative authors are free to draw on aspects of their work necessary for these tasks.

It is worth noting, in conclusion, that copyright law's originality requirement harmonises well with the first principle of public reason outlined above – the principle of authority. Copyright's originality requirement applies to both new and transformative work and, in both cases, the key to determining originality rests on the question of the source of the work – to count as original for the purposes of copyright it '. . . must not be copied from another work . . . it should originate from the author'.[80] Understanding originality in this sense as *origination*, we might introduce the distinction between derivative and non-derivative forms of communication, which underlies the principle of authority. A transformative work of authorship whose authority is actually derived from a primary work cannot be classed as having 'originated' from the transformative author – in this sense, works of authorship that count as 'derivative' under the principle of authority would likewise not count as 'original' for the purposes of copyright protection. On the other hand, provided the transformative work's authority is derived from the transformative author's own communication, the transformative work would count as 'non-derivative' under the principle of authority – and, for the purposes of copyright protection, it would count as original. Although a fuller exploration of copyright's originality requirement is well beyond the scope of this chapter, the above analysis suggests that principles of public reason might fruitfully be appealed to when attempting to explain why some transformative works warrant copyright protection and others do not.

[80] *University of London Press Ltd* v. *University Tutorial Press Ltd* [1916] 2 Ch 601, Peterson J.

2. Trade mark law

Now that I have discussed some possible ways in which we might apply Kantian principles of public reason to problems about the expansion and propertisation of copyright law, I would like to consider whether Kantian arguments of this sort have application beyond copyright law; after all, as I pointed out in my introduction, concerns about propertisation also arise in trade mark and patent law. I shall begin in this section with a discussion of trade mark law, where a similar attempt has been made by Michael Spence to appeal to speech-based arguments, without explicit appeals to Kant's writings.[81] Having drawn attention to a debate about the recent expansion of trade mark law to cover 'allusive' uses of marks, I shall illustrate how the Kantian account of public reason, outlined above, can be applied to this problem in a fresh and novel way.

2.1 Speech vs. property

In the historical development of trade mark law, there was no counterpart term to copyright's 'literary property' or patent law's 'industrial property'. It is clear that the law currently views trade marks in proprietary terms; as Bently and Sherman state, it views them as 'forms of property in their own right'.[82] But it is interesting from the perspective of the analysis I have offered that trade marks have also been seen in communicative terms, as part of the law governing the regulation of speech. This division between speech and property is not meant to be mutually exclusive; rather, it seems that some functions of trade marks are more communicative than they are proprietary, and vice versa.

The most extensive discussion of the classification of trade marks as 'speech' and 'property' is found in the work of Michael Spence, who begins an influential article on the subject with the interesting claim that legal doctrines develop 'in the interplay of topoi', or categories of classification. Just as contract law is partly shaped by the law of promise and partly by the law protecting justified reliance so, he argues, can intellectual

81 As noted above, Borghi and Drassinower have both applied Kantian arguments about authorship to trade mark law to illustrate how copyright's subject matter is quite distinct from that of these other areas of intellectual property law, even if they are viewed in communicative terms (Borghi, 'Copyright and Truth' and Drassinower, 'Authorship as Public Address'). My argument here does not address the point that copyright, patent and trade mark law may protect quite different *species* of communication; rather, it simply highlights that they can all be classified under this *genus*.

82 L. Bently and B. Sherman, *Intellectual Property Law* (Cambridge University Press, 2005), p. 946.

property law – trade mark law in particular – be shaped both by the law of property and the law regulating speech and communication. As he notes:

> The law of trade marks wanders between the *topos* of 'property' and the *topos* of 'speech' ... The law of trade marks is undoubtedly part of the law of intangible property. But trade mark law also restricts what people may say about themselves and other people, and about their own and other people's goods and services.[83]

Spence goes on to note that the property 'topos' has been far more powerful in recent years, but argues that viewing trade mark law as a system for regulating speech is 'normatively far more attractive than a description that focuses upon its operation as a system of property rights'.[84] The reasons he offers for this claim are worth further consideration, since they connect back to the questions about the propertisation of intellectual objects with which this chapter began.

The first reason Spence gives for preferring the classification of trade marks as speech is that, from a rhetorical standpoint, such classification places the burden of justification on the trade mark holder to show why he should be allowed to restrict the speech of others:

> The rhetorical power of the 'property' *topos* is the implication that such control [over uses by others] is given: invoking the 'property' *topos* challenges those who would derogate from the owner's presumptive right of control to make their case ... the trade mark owner has the whip-hand in disputes about the pursuit of particular signs ... by contrast, to say that something is 'speech' is usually by presumption to suggest that it ought to be the subject of minimal regulation, that it ought to be free ... if trade mark law is at its very heart a system for the regulation of speech, then the person whose speech trade mark law would restrict presumptively has the whip-hand.[85]

This argument should strike us as familiar. Spence is suggesting that invoking the property 'topos' places the burden of justification on users of marks to explain how their use is compatible with the prior existence of the owner's property right. Of course, this need not be the case, since some private property rights can be highly circumscribed; moreover, in systems of common ownership, not even use-rights need to be presumptively justified. But Spence is correct to say that, according to conceptions of strong private ownership, property owners have the 'whip-hand' in disputes about uses of their property by others, and perhaps such conceptions of ownership are predominant from the standpoint of rhetoric. On the other hand, when the topos of speech is introduced, the burden of justification appears to lie in the other direction; why should a trade mark

[83] Spence, 'The Mark as Expression/the Mark as Property', 491. [84] Ibid., 492.
[85] Ibid.

holder be allowed to take from the stock of language and control uses of his mark or sign by others?

Spence goes on to make a second claim, namely, that trade mark law has expanded greatly in recent years – partly, he believes, under the influence of the property *topos*. He notes that the 1994 Trade Marks Act (UK) extended the power of trade mark holders to 'license trade mark rights in much the same way as personal property'.[86] Moreover, the Act broadened the scope of trade mark infringement in certain ways. One of the fundamental goals of trade mark protection is the prevention of consumer confusion – cutting down on consumer search costs, and stopping other traders from misrepresenting trade-marked goods. But, Spence notes:

> ... infringement can now be found in certain circumstances in which there has been, not confusion, but allusion by a competitor to the owner's mark. That is, the owner can prevent others not only from making misrepresentations, but also true statements that allude to the owner of the mark or her goods and services.[87]

Trade mark infringement by allusion or dilution certainly broadens the class of actions that infringe a trade mark beyond simple cases of misrepresentation. Spence blames the property *topos*, arguing that '[i]n a legal environment in which the language of property is predominate [*sic.*] ... the presumption all too soon becomes that the owner of the trade mark ought, absent good reason to the contrary, to control all its potential uses'.[88] But rather than immediately blaming an exclusive reliance on proprietary conceptions of trade marks for this phenomenon, let us first consider the extension of trade mark protection in more depth. The question that needs to be addressed is whether the law of trade marks ought to be extended in this way, preventing not only acts that directly misrepresent goods, but those that do so indirectly through 'allusion' to the mark. In the course of doing so, we shall also consider Spence's own argument for viewing some allusive uses of trade marks as cases of 'compelled speech'.

2.2 *Allusive uses of trade marks*

Before moving on to consider whether or not trade mark infringement ought to extend to allusive uses of marks, it is important to clarify further what is meant by allusion, which also comes under the heading of trade mark 'dilution'. According to section 10(3) of the Trade Marks Act 1994, infringement by allusion is defined as follows:

[86] Ibid., 495. [87] Ibid., 492. [88] Ibid., 496.

A person infringes a registered trade mark if he uses in the course of trade, in relation to goods and services, a sign which is identical with or similar to the trade mark, where the trade mark has a reputation in the United Kingdom and the use of the sign, being without due cause, takes unfair advantage of, or is detrimental to, the distinctive character or the repute of the trade mark.

Particularly relevant to the question of allusion are the two kinds of detriment mentioned at the end of the section: actions that are detrimental either to the distinctiveness of the trade mark, or to the repute of the trade mark. In US law, the first kind of detriment, pertaining to loss of distinctiveness, is known as 'blurring', defined as 'association arising from similarity between a mark or trade name and a famous mark that impairs the distinctiveness of the famous mark'.[89] A notable US case is that of the jeweller Tiffany, who was able to prevent use of that name by a perfume company, a Boston bar and a motion picture company.[90] The concern underlying these cases was that, rather than referring to the activities of a jeweller, Tiffany would begin to designate 'generalised notions of quality, luxury and prestige',[91] thereby losing its distinctiveness. This raises a very interesting question about the relationship between trade marks and brands; after all, in addition to informing Tiffany's consumers about the origin of the goods they purchase, the mark conjures up 'brand values', which reach far beyond informing the consumer that their product comes from a reliable source. Should Tiffany's trade mark extend to the protection of these generalised brand values? I return to this question below.

What about the second form of allusion? This is known as 'tarnishment', defined in the Lanham Act as 'association arising from the similarity between a mark or trade name and a famous mark that harms the reputation of the famous mark'. As an example, many cite the US case in which the cheerleaders of the Dallas Cowboys were able to prevent the use of a uniform similar to their own in a pornographic film.[92] The concern at the heart of this form of infringement is that the mark can no longer be used in the same way as it could before the infringement, since the allusive uses of it have created unpleasant connotations that damage the reputation of its owner. Another case often mentioned is that of *Mattel Inc.* v. *Walking Mountain Productions Co.*, in which Mattel wanted to prevent an artist from using the 'Barbie' trade mark in a protest work, but were unsuccessful in doing so. Both section 10(3) of the UK Trade Marks

[89] Lanham (Trademark) Act, 15 USC 1052, s. 45.

[90] *Tiffany & Co.* v. *Tiffany Productions, Inc.* 188 NE 30 (NY 1933); *Tiffany & Co.* v. *Boston Club, Inc.* 231 F. Supp 836 (D. Mass. 1964); *Tiffany & Co.* v. *L'Argene Products Co.* 324 NYS 2d 326 (NY App. Div. 1971).

[91] Spence, 'The Mark as Expression/the Mark as Property', 500.

[92] *Dallas Cowboy Cheerleaders, Inc.* v. *Pussycat Cinema Ltd* 604 F.2d 200 (1979).

Act and section 45 of the US Lanham Act make it clear that confusion is not required in order for a trade mark to be protected against dilution; rather, both acts prevent not confusion, but allusion to a registered mark. Now that we are in a better position to understand what is meant by an allusive use of a trade mark, let us consider how Kantian styles of argument might be brought to bear on the question of whether trade mark protection ought to extend to allusive uses of marks in this way.[93]

2.3 *Allusion and speech: Kantian communication*

Spence noted above that the speech *topos* usually places the burden of justification on the trade mark holder to show why they should be allowed to restrict others' speech by preventing them from using their mark allusively. We might assume that the question could be solved fairly quickly, then, against the trade mark holder and in favour of those who would wish to make allusive uses of trade marks. In the case of *Mattel* v. *Walking Mountain Productions Co.*, mentioned above, an artist produced a series of photographs showing mutilated Barbie dolls, and Mattel's attempt to prevent their release using trade mark law was shot down by the courts on grounds that to do so would be to violate the artist's freedom of speech.

However, Spence reaches a somewhat more complex answer to the question of how, under the speech *topos*, we should view the problem of trade mark infringement by allusion. Rather than siding automatically with those who would make allusive use of marks, Spence argues that some such allusive uses are violations of the expressive autonomy of the trade mark holder. In discussion of the *Mattel* case, Spence worries 'whether adequate account had been taken of Mattel's expressive autonomy', even though he accepts the overall ruling. 'Expressive autonomy' is a phrase we encountered above in discussion of copyright's communicative dimensions.[94] I dissociated it from Kantian autonomy, and noted that it was a paradigm example of individual, not Kantian, autonomy. But that is not to say that Kantian arguments are irrelevant to the question at hand; after all, expression and communication are importantly connected, and Kant had much to say about the communicative function of intellectual property. But to begin, let us consider Spence's argument for broadening the scope of trade

[93] For discussion of whether utilitarian and Lockean accounts might support the expansion of trade mark protection in this way (and with particularly strong arguments against the Lockean case for expansion), see the illuminating account offered by D. Scott, A. Oliver and M. Ley Pineda, 'Trade Marks as Property: A Philosophical Perspective', in L. Bently, J. Davis and J. Ginsburg (eds), *Trade Marks and Brands: An Interdisciplinary Critique* (Cambridge University Press, 2008), pp. 285–306.

[94] See section 1.2.2 above.

mark protection as considered under the *topos* of speech to cover allusive uses of marks. His argument is not put forward as Kantian in nature, but as rooted in a conception of 'personal autonomy'.[95]

The argument begins by drawing attention to the expressive function of trade marks in more depth. Spence draws attention to the point, noted above, that a trade mark communicates 'not only the trade origin of goods, but also a whole range of associated values'.[96] For example, the name 'Pepsi' embodies the values associated with the Pepsi Generation, and does not simply inform consumers that the relevant product was made by PepsiCo. Generally speaking, almost any trade mark might be said to have not only an *informative* function, but also a *persuasive* or emotive function which extends beyond the mere communication of facts to communication of the brand value of products attached to the mark. Spence argues that both informative and persuasive forms of communication are within the scope of the trade mark holder's 'expressive autonomy', and should be protected as such.

The next stage of Spence's argument rests on the point that free speech includes not only a right to refrain from speech, but a right 'to control the meaning of speech, particularly ongoing speech such as a mark'.[97] He cites some First Amendment cases involving courts intervening to prevent compelled speech,[98] and argues that the right to resist compelled speech is justified 'on the basis that affording control over when and how a person expresses herself, including control over when and how she refrains from doing so, is an important part of protecting her autonomy'. Spence applies similar logic to the issue of trade mark dilution: when a second trader uses a sign that merely alludes to a trade mark, they may be involved in 'compelling speech', 'forcing the trade mark owner to participate in speech with which she would disagree or in making her mark subsequently bear a meaning from which she would be dissociated'. Courts should therefore intervene, along similar lines, to prevent these cases of compelled speech. He draws attention to the case *Girl Scouts of the United States of America* v. *Personality Posters Manufacturing Co.*, which concerned the creation of a

[95] Indeed, Spence briefly mentions Kant's distinction between books as 'speech' and visual works of art as alienable property and concludes that Kant would not have viewed trade marks in communicative terms (Spence, 'The Mark as Expression/the Mark as Property', 505). However, he seems to mischaracterise the point of Kant's distinction, which is actually introduced in order to distinguish between different kinds of copying. Moreover, the majority of trade marks are clearly forms of written communication because they are words rather than pictures.

[96] Spence, 'The Mark as Expression/the Mark as Property', 504. [97] Ibid., 505.

[98] *Pacific Gas and Electric Company* v. *Public Utilities Commission of California* 475 US 1 (1986); *Hurley* v. *Irish American Gay, Lesbian and Bisexual Group of Boston* 515 US 557 (1989); *Boy Scouts of America* v. *Dale*, 530 US 640 (2000).

poster of a pregnant Girl Scout wearing the Scouts' uniform marked with its trade mark, and next to it the Scouts' motto 'Be Prepared'. This case appears to fit Spence's sense of 'compelled speech', because the Girl Scouts were being associated with a message with which they disagreed; moreover, having seen the poster, it might be argued that the Girl Scouts' motto would be forever 'tarnished' in the public mindset.[99]

What are we to make of Spence's argument? Questions could be asked about both of its stages. First, there is a question about the nature and scope of a trade mark holder's expressive autonomy. Why should the trade mark holder's expressive autonomy be said to include control over both the informative and persuasive functions of their mark? Second, there is a question about the characterisation of allusion as 'compelled speech', especially when allusive uses of marks are speech acts carried out under the identity of a different trader, and there is no confusion in the public mindset about the identity of each speaker. Finally, why does Spence feel that bringing trade marks under the speech *topos* is 'normatively more attractive' than bringing it under the property *topos*? After all, he has reached exactly the conclusion he blamed the property *topos* for supporting – viz., justifying an extension of trade mark infringement to cover allusive uses of marks. To be fair, Spence ultimately reaches a more nuanced account of infringement by allusion than that which he attributes to the property *topos*, and goes on to explain some cases in which allusive uses of marks by other traders are in keeping with their expressive autonomy. But the difficult challenge Spence faces is to show why, in cases where the expressive autonomy of both parties is appealed to, one party has the upper hand, rather than both parties being in deadlock.

At this point, we might wonder whether Kantian arguments could be of use in analysing these questions. Let us begin by addressing the question about the nature and scope of a trade mark holder's expressive autonomy – bearing in mind, of course, the point that on Kantian accounts the notion of 'expressive autonomy' makes little sense; the question is better phrased in terms of the nature and scope of the author's communication. I noted in my discussion above that Kant was concerned with enabling authors to communicate in their own name, and that transformative uses of works should not be carried out in the name of the primary author. This appears similar to Spence's claim that some allusive uses of trade marks implicate 'the owner of a trade mark in the expression of a message with which she would wish to be dissociated'. At first blush, that is, we might think that

[99] The court in question did not accept this as a case of tarnishment but, according to Spence, this was mainly due to the fact that, at that time, it was necessary to show 'confusion' as well as allusion for proof of infringement by tarnishment.

Kantian arguments would justify extending the scope of trade mark infringement beyond misrepresentation and towards allusion on speech-based grounds in much the same way as Spence's argument allows.

However, closer reflection reveals that this conclusion does not follow. In consideration of the informative function of trade marks and their protection against misrepresentation, Kantian arguments can certainly be appealed to in order to protect the communications of trade mark holders. After all, if a second trader passes off their goods as belonging to the trade mark holder, the second trader is clearly communicating in the name of the trade mark holder (without the trade mark holder's authorisation). This is ruled out on Kant's account as a 'derivative' misuse of another's communication. But this is not to say that Kantian arguments can be applied, in the same way, to prevent all allusive uses of marks. Indeed, Kant argued that transformative uses of primary communications were legitimate when carried out in the name of the transforming author, or carried out non-derivatively. This is the standard of public reason we termed 'authority', or speaking in one's own name. Allusive uses of trade marks fit into this category, since they are carried out in the name of the second trader, even if the second trader needs to refer to or use the first trader's name in order to communicate their message effectively. So in consideration of this standard of public reason, there appears to be little scope for extending trade mark protection beyond cases of misrepresentation, because allusive uses of marks are carried out in the name of the second trader, not the trade mark holder.

What about the standard of intelligibility? It seems clear that acts of misrepresentation can damage the intelligibility of a trade mark's communication, and this is evidenced through consumer confusion. Under this principle of public reason, too, misrepresentation is unjustified. However, the opposite conclusion is reached with many cases of allusion. After all, in a variety of these cases, the second trader quite often needs to allude to the trade mark in order to make their communication intelligible; the message at the heart of Tom Forsyth's 'food chain Barbie' would have been obscured if the artist had been unable to depict Barbie in his work. Indeed, in certain cases of allusion, it is central to the very meaning of the message being communicated – whether by parody or irony – that the mark is alluded to. Spence himself agrees that allusive uses of a mark are permissible when 'it is necessary to use the mark in order adequately to comment upon, or even identify, the mark'.[100] But he goes on to argue that cases which go beyond comment or identification are cases of 'compelled speech'.

[100] Spence, 'The Mark as Expression/the Mark as Property', 510.

At this point, we can call into question Spence's characterisation of allusion as compelled speech, drawing on the Kantian principle of intelligibility. Suppose that somebody uses the Mickey Mouse mark on T-shirts protesting against American foreign policy. In such a case, Spence argues, 'a person is not merely commenting upon either Mickey Mouse or the Disney Corporation. She may be conscripting them to participate in a political cause that the company has no desire to join; she may be doing so even if those who observe the protest know that there is no connection between her and the Disney Corporation.'[101] But in considering this last clause, we appreciate why Kantian arguments, understood in light of the second principle of public reason, lead to quite a different conclusion. If the audience is capable of understanding the lack of connection between, say, the Disney Corporation and the anti-American message about foreign policy, the intelligibility of the primary meaning of the trade mark is preserved, and it is very difficult to see how such a case could be viewed as 'compelled speech'.

Finally, what about the standard of public reason we termed consistency? It can be argued that all communicators must be willing to subject their communications to public scrutiny, criticism and mutual questioning. It is natural that, as a result of such questioning, criticism and public exposure, the meaning of the mark might change. If the meaning of the mark changes in a way that prevents the trade mark holder from adequately communicating its primary message and its intelligibility is called into question then, on the standard of consistency, it seems right to limit such 'misrepresentative' uses of trade marks. But if the primary meaning of the mark is intact, which is true in a number of allusion cases, there seems little justification for giving the trade mark holder control over all subsequent uses of their mark, or the meaning that people come to attach to it after it has been made public. As Tushnet points out, 'dilutive uses [of marks] may increase the richness of a term's associations'.[102] Indeed, such changes of meaning and association are part and parcel of the dynamic nature of language and communication, and the standards of public reason that are said to underlie it on the Kantian account.

A further question to ask when thinking about how consumers come to attach subsequent meaning to trade marks after they have been made public is the extent to which the ability to use such marks freely, even by allusion, is part of the so-called expressive autonomy of consumers and

[101] Ibid., 509.

[102] R. Tushnet, 'Gone in Sixty Milliseconds: Trademark Law and Cognitive Science' *Texas Law Review* 86 (2008) 538.

the public, rather than of trade mark holders. As Bently and Sherman aptly put it, 'while the associations between the mark and a source of goodwill may be instigated and nurtured by the trader, they are as much created by the customers and the public'.[103] That is to say, the brand values associated with marks acquire their meaning, after the creation of the mark, as a result of the psychological associations in the minds of consumers, as well as the efforts of traders. Spence admits that '[a] mark can be used in an enormous variety of expressive acts . . . and its meaning altered in an enormous number of ways'.[104] He goes on to argue that allusive uses of marks are permissible when 'the mark has already acquired an important indexical function', such as 'Barbie' serving as an 'index for a particular understanding of womanhood'.[105] In such cases, when marks have become 'important cultural indices', the law ought to protect the 'expressive autonomy, not only of the owner of the mark, but also those who would allude to it'.[106] Rather than putting the issue in terms of the difficult question of balancing claims of expressive autonomy, though, I would suggest that there are alternative Kantian grounds, based on the principle of consistency, for ensuring public communication is a dynamic process in which meaning and associations are created and altered over time, rather than monopolised or controlled without good reason. This argument is rooted not in a conception of individual expression, but in the normative commitments that lie at the heart of a conception of reasoned communication.

In sum, Spence's argument from 'expressive autonomy' appeared to leave us with no strong reason to think that the speech *topos* was preferable to the property *topos*, and it also appeared to lack the resources to deal with conflicting claims of 'expressive autonomy' in a principled way. But through consideration of the application of Kantian public reason to the problem at hand, we reached a more satisfactory solution to the question of whether trade mark law should be extended to cover certain allusive uses of marks. There seems to be little support for such an extension within the Kantian account developed here, except for cases which also cause confusion and damage the intelligibility of the communicative message embodied in the trade mark. This is not to say that the Kantian account outlined here could be applied to justify or limit every case of trade mark allusion, and to consider such a claim would be beyond the scope of my discussion; rather, the purpose of the discussion has

[103] Bently and Sherman, *Intellectual Property Law*, p. 699.
[104] Spence, 'The Mark as Expression/the Mark as Property', 512. [105] Ibid., 511.
[106] Ibid.

been to move this particular debate about the 'expressive autonomy' of trade mark holders forward in a new and promising direction.

3. Patent law's information function

I would like to finish by considering the possible application of Kantian arguments about public reason to patent law. This might seem like an unusual connection to make, since in patent law, consequentialist justifications are far more dominant than either Lockean or Kantian justifications; indeed, Kant's writings on intellectual property have only very recently been applied to the justification of patents – by Borghi and Drassinower – and in this context they have been applied to illustrate the distinctiveness of the subject matter of copyright law, rather than any particular justificatory position about the scope or nature of patent protection.[107] Accordingly, I shall now consider whether Kantian arguments about communication have application to patent law, focusing in particular on its so-called 'information function', and explaining a way in which the currently popular consequentialist justification for patents might usefully incorporate some principles of public reason.

The most familiar version of the consequentialist justification for patents states that the public should 'only have to endure the harm caused by the grant of a patent if they receive some corresponding benefit'.[108] How exactly we characterise this benefit is a source of much debate, which is a symptom of the fact that consequentialist reasoning often depends on both empirical facts and on contested approaches to defining and measuring 'utility'. The most standard rationale appeals to the claim that the patent system induces intellectual innovation, encouraging research efforts that result in genuinely new inventions. As Lord Oliver has stated, 'the underlying purpose of the patent system is the encouragement of improvements and innovation. In return for making known his improvement to the public the inventor receives the benefit of a period of monopoly during which he becomes entitled to prevent others from performing his invention except by his license'.[109] At its foundation, patent law is said to be committed to this policy balance between incentives to innovate on the one hand, and enjoyment by the public of the fruits of innovation on the other. Any restrictions

[107] Borghi, 'Copyright and Truth' and Drassinower, 'Authorship as Public Address'.
[108] Bently and Sherman, *Intellectual Property Law*, p. 327.
[109] *Asahi Kasei Kogyo, KK's Application* [1991] RPC 485, quoted in Bently and Sherman, *Intellectual Property Law*, p. 485.

on access to innovations that result from the grant of the patent are justifiable only as an unavoidable part of this bargain.

According to this consequentialist argument, whether or not we should have a strong or a weak system of patent protection in certain sectors could depend on exactly how we assess the benefits that result from the provision of new innovations. On the one hand, weakening existing patent protection may prevent substantial progress in the development of new technology and new products. Innovation seems to contribute to the global public interest, while failing to innovate does not. If, on the other hand, the consequences of having strong patents were shown to be detrimental to the global public interest in other ways – because the wrong sort of incentives are created, because monopoly pricing becomes prohibitive, and so on – the same consequentialist rationale would support a weaker system of patent protection. Consequentialist justification as such, then, provides no principled reason for thinking that we need either a strong or a weak patent system, since everything depends on the calculations of costs and benefits. At present, the consequentialist rationale is mainly being used to defend a strong, globalised patent system. But this way of using consequentialist reasoning has also been called into question.[110]

Rather than attempting to add another voice to this debate about the relative costs and benefits of a strong or a weak patent system, I would like to approach the debate from a different perspective, and argue that the traditional consequentialist rationale might be broadened to take account of the values developed in our discussion of public reason – authority, intelligibility and consistency. In discussing the information function of patents below, I am going to focus specifically on the value of intelligibility. If we cannot escape the influence of consequentialism on patent law, as most commentators seem to think, then we can at least develop more sophisticated consequentialist analyses that include within their specification of 'utility' non-economic benefits such as public reason. In doing so, we recognise that patents are not simply tools for allowing investors to recoup costs, nor for inventors to make a profit; they can also be used to promote broader, non-economic goals.[111]

[110] A. Hollis and T. Pogge, *The Health Impact Fund: Making New Medicines Accessible for All* (Incentives for Global Health, 2008), p. 65.

[111] Bently and Sherman have noted that 'whenever non-economic factors such as health, human rights, the environment or ethics are discussed [in the context of patents], they are usually treated as external (negative) constraints upon the core activities of the patent system, or as undesirable side effects that need to be mitigated' (*Intellectual Property Law*, p. 329). In my view, such negativity usually accompanies the narrow consequentialist rationale for patents which we need and indeed ought not to accept. Bently and Sherman argue that there is nothing in principle to stop the patent system from being used as a

3.1 *Public reason: information and intelligibility*

To illustrate how the consequentialist analysis might be broadened to encompass the standards of public reason, I shall briefly consider patent law's 'information function'. This is rooted in the fact that patents require innovators to 'lay open' the details of their invention as a condition for their patent being granted.[112] Indeed, this should be clear from the very etymology of the word 'patent', which is derived from the Latin 'patere' meaning 'to lay open'. This function of patents requires information about possibly useful products and processes to circulate. In discussion of the information function in the case of the patenting of DNA, Ossorio notes:

> When a patent claims a particular DNA sequence, it must teach others how to make that sequence – the patent must give enough information that another investigator can synthesise the sequence de novo or clone the sequence herself.[113]

Whatever we think about the moral issues surrounding the patenting of DNA sequences, which is well beyond the scope of this chapter,[114] most would agree that the disclosure of information about manipulating and isolating DNA sequences is valuable and certainly in the public interest. However, as we noted in our discussion of Kantian public reason, mere disclosure or expression of information is not sufficient for communication to meet the standards of public reason – other standards besides accessibility of information are needed. This is where we can introduce the standard of 'intelligibility'. In addition to innovators disclosing information about patents, they must also do so in a way that makes such information intelligible by relevant audiences – that is, individuals skilled in the 'prior art' who are thereby able to make use of the information disclosed.

It should be pointed out that patent law already recognises the need to impose standards on the disclosure of information contained in patent claims. A patent application achieves its information function by disclosing 'the invention in a manner that is clear enough and complete enough for it to be performed by the person skilled in the art', which is a requirement of patentability.[115] This is usually known as the requirement of

regulatory tool for the promotion of non-economic ends. Broadening our rationale away from the narrow utilitarian view, which focuses largely on profit and incentives for market return, we gain greater understanding of this point.

112 See, e.g., Bently and Sherman, *Intellectual Property Law*, p. 327.

113 P. Ossorio, 'Legal and Ethical Issues in Patenting DNA', in J. Burley and J. Harris (eds.), *A Companion to Genethics* (Oxford, Basil Blackwell, 2002), p. 412.

114 For overview and analysis of this debate, see A. Lever, 'Is it Ethical to Patent Human Genes?', in Gosseries, Marciano and Strowel (eds), *Theories of Justice and Intellectual Property*, pp. 246–65.

115 Bently and Sherman, *Intellectual Property Law*, p. 489. See also s. 14(3) of the Patents Act 1977.

'sufficiency of disclosure'. Such a requirement seems to fit the standard of intelligibility, since although the relevant information might not be intelligible to all audiences (understandable given the technical nature of many inventions), it must be intelligible to relevant audiences – namely, those who are skilled in the art. But there are questions to be raised about the extent to which inventors really are encouraged to make their patent claims fully intelligible under current requirements; after all, on the traditional consequentialist analysis, 'it is necessary to ensure that patents offer sufficient rewards to encourage organizations to become involved in the patent process in the first place'.[116] Partly for this reason, the onus is very much on the defendant to challenge the patent on grounds that it has not been sufficiently disclosed; only when there are 'serious doubts' about its intelligibility will the patent be revoked.

Indeed, a further question has been asked in this context, about whether or not patent law currently allows other innovators to make optimal use of the information that patents disclose, or whether the constant drive to encourage new inventions has led to deterioration in the quality of information made available. As more and more patents are sought and granted – perhaps, it might be argued, under the influence of the narrow consequentialist rationale – the scientific commons has become increasingly privatised and access to scientific knowledge has become more circumscribed.[117] Given patent law's information function, this development is surprising and somewhat paradoxical: surely an increased number of patents ought to increase rather than limit the amount of scientific knowledge available for others to draw upon, due to the fact that patents allow information about products and processes to circulate? But it should also make us stop and think about the relationship between the proliferation of patents and the effectiveness with which patent law's information function is met.

Some jurisdictions incorporate a requirement that patent applicants disclose 'the best mode' of performing the invention as a condition of patentability.[118] Thambisetty points out that, historically, 'a statement of the best method of performance of the invention ... was required [in the common law] even before statutes expressly required it'.[119] This duty on

[116] Bently and Sherman, *Intellectual Property Law*, p. 489.
[117] See Merges, 'Property Rights Theory and the Commons'.
[118] In the United States and Australia, for example. See S. Thambisetty, 'Sufficiency of Disclosure in the Common Law: Complexity, Divergence and Confusion', in C. Ng, L. Bently and G. D'Agostino (eds.), *The Common Law of Intellectual Property: Essays in Honor of Professor David Vaver* (Oxford and Portland, Oreg.: Hart Publishing, 2010), pp. 203–8.
[119] Thambisetty, 'Sufficiency of Disclosure in the Common Law', p. 206.

behalf of the patent applicant existed in the UK until 1977, and continues in the United States, Australia and New Zealand. The rationale behind the requirement to disclose 'the best mode' of performing the invention is to prevent patentees from withholding information, 'in effect maintaining part of the invention as a trade secret while protecting the whole under patent law'.[120] Nevertheless, questions need to be asked about the extent to which this goal is being met under 'best mode' requirements as they currently stand. The first problem is that, in both US and Australian law, there is no requirement that patent applicants actually *identify* the best mode, 'increasing the possibility of voluminous applications where a number of modes of performing the invention may be safely buried'.[121] Rather than helping to solve problems associated with the proliferation of patents and the decline in the availability of useful information, best mode requirements can actually contribute to this problem. The second problem is that, at least under Australian law, patent applicants can amend the information they disclose right up until the date the patent is granted, 'allowing the patentee to monopolise a greater field than has been disclosed to the public'.[122] Both problems illustrate the point that it does not follow from the sheer existence of patents or the sheer disclosure of information about invention on behalf of patentees that others can find, follow or use such information optimally. As we noted in our discussion of public reason, mere expression or disclosure of information is not sufficient for communication in the sense of enabling relevant audiences to follow and assess it intelligibly. If the consequentalist rationale took account of this insight – broadening its conception of utility to encompass standards of public reason – I believe it might find the resources to tackle some of the above problems in a fresh and novel way.

Conclusion

This chapter has covered a lot of ground. Its main purpose is to illustrate some ways in which a Kantian account of public reason has novel and important application to contemporary debates about the expansion and strengthening of intellectual property regimes. First, I have stressed the need for copyright scholars to focus on the true relevance of Kantian autonomy to debates about the connection between copyright and freedom of expression, paying attention to the distinction between self-expression and public communication. Second, I have shown that Kantian arguments about public reason can shed light on trade mark law's communicative function; in particular, by limiting the classes of

[120] Ibid., p. 207. [121] Ibid. [122] Ibid.

action that might be said to count as infringement by 'allusion'. Finally, I have highlighted the important connection between Kantian public reason and patent law's information function. Although I have not been able to enter into a detailed discussion of each of these highly complex issues, I have suggested that a Kantian approach to their analysis is both plausible and attractive and, in so doing, I hope to have added a fresh perspective to some currently contested debates in the literature.

10 Illegal downloading, free riding and justice

*Geert Demuijnck**

1. Introduction

My children are totally uninhibited when they wish to download (illegally) a song or a film. When I tell them that this is illegal, they laugh and say that everyone in their school downloads music.[1] They are absolutely not disturbed by any sense of injustice or unfairness, nor are their friends.[2] Nor are students in general. During the last academic year, I mentioned the documentary film *Inside Job* during a class on ethics and finance. The students knew all about it and, moreover, they all had it on their laptops. Interestingly, they came from about fifteen different countries. I will focus mostly on music here for two reasons: first, some participants in the music record industry are in a serious crisis because of the massive illegal downloading, which is not yet the case for those involved in the film industry. Second, with the notorious exception of Hollywood, film production in almost all countries is directly or indirectly sponsored by the government, unlike music production.

In this chapter, I want to argue that, despite the illegal character of these practices, the moral intuitions of these young people, on a fundamental normative level, are not so obviously wrong. More precisely, I want to argue that the kind of peer-to-peer (P2P) downloading of music

* This is a rewritten and expanded version of my 'Is P2P Sharing of MP3 Files an Objectionable Form of Free Riding?', in A. Gosseries, A. Marciano and A. Strowel (eds.), *Intellectual Property and Theories of Justice* (Basingstoke and NY: Palgrave Macmillan, 2008). I am grateful to Palgrave for permission to use this material. I further thank Axel Gosseries, Alain Marciano, Alain Strowel and Annabelle Lever for their helpful comments.

[1] Illegal downloading seems to be particularly widespread in France nowadays. Piracy is estimated to be twice as common as in other Organization for Economic Co-operation and Development countries. See the recent estimates mentioned and discussed in the newspapers *Les Echos* (6 September 2007, p. 23) and *Le Monde* (24 November 2007, p. 24).

[2] And neither are the teachers of these kids. Curtis Cook mentions a survey of teachers conducted in the state of Illinois which shows that this group of the population feels quite justified when infringing copyright law. C. Cook, *Patents, Profits & Power: How Intellectual Property Rules the Global Economy* (London: Kogan Page, 2002), pp. 124–5.

files these people are practising is only exceptionally an objectionable kind of free riding.

Copyright protection of digital artistic production is a rapidly evolving area, not only in its legal aspects, but also concerning the technical possibilities of copying and protecting. Moreover, it is surprisingly unclear what the economic effects of the growing possibilities of piracy, as well as of commercialization based on downloading or 'streaming' (interactively choosing music tracks without storage on the computer of the consumer), will be in the long run.[3] This chapter aims neither to explore these possibilities, nor to predict what will happen. It merely focuses on the moral legitimacy of the prevailing copyright rules. More particularly, it examines whether or not people who share music files on the Internet are acting like *unfair free-riders*.

The main arguments in favour of P2P sharing – that is, arguments that show that it is not always an unfair form of free riding – originate with, and are inspired by, the ideas of David Gauthier, although they do not depend on endorsing his Lockean theory of property in all particulars.[4] The first argument starts from the contractarian basis of morality. We are supposed to respect rules of fairness insofar as compliance with these rules creates a cooperative surplus. When the rules create a general loss, they have no legitimacy. The second argument defends the idea that, although copyright is an institutional scheme which aims to cope with the 'public good' aspect of information, free riding may be morally justified if the institutional scheme is unfair. The third argument starts from David Gauthier's version of the Lockean proviso: negative externalities imposed on others with whom there is no market interaction at all do not adversely affect the terms of trade, and therefore do not require compensation. Some piracy does not replace any market interaction and therefore, falls under this scheme. This point will be related to some aspects of the 'fair use' exception.

None of these arguments is conclusive, but they all show, nevertheless, that, in many cases, piracy is not morally condemnable on the basis of the free-riding argument. The arguments highlight the ways in which the current copyright protection system is ill-adapted to stimulate creativity,

[3] Einhorn mentions the possibility of streaming as a substitute for actual downloading. See M. Einhorn, *Media, Technology and Copyright: Integrating Law and Economics* (Cheltenham: Edward Elgar, 2004), p. 106. Liebowitz risks some predictions about the future of copyright infringement. See S. Liebowitz, 'Back to the Future: Can Copyright Owners Appropriate Revenue in the Face of New Copying Technologies?', in W. Gordon and R. Watt (eds), *The Economics of Copyright: Developments in Research and Analysis* (Cheltenham: Edward Elgar, 2003), p. 20. Both of these predictions turn out to have been confirmed at this stage.

[4] David Gauthier, *Morals by Agreement* (Oxford: Clarendon Press, 1986).

however justified the goal. The quick development of digitalization and sharing techniques simply makes this more obvious. In the final section, I will argue that governments who try to enforce compliance with currently prevailing legislation are failing to improve the situation and, even, adding new forms of injustice.

2. Is free riding immoral?

One moral objection to P2P downloading is that downloaders are *free-riders*, and, therefore, behave unfairly. The validity of this objection depends crucially on how we define free riding and on whether or not all cases of free riding, according to the definition we adopt, are unfair.

A good starting point for a discussion of the possible unfairness of free riding is David Gauthier's contractarian theory of economic justice.[5] According to Gauthier, perfect market interaction is the paradigm of rational and moral interaction. If I sell goods that I have produced, I am the legitimate owner of what the transaction yields. Market exchanges, like selling my products, are both rational and impartial, and beyond the debate about distributive justice. Two important conditions have to be respected, though. First, production should be based on my labour and on resources that are also available to others at the current market price. In other words, exchanges would become morally questionable if I were to take advantage of a monopolistic possession of a production factor, i.e. if I were to benefit from what Gauthier calls a 'factor rent'. Second, exchanges would also become morally questionable if I were to impose part of the production cost on others, i.e. if production created negative externalities, or, at least according to Gauthier, if production took advantage of positive externalities created by others' activities without paying for them.

The topic of free riding comes into focus when the second condition is not satisfied, that is, in situations in which there are *externalities* at play, situations in which consumption or production decisions of some agents affect other agents' utility. These external effects, whether they are positive or negative, according to Gauthier, give rise to two types of immoral behaviour: being either a free-rider or a parasite. 'A free-rider obtains a benefit without paying all or part of its cost. A parasite in obtaining a benefit displaces all or part of the cost.'[6]

The aim of any set of moral rules and regulations, according to Gauthier, is to eliminate free-riders and parasites.[7] The whole purpose of moral rules in the economy can therefore be related to the failures of the market. Faced

[5] *Ibid.*, [6] *Ibid.*, p. 96. [7] *Ibid.*

with these failures, rational people try to find solutions which are both impartial and rational. The discussion of Gauthier's particular solution is beyond the scope of this chapter. What matters here is the moral rejection of free-riders and parasites. In general, Gauthier's moral objection is against what he calls 'taking advantage of' someone else. Justice is defined by Gauthier as 'the disposition not to take advantage of one's fellows, not to seek free goods or to impose uncompensated costs, provided that one supposes others similarly disposed'.[8]

The concept of a parasite is quite clear: in more common language, it comes down to imposing negative externalities on others, in other words, harming other people. Gauthier gives an example: 'The factory owner who disposes of her gaseous wastes by polluting the atmosphere without compensating those who suffer the pollution she causes is a parasite, displacing part of the costs of her activities on to others'.[9] Parasitism is obviously unfair.

Gauthier also gives an example of free riding: 'The ship-owners whose vessels take navigational advantage of a lighthouse although they have contributed neither to its erection nor to its maintenance are free-riders.'[10] The ship-owners 'obtain a benefit' from a positive externality. However, it is unclear whether 'obtaining a benefit' from a positive externality, without paying, *necessarily* means *unfairly* 'taking advantage of', as Gauthier's definition suggests. Consider the example of someone who has nice flowers in front of his house. Of course, the owner of the flowers is probably the person who sees these most often, but other people passing by also enjoy the sight. And yet it seems completely absurd to claim that the owner of the flowers should be allowed to constrain the passers-by to pay for the view of the flowers they did not ask for. Similarly, and more closely related to the issue at stake, my neighbour Vincent is a professional musician, and sometimes, when I am sitting in the garden, I enjoy listening to him playing the violin. Still, that is clearly not a sufficient reason for him to charge me. And yet, I benefit from an action which I did not pay for.[11]

Therefore, free riding as taking advantage of positive externalities seems *prima facie* morally acceptable.[12] The flipside of this point is that there is no reason to allow the producer of positive externalities to appropriate them.

[8] *Ibid.*, p. 113. [9] *Ibid.*, p. 96. [10] *Ibid.*

[11] A similar example is given by Robert Nozick: 'You may not decide to give me something, for example a book, and then grab money from me to pay for it, even if I have nothing better to spend the money on' (R. Nozick, *Anarchy, State, and Utopia* (New York: Basic Books, 1974), p. 95). Nozick's argument is especially aimed at the claim that people can be coerced to participate involuntarily in a cooperative scheme.

[12] One could argue that diminishing prices caused by a more severe competition similarly decreases profits and increases the consumer surplus. One could even argue that increasing the consumer surplus comes down to increasing the positive externalities (M. Lemley,

3. Free riding and public goods

However, this is too quick. As Gauthier's lighthouse example suggests, free riding on externalities cannot always be condoned from a moral point of view. At first sight, the distinction between morally acceptable forms of free riding and unfair forms of free riding seems related to whether or not one is free riding on a good which is in some sense *public*. Technically, public goods are characterized by *non-excludability*: once they exist, no one can be excluded from benefiting from them. A further characteristic is *non-rivalry*: the fact that I enjoy the good does not impinge on other people enjoying the same good at the same time.[13]

If a good is a public good in this technical sense, free riding may lead to its non-production.[14] Public goods are characterized by positive externalities to the extent that they cannot be produced by the standard market economy because their positive externalities prevent their production: the return on investment is less than the investment needed to produce them. For instance, it would never be worthwhile for an individual ship-owner to bear the cost of the construction of a lighthouse.[15] To the extent that non-rivalry and non-excludability may be a matter of degree, goods to some extent may be 'public', and, as a consequence, 'under-produced'.[16]

If goods are 'public' in this sense, citizens will not gain potential benefits unless they find an alternative to the ordinary combination of private entrepreneurship and a competitive market. Typically, many common collective goods (e.g. street-lighting, lighthouses and security) are technically public goods. If everyone were to free-ride on them, they would not be provided. But in such cases, and only to the extent that we collectively judge that these goods are *socially desirable* and therefore *should* be

'Property, Intellectual Property, and Free Riding' *Texas Law Review* 83 (2005) 1046–7): the fact that I would be willing to pay a particular amount of money for a book and that it is available at a lower price thanks to market competition means that I do not have to pay what I consider to be the full price. See also the 'Introduction' in Gordon and Watt, *The Economics of Copyright*.

[13] These are often-mentioned characteristics of public goods. However, the literature on public goods sometimes mentions other, mostly related characteristics, such as 'jointness in supply', i.e. once a good is available to one consumer it is available to others at no supplementary cost, 'indivisibility', etc. G. Cullity, 'Moral Free Riding' *Philosophy and Public Affairs* 24 (1995) 3–4.

[14] S. Parsons, 'Fair-Play Obligations: A Critical Note on Free Riding' *Political Studies* 53 (2005) 643.

[15] Note that here again, just as in the previous examples, free riding does not harm anyone.

[16] Non-rivalry is sometimes a matter of degree: if I watch the Old Faithful geyser at Yellowstone Park, I am not bothered by the fact that someone else is looking too. However, if there are several thousands of tourists similarly watching, that may diminish the pleasure I derive from the amazing phenomenon. Excludability may be a matter of degree when preventing someone from enjoying a good may be excessively costly.

produced, we can indeed opt for alternatives to the standard case, i.e. market production in which the appropriation (the 'internalization') of the positive utility that one creates for others is possible (and to this extent is not an externality) and allowed.

A first possibility is that the government may provide the good, in the form of a collective good. In this case the taxpayers contribute, independently of whether or not they benefit from the good produced. If the decision to produce the good is taken democratically, we may assume that the total value of the good exceeds the total cost. Moreover, the government, unlike a monopolist, does not capture this surplus.

A second solution, in the case of tangible goods, is to set up an institution such that the good is no longer a public good in the technical sense. One may, for example, grant a right to an investor to exploit privately the 'public' good. Concrete examples are private toll roads, but recently this strategy has also been used for the construction of tunnels and airports. This presupposes that excludability is to some extent realizable.[17] Unlike an ordinary street which may be used by anybody, private toll roads have access control. In this case it is important to stress that private investors need not capture completely the positive externalities created by their investment, but just *enough* for their investment to be profitable. This explains why governments grant temporary exploitation licences for which different companies compete. The latter strategy comes down to grant the right to internalize (part of) the positive externalities.

Whatever the specific exceptional institutional arrangement which copes with the 'public good' characteristic, it comes down to an institutional 'scheme' that 'confers benefits by making requirements of beneficiaries', either tax revenue or specific fares, for the benefits.[18] As several authors have noted, it seems *prima facie* unfair to free-ride on such a scheme, which is only viable when most other people satisfy the requirements.[19] Not only would widespread free riding undermine the very institutional scheme, it is moreover unfair to accept the benefit from such an institutional arrangement by taking advantage of others' benefit-producing compliance.

However, this delineation between fair and unfair free riding (i.e. taking a free ride is acceptable unless it is on an institutional scheme which copes with a public good problem) is again too hasty. Garrett Cullity has

[17] Lemley, 'Property, Intellectual Property, and Free Riding', 1050.

[18] Cullity, 'Moral Free Riding', 14.

[19] See, e.g., R. Arneson, 'The Principle of Fairness and Free-Rider Problems' *Ethics* 92 (1982) 616–33.

convincingly argued that free riding on cooperative schemes which are set up to resolve 'public good' problems is only unfair when three conditions are satisfied. If they are not, free riding may, arguably, be fair. The conditions that allow us to say that taking a free ride on an institutional scheme is unfair are the following.

First, the practice of participation in the institutional schema represents a net benefit for the potential free-rider. No free-rider can be blamed if his regular participation in the scheme would have made him worse off than he would have been without the existence of the scheme. For example, suppose that I am poor and that there is a collectively organized cleaning system which sweeps the streets twice a day, bringing them to an exceptional standard of cleanness.[20] Even if the cost is fairly distributed among the citizens and street cleaning is a non-rival and non-excludable public good, my participation in the scheme (since I am poor and am not really concerned with exceptionally clean streets) makes me worse off than I would be in the absence of the scheme. In this case, it seems questionable to condemn free riding as unfair. However, if I have a net benefit from the scheme, free riding is unfair, that is, if the two other conditions are satisfied as well.

The second condition is that the scheme as a whole makes practically everyone better off when *fairly generalized.* For imagine a scheme that is organized in a fair way, that is, the requirements it imposes on everyone are fairly distributed, but the scheme is inefficient overall: in this case it is not obvious to call free riding unfair. Cullity gives the example of a system in which everyone would be liable to pay all unsolicited benefits that are worth their cost.[21] This system would be fair in the sense of the first condition, but so inefficient that it would impoverish most people.[22]

The third condition concerns the absence of general moral objections to the scheme. One could think of a scheme which is itself unfair, or of a fairly distributed scheme among gangsters which exploits others. When these three conditions are met, taking a free ride on an institutional scheme which copes with a public good problem is unfair.[23]

Prima facie, insofar as the copyright protection can indeed be considered as a cooperative device to overcome a public good problem, P2P sharing is an example of unfair free riding, unless one of Cullity's

[20] This example is taken from Cullity, 'Moral Free Riding', 17. [21] *Ibid.*, 14.

[22] Most and not all because, as Cullity points out, it is possible to conceive overall inefficient systems from which some individuals would benefit.

[23] I leave aside here the issue of whether or not the unfairness of free-riding behaviour is a sufficient reason to coerce free-riders to comply with the requirements of the scheme.

conditions would not be met. Cullity's conditions with respect to questions at stake come down to this. Insofar as copyright is an institutional device to cope with a public good problem, P2P sharing of music files would be unfair if (1) the potential downloader, if he did *not* download, still benefited from the current copyright protection, i.e. his utility would decrease if the system did not exist at all; (2) almost everyone concerned benefits from the current copyright protection; and (3) the copyright protection cannot be morally blamed in any aspect.

4. Intellectual goods as public goods

The 'public good' aspect of intellectual property is related to a particular technical characteristic of intellectual goods. The cost of creating goods such as films, songs and books is often high, but the cost of reproducing them is typically very low.[24] Strictly speaking, goods as books, songs and films are excludable, and to some extent rival, goods. However, the marginal cost to produce a supplementary copy is extremely low and, since the introduction of digitalization, it is close to zero. The ratio of fixed to marginal costs especially is incomparably higher than that for material goods. Furthermore, as in all competitive markets, the price would be close to the marginal cost in the absence of an exclusive right to copy. Together, these elements imply that, given this particularly high fixed-costs/marginal cost ratio, producers cannot cover their fixed-cost investment. As a consequence, the good cannot be produced by the private market, since no one will invest when there is a negative expected return. For example, if the price of a CD falls to the marginal cost of the production of the disk itself, the producers will not be able to capture the costs of making the recording.

Copyright, and intellectual property rights in general, are precisely a solution for this 'public good' problem. By limiting the right to copy, or the right to take advantage of a new idea, they create scarcity in order to boost returns on creative investments.[25] To be clear, the expected return should cover not only the production costs, but also the risks, which, in creation, are understandably high.[26]

On the other hand, this exception to the general rule of the market mechanism – in which charging people for positive externalities is disallowed – does not imply that the creators of intellectual goods should have

[24] W. Landes and R. Posner, 'An Economic Analysis of Copyright Law' *The Journal of Legal Studies* 18 (1989) 326.
[25] Lemley, 'Property, Intellectual Property, and Free Riding', 1031.
[26] Landes and Posner, 'An Economic Analysis of Copyright Law', 327.

full control over these goods. On the contrary, a major goal of intellectual property rights is to prevent people keeping their ideas and inventions secret by guaranteeing a sufficiently long-term monopolistic exploitation. After this monopolistic term, the intellectual goods are 'free' and people are permitted to take advantage of uncompensated positive externalities.[27] This system has a lot in common with the system of private toll roads: it grants the right to internalize positive externalities. As a consequence, copyright necessarily produces deadweight loss.[28]

However, the point of copyright protection is *also to promote* uncompensated positive externalities: 'Copyright protection, [...] trades off the costs of limiting access to a work against the benefits of providing incentives to create the work in the first place. Striking the correct balance between access and incentives is the central problem in copyright law.'[29]

The exception to the general rule of free competition seems necessary in order to stimulate creativity, but it also seems important to minimize any market distortion and not to overprotect intellectual goods. From this perspective, it is important, as Lemley stresses, to take into consideration that intellectual property rights are 'a form of legal protection to deal with public goods problems'.[30] Therefore, they should be compared with other forms of government intervention in the economy (e.g. subsidies, taxes etc.) rather than with 'real' property.

From this argument, it follows, *prima facie*, that P2P sharing should be deemed unfair. This unfairness is about the radical market segmentation between payers and free-riders. Film and music files that are downloaded with P2P sharing systems are made on the basis of real, existing CDs and DVDs. The fact that the CDs are still produced and sold, albeit to a lesser extent, proves that they can still be produced by the market. The fact that profits diminish and that, therefore, the 'consumer surplus' increases, is a normal phenomenon of the market economy. The question of whether P2P downloading makes their production impossible is pointless with respect to these files.

Piracy is only conceivable on the basis of produced work, and it therefore presupposes that the investment is valuable. Still, P2P sharing can only exist to the extent that some clients pay for their CDs. It presupposes, therefore, that in the market segment of the CDs, copyright is not infringed. The only morally problematic point here concerns the division of the consumer surplus, i.e. the decrease of the deadweight loss due to the

[27] Lemley, 'Property, Intellectual Property, and Free Riding', 1052.
[28] Gordon and Watt, *The Economics of Copyright*, p. xvii.
[29] Landes and Posner, 'An Economic Analysis of Copyright Law', 326.
[30] Lemley, 'Property, Intellectual Property, and Free Riding', 1030–1.

P2P sharing: some consumers pay the former price (full deadweight included) and some pay nothing. This radical form of market segmentation is clearly unfair. However, it is unfair with respect to the paying consumers who finance the production, but not necessarily unfair to the creators (see below).

If, *prima facie*, it seems clear that P2P sharing is an example of unfair free riding, whether or not free riding on this institutional scheme of legal protection is unfair depends ultimately on whether the three conditions outlined in the preceding section are satisfied.

5. Is P2P sharing of MP3 files unfairly free riding on 'public goods'?

Since the copyright system can be thought of as an institutional scheme to overcome a public goods problem, we need to ask whether Cullity's conditions are met before concluding that illegal downloading is unfair. In this section I focus on the second and third condition, leaving the first to the next section.

A crucial background element of our discussion of both of these conditions is the particular structure of the music business. The market of creation is of the 'winner-takes-all' type. In such a market, reward depends heavily on relative, and not absolute performance. When a farmer is slightly less productive than his neighbour, he will have a slightly smaller income. In the world of music, there is no such proportionality. Robert Frank and Philip Cook give the following example: 'At the turn of the century, Iowa alone had more than 1,500 of them [opera houses]. Thousands of sopranos earned adequate, if modest, livings from their live performances. But now, thanks to modern recordings, the world's best soprano can be literally everywhere at once.'[31] This winner-takes-all characteristic of the market of recorded music has dramatic consequences with respect to Cullity's conditions.

Cullity's second condition states that the system should make (almost) everybody better off than either an alternative system or no system at all. The current system of copyright protection is highly questionable in this respect. For creativity seems to be overcompensated – this is not unrelated to the phenomenon of the popular music market as a

[31] R. Frank and P. J. Cook, 'It's a Winner-Take-All Market – Top Money goes to Top Performing People or Products' *Washington Monthly*, Dec. 1995. For a theoretical discussion of the particular winner-takes-all market of popular entertainment, see R. Rosen, 'The Economics of Superstars' *American Economic Review* 71 (1981) 845–58 and M. Adler, 'Stardom and Talent' *American Economic Review* 75 (1985) 208–12.

winner-takes-all market – which leads to situations of rent. At the same time, the system does not allow the production of recordings of some intrinsically valuable music. Finally, the system of copyright protection has questionable side-effects on the development of mass culture and taste.

One can quite confidently argue that famous rock stars are in factor rent situations (i.e. rent related to the monopolistic possession of a rare production factor, such as a special talent). Admittedly, precisely defining rent is a tricky matter. Gauthier defines factor rent as 'a premium certain factors' services command, over and above the full cost of supply, because there is no alternative to meet the demand'.[32] He specifies that this means, for the owner of rare talent, 'to extract payment for his services over and above the cost to him, including the opportunity cost, of supplying those services'.[33] Although this definition to some extent may be imprecise, it is not difficult to suppose that, say, David Bowie would have composed his songs for less then he currently earns on the basis of copyright. The standard of living of a famous rock star is widely described and photographed in popular magazines. As children are illegally downloading music of this kind of contemporary nobility, they may justify it with a Robin Hood argument: these people are so rich that a small decrease in their copyright revenue is recommendable.

On top of the unfairness of this system, it has some other troubling features which are worth spelling out. First, the winner-takes-all phenomenon is partly reinforced and explained by the rent-seeking behaviour of the publishers, who are the actual owners of the copyright.[34] The music industry is highly concentrated and the 'majors', which also own the channels by which the 'content' is distributed, want their artistic material (of which they own the copyright) distributed and bought. Marketing is aggressive, as Joost Smiers puts it, 'to the degree that alternate cultural options will be pushed away from many people's mental map'.[35] Following the commercial logic, money for marketing and promotion creates 'stars'.

[32] Gauthier, *Morals by Agreement*, p. 272. [33] Ibid.

[34] They pay so-called 'royalties' to the real creators: 3% except for big stars' 15%: 'Artists receive a certain percentage of the revenue their songs generate. The initial rate is mostly between 7 and 15%, but different reductions lead to a final royalty percentage of about 3%.' See T. Regner, 'Innovation of Music', in Gordon and Watt, *The Economics of Copyright*, p. 109.

[35] J. Smiers, 'The Abolition of Copyrights: Better for Artists, Third World Countries and the Public Domain', in R. Towse (ed.), *Copyright in the Cultural Industries* (Cheltenham: Edward Elgar, 2002), pp. 119–39.

One obvious effect of this marketing system that aims at exploiting copyright property is the star system. The mechanism and its catastrophic artistic consequences were analysed in the 1940s by Max Horkheimer and Theodor W. Adorno, who showed how the mutual influence of the mass media, together with development of a mass culture, would narrow artistic creation to standardized, fully interchangeable consumption products: i.e. songs of 3 minutes, TV soaps of 26 minutes, etc., based on stardom.[36] Their prediction turned out to be basically correct. The overall effect of this commercial 'culture industry' is levelling down the intrinsic quality of cultural productions. Much of the music pupils are downloading is artistically more-or-less worthless. It is highly probable that a significant minority, or even a majority of the population, judges the music my son likes as ugly noise. The point is that the current copyright protection rules make investment in this kind of aggressively promoted records profitable, and pupils are the most obvious consumers. Therefore, it cannot be argued that the production of these goods demands an institutional device to overcome the 'public good' problem, because they are the rather unlucky side-effects of the current overprotection of copyright.

Second, the flipside of this mass culture marketing system is that, paradoxically, current copyright protection may also be insufficient as an incentive for artistic production. For example, copyright protection alone would never make it possible to record the wonderful traditional Baka music. I suppose that many people would be willing to pay a trivial sum to contribute to the recording of world heritage music such as the Baka's, but unwilling to pay the equivalent of the price of a CD. In this case, the typical 'public good' problem cannot be resolved by the current copyright protection. Although it overcompensates creators, it is, at least in some cases, insufficient. Luckily, public institutions like the United Nations Educational, Scientific and Cultural Organization fill this gap.[37]

To conclude, we pay, together, too much rent to some artists, and in general, because of the rent created by the system, basically we pay for music which is cheap mass culture. Therefore, and *only* insofar as people mostly download winners' music, P2P sharing cannot be qualified as unfair, at least not unfair to these winner musicians. Some have even argued that one of the positive side-effects of the current crisis in the

[36] M. Horkheimer and T. W. Adorno, 'Kulturindustrie', in their *Dialektik der Aufklärung: Philosophische Fragmente* (Frankfurt: Fischer Verlag, 1944 [first published in English 1972]), pp. 109: 'In der Tat ist es der Zirkel von Manipulation und rückwirkenden Bedürfnis, indem die Einheit des Systems immer dichter zusammenschießt.' See also their analysis of the star system on p. 120 ff.

[37] Cameroon Baka Pygmy Music. Unesco collection Auvidis. Musics & Musicians of the World. D8029. ©Auvidis/IICMSD/Unesco 1990.

commercial music sector, arising from digitalization and illegal downloading, might be that it leads to a less concentrated music offering and to a situation in which more people are able to make a living out of music, albeit a less lavish one than famous rock stars enjoy.[38] To conclude, Cullity's second condition (the overall necessity and beneficial effect on society's well-being) is clearly not met. Therefore, free-riders should not necessarily be considered as selfish. They may be willing to pay for music in general, but motivated by the refusal to be complicit with an intrinsically ill-conceived system. If everyone would follow them, a better business model for music could emerge.

Nor is the third condition (i.e. the overall fairness of the system, beyond the fairness among contributors) satisfied, because winner-takes-all markets are essentially unfair. The problem here is not the unfairness of free riding, but the unfairness on the side of those who receive the benefits. It is obvious that, with respect to musicians in general, the current system is not really an example of distributive justice. Creators are remunerated very unequally.

Anyone who spends time where live music is performed knows that there are many excellent musicians around. Even during 'open mike' sessions, one wonders why these people are not famous whereas others, barely better or sometimes worse performers, live like royalty. Of course, sometimes the 'system' picks up a street musician (Damien Rice is an example), but the artistic labour market is deeply divided between a few stars on the one hand and an army of losers on the other. As mentioned above, the high incentives for winners attract too many people to the market of creation, and all the more so the stronger the copyright protection is.[39] The system of excessive reward creates 'a few big winners and lots of losers who have wasted their time'.[40] As Lemley and others[41] point out: 'Virtually no musicians actually make money. Potential creators are drawn by the lure of the big score like moths to a flame, and most of the effort turns out to be wasted.'[42]

38 See Smiers, 'The Abolition of Copyrights', p. 133, for some more detail.

39 Frank and Cook explain this by the fact that many people overestimate their chances of 'winning'. For one thing, people much more often see the winners rather than the losers, and for another, people are notoriously inadequate in estimating their own talents against those of others.

40 Lemley, 'What's Different About Intellectual Property?' *Texas Law Review* 83 (2005) 1103.

41 For example, Regner, 'Innovation of Music' and Smiers, 'The Abolition of Copyrights'.

42 Lemley, 'What's Different About Intellectual Property?'

As a consequence, the system of copyright protection combined with the typical winner-takes-all market structure explains why the great majority of musicians earn relatively little from copyright. Most of the income generated by copyright work goes to the publishers and to a small minority of high-earning performers.[43]

To conclude this section, Cullity's second and third conditions are clearly not met: the current system does not make (almost) everyone better off and the distribution of its advantages is, at least among creators, quite unfair. Therefore, free riding is not necessarily morally condemnable. Concerning the last condition, again free-riders can argue that they are not merely motivated by selfishness, but also by the rejection of complicity with an unfair distributional system.

6. Harmless copying in the absence of market interaction

Let me turn now to a second line of argument which shows that illegal downloading or copying is not necessarily a form of morally reprehensible free riding, even if the market for music were not of the winner-takes-all type, and if copyright were pitched at a perfectly adequate level. It may be argued that some groups of downloaders do not have the means to buy some of the music they download – students, and also people living in poor regions. The point we defend here, basically, is that since these are very poor free-riders who would never be able to buy CDs in a regular way, they cannot be considered as unfair free-riders. Four arguments may be deployed to support this view.

A first argument starts again from Gauthier's theory of justice. Besides the basic conditions we mentioned above, Gauthier advances a further background condition to guarantee the impartiality of market exchanges – namely, that interacting parties should not worsen each other's initial position before they start their market relations. It is his very much weakened version of the well-known Lockean proviso, which says that one may convert natural resources into private property as long as one leaves sufficient of these to the others.

Gauthier gives the following example: 'Suppose that we live as fisherfolk along the banks of a river. [...] But if you, living upstream from me, merely use the river for the disposal of your wastes, then even though you thereby kill many of the fish in my part of the stream, you do not violate the proviso. For although you worsen my situation in relation to what I should expect in your absence, you do not better your own situation

[43] Regner, 'Innovation of Music', 109.

through interaction with me.'[44] However, things change as soon as we start trading. The terms of trade are influenced by the supply of fish, which in turn is influenced by your polluting: 'You benefit from polluting my water; you better your situation through interaction that worsens mine'.[45] Gauthier argues that this harm should be compensated for in order to create fair market conditions.

The situation that interests us here is the first, the one in which there is no commercial interaction. In that case, externalities, whether positive or negative, do not influence the terms of trade, because there is no trade.[46] Imagine the not so implausible case that dumping your waste in the stream gives more food to the fish in the river so that I benefit from positive externalities. In this case, the question of compensation in the absence of market interaction would be totally pointless. Moreover, it is not obvious at all that these positive externalities should be compensated for: insofar as the people downstream did not ask for them, claiming compensation would be illegitimate.

The relevance of this proviso for our topic is that, in the absence of regular market interaction, benefiting from externalities cannot make interactions unfair and is therefore not morally condemnable. This point becomes interesting if one takes into consideration that the reason why it may be impossible to establish a market interaction is not necessarily, as in Gauthier's hypothetical example, unawareness of each other's existence, but, more commonly, poverty. Since poor 'pirates' would simply never have bought the CD anyway, they do not worsen the market exchanges of the musicians.[47]

A second argument relies on Cullity's first condition to qualify free riding as unfair which I mentioned in section 3. Free riding cannot be qualified as unfair if normal participation in the institutional scheme that is set up to overcome a 'public good' problem (here the non-rivalry of music files) does not bring about a net benefit to the participant compared to the absence of the scheme. The current copyright system does not improve the situation of very poor people, insofar as they lack the purchasing power to buy CDs. Therefore, their free riding cannot be qualified as unfair.

A third argument is a variant of the second. Its background is the 'fair use' jurisprudence, which echoes the preceding point to some extent. 'Fair use' identifies some exceptional situations in which copying does

[44] Gauthier, *Morals by Agreement*, pp. 211–12. [45] *Ibid.*

[46] Note that David Gauthier's example mentions only negative externalities. This is not clear from the quotation, but is obvious in the passage from which it is taken. Gauthier says that my desire to buy your fish is increased by your pollution.

[47] Gordon and Watt, *The Economics of Copyright*, p. 11.

not in any respect harm the copyright owner and can therefore not be considered as legally condemnable. As I stressed earlier, free riding never causes harm directly, it causes harm to the extent that it undermines the institutional scheme that was set up to resolve a 'public good' problem. The basic argument is always the no harm principle.

Fair use is quite a vague term used to refer to a set of situations that allow different kinds of exceptions to the copyright law. Some copying of a copyrighted work does not make the copier an infringer. Section 107 of the US Copyright Act 2000 mentions four major factors, drawn from prior judicial decisions, to be considered in judgments under the fair use doctrine.[48] The first is the purpose and the character of the use. It makes a difference, for example, whether the copier is a firm selling copies or not.[49] Similarly, it seems obvious that it should be permitted to make one copy for personal use, or to share copies within families. I come back to this point below. A second factor which justifies the fair use exception is the nature of the copyrighted work: it is considered less harmful to copy factual information than creative information, and material already published rather than unpublished. Third, the amount that is copied also matters. For example, less than a chapter of a book is acceptable. The final factor is the one which interests us particularly here: the degree to which the effect of copying on the potential market for the copyrighted work is negligible. If the copier is not a potential purchaser of copies, his use does not affect the demand for them, nor the supply. This, in general, is the factor which is most often invoked to justify the fair use exception.[50] One reason why the copier will not have an effect on the market may be poverty. Poverty may explain why the copier would never buy copies. And, indeed, some of the explicitly mentioned exceptions in the jurisprudence of copyright concern the category of poor consumers.[51] Moreover, there are exceptions to the application of copyright related to the poverty of creators. For example, the US Copyright Act 2000 'includes a provision that permits live performance of musical works and nondramatic literary

[48] Similar laws apply in other legislations. For exemple, the French *Code de la propriété intellectuelle*, Art. L122–5, mentions similar exceptions.

[49] Landes and Posner, 'An Economic Analysis of Copyright Law', p. 357. Recall the example of me listening to my neighbour Vincent playing the violin. I do not make records of his playing to sell them without paying him. In the latter case, I would make a profit by making Vincent unknowingly cover part of the production cost. Therefore, there is an important difference between simply enjoying a positive externality on the one hand, and using this externality to make a further profit.

[50] See B. Beebe, 'An Empirical Study of U.S. Copyright Fair Use Opinions, 1978–2005' *University of Pennsylvania Law Review* 156(3) (2008) 549–624.

[51] See M. Shaffer Van Houweling, 'Distributive Values in Copyright' *Texas Law Review* 83 (2005) 1545, for examples.

works so long as the performance does not have a commercial purpose, the performers are not paid, and no admission fee is charged'.[52]

In different papers, Wendy Gordon has argued for a broader interpretation of 'fair use' precisely in this perspective. She argues that the main distinction is between 'harmless' and 'harmful' use of copyrighted works. Harm is defined as a negative divergence from a baseline, which, in turn, is defined as 'the welfare of the party in a world where the other person's actions had not occurred'.[53] She refers metaphorically to the old tradition of 'gleaning': after the farmer reaped his harvest, the poor had the right to collect the remaining wheat. It is an example of a practice of taking advantage from the effort of others which is not judged as theft.

A last, more fundamental reason and why a comparison between copying without paying copyright and stealing tangible goods – and therefore that free riding may sometimes not be unfair – does not hold, is that cultural goods have an intrinsic value, which has to be clearly distinguished from their market value. Creators want to make a living from their work, but they also want their work to be read, listened to, or performed. Following this logic, creative artists want to be recognized in the first place. If a literary critic discusses a novel, the author will not be bothered to know whether the critic bought the book in a shop or picked it up in a public library. Especially with respect to real fans who do not have the means to buy an expensive copy, artistic creators somehow lose their artistic soul when they blame illegal downloading.

This last argument needs some further comment related to the fair use exception. The ambition to be recognized and famous has implications for the use of copies. If you want to be renowned you have to accept that people talk about your work, share their opinions and occasionally borrow things from each other. This kind of sharing, which does not need any copying, may nevertheless affect the market. Take the following example. A friend of mine is a member of a reading group. The group of about twelve members meets every year to discuss the new novels that seem worth reading. They agree on a list, each buys one of the books, reads it and transmits it to another member the next month. At the end of the year, they have read twelve books, but paid for only one. Although their main motivation is not to save money, it is rather a strange device to be mutually stimulated to read novels because they think that reading novels is important. However, their mutual constraint based on sharing books makes them avoid copyright payment. One could say that in this case there is no

[52] *Ibid.*, 1535.
[53] W. Gordon, 'Harmless Use: Gleaning from Fields of Copyrighted Works' *Fordham Law Review* 77(5) (2009) 2427.

infringement of copyright, since no copies are made. But the books are shared.[54]

The sharing of copyrighted material in small circles is explicitly accepted in the legislation. The French legislation on fair use, which is referred to as the 'private copy' exception, mentions the right to give free representation in 'the family circle'.[55] At first sight, one could argue that P2P sharing is just an extended version of sharing in a family environment, especially when it does not need any copying. However, this way of considering P2P sharing clearly contradicts the fourth justificatory ground of the fair use exception, i.e. the effect on the market. Unlike small-scale sharing, P2P sharing among people who do not know each other is likely to have a considerable impact on the demand side of the market. It would therefore probably imply substantial unfair behaviour.

8. Adding insult to injury: the unfairness of punishing illegal downloaders

Some artists, and especially music producers, have been in a serious crisis over the past decade. According to some sources, the business volume has been divided by three between 2002 and 2010.[56] This does indeed sound problematic at first. But on the other hand, young people are still discovering new groups, new talents break through, and they all make records. At this stage, we do not observe something like shortage or under-production. This may be related to different factors. One is perhaps that it is nowadays relatively cheaper to make a recording of an acceptable quality level than it was in the days of the Beatles. Many new or amateur artists sell CDs after their concerts which have not been produced by the majors, but that are nevertheless decent in terms of quality. Of course, new groups also share their music on the internet, on *YouTube* for example. People who follow the evolution of particular trends or music styles have their numerous specific websites and forums. Even some established artists have radically changed their commercial strategy. In 2007, Radiohead shocked the record industry by letting

[54] This was already explicitly defended by Proudhon: 'Défendrez-vous à l'amateur, qui vient de payer un livre, de réunir chez lui une douzaine d'amis, de faire des lectures, de prêter et faire circuler son volume?' (P.-P. Proudhon, *Les majorats littéraires: Examen d'un projet de loi ayant pour but de créer au profit des auteurs, inventeurs et artistes, un monopole perpétuel* (Brussels: Office de la Publicité, 1862), p. 39.

[55] Code de la propriété intellectuelle, Art. L122–5: 'Lorsque l'œuvre a été divulguée, l'auteur ne peut interdire : 1° Les représentations privées et gratuites effectuées exclusivement dans un cercle de famille.'

[56] See the French financial newspaper, *Les Echos*, 1 June 2011 and also of 20 January 2010.

people download one of their albums (*In Rainbows*) for whatever they were willing to pay. In July of the same year, Prince offered three million copies of his new CD (*Planet Earth*) to the readers of the British newspaper, *Mail on Sunday*, during the period in which he gave a series of concerts in London.

The conclusion we can draw from these observations is that it is obviously not impossible to make a living out of music, thereby offering recorded music to the people, on a basis different from the current copyright system. And yet, we have observed strong lobbying from the side of artists and producers with governments and the European Union, in order to maintain and enforce compliance with the current legal copyright framework.[57] I would like to argue two points with respect to this conservative move. First, it seems like a hopelessly rearguard action, shutting the stable door after the horse has bolted, so to speak. Second, and most importantly with respect to the main issue of this chapter, legal measures, such as the recent 'Hadopi' legislation in France, exacerbate the unfairness created by the copyright system, as the people they are most likely to punish are unlikely to be those who download the most music. The conservative move is hopeless for two reasons. First, it is simply technically impossible to enforce compliance. People who have some knowledge of information technology know many ways how not to get caught, and they spread the word on the Internet. For example, you can hire for a period of time for almost nothing an IP address, based in some East-European country or in Asia, and download files indirectly, via the computer based abroad. Of course, it is technically possible for the police to track the real identity of the 'foreign' downloader, and such steps can indeed be made for serious crimes, but one cannot imagine diplomatic steps and international police coordination to track someone who downloaded songs of Lady Gaga or a Harry Potter film. More radically, there are new forms of sharing and downloading which no longer rely on P2P technology: someone offers storage on a computer, again based, for example, in a former USSR country, on which people put files which others can download. The site owner earns money (covers the storage costs and makes a profit) with advertising on the site and with a pay system which allows people to download very quickly if they pay a trivial sum.

[57] Recently, the International Confederation of Societies of Authors and Composers, presided over, typically, by a musician whose greatest hits date from more than 20 years age, called for stricter enforcement of European Union copyright rules and urged the European Commission to make Internet service providers play a greater role in the process (*Wall Street Journal*, 9 June 2011).

Information about possibilities such as this can be found on specialized websites and in specialist magazines.[58]

During the 'Hadopi' debate in France (to which I turn in a moment) it became clear that the politicians who had to make decisions about copyright law are wholly unaware of these technical possibilities. The people who operate the French satirical website www.bakchich.info asked politicians of the commission which prepared the law what 'peer to peer' meant. The answers were totally absurd and irrelevant.[59] In fact, not much has changed since President Jacques Chirac's hilarious question during the inauguration of the Bibliothèque François Mitterrand in 1996, 'La souris, qu'est-ce que c'est (The mouse? What's this?) ?'[60] Such obvious lack of technical knowledge may explain some of the absurdity in the 'Hadopi' debate.

'Hadopi' stands for 'Haute Autorité pour la diffusion des œuvres et la protection des droits sur Internet' (High Authority for the diffusion of artistic work and the protection of rights on the internet). It is an authority created in France by the law, and its abbreviation is also used as a shortcut to refer to the law.[61] The main aim of the law was to find appropriate answers to the increasing number of violations of the copyright legislation. I will not go into detail concerning the history of the legislation, but it is important that, until 'Hadopi', the violation of intellectual property rights was considered a *crime* under French law, and could be punished with a fine of up to €300,000 and imprisonment. The most recent legislation, called DADVSI, also an acronym,[62] created in 2006, had *announced* a more gradual answer to this specific illegal behaviour, but the implementation did not follow. The 'Hadopi' provided this gradual answer. Its aim was to create an independent institution with the following main mission: the newly created authority should implement a specific administrative sanction, i.e. a sanction decided by the administration and not by the criminal court, to sanction illegal downloaders. Moreover, the sanction should be gradual: the Hadopi authority should first send an e-mail with a warning to the illegal downloader (his or her IP address should be transmitted to Hadopi by the copyright owners); a second step, if the downloader persists in his or her misbehaviour, should be a registered letter with a last warning; the final step is an order to the Internet Service Provider to cut the connection of the downloader. Of course, the previous

[58] Like, e.g. www.libertyland.tv (which was set up a few days after the previous version of *libertyland* was shut down and three people arrested for violation of copyright, see *Ouest France*, 28 May 2011), or magazines like, e.g., the French *OInet*. Moreover, there are many discussion forums where people exchange tips.

[59] www.bakchich.info/Hadopi-le-pire-du-pire-de-l,07562.html.

[60] *L'Express* (weekly), 26 December 1996. [61] Loi no. 2009–669 of 12 June 2009.

[62] DADVSI: Droit d'auteur et droits voisins dans la société d'information.

legislation still prevails. If the content owner initiates a lawsuit against downloaders, the latter still risk a fine and imprisonment.

The whole project was controversial from the start, for reasons of feasibility, but also for more fundamental problems: the protection of privacy and basic liberties. The Commission nationale de l'informatique et des libertés (CNIL), which is the independent authority that watches the respect of privacy and fundamental liberties in the domain of information technology, had different objections against the initial version of the law as it was proposed. The main one was that the sanction to sever someone's access to the internet without the possibility of contesting the accusations in a court seemed unacceptable. The *Conseil Constitutionnel*, the body which controls whether new legislation accords with the constitution, followed the CNIL in this, and the final version which was passed, stated that all sanctions must be pronounced by a judge. The CNIL also had its own objections, concerning the collection of IP addresses. However, the legislator ignored the negative advice from the CNIL on this matter.[63] The law provoked a wave of protest and its possible threat to fundamental liberties was also discussed in the European Parliament, which passed amendment 138 which, roughly, forbids restricting people's liberties without a sanction pronounced by a judicial authority.[64]

That the technical and ideological objections to the project were formulated and debated at both national and EU level is important, and illustrates the short-sightedness of the French government. However, it is also interesting to know the impact of this legislation. Recently, the right-wing economic newspaper, *Les Echos*, frankly admitted that the whole project, one year after its launch, does not seem to have had any effect at all.[65] There is no evidence that P2P sharing is diminishing, despite the 400,000 warning letters Hadopi has mailed.[66]

I can add two points here. First, it is unlikely, without a radical limitation of people's freedom on the internet, that legislation such as Hadopi will ever have an impact, and second, if it does, it will increase unfairness. A long tradition going back to Rousseau and Hume amongst others, considers property rights as conventions that have to be deemed legitimate in order to be obeyed. As soon as the beliefs of the majority of the

[63] As the CNIL (the commission whose task it is to protect citizens' public liberties and their privacy) explicitly remarked in its report, the Hadopi legislation was set up to protect the copyrighted content owners. Downloading was qualified as theft from the start. See *La Tribune*, 3 November 2008.

[64] http://europa.eu/rapid/pressReleasesAction.do?reference=MEMO/08/681&format=HTML&aged=1&language=EN&guiLanguage=fr.

[65] *Les Echos*, 1 June 2011, p. 14. [66] *Le Figaro*, 6 June 2011.

people about the legitimacy of property are undermined, it becomes difficult to enforce compliance. In the case of copyright, the belief in the legitimacy is seriously undermined nowadays, and there seem to be no reasons to justify the current level of copyright protection that will make people change their minds.

Second, given what we have seen about the means to download illegally without being detected, it is likely that those caught and sanctioned by Hadopi will be the most naive and ignorant downloaders, rather than those who do so most often. In fact, already there are examples of strikingly arbitrary and disproportionate sanctions resulting from the legislation.[67] Enforcing the prevailing system will multiply such painful situations.

9. Conclusion

This chapter is not an argument in favour of the abolition of copyright. It is obvious that we should clearly be aware of the reasons why copyright was invented in the first place: without copyright as a device to cope with the 'public good' character of art creations, many authors and musicians would have been unable to create their work, to their detriment and to the detriment of the consumers. However, faced with the new technological developments which tend to facilitate downloading, some ask whether copyright is not quickly becoming obsolete. Technological as well as philosophical arguments to reconsider the legal framework of artistic creation and the market of cultural goods have been advanced. In this chapter, I have qualified an often heard argument, advanced by those who defend the prevailing copyright system, i.e. that illegal downloaders are morally objectionable 'free-riders'. They may be, but certainly not all the time. We have indicated two different configurations in which this qualification of unfair behaviour does not hold: insofar as they download 'winners', they take a free ride on an unfair system; and insofar as they lack purchasing power, they are excluded from the regular market, which makes it questionable whether their free riding is unfair. However, I am aware that, in both cases, it may be very difficult to draw a line between fair and unfair downloaders. The threshold which defines a musician as a 'winner', as well as the threshold for determining when someone is so poor as to be excluded from the market, is difficult to fix, and applying these thresholds would presuppose much empirical data that we do not have.

[67] In 2009, a single mother from Minnesota was fined $1.9 million for having downloaded 24 songs. See http://articles.cnn.com/2009-06-18/justice/minnesota.music.download.fine_1_jury-instructions-fined-sheryl-crow?_s=PM:CRIME.

Publishers may adopt a defensive strategy against free riding and try to develop 'self-help' systems, that is, systems which make copying (also copying on your own computer) impossible. However, the development of such systems will be an infinite and costly race against people who break these systems. Therefore, it might be more interesting to think of alternative ways of coping with the public good aspect of creative material, like a package deal in which, together with the bill of their internet provider, people pay a fixed copyright tax. One of the positive side-effects of such an alternative may be a more equitable allocation among artists which, consequently, if my preceding arguments are correct, would make the scope of possibly 'unfair' free riding much smaller.

To conclude, as Paul Krugman has argued in a column in *The New York Times*, digitalization cannot be stopped, and book publishers are likely to undergo a similar crisis to the record industry: 'Bit by bit, everything that can be digitized will be digitized, making intellectual property ever easier to copy and ever harder to sell for more than a nominal price. And we'll have to find business and economic models that take this reality into account.'[68] The only way to face this evolution is to think about new business models within which there are sufficient economic incentives to stimulate creativity.

[68] *The New York Times*, 6 June 2008.

11 The virtuous p(eer): reflections on the ethics of file sharing

*David Lametti**

Introduction

File sharing in the digital world, and particularly the sharing of music files, is as criticised as it is commonplace. Labeled 'piracy', 'theft' and 'free-riding' by its detractors, file sharing is lauded by its supporters and practitioners and, dare I say, even some legal experts and musicians. Whatever the case, the practice has continued unabated and may have led to the death of an economic model for an entire industry, that of the sale of recorded music.[1] Music listeners have voted with their feet, or, more accurately, with their mice, hard drives, iPads, iPods and MP3 players. And this, despite the negativity of the demonising rhetoric and the substantial resources dedicated to the media campaigns[2] 'educating' people on the vices of file sharing.

Clearly, the phenomenon of file sharing, especially that of music file sharing, is much more ethically complex than the media campaigns decrying file sharing as piracy and theft would have us believe. The fact that the practice of file sharing of music continues raises a number of

* I would like to thank the participants of the Philosophy and IP Conference, London School of Economics, May 2009, especially Annabelle Lever, Abraham Drassinower, Laura Biron, Lionel Bently, Geert Demuijnck, Anne Baron, Roberto Caso, Simone Bittman, Magda Woscszyk, Keiran Gibbs, Ian Dahlman and Ellen Bourque. I wish to thank Sandy Pearlman for various conversations over the years. Research assistance was supported by the Social Sciences and Humanities Research Council of Canada.

1 The decline and fall of the market for recorded music is documented in a number of places over the past number of years. See most recently, M. Sweeney, 'Global Recorded Music Sales Fall almost $1.5bn amid Increased Piracy', *The Guardian*, 28 March 2011, www.guardian.co.uk/business/2011/mar/28/global-recorded-music-sales-fall. Of course, figures almost always come from producers. Moreover, one has to put the decline in sales in context: CD sales rose in the 1980s and 1990s – perhaps the heyday of recorded music sales – as a generation of buyers moved to replace their existing vinyl and cassette collections, effectively re-buying a great deal of recorded music and inflating sales figures.

2 See 'Music Matters to New Anti-piracy Campaign', *The Guardian*, 24 March 2010, www.guardian.co.uk/music/2010/mar/24/music-matters-anti-piracy-campaign. More recently, see the video clip of Arnold Schwarzenegger and Jackie Chan: www.youtube.com/watch?v=cKPs06vFihI.

serious ethical and normative questions: what makes 'good' people engage in this 'bad' form of behaviour?[3] Is recorded music in some way distinct, either as an object of an intellectual property right (namely, copyright), or in its larger context as part of an industry model, from other kinds of digital 'goods' that are shared? Is there a problem for normative ordering when the gap between formal norms and informal practices is effectively a chasm?

The starting point for this reflection is an article by Geert Demuijnck.[4] Working from a law and economics perspective, as well as justice-based reasoning, Demuijnck has questioned whether the sharing of MP3 files is an objectionable form of free riding. His conclusion is negative. For reasons that are grounded in the nature of the market, the nature of the industry and the nature of the target market for popular music – adolescents, in particular – Demuijnck concluded that the sharing of music files is not a type of free riding that is ethically problematic.

Demuijnck's point is fundamentally sound. From a contextual perspective, many of the adolescents who share such music files were never in the market for recorded music anyway, and never have been. While to some extent younger people have bought some popular music, the majority of them, even prior to the Internet, had never paid for all of the popular music that they obtained.[5] Sharing has always been commonplace, especially through taping and burning CDs.[6] So here, Demuijnck's argument is another variant of the target market argument with which copyright is already quite familiar in discussing the audience or target market for the purposes of fair use or fair dealing analysis: does the copying by adolescents affect the market for the original? It is also true that, while copying necessarily must reduce at least some of the potential market for the original work, by how much it reduces that market is unclear. The same is true for the question of whether that potential market (from the point of view of the copyright holder) is so

[3] A. Peukert, 'Why do "Good People" Disregard Copyright on the Internet?', in C. Geiger (ed.), *Criminal Enforcement: A Blessing or a Curse for Intellectual Property?* (Cheltenham: Edward Elgar, 2010); electronic copy available at ssrn.com/abstract=1660319.

[4] G. Demuijnck, 'Is P2P Sharing of MP3 Files an Objectionable Form of Free-Riding?', in A. Gosseries *et al.* (eds.), *Intellectual Property and Theories of Justice* (London and New York: Palgrave Macmillan, 2008), p. 141.

[5] Of course, the phenomenon of music file-sharing is not strictly generational: it is more a question of people of whatever generation who are not accustomed to or have rejected the legitimacy of the concept of recorded music as a material product, although I think that it is fair to say that young people, at least at the outset, belong mainly to the former category.

[6] J. Litman, 'Sharing and Stealing' *Hastings Communication and Entertainment Law Journal* 27 (2004) 1.

large so as to include every piece of music ever obtained by an adolescent. This latter market, in my view, has always been purely hypothetical, though some artists have managed to exploit it better than others, often by expressly marketing to that demographic group.[7]

Finally, according to Demuijnck, the nature of the music industry was (and, I suppose, still is) such that it was not fully 'just' in its allocation of revenues, such that the 'tapping into' of the revenue streams of recorded music through file sharing was not additionally unjust to artists, who saw little of the revenues anyway. It is also true that the market for the sale of musical recordings is a relatively recent phenomenon, made technologically possible and spanning only the last sixty-odd years, and as such should not be treated as a natural phenomenon or natural order of things: technology giveth and technology taketh away.[8]

In addition to these economic arguments, I wish to bolster the argument that the sharing of *music* files – if not absolutely justified in all – is at least justifiable in many circumstances. Perhaps, as an act, one might say that sharing music files is ethically neutral: justified in some circumstances, though perhaps not in others. Certainly, the words 'theft' and 'piracy' are generally instances of overblown hyperbole in most cases. Legal norms are often complex or do not coincide with common practice. This normative gap may be exacerbated by a generational gap: while I am not supposing that there is a generation gap that is equivalent in all spheres, or that the phenomenon of elected, often older, persons legislating for non-elected, often younger, persons is in any way illegitimate, the fact remains that in this case there is a divergence between a generation that is accustomed to the materiality of purchased music – and these are often older, empowered persons – and another generation that is not – and these are often younger persons. In all cases, the individual actor must make ethical choices to act virtuously as regards the sharing of recorded music. Given the nature of music, the music industry and the situation of the actors, in many such cases sharing music files may very well be the virtuous response or based on a legitimately-held though subjective belief that it is virtuous.

Music file sharing as virtuous

I wish to pursue this tack in a couple of specific directions. The first is built upon the ethical foundation that is coming to be known as 'virtue

[7] As is currently being done by Katy Perry, Lady GaGa and Justin Bieber, or as did before them Hannah Montana, New Kids on the Block, Spice Girls, Madonna or Duran Duran.

[8] I thank Ian Dahlman for suggesting this turn of phrase, who in turn credits a speech by Neil Postman in 1998: www.cs.ucdavis.edu/~rogaway/classes/188/materials/postman.pdf.

ethics'.[9] The second is based upon the contextual idea that social norms as regards copyright and copying, or 'copynorms',[10] inform file sharing.

i. The virtue ethics of copyright

Virtue ethics is the label given to what might be called a rediscovered emphasis on ethical action in specific contexts or situations. These situations challenge us to act and, in doing so, force us to define what is right and wrong and as a consequence, effectively define and better ourselves.

Inspired by the writing of Aristotle (and to a lesser extent Aquinas) and re-formulated by a new generation of scholars,[11] virtue ethics purports to provide the guidelines or the right questions to ask in a situation of ethical decision-making. Such decisions, following Aristotle's concept of practical reasonableness and attention to context, make the 'positionality' of the ethical decision-maker central to deciding how to act in any given circumstances.[12] That is, all norms are culture-relative and supported by intuitions that are grounded by community traditions; these norms are understood and inculcated in the members of a community over time. The hermeneutic tradition that supports this understanding of normativity and the transmission of norms will not necessarily tell agents – us – what the right answer is in all cases, but rather, will help us to find the right answer for ourselves. Although set rules form part of the basis for what it means to act virtuously, rules are often less than clear, limited, contradictory and opaque; hence, rule-following is incomplete as an ethical stance, outlook or way of life. Put simply, we need to do more than follow rules in order to do what is right. Indeed, there is a sense in which one can even in principle, disregard, certain rules while remaining faithful to law.

[9] The following paragraphs are loosely reworked from my previous, more Canadian-centred article: 'How Virtue Ethics Might Help Erase C-32's Conceptual Incoherence', in M. Geist (ed.), *From 'Radical Extremism' to 'Balanced Copyright': Canadian Copyright and the Digital Agenda* (Toronto: Irwin Law, 2010), p. 309.

[10] M. F. Schultz, 'Copynorms: Copyright Law and Social Norms', in P. Yu (ed.), *Praeger's Intellectual Property and Information Wealth: Issues and Practices in a Digital Age* (London: Praeger Perspectives, 2006), vol. I, p. 201; available at ssrn.com/abstract=933656.

[11] The best introductory work is S. van Hooft, *Understanding Virtue Ethics* (Stocksfield, UK: Acumen, 2006). See also R. Hursthouse, *On Virtue Ethics* (Oxford University Press, 1999); D. Statman (ed.), *Virtue Ethics: A Critical Reader* (Edinburgh University Press, 1997); and R. Crisp and M. Slote (eds), *Virtue Ethics* (Oxford University Press, 1997). See also O. O'Neill, *Towards Justice and Virtue* (Cambridge University Press, 1996) and C. Taylor, *The Sources of the Self* (Cambridge, Mass.: Harvard University Press, 1989).

[12] The best discussion of 'positionality', in my view, is contained in K. Bartlett, 'Feminist Legal Methods' *Harvard Law Review* 103 (1990) 829. While that article pre-dates the use of the term 'virtue ethics', the Aristotelian and neo-Aristotelian sources and substance indicate that Bartlett's positionality narrative fits well within the description of virtue ethics.

The advantage of a virtue ethics approach or stance is that it helps individuals to make decisions in concrete situations, either in life's various circumstances or in copyright-specific cases. What is required is individual judgment or self-reflection in service of the balanced decision-making that Aristotelians and neo-Aristotelians have favoured in their ethics. The fact that these virtues and values are widely shared in a society, deeply understood and intrinsically appreciated means that such an ethic is not merely a breed of moral relativism, and positionality, while situated, is not simply a species of situation ethics.[13]

Put in other terms that might be familiar along Lon Fuller's lines, I am advocating an 'ethics of aspiration'[14] in which we aim (as individuals, or in framing the law or the legal system, or the normative order) to aspire to the best exemplars of actions or norms. This kind of ethics goes beyond formal norms: it is not mere rule-following. This ethic might serve as the basis for a specific duty, such as a duty to aspire to a certain standard of behaviour,[15] but it does not always conform to rules and it goes beyond an ethic of duty to strictly follow rules. However, rules are a part of the ethical mix and ought to be followed generally as exclusionary reasons for action.[16] Good ethical reasons, based on a determination made using practical reasonableness (phronesis) while embedded in a contextual vantage point (positionality), might allow us to look beyond exclusionary reasons in some circumstances in service of some higher value or virtue. Moreover, the fact that such informal, ethical standards are so widely and deeply understood helps to lower the potential so-called information costs of relying on contextual standards as opposed to fixed rules.

[13] This suffices for now, though I appreciate that these claims will always be contested. A good analysis, containing a defence of virtue ethics against the charge of moral relativism and differentiating virtue ethics from a duty-based ethics is contained in van Hooft, *Understanding Virtue Ethics*, p. 7.

[14] L. L. Fuller, *The Morality of Law* (New Haven, Conn.: Yale University Press, 1969). Happily, I have been 'accused' of falling into this camp already: see D. Lametti, 'The Morality of James Harris's Theory of Property', in T. Endicott, J. Getzler and E. Peel (eds.), *The Properties of Law: Essays in Honour of James Harris* (Oxford University Press, 2006), p. 164, n. 44; available at ssrn.com/abstract=1758880.

[15] To adopt the language of clear 'rules' and open-ended 'standards': for a recent discussion in a property context, see A. Lehavi, *The Dynamic Law of Property: Theorizing the Role of Legal Standards*, at ssrn.com/abstract=1618768.

[16] A concept elaborated by Joseph Raz: J. Raz, *The Authority of Law: Essays on Law and Morality* 2nd edn. (Oxford University Press, 2009), p. 22 ff. An exclusionary reason, such as a law, gives a person a reason for acting without forcing or requiring the person to provide any other reason or seek any other justification for acting. A stop sign gives a person an exclusionary reason for stopping; it does not mean, however, that in an emergency a person would not be ethically prohibited from safely running that same stop sign (my example).

Virtue ethics is useful in understating the nature of intellectual property and especially in comprehending the nature of copyright, because it helps to identify the boundaries and substance of open-ended terms like 'fair', 'just' and 'balance', which are critical for understanding a number of the most basic copyright concepts like the idea–expression dichotomy[17] or fair dealing.[18] These open-ended standards do not have bright-line interpretations, but rather require exercises of interpretive judgment. Likewise, the same is true for traditional property.[19]

The virtue ethics of copyright are in plain view in its justificatory foundational discourses, in its teleology and function, and in its doctrines and the interpretive standards used to elaborate them. The starting point is the idea that copyright is a limited right. While most citizens, legislators and scholars are now comfortable with the idea of labelling copyright's rights as a species of *property* rights, in the sense that they have economic value,[20] have an *in rem* and exclusive aspect, and are treated as such in statutes[21] and in practice,[22] this is by no means accompanied by the underlying idea that such rights are absolute.[23] Numerous scholars have noted, in the common law tradition, the statutory origins of the rights in question and the fact that such rights are not rights *in gross*. Rather, there are serious limits on duration and scope of the (specific) rights of copyright holders. The same is true in the civil law *droit d'auteur* tradition, even though it is perceived as being more absolute from the outset. Moreover, various substantive doctrines, notably fair use or fair dealing in copyright, or copyright misuse, have further emphasised this seemingly banal point by limiting even the exercise of rights by a right holder.[24]

17 *Nichols* v. *Universal Pictures Corporation et al.*, 45 F.2d 119 (2d Cir. 1930).

18 In the Canadian context, in the case of former Bill C-32, virtue ethics helps individual actors in the copyright context – users and copyright holders – to resolve the conceptual incoherence of the copyright and paracopyright elements that had been forced to cohabit in the bill; see Lametti, 'How Virtue Ethics Might Help Erase C-32's Conceptual Incoherence', 309.

19 See D. Lametti, 'The Objects of Virtue', in G. S. Alexander and E. M. Peñalver (eds.), *Property and Community* (New York: Oxford University Press, 2010), p. 1, available at ssrn.com/abstract=1758859. See also D. Lametti, 'Laying Bare an Ethical Thread: From IP to Property to Private Law?', in S. Balganesh (ed.), *Intellectual Property and the Common Law*, forthcoming.

20 Or, in civil law terms, are 'patrimonial'.

21 As an example, the Canadian Copyright Act uses the term 'ownership'.

22 Think only of the use of IP rights as collateral for secured lending.

23 D. Lametti, 'The Concept and Conceptions of Intellectual Property as seen through the Lens of Property', in G. Comandé and G. Ponzanelli (eds.), *Scienza e Diritto nel Prisma del Diritto Comparato* (Torino: Giappichelli, 2004), p. 269, available at ssrn.com/abstract=1758894.

24 Even those intellectual property rights that have their origins not in statute but in the common law, such as passing off, are by no means unlimited: see J. Litman, 'Breakfast with Batman: The Public Interest in the Advertising Age' *Yale Law Journal* 108 (1999)

What is more, one needs to acknowledge and underscore the very explicit, overtly ethical teleology of intellectual property, and especially copyright. The purpose of these intellectual property rights is to favour artistic creativity and the promotion of useful inventions, as evidenced in a variety of foundational documents. More specifically with respect to copyright, the Statute of Anne in 1710, in its very title, states that the *Act*'s purpose is for 'the Encouragement of Learning'.[25] The Constitution of the United States, in protecting patent and copyright under federal jurisdiction, does so in order 'to promote the Progress of Science and useful Arts, by securing for limited Times to Authors and Inventors the exclusive Right to their respective Writings and Discoveries'.[26] The first US federal Copyright Act of 1790 picked up the language of the Statute of Anne, and was 'an Act for the encouragement of learning, by securing the copy of maps, charts, and books, to the authors and proprietors of such copies, during the times therein mentioned'. Thus in both copyright and patent there is an idea that the grounds for intellectual property protection, in its barest terms, is overtly consequentialist or utilitarian: the according of precise, limited, and exclusive (and thus property-like) rights is done in order to foster specific desirable, and indeed, ethical goals.[27] The question is one of balance.

Certainly one might take an impoverished view of the above and reduce the idea of promoting creativity as the furnishing of incentives simply to economic terms. This reduction, however, would not accurately describe the full amplitude of the notion of progress or creativity, and their ties to

1717; M. A. Lemley, 'The Modern Lanham Act and the Death of Common Sense' *Yale Law Journal* 108 (1999) 1687; and S. L. Dogan and M. A. Lemley, 'The Merchandising Right: Fragile Theory or *Fait Accompli*?' *Emory Law Journal* 54 (2005) 461. Shyamkrishna Balganesh has argued that we might return, fruitfully, to the methodology and substance of the common law of IP, still present in the interstitial aspects of state common law IP rights. But this, too, is not an argument for absolute IP rights across the various domains; rather, it is a system in which rights are discerned through a process of 'pragmatic incrementalism': see S. Balganesh, 'The Pragmatic Incrementalism of Common Law Intellectual Property' *Vanderbilt Law Review* 63(6) (2010): 1564.

25 An Act for the Encouragement of Learning, by Vesting the Copies of Printed Books in the Authors or Purchasers of such Copies, During the Times therein mentioned, 1710, 8 Anne, c.19.

26 US Constitution, Art. I, s. 8, cl. 8. Note that this provision also underscores the limited nature of these exclusive rights.

27 Recent psychological evidence is questioning the foundational idea that people most effectively create, innovate or invent when presented with financial rewards. Indeed, in many cases this reward has the opposite effect: less creativity or innovation in terms of both quality and quantity. For an introduction, see D. H. Pink, *Drive: The Surprising Truth About What Motivates Us* (New York: Riverhead, 2009). The impact of this on copyright's balances is a matter for another day, though in general it does support the idea of less-absolute copyright rights and increased user rights and privileges, including sharing, and especially sharing to create.

the promotion of knowledge, learning and the advancement of scientific and artistic ideas.[28] Nor would it capture the concept of human flourishing,[29] the idea of the social benefits of copyright,[30] or the role that a robust public domain of ideas necessarily has in providing the backdrop for progress.[31] The institution of copyright is not uniquely about according economic rights to the creator, but rather, the process of the 'bringing about' of the creation itself: the promotion of the useful arts, and the encouragement of learning. This is not something that can be measured in simple *utils*. Rather, there is an ethical direction to the whole of copyright. This is exemplified in the balance of according rights limited in scope in exchange for promoting the public's access to the arts and providing incentives for authors, all in service of the public good.

Perhaps the best illustration of this point is the discussion regarding a central limitation of copyright: fair use or fair dealing. That voluminous discussion of what is either a central limit to copyright's property-like rights or an instance of 'user's rights'[32] is an explicitly moral discussion. A glance at section 107 of the US Copyright Act and its criteria for fair use brings out this ethical picture quite nicely. The purposes which justify fair use – 'criticism, comment, news reporting, teaching (including multiple copies for classroom use, scholarship, or research)' – are purposes that go to the heart of what we feel our society is about: knowledge and knowledge transfer, public debate and discourse, teaching and scholarship and learning. The enumerated factors that follow in section 107 are meant to provide a specific set of open-ended criteria that provide the basis for making such determinations.

Another interesting example is the emerging doctrine of copyright misuse. Based on the notion of patent misuse, copyright misuse is a

[28] See, e.g., M. J. Madison, 'Beyond Creativity: Copyright as Knowledge Law' *Vanderbilt Journal of Law and Technology* 12 (2010) 817. Available at ssrn.com/abstract=1599621 (knowledge and learning as the central goals of copyright norms).

[29] See, e.g., W. W. Fisher III, 'The Implications of Law of User Innovation' *Minnesota Law Review* 94 (2010) 1463 ff (human flourishing as a part of the law of copyright); A. Drassinower, ch. 8 above (Kantian view of copyright and human flourishing).

[30] See B. M. Frischmann, 'Spillovers Theory and Its Conceptual Boundaries' *William and Mary Law Review* 51 (2009) 801 (social benefits of IP depend on spillovers for which standard economic utilitarian theories cannot account).

[31] See J. Litman, 'The Public Domain' *Emory Law Journal* 39 (1990) 965; J. Boyle, *The Public Domain: Enclosing the Commons of the Mind* (New Haven, Conn.: Yale University Press, 2008), p. 179 (on the intellectual commons as a source for creative work); and A. Drassinower, 'Taking User Rights Seriously', in M. Geist (ed.), *In the Public Interest: The Future of Canadian Copyright Law* (Toronto: Irwin Law, 2005), p. 462 (on the intertextuality of creation).

[32] See, e.g., in Canada, *CCH Canadian Ltd* v. *Law Society of Upper Canada*, [2004] 1 SCR 339 (effectively importing into Canadian 'fair dealing' jurisprudence a US-like 'fair use' test).

doctrine that has increasingly been cited as a check or a brake upon the unfettered rights of copyright holders, *even within the normal scope of rights held*. The parameters of the doctrine are being worked out, but what is of significant interest is the focus on the actions of the right holder and the purposes to which the actions were taken.[33] Thus in Canada, the actions of a multinational food company were scrutinised under this doctrine when copyright was used to vindicate a putative exclusive right to import popular Belgian chocolates, when neither trade mark nor competition law afforded a remedy to the company and where the competitor, a small local importer, broke no laws and paid all fees.[34] In the view of some scholars, in this David and Goliath scenario the multinational was being unethical, plain and simple.[35] An obvious parallel is the concept of abuse of rights, or *abus de droit*, in the civil law, a doctrine which, as is argued below, may very well be seeping into the common law, or has indeed already crept in from time to time.[36]

What is critical to all of these discussions – the scope of rights, the nature of limitations, doctrines such as fair use and misuse – is context. In all of these instances, there is a requirement to look at the context of right holders and non-right holders, and come up with a balanced answer based on positionality. If you will, the position of right holders needs to be examined and understood, and the nature of copyright protection, its purpose and scope and its limits, all need to be discerned. The same is true for the position on non-right holders – i.e., users – in the context of *their* relation to the work and the scope of copyright protections, their reasons for use and their actual uses, etc. There is often no clear, bright-line answer that is easily discernible in advance. Part of the context is the ultimate goals to be serviced and their application to specific circumstances. The Aristotelian concept of practical reasonableness, both as a

[33] See generally, K. Judge, 'Rethinking Copyright Misuse' *Stanford Law Review* 57 (2004) 901: in her view, any attempt by a copyright holder effectively to expand the purview of copyright protection to gain control over an idea or deter fair use constitutes misuse. For an application to digital copyright, see D. L. Burk, 'Anti-Circumvention Misuse' *UCLA Law Review* 50 (2003) 1095. For a specific critique of copyright holders' non-existent or overbroad (copy)rights, see J. Mazzone, 'Copyfraud' *NYU Law Review* 81 (2006) 1026.

[34] *Euro Excellence Inc.* v. *Kraft Canada Inc.* [2007] 3 SCR 20, 2007 SCC 37 (concurring reasons of Bastarache J and the warning expressed regarding copyright overreach in the concurring reasons of Fish J). The majority ignored the copyright 'abuse' claim on technical grounds.

[35] P.-E. Moyse, 'Kraft Canada c. Euro-Excellence: l'insoutenable légèreté du droit' *McGill Law Journal* 53 (2008) 74, available at ssrn.com/abstract=1761002; A. Drassinower, 'The Art of Selling Chocolate: Remarks on Copyright's Domain', in Geist (ed.), *From 'Radical Extremism' to 'Balanced Copyright'* p. 121.

[36] *Contra*, see L. Katz., 'A Jurisdictional Principle of Abuse of Right' (8 February 2010), ssrn.com/abstract=1417955.

value itself as well as a method of determining other values, is also part of the normative structure and is linked to the idea of positionality: from one's particular context, one reasons practically.

Context and positionality *are* by their very nature the realm of virtue ethics. In other words, it is a small step from these relatively uncontroversial descriptive points about the nature of copyright to an understanding of its teleology and context, or to the classification of the ethics of this institution as an ethics of virtue. My central point here is that this discussion of the teleology of copyright is explicitly *moral*, and, while it is very much teleological, any discussion that purports to reduce this teleology to merely acontextual, economic terms will miss much, if not most, of its richness and import.[37] It will in effect short-circuit the teleology of the institution.

As I have noted already, the copyright tradition – comprised of statutes, norms and doctrine – is best characterised by the notion of balance. While a fundamental statute such as the Copyright Act in the United States, the UK or Canada remains the ultimate basis for action, leading cases and the fundamental underlying principles enunciated therein also form part of the underlying normativity of copyright. It is also true that foundational ideas such as the goals that copyright is meant to serve, like the promotion of the arts, learning, literature and creativity, generally enshrined in seminal copyright documents like the Statute of Anne and the US Constitution, and often applied directly and indirectly, forming part of the hermeneutics of copyright, also play a large role in our understanding of copyright's normativity. Equally true and emanating from all of the above is that ideas of fairness – to authors and users – form part of copyright's context. Transcendent values, such as the promotion of knowledge, are part of copyright's core. Sharing and friendship, long-standing virtues in ethics, are increasingly seen to be important to the explanation of current internet practices, as is evident in social networking and the Wiki as cultural phenomena.

So, while much of copyright is formal – i.e. contained in legislation, codes and case law – a great deal is also informal, captured in the discourse surrounding copyright. These normative standards simply cannot be ignored, as they inform much of our understanding of what we must do as individual agents seeking to come to terms with lacunae, contradictions and other ambiguities in the formal normativity of statutes and cases. It mirrors the Aristotelian discussion of *epikeia* in the *Ethics*.[38]

[37] Indeed, this might very well be the *ethical* problem with the Digital Millennium Copyright Act of 1998 (Pub L No 105–304, 112 Stat 2860) and other copyright-plus or paracopyright initiatives: they depart quite markedly from the traditional teleology of copyright.

[38] In the *Nicomachean Ethics*, Book V, ch. 10, Aristotle uses the example of equity filling gaps in the general statements of the law:

ii. The context of copyright: 'copynorms'

In order to truly understand the potential for and the impact of an ethics of virtue, one needs to understand more fully the impact that the context of copyright has on normativity. Scholars have more recently come to understand the importance of the complexities of legal pluralism and in particular the role that informal norms play in our everyday lives.[39] These norms are powerful, and indeed are often more powerful than formal law. The burgeoning literature on 'social norms', by writers such as Richard McAdams, Lior Strahilevitz, Dan M. Kahan and Mark Schultz, has expanded the understanding and scope of application of the role and power of informal normativity.[40] The 'emerging picture', to paraphrase Schultz, of the role of social norms is a powerful one, in which laws influence the content of social norms by 'expressing' or articulating the law, and which also underscores the role – even the primary role – that informal social norms have in ensuring compliance with the law. Social norms can even replace the law, where gaps exist,[41] or establish different default rules.[42] These social norms have a number of sources – religious, philosophical, commercial, etc. – with a variety of means of inculcation.[43] Their normative power or punch gives them legitimacy. Finally, in characterising the source and nature of such social norms, Robert Cialdini has

> The reason is that all law is universal, and there are some things about which one cannot speak correctly in universal terms. . . . And this is the very nature of what is equitable – a correction of law, where it is deficient on account of its universality.

Nicomachean Ethics, R. Crisp (trans. and ed.) (Cambridge University Press, 2000), p. 100 (1137b–1138a).

39 R. A. Macdonald, *Lessons of Every Day Law/Le droit du Quotidian* (Montreal-Kingston: McGill-Queen's University Press, 2002); R. C. Ellickson, *Order Without Law: How Neighbors Settle Disputes* (Cambridge, Mass.: Harvard University Press, 1991).

40 See generally, R. H. McAdams, 'The Origin, Development, and Regulation of Norms' *Michigan Law Review* 96 (1997) 338; Schultz, 'Copynorms: Copyright Law and Social Norms', 309; L. Strahilevitz, 'Charismatic Code, Social Norms, and the Emergence of Cooperation on the File-Swapping Networks' *Virginia Law Review* 89 (2003) 505; and D. M. Kahan, 'The Logic of Reciprocity: Trust, Collective Action, and Law' *John M. Olin Center for Studies in Law, Economics, and Public Policy Working Papers* (2002), Paper 281. I am generally following the structure of Mark Schultz's argument in the following paragraphs.

41 As I have argued generally in Lametti, 'How Virtue Ethics Might Help Erase C-32's Conceptual Incoherence', 309.

42 I often use the example of overhanging tree branches under the Quebec Civil Code: art. 985 states that a neighbour may request an owner to cut overhanging branches that seriously obstruct the neighbour's use, or compel the owner to do so. The social norm in practice, widely followed, is that the neighbour simply has the tree trimmed himself and, only where serious, bills the owner. See Civil Code of Quebec, S.Q. 1991, c.64, art. 985.

43 See R. McAdams and E. B. Rasmussen, 'Norms and the Law', in A. M. Polinsky and S. Shavell (eds.), *The Handbook of Law and Economics* (North-Holland: Amsterdam, 2007). Virtue ethics, in my view, is a strong candidate for helping to understand *and regulate* copyright questions, especially as regards music.

usefully characterised norms as 'descriptive' (how one perceives others' actual behaviour) or 'injunctive' (how one perceives how others believe that one ought to behave).[44] Injunctive norms require an internalised sense of morality or some group influence or pressure, while descriptive norms are strong cues read or imitated from the group. One follows the first type because they feel that they ought to because the norms are right, or because of a feared punishment. One follows the second type out of conformity or imitation.

As regards copyright, what I suppose is best described as a sub-concept of social norms – 'copynorms' – has been used to describe this phenomenon of informal normativity. Mark Schultz and Lawrence Solum have popularised the word copynorms, as regards the congeries of informal norms, both descriptive and injunctive, that characterise copyright.[45] Their importance needs to be understood and recognised:

> There is no reason to believe that social norms affect copyright less than any other type of law. In fact, social norms may be more important to understanding copyright law than most other laws. Copyright is largely a private right. Therefore, copyright owners may choose whether and how to enforce their rights – a choice that often is influenced by social norms. Even when copyright owners do choose to enforce their rights, however, their efforts are often easy to elude. In many situations, copyright infringement is difficult to detect. The user's choice whether to comply with copyright is also often influenced by social norms. Copynorms thus greatly influence how copyright is enforced and observed.[46]

Schultz lists a number of examples of both injunctive and descriptive norms in the context of copyright. Among those injunctive norms explicitly articulated and consciously advocated are the Creative Commons movement, ethical limits and conventions on the understanding of plagiarism, open source and free software movements, library norms, hacker norms and warez[47] trading norms. Examples of descriptive norms identifying social practices that are prevalent and consistent enough to inform behaviour include search engine indexing and archiving, email replying and forwarding, blogger norms, format and time shifting, and file sharing. In all cases, these practices amounting to social norms often involve some type of copyright infringement in formal legal terms, but are otherwise

[44] R. B. Cialdini, C. A. Kallgren and R. R. Reno, 'A Focus Theory of Normative Conduct: A Theoretical Refinement and Reevaluation of the Role of Norms in Human Behavior' *Advances in Experimental Social Psychology* 24 (1991), 201, available at http://psp.sagepub.com/content/26/8/1002.

[45] L. Solum, 'The Future of Copyright' (Review of L. Lessig, *Free Culture*) *Texas Law Review* 84 (2005) 1137; Schultz, 'Copynorms: Copyright Law and Social Norms', 201.

[46] *Ibid.*, 5. [47] That is, illegal copies of computer software.

justified by an accepted internal ethic (i.e. in the injunctive norms category) or are simply widely done (i.e. in the descriptive norms category).

Most would likely place music file sharing in the realm of what Schultz calls 'descriptive' copynorms: 'Everyone else is doing it, so why can't we?' to borrow a phrase from a once popular Irish rock band. Lior Strahilevitz has argued that file-sharing software has facilitated such descriptive normativity.[48] Schultz points out that the record industry's media blitzes that drew attention to the prevalence of file sharing activity, while condemning it, effectively further entrenched the descriptive norm.[49]

In my view, the copynorms of music file sharing may very well be more than descriptive. I wish to suggest that virtue ethics, as regards music, and notwithstanding Schultz's partial counter-example,[50] moves music file sharing from the descriptive ('everyone is doing it') to the injunctive ('why it is acceptable'). That is to say that within the very understanding of both copyright and music, in its formal and informal normativity, is a set of ethical arguments that justifies the practice – the virtue, if you will – of sharing music files. This must be done by returning to the ethical discourse underlying copyright and its interaction with music, and using the insights of copynorms.

iii. Sharing music

There are two dynamics, necessarily intertwined and most definitely contextual, which are both present in a virtue ethics understanding of music file sharing. The first dynamic pushes us to try to understand the particular virtues served by music file sharing, while the second, related dynamic points to specific characteristics of music which amplify, for lack of a better expression, the virtue aspects of the relation.[51]

What virtues might be fostered, served, enhanced, strived for, or perfected by the sharing of music files? Deeply embedded within the Anglo-American

[48] Calling the software 'charismatic code': see Strahilevitz, 'Charismatic Code, Social Norms, and the Emergence of Cooperation on the File-Swapping Networks', 505.

[49] Schultz, 'Copynorms: Copyright Law and Social Norms', 228.

[50] Of 'jambands' such as the Grateful Dead and Phish, in which certain kinds of uses and sharing are deemed socially acceptable by the band and users, while others not. The ethic is one of reciprocity: see M. F. Schultz, 'Fear and Norms and Rock and Roll: What Jambands Can Teach Us About Persuading People to Obey Copyright Law' *Berkeley Technology Law Journal* 21 (2006) 651.

[51] Effectively mirroring my own property analysis and methodology of looking at the property relation and what specific particularities the object of the relation might bring back to the relation, i.e. as a filter for that relation: see D. Lametti, 'The Concept of Property: Relations *through* Objects of Social Wealth' *University of Toronto Law Journal* 53 (2003) 325.

copyright tradition is the idea that creativity and the promotion of knowledge were important goals to be served. This discussion has traditionally focused on creativity, but as pointed out above, knowledge and education are being increasingly recognised as part of this 'creative' function.[52] Moreover, the proper understanding is much more rich or 'thick' than a merely instrumental reading of the goals of copyright; rather, we focus on all aspects of the educative, knowledge-imparting and expressive creative act. The sharing of files most certainly assists this process.

This is particularly true when one factors the discourse of the public domain into the knowledge-generating, creativity equation. The public domain is comprised of ideas which are not the subject matter of copyright protection, including the commonplace manifestation of standard ideas such as archetypes, *scènes-à-faire*, etc., as well as fixed expressions of ideas whose protection has expired. It represents the vast area of knowledge and creativity which forms the basis for all future expression and creativity. Scholars of the public domain have exhorted us to care for that resource, as we would any other valuable resource. This too, then, would be a virtue, and sharing music (as opposed to putting it under lock and key through an access-inhibiting digital lock, for example) might well be a virtuous way of enhancing creativity and knowledge.

Similarly, the nature of music creation involves being inspired by and borrowing from the previous stock of musical expression in the public domain. Sampling is only the most recent form of the borrowing of previously written musical expression, as common to Haydn (who borrowed from Mozart) to Jay-Z (who borrowed from the Beatles) or Danger Mouse (who mashed both the Beatles and Jay-Z). How much poorer we would be had this stringent, overly rights-based view of copying and copyright currently espoused in certain music industry quarters prevailed when classical composers borrowed from each other, or much later when rock and roll borrowed from gospel, hillbilly and blues music.[53]

Sharing itself is a virtue with a long pedigree tracing back to Aristotle. Sharing is meant to enrich all parties, and, in the Aristotelian picture, the sharing of private property was meant to enhance friendship and foster

[52] Especially by Madison, 'Beyond Creativity: Copyright as Knowledge Law', 817; and Fisher, 'The Implications of Law of User Innovation', 1473; and, I suppose, by me.

[53] As Madison points out, van Gogh quite literally copied paintings from French realist painter Millet, adding colour and 'impression'. In his letters to his brother Theo, he called the process 'translation'. Are we to call van Gogh a copyright infringer? We are much better off for this 'translation'. See Madison, 'Beyond Creativity: Copyright as Knowledge Law', 835–42. For a view of the paintings in question, see www.vggallery.com/influences/millet/main.htm. My thanks to both Michael Madison and Adam La France for providing the pictorial record for Madison's (and van Gogh's) narrative.

generosity.[54] Indeed, while private property was 'private in possession', it was to be 'common in use'. As I have argued elsewhere, the 'common in use' points to a notion of destination or vocation for the resource, and here the creation of new works and education – knowledge function of sharing fits well within the Aristotelian picture.[55]

So perhaps the strongest ethical arguments are contextual, combining the virtues of sharing with the overall teleology of creativity and the fostering of knowledge and education. In favour of some forms of music sharing are those that point to the way in which listening to music helps to inspire new forms of music. In some cases, blatant copying is part of the picture: think of the digital sampling and re-mixing that leads to new musical creations. New works are made, with or without audible recognition of the sampled original. At bottom, this process is really no different than the way in which music was borrowed, was copied, or had provided inspiration in the past, except that one can now take exact samples and need not replay the music on new instruments; in effect, the computer is the instrument.[56] Any changes can be brought to the sample at any point. The fact of the matter is that much new music is created here, and, ethically, one can argue that one has not really done anything different than in the past when one borrowed a riff or a chord structure – often note for note – from another group. Indeed, the reality of what has changed in the digital world is not the borrowing itself, but rather that the borrowing is literal and the original group now has the ability to trace its music more effectively (and demand a fee with a greater chance of success). One might even argue that this is the logical extension or progression of the technology that made recorded music a commodity in the first place.[57]

I am mindful, as well, of a powerful argument that copyright rights, and the stringent enforcement of them, actually stifle creativity.[58] The misunderstanding, exaggeration and misinterpretation of copyright's rights channels and inhibits the creation of new work by hindering borrowing and duplication, necessary components of the creative process. The formal normativity of copyright is too cumbersome to adapt to new methods of creation and expression, forcing this form of creative activity to law's

[54] See Lametti, 'The Objects of Virtue', 1. [55] *Ibid.*

[56] For example, Girl Talk; B. Gaylor, *RiP! A Remix Manifesto* (Canada: National Film Board, 2008), www.nfb.ca/film/rip_a_remix_manifesto/.

[57] I thank Ian Dahlman for suggesting this point.

[58] See J. Demers, *Steal this Music: How Intellectual Property Law Affects Musical Creativity* (Athens, Ga.: University of Georgia Press, 2006); K. McLeod, *Freedom of Expression®: Overzealous Copyright Bozos and Other Enemies of Creativity* (New York: Doubleday, 2004), esp. ch. 2; and S. Vaidhyanathan, *Copyrights and Copywrongs: The Rise of Intellectual Property and How It Threatens Creativity* (New York University Press, 2001).

shadows. Here, copynorms might arise to help foster new work and legitimate it. Strict enforcement of rights, or even attempted compliance with rights, can be costly and further chill creative impulses and methods. Such arguments, recognising the realities of power politics and societal influence, further legitimate sharing in service of expression and creativity. Indeed, the fact that record labels are now routinely allowing other artists from other labels to sample their music in a form of reciprocal permission as among labels is in and of itself an emerging social norm that recognises the creativity of sampling. This perhaps also explains why Girl Talk, labelled a 'pirate' by many and with extraordinary visibility in the sampling world, has never been sued: what he does is acceptable by social norms, and, indeed, most creative.

Another contextual consideration, the social nature of music – metaphorically music is the object of the copyright relation, and mediates the relationship between creator and audience – also points to virtues in sharing. Here the focus is on the relationships fostered by music, the emotions it evokes and the bonds of attachment and memory that it fosters. One might also add to the kinds of virtues that human action attempts to foster through sharing: friendship, sociality and socialisation.

Music has a social function.[59] My children listen to music, and interact with their friends (and, I must add, their parents – they are now dragging me to concerts) through music. Like their parents did, they, too, listen to music together, as often as not sharing an ear-bud as opposed to listening to an LP or CD (and tapes) in a friend's basement or in a car. Indeed, in my experiences, the car is one of the places where one still listens to music with others, and satellite radio is helping to maintain this shared space. It is also true that the act of giving the cassette tape was a gift, as was the time and effort made to select and record the music – the mix-tape – for a friend.[60] So, as my generation made cassette tapes, a younger generation (and indeed, older people as well) shares files on their MP3 players. The main difference is that in previous generations, the original record was bought by someone: a parent, an older sibling, or a friend thrice removed. Now it is simply downloaded from a bit torrent site. Whatever the source, this sharing, it seems to the lay observer (and parent), is a kind of socialisation and is a necessary part of adolescence

[59] See generally, A. P. Merriam, *The Anthropology of Music* (Evanston, Ill.: Northwestern University Press, 1964).

[60] Think of English author Nick Hornby's superb novel, *High Fidelity*, in which the central character makes mix-tapes for the purposes of 'courtship' (London: Riverhead, 2000). I thank Ian Dahlman for reminding me of this.

(and beyond). I would argue that this virtue of sharing and fostering of friendship is a strong counterweight to legal impediments to sharing.

There is even a naturalistic basis for this social function: Dan Levitin has written that our brains are hard-wired for music, and part of its impact is social, as one might see with its link to dancing, for example.[61] The brain (modern or pre-modern) needs music and has a special, physical place reserved for it. Again, this points to a developmental desirability, if not necessity, to have access to and for the sharing of music, and the kind of file sharing that goes on does at least serve this purpose.

All of this points to ethical considerations of human development and flourishing (social and individual), of copyright's role in that flourishing, and of the particularities of the context of copyright as applied to music, that point to a strong argument in favour of an injunctive copynorm as regards music file sharing. Everyone is doing it, and it is not necessarily theft, piracy or even wrong; it may be beneficial to one's emotional and social development, and thus justified, ethical and virtuous. And even in most 'illegal' manifestation, piracy can have beneficial effects, often being a creative force behind artistic and scientific (and social) progress.[62]

Of course, Aristotelian ethics import their own limits – it is, after all, about finding a mean – and the same is true here. Hence, none of the above means that all kinds of copying should be allowed. Obviously, if one takes a substantial part of a song or most of it, especially when taken for economic purposes – whether using analogue or digital technology, or simply re-playing the music – one should have to pay a licensing fee to the copyright holder. And we should consider downloading for non-creative purposes: the adolescent who is a serial uploader and downloader, but never pays a cent for music and merely uploads to make it available to strangers and downloads at will. To some extent, some of the virtue arguments apply (sharing knowledge, friendship, creating, inspiring, etc.), as do the (non-) market arguments (would not have bought anyway). It is also true that torrent communities do provide a service that is simply unavailable elsewhere, mainly for copyright-protection reasons: they provide easy access to just about any piece of music ever recorded, the universal jukebox.[63]

[61] D. J. Levitin, *This is Your Brain on Music: The Science of a Human Obsession* (New York: Dutton, 2006).

[62] A. Johns, *Piracy: The Intellectual Property Wars from Gutenberg to Gates* (University of Chicago Press, 2009). A similar argument has been made in the larger context of property reform: E. M. Peñalver and S. K. Katyal, *Property Outlaws: How Squatters, Pirates and Protesters Improve the Law of Ownership* (New Haven, Conn.: Yale University Press, 2010).

[63] See, e.g., the history of OiNK: www.demonbaby.com/blog/2007/10/when-pigs-fly-death-of-oink-birth-of.html.

That being said, it is still equally true that some of this music was also bought and paid for in the past, so the free downloading is by some measure unfair. Aristotelian ethics allow one to criticise or condemn this person and offer up a better contextual understanding of the ethics of the act of copying. These correctives will be offered to change behaviour. (As a parent, this is what I try to do all the time.) It may even be so over-the-top that legal action is warranted, although my experience is that the informal pressure and normativity will work a whole lot more effectively and efficiently. Surely this has greater potential to channel behaviour than legal action against file sharers.

It is important to note the role that the normativity of copyright – formal and informal – plays in allowing us the ethical stance from which to judge fairness or condemn the unethical. In the Aristotelian structure, some will be less than ethical and will never 'get it'. Education, the example of the virtuous, legal norms and rules, standards and possibly even threat of legal action, all continue to play a role in helping individuals understand their ethical choices.[64]

So, in the end, the ethic of virtue means that, as a user, you ought to deal with all musical works 'fairly', using the various copyright norms as your guide – not only the works in which you are claiming a fair dealing right, but in all works. As a result, if you are in the habit of sampling music in order to decide what music you will later purchase, that practice is ethically justifiable, as one might have done with a cassette in the past; but, in my view, you have to purchase enough music to justify your sampling. In the same vein, if you are sampling to create, then you have to create and, in turn, be willing to share what you have created to some extent.[65] If you do purchase you should be able to expect, whatever the licence agreement,[66] that you can make a copy for your kids, your brother and your best friend in a format that is compatible to your hardware. This, in my view, is the way that it has always been. Digital locks should not be able to prevent that. Clearly, there are no bright-line answers to questions such as what constitutes 'enough

[64] I thank Magda Woszczyk for pressing me on this point.

[65] Bill C-32 incorporates a non-commercial, user-generated content exception, reinforcing formally what informally is virtuous or ethical.

[66] In my view, in ethical terms, purchasing a copy of a work and thus remunerating the creator/right-holder might give the owner of the purchased copy additional moral weight in making ethical decisions to make copies, or do other acts with the copied work: lend it to a friend, make a back-up, alter the material support, etc. This is evidenced by the first-sale doctrine in Anglo-American copyright. A licence, on the other hand, being more limited, might ground less extensive rights, although making a back-up copy of software purchased by licence seems to me to be completely ethical. Again, I suppose context is determinative: is the work normally purchased or licensed?

music', how you 'create', or who is a 'best friend', but context should help determine appropriate answers in any given circumstance.

To this might be added Geert Demuijnck's economic analysis about the at times unethical nature of the record companies, and the imperfections of the market, as further fodder for the injunctive copynorm that is justified as regards music file sharing. I would add that sharing has always aided creators, even in the pure economics of the market. The recorded music market was dependent on a less-than-perfect, anti-copying and performance regime for free publicity. I doubt the DJs at my college pubs and dances in the 1980s and 1990s paid for all their recorded music or paid any sort of licensing fee for what they played, but I heard and bought a whole lot of (sometimes life-changing) recorded music based on what they played. Ditto for recorded tapes and burned CDs from friends, later from nieces and nephews, and finally from students. Back then there was still conventional radio for new music, where a tariff is indeed paid, but these forms of dissemination have been overtaken by sharing on the web, through MySpace and other social networking sites, YouTube, etc. Without some forms of sharing and 'leakage', everyone loses out financially. This has always been the case.

Finally, one might also add a gloss to Demuijnck's economic analysis of the nature of the record companies by noting what one might call the 'ethics of protest' or 'ethics of objection'. Here, downloading music is seen as an act of civil disobedience in protest against the economic and political power of larger music interests as a result of previous perceived bad behaviour as 'middlemen', or as a means to weaken their economic or political power in the present and future. This might be linked to the idea already identified of trying to change normativity by working on the informal, given that access to the political levers of change as regards formal normativity is beyond the reach or the means of the protesting group. It is sometimes done in the name of helping musical artists. So here the ethical decisions are made in the name of doing what is perceived to be right and virtuous.

The actions of copyright holders must also be assessed under the light of this approach. As the copynorms analysis makes clear, these ethical and social norms apply not only to users (in sharing), but to copyright holders in understanding, applying and enforcing their rights (say, in deciding whether or not to use digital locks).[67] In the context of music, in light of what has been said above, one wonders whether a copyright

[67] As I have argued in Lametti, 'How Virtue Ethics Might Help Erase C-32's Conceptual Incoherence', 309.

holder ought ever, *ethically*, to impose a digital lock that restricts access to the musical work, or its copying and sharing for the legitimate purposes identified above.[68]

So, ethically, a copyright holder ought to consider the object of protection – recorded music – before imposing limits. Music sharing helps to advance creativity, it enriches the public domain and inspires others to create in turn. It is in some sense the foundation for a continued transmission of culture and knowledge. Its sharing serves to develop other social virtues. Others might reasonably be expected to want to deal fairly in order to re-create and format shift. And the development of the musical artefact owes its origins to adaptation from the public domain or the pool of creative knowledge. Hence, my strong ethical intuition is that one should *never* put up a digital barrier or fence around music, whatever the law might allow, but rather, trust the traditional balances of copyright to balance the interest of the right holder and users or society.

Here the analogy to concepts such as the American doctrine of copyright misuse,[69] as seen above, or the concept of *abus de droit* in civil law,[70] is appropriately drawn. One's right does not allow a person to exercise that right in any conceivable fashion.[71] In all such cases the exercise of the right must be undertaken to foster the overall purposes or teleology of the statute, in the case of copyright misuse, or of both a civil law norm and the larger normative order, in the case of civil law. Misuse

[68] Given the effectively temporary nature of digital fences (all locks can be picked, all fences can be breached) and the persistence of hacking, one wonders if this inevitability would cause anyone ever to opt for a fence, incurring development costs and occasionally the scorn of its customer base. Certain elements of the music industry have begun to understand this and have tried to work around the digital age by developing new business models. Such is the case especially after the Sony 'Rootkit fiasco', where many consumers and artists reacted quite strongly against such measures: see 'Sony's Rootkit Fiasco' *CNET News* (November 2005), news.cnet.com/Sonys-rootkit-fiasco/2009–1029_3–5961248.html; and J. F. deBeer, 'How Restrictive Terms and Technologies Backfired on Sony BMG' *Internet and E-Commerce Law in Canada* 6 (2005–6) 93. A number of these models are based on sharing, user interaction, or both. Some artists simply want their music to be heard, tolerating and even encouraging sharing. Profit can be found in other aspects of the business, even including some sale of recorded music. This seems to me to be a virtuous approach. It may also end up being profitable, especially for artists.

[69] See generally Judge, 'Rethinking Copyright Misuse', 901: in her view, any attempt by a copyright holder effectively to expand the purview of copyright protection to gain control over an idea or deter fair use constitutes misuse. See also D. L. Burk, 'Anti-Circumvention Misuse' *UCLA Law Review* 50 (2003) 1095.

[70] See, e.g., in Quebec, Civil Code of Quebec, S.Q. 1991, c.64, art. 6.

[71] One may call upon the tradition of analytic philosophy to make a similar point. See, e.g., Judith Jarvis Thomson's analysis, coming to the conclusion that rights are not absolute and that holding a right does not mean that one can exercise it in all cases: J. J. Thomson, *The Realm of Rights* (Cambridge, Mass.: Harvard University Press, 1990), 'Introduction' at p. 4, and chs. 3–4. I thank Annabelle Lever for reminding me of this.

or abuse of the right undermines the very principles upon which the right holder's rights are grounded. Hence, all are to exercise their rights in good faith. Moreover, these doctrines focus on action, target standards of behaviour, and are contextual in terms of their specific substantive understanding and application within a given set of circumstances. And, in a very real sense, none of these doctrines or the principles underlying them is foreign to copyright law: thanks to international treaties[72] on copyright, the civil law of *droit d'auteur* is part of our copyright tradition in Canada, and we are closely linked to our American cousins in terms of Anglo-American copyright doctrine and practice.[73] In short, there is no good reason to seal hermetically Anglo-American copyright from principles that are already familiar and that focus on virtuous behaviour.

Finally, in light of the changing remuneration model in the music industry, I believe that there is an ethical duty (based on the aspiration to be fair) to explore, consider and support other models for artists. The old industry business model for recorded music – a small group of record labels with artists signed to them, giving exclusive rights to the label, and allowing the label to market for them – is drawing to an end. It has lasted around fifty years,[74] with its banner years from the sixties to the nineties and especially this last decade when many customers repurchased works in digital form on CD at a price point much higher than production cost. As with other industrial revolutions, a series of technologies brought the old model to its knees. Artists are already beginning to use social networking and other distribution models for the dissemination of and remuneration for their works.[75] This decline is as much a

[72] For example, Berne Convention, art. 6bis on moral rights.

[73] Indeed, while there is an easy case to be made on the ethical threads present in the Quebec Civil Law, familiar to many Canadians, the argument is increasingly being pitched in the common law tradition as well; see Lametti, 'Laying Bare an Ethical Thread: From IP to Property to Private Law?'.

[74] See J. Sterne, 'Is Music a Thing?', in his *MP3: The Meaning of a Format* (Durham, NC: Duke University Press, forthcoming).

[75] Of course, the now standard example is Radiohead's initial sale of *In Rainbows* directly over the Internet – if memory serves, I paid £ 7 sterling – but there are numerous other examples from a variety of sources: see, e.g., S. Frere-Jones, 'The Dotted Line: What do Record Labels do now?' *The New Yorker* (16 and 23 August 2010), 92 (discussing bands Arcade Fire and Vampire Weekend and their respective independent labels, Merge Records and XL Recordings, that have used alternative business models from the outset, including social networking and grass-roots marketing). At McGill, the Faculties of Law, Management and Music over the past four years, have mounted a course focused precisely on developing new business models for remunerating artists, many of which have been focused on educating consumers and social networking. It is hoped some of these solutions will find their way to the industry-sector market and governance policies.

cause for celebration – many artists were not, to put it euphemistically, well dealt-with under the old model – as it is a cause for mourning. Yet, there is no doubt that some artists and people previously employed in the industry are suffering.

Virtue ethics address this situation as well. In my view, it is simply unethical for consumers not to seriously consider and perhaps even actively support some form of remuneration model, such as a tax or tariff on Internet Service Providers,[76] or hardware that puts money back into the hands of artists and value-adding persons in the recorded music industry through donations.[77] There is no shortage to the solutions that some applied (virtuous) good faith and intellectual diligence will unearth.

Finding the mean

The context of music file sharing is far from black and white, and simply defies labels such as 'theft', 'piracy' and 'free riding'. Rather, the ethics of copyright in its teleology and foundational discourses, and its balancing doctrines, displays a number of contextually dependent determinations which are better understood as being in part governed by virtue. Moreover, the informal normativity of copynorms provides not only a descriptive example of normativity, but also a powerful type of injunctive normativity that explains and is seen as binding by a community of adherents: here, virtue informs and justifies certain types of file sharing. Finally, the specific context of music file sharing paints a picture in which file sharing ought to be understood.

All of this points us to the aspirational morality of copyright and its application to music. Here we seek to articulate and understand the determination of what is 'fair' and 'just', 'balanced' and 'virtuous', eschewing facile labels. Thankfully, copyright's traditional discourses already point in this direction: this chapter has attempted only to bring these under a better light. In this sense, this aspirational morality is by no means unrealistic. It is certainly no less unrealistic than trying to stop music file sharing through lawsuits or piracy publicity!

[76] See, e.g., N. W. Netanel, 'Impose a Noncommercial Use Levy to Allow Free Peer-to-Peer File Sharing' *Harvard Journal of Law and Technology* 17 (2003) 1. Available at ssrn.com/abstract=468180 or doi:10.2139/ssrn.468180; and Terry Fisher's and Paul Hoffert's *noankmedia* project (tariff models): cyber.law.harvard.edu/research/noankmedia.

[77] For voluntary schemes, see, e.g., Litman, 'Sharing and Stealing', 1; and L. Helman, 'Pass the Hat: Voluntary Payment as a Complementary Model for Music Copyright' (23 August 2010), available at ssrn.com/abstract=1664034.

Music file sharing is a phenomenon that is widespread, and likely enduring. In this context, it is not only legitimate, but also desirable to rely on an ethics of virtue to lead us through the process of finding the right balances – the just mean of virtue – for norms governing the sharing of music files to be reflected in both formal and informal normativity.

Bibliography

Academy of Medical Science and Royal Academy of Engineering, *Systems Biology: A Vision for Engineering and Medicine* (London: AMS and RAE, 2007)

Adler, M., 'Stardom and Talent' *American Economic Review* **75** (1985): 208–12

Advocacy Project, 'On the Record – The Rio Negro Campaign' 11 (no. 5, 17 April 2000)

Amos, M., *Genesis Machines: The New Science of Biocomputing* (London: Atlantic Books, 2006)

Anderson, E., *Value in Ethics and Economics* (Cambridge, Mass.: Harvard University Press, 1995)

Anon., 'Forum on Synthetic Biology' *BioSocieties* **4**(2–3) (2008): 273–4

Appiah, K. A., *The Ethics of Identity* (Princeton University Press, 2005)

Aristotle, *Nicomachean Ethics* (trans. and ed. R. Crisp) (Cambridge University Press, 2000)

Arneson, R., 'The Principle of Fairness and Free-Rider Problems' *Ethics* **92** (1982): 616–33

Attas, D., 'Fragmenting Property' *Law and Philosophy* **25** (2006): 119–49

'Lockean Justifications of Intellectual Property' in A. Gosseries, A. Marciano and A. Strowel (eds), *Intellectual Property and Theories of Justice* (New York and London: Palgrave Macmillan, 2008)

Austin, L., 'Privacy and the Question of Technology' *Law and Philosophy* **22**(2) (2003): 119

Australian Law Reform Commission, *Genes and Ingenuity: Gene Patenting and Human Health* (Report 99) (2004)

Avise, J. C., *Inside the Human Genome: A Case for Non-Intelligent Design* (New York: Oxford University Press, 2010)

Aybar, S., Harlan, J. and Lee, W., 'John Rawls: For The Record' *Harvard Review of Philosophy* **1** (1991): 38–48, at 45. Online at www.hcs.harvard.edu/~hrp/issues/1991/Rawls.pdf

Bagley, M., 'Patent First, Ask Questions Later: Morality and Biotechnology in Patent Law' *William and Mary Law Review* **45**(2) (2003): 469

Baker, D., Church, G., Collins, J., Endy, D., Jacobson, J., Keasling, J., Modrich, P., Smolke, C. and Weiss, R. (The Bio Fab Group), 'Engineering Life: Building a FAB for Biology' *Scientific American* June (2006): 34–9

Balganesh, S., 'The Pragmatic Incrementalism of Common Law Intellectual Property' *Vanderbilt Law Review* **63**(6) (2010): 1564

Ball, P., *Critical Mass: How One Thing Leads to Another* (London: William Heinemann, 2004)

Banerjee, A., Hollis, A. and Pogge, T., 'The Health Impact Fund: Incentives for Improving Access to Medicines' *Lancet* **375** (2010): 166–9

Barclay, L., 'Autonomy and the Social Self', in C. Mackenzie and N. Stoljar, *Relational Autonomy: Feminist Perspectives on Autonomy, Agency and the Social Self* (New York: Oxford University Press, 2000), pp. 52–71

Barder, O., Kremer, M., Levine, R. and Albright, A., *Making Markets for Vaccines: From Ideas to Actions* (Washington DC: Center for Global Development, 2005)

Barendt, E., *Freedom of Speech* (Oxford University Press, 2005)

Barron, A., 'Kant, Copyright and Communicative Freedom' *Law and Philosophy* **30**(1) (2012): 1–48

Bartlett, K., 'Feminist Legal Methods' *Harvard Law Review* **103** (1990): 829

Basheer, S. (with Purohit, S. and Reddy, P.), 'The *Ordre Public* and Morality Exclusions', in L. Bently *et al.*, *Exclusions from Patentability and Exceptions and Limitations to Patentee's Rights – A Study prepared for the World Intellectual Property Organisation* (Geneva: WIPO, 2010), Annex I

Bechtel, W., *Discovering Cell Mechanisms: The Creation of Modern Cell Biology* (New York: Cambridge University Press, 2006)

Becker, L., *Property Rights: Philosophical Foundations* (New York: Routledge, 1981)

Beebe, B., 'An Empirical Study of U.S. Copyright Fair Use Opinions, 1978–2005' *University of Pennsylvania Law Review* **156**(3) (2008): 549–624

Beitz, C., 'The Moral Rights of Creators of Artistic and Literary Works' *Journal of Political Philosophy* **13**(3) (2005): 330–58

Benhabib, S. and Dallmayr, F., *The Communicative Ethics Controversy* (Cambridge, Mass.: MIT Press, 1990)

Bentham, J., *Rights, Representation, and Reform – Nonsense upon Stilts and Other Writings on the French Revolution*, Philip Schofield, Catherine Pease-Watkin and Cyprian Blamires (eds) (Oxford: Clarendon Press, 2002)

Bently, L., Sherman, B., Boges Barbosa, D., Basheer, S., Visser, C. and Gold, R., *Exclusions from Patentability and Exceptions and Limitations to Patentee's Rights – A Study prepared for the World Intellectual Property Organisation* (Geneva: WIPO, 2010)

Bently, L., Davis, J. and Ginsburg, J. (eds), *Trade Marks and Brands: An Interdisciplinary Critique* (Cambridge University Press, 2008)

Bently, L. and Sherman, B., *Intellectual Property Law* (2nd edn., Oxford University Press, 2005)

Beyleveld, D. and Brownsword, R., *Mice, Morality and Patents* (London: CLIIP, 1993)

Bird, R. C., 'Developing Nations and the Compulsory License: Maximizing Access to Essential Medicines while Minimizing Side-effects' *Journal of Law, Medicine and Ethics* **37**(2) (2009): 209

Birnhack, M., 'A Quest for a Theory of Privacy: Context and Control' *Jurimetrics: The Journal of Law, Science and Technology* **51**(4) (2011): 514

Blackstone, W., *Commentaries on the Laws of England*, in H. Broom and E. Hadley (eds) (London, William Maxwell & Son, Henry Sweet, and Stevens & Son, 1869, 1st pub. 1766)

Blair, R. and Cotter, T., *Intellectual Property. Economic and Legal Dimensions of Rights and Remedies* (Cambridge University Press, 2005)

Borghi, M., 'Copyright and Truth' *Theoretical Inquiries in Law* **12**(1) (2011): 1–27

'Owning Form, Sharing Content: Natural-Right Copyright and Digital Environment', in F. Macmillan (ed.), *New Directions in Copyright Law* (Cheltenham: Edward Elgar Publishing, 2007), vol. V

and Karapapa, S., 'Non-Display Uses of Copyright Works: Google Books and Beyond' *Queen Mary Journal of Intellectual Property* **1**(1), (2011): 21

Boxill, B., 'A Lockean Argument for Black Reparations' *Journal of Ethics* **7** (2003): 63–91

Boyle, J., *The Public Domain: Enclosing the Commons of the Mind* (New Haven, Conn. and London: Yale University Press, 2008)

Bratman, M., *Structures of Agency: Essays* (New York: Oxford University Press, 2007)

'Breakthrough Accord Could Bring Reparations for Guatemala Massacre Survivors', *NowPublic*, 3 (December 2008)

Brennan, G. and Pettit, P., 'The Feasibility Issue' in F. Jackson and M. Smith (eds), *The Oxford Handbook of Contemporary Philosophy* (Oxford University Press, 2005), pp. 258–79

Brooke, J. H., 'Wöhler's Urea and the Vital Force – A Verdict from the Chemists' *Ambix* **15** (1968): 84–114

Science and Religion: Some Historical Perspectives (Cambridge University Press, 1991)

Brown, W., 'Suffering Rights as Paradoxes' *Constellations: An International Journal of Critical and Democratic Theory* 7(2) (2000): 208–29

Buchanan, A., Cole, T. and Keohane, R. O., 'Justice in the Diffusion of Innovation' *Journal of Political Philosophy* **19**(3) (2011): 306–32

Burk, D. L., 'Anti-Circumvention Misuse' *UCLA Law Review* **50** (2003): 1095

and Lemley, M., 'Policy Levers in Patent Law' *Virginia Law Review* **89**(7) (2003): 1575–696

Burrell, R. and Coleman, A., *Copyright Exceptions: The Digital Impact* (Cambridge University Press, 2005)

Butler, J., *Excitable Speech: A Politics of the Performative* (New York: Routledge, 1997)

Gender Trouble: Feminism and the Subversion of Identity (New York: Routledge, 1990)

Butt, D., *Rectifying International Justice: Principles of Compensation and Restitution Between Nations* (Oxford University Press, 2009).

Calvert, J., 'Synthetic Biology: Constructing Nature?' *The Sociological Review* **58**(1) (2010): 95–112

Cane, P., 'Corrective Justice and Correlativity in Private Law' *Oxford Journal of Legal Studies* **16** (1996): 471–88

Capurro, R., 'Das Internet und die Grenzen der Ethik', in M. Rath (ed.), *Medienethik und Medienwirkungsforschung* (Weidebaden: Westdeutscher Verlag, 2000), pp. 105–26

Carignan, M., 'Analogical Reasoning in Victorian Historical Epistemology' *Journal of the History of Ideas* **64**(3) (2003): 445–64

Cello, J., Paul, A. V. and Wimmer, E., 'Chemical Synthesis of Poliovirus cDNA: Generation of Infectious Virus in the Absence of Natural Template' *Science* **297** (2002): 1016–18

Christman, J., *The Myth of Property: Towards an Egalitarian Theory of Ownership* (New York: Oxford University Press, 1994)

(ed.), *The Inner Citadel: Essays on Individual Autonomy* (New York: Oxford University Press, 1989)

'Distributive Justice and the Complex Structure of Ownership' *Philosophy and Public Affairs* **23**(3) (1994): 225–50

The Politics of Persons: Individual Autonomy and Socio-Historical Selves (Cambridge University Press, 2009)

'Autonomy in Moral and Political Philosophy', in E. Zalta (ed.), *The Stanford Encyclopedia of Philosophy* (2003) (http://plato.stanford.edu/contents.html)

'Autonomy, Self-Knowledge, and Liberal Legitimacy', in J. Christman and J. Anderson (eds), *Autonomy and the Challenges to Liberalism: New Essays* (Cambridge University Press, 2005), pp. 330–57

'Saving Positive Freedom' *Political Theory* **33**(1) (2005): 79–88

Cialdini, R. B., Kallgren, C. A., and Reno, R. R., 'A Focus Theory of Normative Conduct: A Theoretical Refinement and Reevaluation of the Role of Norms in Human Behavior' *Advances in Experimental Social Psychology* **24** (1991): 201–34, available at http://psp.sagepub.com/content/26/8/1002

Cohen, A. I., 'Compensation for Historic Injustices: Completing the Boxill and Sher Arguments' *Philosophy and Public Affairs* **37** (2009): 81–102

Cohen, J. 'Procedure and Substance in Deliberative Democracy', in S. Benhabib (ed.), *Democracy and Difference* (Princeton University Press, 1996)

'Deliberation and Democratic Legitimacy', in J. Bohman and W. Rehg (eds), *Deliberative Democracy* (Cambridge, Mass.: MIT Press, 2002), pp. 67–92

Philosophy, Politics and Democracy (Cambridge, Mass.: Harvard University Press, 2009)

and Rogers, J., *Associations and Democracy* (London: Verso, 1995)

Cook, C., *Patents, Profits & Power: How Intellectual Property Rules the Global Economy* (London: Kogan Page, 2002)

Copp, D., 'Social Unity and the Identity of Persons' *The Journal of Political Philosophy* **10**(4) (2002): 365–91

Couzin, J., 'Active Poliovirus Baked from Scratch' *Science* **297** (2002): 174–5

Cowen, T., 'Discounting and Restitution' *Philosophy and Public Affairs* **26** (2006): 165–85

Crager, J. and Price, M., 'Prizes and Parasites: Incentive Models for Addressing Chagas Disease' *Journal of Law, Medicine and Ethics* **37**(2) (2009): 292–304

Crespi, S., 'Biotechnology Patenting: The Wicked Animal Must Defend Itself' *European Intellectual Property Review* **17**(9) (1995): 431

Crews, K. D., 'Fair Use of Unpublished Works: Burdens of Proof and the Integrity of Copyright' *Arizona State Law Journal* **31** (1999): 1

Crisp, R. and Slote, M. (eds), *Virtue Ethics* (Oxford University Press, 1997)

Crittenden, J., *Beyond Individualism: Reconstituting the Liberal Self* (New York: Oxford University Press, 1992)

Cronin, L., Krasnogor, N., Davis, B. G., Alexander, C., Robertson, N., Steinke, J. H. G., Schroeder, S. L. M., Khlobystov, A. N., Cooper, G., Gardner, P. M., Siepmann, P., Whitaker, B. J. and Marsh, D., 'The Imitation Game – A Computational Chemical Approach to Recognizing Life' *Nature Biotechnology* **24** (2009): 1203–6

Cullity, G., 'Moral Free Riding' *Philosophy and Public Affairs* **24** (1995): 3–34

Dagan, H., *The Law and Ethics of Restitution* (Cambridge University Press, 2004)

Davies, P., *The Origin of Life* (London: Penguin, 1999)

Dawkins, R., *The Selfish Gene* (30th ann. edn, Oxford University Press, 2006)

De Beer, J. F., 'How Restrictive Terms and Technologies Backfired on Sony BMG' *Internet and E-Commerce Law in Canada* **6**(12) (2005–6): 93

Deazley, R., *On the Origin of the Right to Copy: Charting the Movement of Copyright Law in Eighteenth-Century Britain (1695–1775)* (Oxford and Portland, Oreg.: Hart Publishings, 2004)

Deligiorgi, K., *Kant and the Culture of Enlightenment* (Albany, NY: State University of New York Press, 2005)

Demers, J., *Steal this Music: How Intellectual Property Law Affects Musical Creativity* (Athens, Ga.: University of Georgia Press, 2006)

Demuijnck, G., 'Is P2P Sharing of MP3 Files an Objectionable Form of Free Riding?', in A. Gosseries, A. Marciano and A. Strowel (eds), *Theories of Justice and Intellectual Property* (Basingstoke: Palgrave Macmillan, 2008), ch. 7, pp. 141–59

Descartes, R., 'Treatise on Man', in S. Gaukroger (ed.), *The World and Other Writings* (Cambridge University Press, 1998)

Dittmar, H. 'Meanings of Material Possessions as Reflections of Identity: Gender and Social-Material Position in Society' in F. W. Rudmin (ed.), 'To Have Possessions: A Handbook on Ownership and Property', Special Issue *Journal of Social Behavior and Personality* **6**(6) (1991): 165–86

Dogan, S. L. and Lemley, M. A., 'The Merchandising Right: Fragile Theory or *Fait Accompli*?' *Emory Law Journal* **54** (2005): 461

Donnelly, D., Cohen, J. and Rogers, J., *Money and Politics (The New Democracy Forum)* (Boston: Beacon Press, 1999)

Drassinower, A., 'A Rights-based View of the Idea/Expression Dichotomy' *Canadian Journal of Law and Jurisprudence* **16** (2003): 3–23

'Sweat of the Brow, Creativity, and Authorship: On Originality in Canadian Copyright Law' *University of Ottawa Law & Technology Journal* **1** (2004): 105

'Taking User Rights Seriously', in M. Geist (ed.), *In the Public Interest: The Future of Canadian Copyright Law* (Toronto: Irwin Law, 2005), pp. 462–79

'Authorship as Public Address: On the Specificity of Copyright vis-à-vis Patent and Trade-mark' *Michigan State Law Review* (2008): 199–232

'From Distribution to Dialogue: Remarks on the Concept of Balance in Copyright Law' *Journal of Corporation Law* **34**(4) (2009): 992–1007

'Canadian Originality: Notes on a Judgment in Search of an Author', in Y. Gendreau (ed.), *An Emerging Intellectual Property Paradigm: Perspectives from Canada* (Cheltenham: Edward Elgar Publishers, 2009), pp. 139–62

'Exceptions Properly So-Called', in Y. Gendreau, and A. Drassinower (eds), *Language and Copyright* (Brussels: Yvon Blais/Carswell and Bruylant, 2009), pp. 205–38

'The Art of Selling Chocolate: Remarks on Copyright's Domain', in M. Geist (ed.), *From 'Radical Extremism' to 'Balanced Copyright': Canadian Copyright and the Digital Agenda* (Toronto: Irwin Law, 2010), pp. 121–50

'A Note on Incentives, Rights and the Public Domain in Copyright Law' *Notre Dame Law Review* **86** (2011): 1869

Dutfield, G., *Intellectual Property Rights and the Life Science Industries: Past, Present and Future* (Singapore: World Scientific, 2009)

'Who Invents Life – Blind Watchmakers, Intelligent Designers or Genetic Engineers?' *Journal of Intellectual Property Law and Practice* **5**(7) (2010): 531–40

Dworkin, G., *The Theory and Practice of Autonomy* (Cambridge University Press, 1988)

Dworkin, R., *Sovereign Virtue: The Theory and Practice of Equality* (Cambridge, Mass.: Harvard University Press, 2000)

Economist, 'Drowning in Data' 26 June 1999, 97–8

Einhorn, M., *Media, Technology and Copyright. Integrating Law and Economics* (Cheltenham: Edward Elgar, 2004)

Ellickson, R. C., *Order Without Law: How Neighbors Settle Disputes* (Cambridge, Mass.: Harvard University Press, 1991)

Engelbrekt, A. B., 'Institutional and Jurisdictional Aspects of Stem Cell Patenting in Europe (EC and EPO): Tensions and Prospects', in A. Plomer and R. Torremans (eds), *Embryonic Stem Cell Patents: European Law and Ethics* (Oxford University Press, 2009), ch. 9

ETC Group, *Extreme Genetic Engineering: An Introduction to Synthetic Biology* (January 2007), available at www.etcgroup.org

European Commission Directorate-General for Research, *Synthetic Biology: A NEST Pathfinder Initiative* (Brussels: European Commission, 2007)

Feinberg, J., *Harmless Wrongdoing (The Moral Limits of the Criminal Law)* (Oxford University Press, 1990)

Finkin M. W., 'Employee privacy, American Values and the Law' *Chicago-Kent Law Review* **72** (1996–7): 221–69

Fischer, J. M. and Ravizza, M., *Responsibility and Control: A Theory of Moral Responsibility* (New York: Cambridge University Press, 1998)

Fisher, T. and Hoffert, P., *Noankmedia* project, http://cyber.law.harvard.edu/research/noankmedia

Fisher, W., 'Theories of Intellectual Property', in S. Munzer (ed.), *New Essays in the Legal and Political Theory of Property* (Cambridge University Press, 2001), pp. 168–200

Fisher, W. W. III, 'The Implications of Law of User Innovation' *Minnesota Law Review* **94** (2010): 1417 at 1463 ff

Flickschuh, K., *Kant and Modern Political Philosophy* (Cambridge University Press, 2000)

Formigari, L., 'Chain of Being', in P. P. Wiener, *The Dictionary of the History of Ideas: Studies of Selected Pivotal Ideas. Vol. I* (New York: Charles Scribner's Sons, 1973–4), pp. 326–36

Frank, R. and Cook, P. J., 'It's a Winner-Take-All Market – Top Money goes to Top Performing People or Products' *Washington Monthly* (December 1995)

Freeman, S., *The Cambridge Companion to Rawls* (Cambridge University Press, 2003)

Frere-Jones, S., 'The Dotted Line: What do Record Labels do Now?' *The New Yorker*, 16/23 August 2010, 92.

Friedel, R., *A Culture of Improvement: Technology and the Western Millennium* (Cambridge, Mass. and London: MIT Press, 2007)

Friedman, M., *Autonomy, Gender, Politics* (Oxford University Press, 2003)

Frischmann, B. M., 'Spillovers Theory and Its Conceptual Boundaries' *William and Mary Law Review* **51** (2009): 801

Fuller, L. L., *The Morality of Law* (New Haven, Conn.: Yale University Press, 1969)

Furby, L., 'Understanding the Psychology of Possession and Ownership: A Personal Memoir and an Appraisal of our Progress', in F. W. Rudmin (ed.), 'To Have Possessions: A Handbook on Ownership and Property', Special Issue, *Journal of Social Behavior and Personality* **6**(6) (1991): 457–6

Gamow, G., 'Information Transfer in the Living Cell' *Scientific American* **193** (1955): 70–8

Gaukroger, S., 'Introduction', in S. Gaukroger (ed.), *The World and Other Writings* (Cambridge University Press, 1998)

Gauthier, D., *Morals by Agreement* (Oxford: Clarendon Press, 1986)

Gaylor B., *RiP! A Remix Manifesto*, National Film Board, Canada, 2008

Geddes, L., 'Rewriting Life in Four-letter Words' *New Scientist*, 20 February 2010: 14

Geller, P. E., 'A German Approach to Fair Use: Test Cases for TRIPs Criteria for Copyright Limitations' *Journal of the Copyright Society of the U.S.A.* **57** (2010): 553

'Beyond the Copyright Crisis: Principles for Change' *Journal of the Copyright Society of the U.S.A.* **55** (2008): 165

Ghosh, S., 'When Property is Something Else: Understanding Intellectual Property Through the Lens of Regulatory Justice', in A. Gosseries, A. Marciano and A. Strowel (eds), *Intellectual Property and Theories of Justice* (Basingstoke: Palgrave Macmillan, 2008), pp. 106–21

Gibbs, W. W., 'Synthetic Life' *Scientific American* (May 2004): 75–81

Gibson, D. G., Glass, J. I., Lartigue, C., Noskov, V. N., Chuang, R.-Y., Algire, M. A., Benders, G. A., Montague, M. G., Ma, L., Moodie, M. M., Merryman, C., Vashee, S., Krishnakumar, R., Assad-Garcia, N., Andrews-Pfannkoch, C., Denisova, E. A., Young, L., Qi, Z.-Q., Segall-Shapiro, T. H., Calvey, C. H., Parmar, P. P., Hutchison III, C. A., Smith, H. O. and Venter, J. C., 'Creation of a Bacterial Cell controlled by a Chemically Synthesized Genome' *Science* **329** (2010): 52–6

Gitter, D., 'Led Astray by the Moral Compass: Incorporating Morality into European Union Biotechnology Patent Law' *Berkeley Journal of International Law* **19** (2001): 1

Gordon, W., 'Harmless Use: Gleaning from Fields of Copyrighted Works' *Fordham Law Review* 77(5) (2009): 2411–35

'An Inquiry into the Merits of Copyright: The Challenges of Consistency, Consent and Encouragement Theory' *Stanford Law Review* **41** (1989): 1343–69

'A Property Right in Self-Expression: Equality and Individualism in the Natural Law of Intellectual Property' *Yale Law Journal* **102** (May 1993): 1533–609

and Watt, R. (eds), *The Economics of Copyright: Developments in Research and Analysis* (Cheltenham: Edward Elgar, 2003)

Gosseries, A., Marciano, A. and Strowel, A. (eds), *Intellectual Property and Theories of Justice* (New York and London: Palgrave Macmillan, 2008)

Gray, J., *Post-Liberalism: Studies in Political Thought* (London: Routledge, 1993)

Greaves, T., 'The Intellectual Property of Sovereign Tribes' *Science Communication* **17** (1995): 203

Greenhalgh, T. and Russell, J., 'Evidence-Based Policymaking: A Critique' *Perspectives in Biology and Medicine* **52**(2) (2009): 304–18

Gregor, M. (ed.), *Immanuel Kant: The Conflict of the Faculties* (University of Nebraska Press, 1979)

The Cambridge Edition of the Works of Immanuel Kant: Practical Philosophy (Cambridge University Press, 1996)

Griffiths, P. E., 'Genetic Information: A Metaphor in Search of a Theory' *Philosophy of Science* **68** (2001): 394–412

Grubb, P. and Thomsen, P., *Patents for Chemicals, Pharmaceuticals and Biotechnology* (5th edn, Oxford University Press, 2010)

Guyer, P. (ed.), *The Cambridge Edition of the Works of Immanuel Kant: Critique of the Power of Judgement* (Cambridge University Press, 2000)

Habermas, J., *Between Facts and Norms* (Cambridge, Mass.: MIT Press, 1996)

Handa, S. *Copyright Law in Canada* (Markham: Butterworths, 2002)

Hanson, M. J., 'Religious Voices in Biotechnology: The Case of Gene Patenting' *The Hastings Center Report: Special Supplement* 27(6) (1997)

Hardin, G., 'The Tragedy of the Commons. The Population Problem has no Technical Solution; it requires a Fundamental Extension in Morality' *Science* **162**(3859) (1968): 1243–8

Hawkes, N. and Cohen, D., 'What makes an Orphan Drug?' *British Medical Journal* **341** (2010): c6459

Haworth, L., *Autonomy: An Essay in Philosophical Psychology and Ethics* (New Haven, Conn.: Yale University Press, 1986)

Hayek, F., 'The Use of Knowledge in Society' *American Economic Review* **35** (1945): 519–30

Hegel, G. W. F., *The Phenomenology of Spirit* (trans. A. V. Miller) (Oxford University Press, 1977)

Heinemann, M. and Panke, S., 'Synthetic Biology – Putting Engineering into Biology' *Bioinformatics* **22** (2006): 2790–9

Heller, M., 'The Tragedy of the Anticommons: Property in the Transition from Marx to Markets' *Harvard Law Review* **111**(3) (1998): 621–88

and Eisenberg, R. S., 'Can Patents Deter Innovation? The Anticommons in Biomedical Research' *Science* **280**(5364) (1998): 698–701

Hellstadius, A., 'A Comparative Analysis of the National Implementation of the Directive's Morality Clause', in A. Plomer and P. Torremans (eds), *Embryonic Stem Cell Patents: European Law and Ethics* (Oxford University Press, 2009)

Helman, L., 'Pass the Hat: Voluntary Payment as a Complementary Model for Music Copyright', 23 August 2010, available at ssrn.com/abstract=1664034

Hendry, J., *Reclaiming Culture: Indigenous People and Self-Representation* (New York: Palgrave Macmillan, 2005)

Hettinger, E., 'Justifying Intellectual Property' *Philosophy and Public Affairs* **18** (1989): 31–52

Heymann, L. A., 'Everything is Transformative: Fair Use and Reader Response' *Columbia Journal of Law and the Arts* **31** (2008): 445

Hobbes, T., *Leviathan, Or The Matter, Forme, & Power of a CommonWealth Ecclesiasticall and Civill* (London: Penguin, 1985, 1st pub. 1651)

Holland, D., Lachiocotte, W., Skinner, D. and Cain, C., *Identity and Agency in Cultural Worlds* (Cambridge, Mass.: Harvard University Press, 1998)

Hollis, A. and Pogge, T., *The Health Impact Fund: Making New Medicines Accessible to All* (Incentives for Global Health, 2008)

Honneth, A., *The Struggle for Recognition: The Moral Grammar of Social Conflicts* (Cambridge, Mass.: MIT Press, 1996)

Honoré, A. M. A., 'Ownership' in A. Guest (ed.), *Oxford Essays in Jurisprudence* (Oxford: Clarendon Press, 1961), pp. 107–47

Hooke, R., *Micrographia: Or some Physiological Descriptions of Minute Bodies Made by Magnifying Glasses with Observations and Enquiries Thereupon* (London: John Martyn and James Allestry, 1664). The relevant section of this work is: Observ. XVIII, *Of the Schematisme or Texture of Cork, and of the Cells and Pores of some other such frothy Bodies.*

Horkheimer, M. and Adorno, T. W., 'Kulturindustrie', in their *Dialektik der Aufklärung. Philosophische Fragmente* (Frankfurt: Fischer Verlag, 1944 7 [1st published in English 1972]), pp. 108–50

Hornby, N., *High Fidelity* (London: Riverhead, 2000)

Hubbard, F. P., ' "Do Androids Dream?" Personhood and Intellectual Artefacts' (2010) at http://ssrn.com/abstract=1725983, Last visited 15 January 2011

Hughes, J., 'Copyright and Incomplete Historiographies: Of Piracy, Propertization and Thomas Jefferson' *Southern California Law Review* **79** (2006): 993–1082

Hughes, T. P., *American Genesis: A Century of Invention and Technological Enthusiasm, 1870–1970* (New York: Viking, 1989)

Hunter, G. K., *Vital Forces: The Discovery of the Molecular Basis of Life* (London and San Diego: Academic Press, 2000)

Hursthouse, R., *On Virtue Ethics* (Oxford University Press, 1999)

Jacob, R., 'Foreword', in C. Ng, W., L. Bently and G. D'Agostino (eds), *The Common Law of Intellectual Property: Essays in Honour of Professor David Vaver* (Oxford and Portland, Oreg.: Hart Publishing, 2010)

Jefferson, T., 'Letter to Isaac McPherson' (13 August 1813), in A. E. Bergh (ed.), *The Writings of Thomas Jefferson* (Washington DC: The Thomas Jefferson Memorial Association of the United States, 1907), vol. XIII, pp. 333–5. Also available at http://etext.lib.virginia.edu/toc/modeng/public/JefLett.html

Johns, A., *Piracy: The Intellectual Property Wars from Gutenberg to Gates* (University of Chicago Press, 2009)
'The Piratical Enlightenment', in C. Siskin and W. Warner (eds), *This Is Enlightenment* (University of Chicago Press, 2010), pp. 301–20
Johnston, B. R., *Chixoy Dam Legacies. Social Commitments and Resettlement Obligations: Promises, Actions, Consequential Damages, and Community Needs* (Center for Political Ecology, 17 March 2005), 5 vols
'Chixoy Dam Legacies: The Struggle to Secure Reparations and the Right to Remedy in Guatemala' *Water Alternatives* **3**(2) (2010): 341–61
Judge, K., 'Rethinking Copyright Misuse' *Stanford Law Review* **57** (2004): 901
Kahan, D. M., 'The Logic of Reciprocity: Trust, Collective Action, and Law', *John M. Olin Center for Studies in Law, Economics, and Public Policy Working Papers* (2002), Paper 281
Kamm, F. M., *Intricate Ethics: Rights, Responsibilities, and Permissible Harm* (Oxford University Press, 2007)
Kant, I., 'On the Wrongfulness of Unauthorized Publication of Books', in Mary J. Gregor (trans. and ed.), *The Cambridge Edition of the Works of Immanuel Kant: Practical Philosophy* (Cambridge University Press, 1996), pp. 23–35
'The Metaphysics of Morals', in Mary J. Gregor (trans. and ed.), *The Cambridge Edition of the Works of Immanuel Kant: Practical Philosophy* (Cambridge University Press, 1996), pp. 353–603
'What is a Book?', in Mary J. Gregor (trans. and ed.), *The Cambridge Edition of the Works of Immanuel Kant: Practical Philosophy* (Cambridge University Press, 1996), pp. 437–9
Katz, L., 'A Jurisdictional Principle of Abuse of Right' (8 February 2010), ssrn.com/abstract=1417955
'The Economics of Intellectual Property Rights' *International Review of Law and Economics* **13** (1993): 337–48
Kay, L. E., *Who Wrote the Book of Life? A History of the Genetic Code* (Stanford University Press, 2000)
Keasling, J., 'Synthetic Biology in Pursuit of Inexpensive, Effective Anti-malarial Drugs' *BioSocieties* **4**(2–3) (2009): 275–82
Keller, E. F., 'What does Synthetic Biology have to do with Biology?' *BioSocieties* **4** (2–3) (2009): 291–302
Kennedy, D., 'The Stakes of Law, or Hale and Foucault!' *Legal Studies Forum* **15** (1991): 327–65
Kershnar, S., 'The Inheritance-Based Claim to Reparations' *Legal Theory* **8** (2002): 243–67
Khan, B. Z., *The Democratisation of Invention: Patents and Copyrights in American Economic Development, 1790–1920* (Cambridge University Press, 2005)
Kitano, H., 'Systems Biology: A Brief Overview' *Science* **295** (2008): 1662–4
Kloc, J., 'Scientists Develop a Visual Language for Mapping Biological Systems that They Hope Will Become "the Circuit Diagrams of Biology"' *Seed Magazine*, 28 Sept. 2009, http://seedmagazine.com/content/article/blueprinting_biology/P1/
Kremer, M. and Glennerster, J., *Strong Medicine: Creating Incentives for Pharmaceutical Research in Neglected Diseases* (Princeton University Press, 2004)

Kymlicka, W., *Liberalism, Community and Culture* (Oxford: Clarendon Press, 1989)

Multicultural Citizenship: A Liberal Theory of Minority Rights (Oxford: Clarendon Press, 1995)

Laddie, H., 'Patents – What's Invention Got to Do With It?', in David Vaver and Lionel Bently (eds), *Intellectual Property in the New Millenium: Essays in Honour of William R. Cornish* (Cambridge University Press, 2004), p. 94

Lakoff, G. and Johnson, M., *Metaphors We Live By* (Chicago University Press, 1980)

Lametti, D., 'The Concept of Property: Relations *through* Objects of Social Wealth' *University of Toronto Law Journal* **53** (2003): 325

'The Concept and Conceptions of Intellectual Property as seen through the Lens of Property', in G. Comandé and G. Ponzanelli (eds), *Scienza e Diritto nel Prisma del Diritto Comparato* (Torino: Giappichelli, 2004), p. 269, available at ssrn.com/abstract=1758894

'The Morality of James Harris's Theory of Property', in T. Endicott, J. Getzler and E. Peel (eds), *The Properties of Law: Essays in Honour of James Harris* (Oxford University Press, 2006) vol. 164, n. 44, available at ssrn.com/abstract=1758880

'How Virtue Ethics Might Help Erase C-32's Conceptual Incoherence', in M. Geist (ed.), *From 'Radical Extremism' to 'Balanced Copyright': Canadian Copyright and the Digital Agenda* (Toronto: Irwin Law, 2010), p. 309

'The Objects of Virtue' in G. S. Alexander and E. M. Peñalver (eds), *Property and Community* (New York: Oxford University Press, 2010), p. 1, available at ssrn.com/abstract=1758859

'Laying Bare an Ethical Thread: From IP to Property to Private Law?', in S. Balganesh (ed.), *Intellectual Property and the Common Law* (forthcoming)

Landes, W. and Posner, R., *The Economic Structure of Intellectual Property Law* (Cambridge, Mass.: Harvard University Press, 2003)

'An Economic Analysis of Copyright Law' *Journal of Legal Studies* (1989): 325

Lanjouw, J., 'Patents, Price Controls and Access to New Drugs: How Policy affects Global Market Entry', Center for Global Development, Working Papers, No. 61

Larmore, C., *The Morals of Modernity* (New York: Cambridge University Press, 1996)

Laurie, G., 'Patents, Patients and Consent: Exploring the Interface between Regulation and Innovation Regimes', in H. Somsen (ed.), *The Regulatory Challenge of Biotechnology: Human Genetics, Food and Patents* (Cheltenham: Edward Elgar 2007)

Leader, S., *Freedom of Association: A Study in Labour Law, and Political Theory* (New Haven, Conn.: Yale University Press, 1992)

Lear, J., *Radical Hope: Ethics in the Face of Cultural Devastation* (Cambridge, Mass.: Harvard University Press, 2006)

Lehavi, A., *The Dynamic Law of Property: Theorizing the Role of Legal Standards* (2010) available at ssrn.com/abstract=1618768

Lemley, M., 'The Modern Lanham Act and the Death of Common Sense' *Yale Law Journal* **108** (1999): 1687

'Property, Intellectual Property and Free Riding' *Texas Law Review* **83** (2005): 1031–75

'What's Different About Intellectual Property?' *Texas Law Review* **83** (2005): 1097–104

Lessig, L., *The Future of Ideas: The Fate of the Commons in a Connected World* (New York: Vintage, 2002)

Free Culture (New York: Penguin, 2004)

Lever, A., 'The Politics of Paradox: A Response to Wendy Brown' *Constellations: An International Journal of Critical and Democratic Theory* 7(2) (2000): 242–54

'Is It Ethical To Patent Human Genes?', in A. Gosseries, A. Marciano and A. Strowel (eds.), *Theories of Justice and Intellectual Property* (New York and Basingstoke: Palgrave Macmillan, 2008), ch. 12, pp. 246–64

'Compulsory Voting: A Critical Perspective' *British Journal of Political Science* **40**(4) (2010): 897–915

On Privacy (London: Routledge, 2011)

Levitin, D. J., *This is Your Brain on Music: The Science of a Human Obsession* (New York: Dutton, 2006)

Liebowitz, S., 'Back to the Future: Can Copyright Owners Appropriate Revenue in the Face of New Copying Technologies?', in W. Gordon and R. Watt (eds), *The Economics of Copyright* (Cheltenham: Edward Elgar, 2003), pp. 1–25.

Lijphart, A., *Thinking About Democracy: Power Sharing and Majority Rule in Theory and Practice* (New York: Routledge, 2007)

Litman, J., 'The Public Domain' *Emory Law Journal* **39** (1990): 965

'Breakfast with Batman: The Public Interest in the Advertising Age' *Yale Law Journal* **108** (1999): 1717

Digital Copyright (New York: Prometheus Books, 2001)

'Sharing and Stealing' *Hastings Communication and Entertainment Law Journal* **27** (2004): 1

Locke, J., *Two Treatises of Government* (Cambridge University Press, 2008)

Lok, L., 'Software for Signaling Networks, Electronic and Cellular' *Science's Signal Transduction Knowledge Environment* **122** (2002): PE11

Love, J. and Hubbard, T., *The Big Idea: Prizes to Stimulate R&D for New Medicines*, KEI Research Paper 2007

Lovejoy, A. O., *The Great Chain of Being: A Study of the History of an Idea.* (Cambridge, Mass.: Harvard University Press, 1936)

Lucretius, *De Rerum Natura (Of the Nature of Things)* (trans. W. E. Leonard). Downloaded from Project Gutenberg Website

Macdonald, R. A., *Lessons of Every Day Law/Le droit du Quotidian* (Montreal-Kingston: McGill-Queen's University Press, 2002)

Mackenzie, C. and Stoljar, N. (eds), *Relational Autonomy: Feminist Perspectives on Autonomy, Agency, and the Social Self* (New York: Oxford University Press, 2000)

Madison, M. J., 'Beyond Creativity: Copyright as Knowledge Law' *Vanderbilt Journal of Law and Technology* **12** (2010): 817, available at ssrn.com/abstract=1599621

Mazzone, J., 'Copyfraud' *NYU Law Review* **81** (2006): 1026

McAdams, R. and Rasmussen, E. B., 'Norms and the Law', in A. M. Polinsky and S. Shavell (eds), *The Handbook of Law and Economics* (Amsterdam: North-Holland, 2007)

McAdams, R. H., 'The Origin, Development, and Regulation of Norms' *Michigan Law Review* **96** (1997): 338

McGrath, A., *Dawkins' God: Genes, Memes, and the Meaning of Life* (Malden: Blackwell, 2005)

McLeod, K., *Freedom of Expression®: Overzealous Copyright Bozos and Other Enemies of Creativity* (New York: Doubleday, 2004)

Maitland, I., 'Priceless Goods: How should Life-saving Drugs be Priced?' *Business Ethics Quarterly* **12**(4) (2002): 451–80

Mele, A. R., *Autonomous Agents: From Self-Control to Autonomy* (New York: Oxford University Press, 1995)

Merges, R., *Justifying Intellectual Property* (Cambridge, Mass.: Harvard University Press, 2011)

'Property Rights Theory and the Commons: The Case of Scientific Research' *Social Philosophy and Policy* **13** (1996): 145–67

Merriam, A. P., *The Anthropology of Music* (Evanston, Ill.: Northwestern University Press, 1964)

Meyers, D., 'Decentering Selfhood: Five Faces of Selfhood', in J. Christman and J. Anderson (eds), *Autonomy and the Challenges to Liberalism: New Essays* (Cambridge University Press, 2005), pp. 27–55

Meyers, D. T., *Self, Society and Personal Choice* (New York: Columbia University Press, 1990)

Mill, J. S., *A System of Logic, Ratiocinative and Inductive: Being a Connected View of the Principles of Evidence and the Methods of Scientific Investigation* (1843)

Principles of Political Economy: With Some of Their Applications to Social Philosophy (5th edn, London: Parker, Son, and Bourn, 1862)

Miller, E. and Feigenbaum, J., 'Taking the Copy Out of Copyright', in T. Sander (ed.), *DRM '01 Revised Papers from the ACM CCS-8 Workshop on Security and Privacy in Digital Rights Management* (London: Springer-Verlag, 2002), pp. 233–44

Mills, O., *Biotechnological Inventions: Moral Restraints and Patent Law* (Aldershot: Ashgate, 2005)

Mitchell, M., *Complexity: A Guided Tour* (New York: Oxford University Press, 2009)

Mitchell, S. D., *Unsimple Truths: Science, Complexity and Policy* (Chicago University Press, 2009)

Mithen, S., *The Prehistory of the Mind: A Search for the Origins of Art, Religion and Science* (London: Thames and Hudson, 1996)

Moore, M., 'Keeping Mum' *British Medical Journal* **334**(7595) (2007)

Morange, M., *A History of Molecular Biology* (Cambridge, Mass.: Harvard University Press, 1998)

Life Explained (New Haven, Conn.: Yale University Press, 2008)

Morris, C. W., 'Existential Limits to the Rectification of Past Wrongs' *American Philosophical Quarterly* **21** (1984): 175–82

Moufang, R. 'Patenting of Human Genes, Cells and Parts of the Body? – The Ethical Dimensions of Patent Law' *IIC* **25**(4) (1994): 487

Moyse, P. E., 'Kraft Canada c. Euro-Excellence: l'insoutenable légèreté du droit' *McGill Law Journal*, **53** (2008): 74, available at ssrn.com/abstract=1761002

Munzer, S. R., *A Theory of Property* (Cambridge University Press, 1990)

'The Special Case of Property Rights in Umbilical Cord Blood for Transplantation' *Rutgers Law Review* **51** (1999): 493–568

'Property as Social Relations', in S. Munzer (ed.), *New Essays in the Legal and Political Theory of Property* (Cambridge University Press, 2001), pp. 36–75

(ed.), *New Essays in the Legal and Political Theory of Property* (Cambridge University Press, 2001)

Munzer, S. R. and Chen Simon, P., 'Territory, Plants, and Land-Use Rights among the San of Southern Africa: A Case Study of Regional Biodiversity, Traditional Knowledge, and Intellectual Property' *William & Mary Bill of Rights Journal* **17** (2009): 831–94

Munzer, S. R. and Raustiala, K., 'The Uneasy Case for Intellectual Property Rights in Traditional Knowledge' *Cardozo Arts & Entertainment Law Journal* **27** (2009): 37–97

'Music Matters to New Anti-piracy Campaign', *The Guardian* 24 March 2010, www.guardian.co.uk/music/2010/mar/24/music-matters-anti-piracy-campaign

Nagel, T., 'The Problem of Global Justice' *Philosophy and Public Affairs* **33** (2007): 113–47

Narverson, J., 'Welfare and Wealth: Provision and Justice in Today's World' *Journal of Ethics* **8**(4) (2005): 305–48

Navarrete Pellicer, S., *Maya Achí Marimba Music in Guatemala* (Philadelphia: Temple University Press, 2005)

Nedelsky, J., 'Reconceiving Autonomy: Sources, Thoughts, and Possibilities' *Yale Journal of Law and Feminism* **1**(1) (1989): 7–36

'Law, Boundaries, and the Bounded Self' *Representations* **30** (1990): 162–89

Netanel, N., *Copyright's Paradox* (Oxford University Press, 2008)

Netanel, N. W., 'Impose a Noncommercial Use Levy to Allow Free Peer-to-Peer File Sharing' *Harvard Journal of Law and Technology* **17** (2003): 1, available at ssrn.com/abstract=468180 or doi:10.2139/ssrn.468180

'Copyright and a Democratic Civil Society' *Yale Law Journal* **106** (1996): 283–387

'Why has Copyright Expanded? Analysis and Critique', in F. Macmillan (ed.), *New Directions in Copyright Law* (Cheltenham: Edward Elgar, 2007), pp. 2–34

Neumann-Held, E. M., 'The Genetic Code: Foundation of Life or Heuristic Device' in Max Planck Inst. for the History of Science, *History and Epistemology of Molecular Biology and Beyond: Problems and Perspectives* (Berlin, 2006): pp. 141–9

Noble, D., *The Music of Life* (Oxford University Press, 2006)

Nozick, R., *Anarchy, State, and Utopia* (New York: Basic Books, 1974)

Nuffield Council on Bioethics, *The Ethics of Patenting DNA: A Discussion Paper* (London: NCOB, 2002)

Nussbaum, M., *Women and Human Development: The Capabilities Approach* (Cambridge University Press, 2001)

OiNK: www.demonbaby.com/blog/2007/10/when-pigs-fly-death-of-oink-birth-of.html

Olby, R., *Francis Crick: Hunter of Life's Secrets* (Cold Spring Harbor Laboratory Press, 2010)

O'Neill, O., 'Ethics for Communication?' *European Journal of Philosophy* **17**(2) (2009): 167

Autonomy and Trust in Bioethics (Cambridge University Press, 2002)

Constructions of Reason (Cambridge University Press, 1989)

Towards Justice and Virtue (Cambridge University Press, 1996)

'Kant on Reason and Religion', in G. Peterson (ed.), *The Tanner Lectures on Human Values* (Salt Lake City: University of Utah Press, 1997), pp. 267–308

'Autonomy, Plurality and Public Reason', unpublished manuscript on file with author

'Kant's Conception of Public Reason', unpublished manuscript on file with author

Oshana, M., *Personal Autonomy in Society* (Aldershot: Ashgate Publishing Ltd, 2006)

Ossorio, P., 'Legal and Ethical Issues in Patenting DNA', in J. Burley and J. Harris (eds), *A Companion to Genethics* (Oxford: Basil Blackwell, 2002), pp. 408–20

Ostrom, E., *Governing the Commons: The Evolution of Institutions for Collective Action* (Cambridge University Press, 1990)

Overland, G., 'The Right to do Wrong' *Law and Philosophy* **26** (2007): 377–404

Palsson, B., 'The Challenges of In Silico Biology' *Nature Biotechnology* **18** (2000): 1147–50

Parfit, D., *Reasons and Persons* (Oxford: Clarendon Press, 1984)

Parsons, S. D., 'Fair-Play Obligations: A Critical Note on Free Riding' *Political Studies* **53** (2005): 641–9

Payne, D. J., 'Desperately Seeking New Antibiotics' *Science* **321** (2008): 1644–5

Pekkarinen, J., Pohjolat, M. and Rowthorn, B., *Social Corporatism: A Superior Economic System (Wider Studies in Developmental Economics)* (Oxford: Clarendon Press, 1992)

Pellegrini Grinover, A., 'Brazil' *Annals of the American Academy of Political and Social Science* **622** (2009): 63–7

Peñalver, E. M. and Katyal, S. K., *Property Outlaws: How Squatters, Pirates and Protesters Improve the Law of Ownership* (New Haven, Conn.: Yale University Press, 2010)

Penner, J., *The Idea of Property in Law* (Oxford University Press, 2000)

Peterson, J., 'Liberalism and the Public Interest in Art', unpublished Ph.D. thesis, University of Toronto, 2008

Peterson, M., Hollis, A. and Pogge, T., 'A Critique in Need of Critique' *Public Health Ethics* **3**(2) (2010): 178–85

Petit, E., 'An Ethics Committee for Patent Offices?' in A. Plomer and P. Torremans (eds), *Embryonic Stem Cell Patents: European Law and Ethics* (Oxford University Press, 2009), ch. 11

Peukert, A., 'Why do "Good People" disregard Copyright on the Internet?', in C. Geiger (ed.), *Criminal Enforcement: A Blessing or a Curse for Intellectual Property*? (Cheltenham: Edward Elgar, 2010), available at ssrn.com/abstract=1660319

Phillips, A., *The Politics of Presence* (Oxford University Press, 1995)
Pievatolo, M. C., 'Publicness and Private Intellectual Property in Kant's Political Thought', in V. Rohden, R. R. Terra, G. A. de Almeida and M. Ruffing (eds), *Law and Peace in Kant's Philosophy* (Berlin: Walter de Gruyter, 2008), pp. 631–42
Pila, J., *The Requirement for an Invention in Patent Law* (Oxford University Press, 2010)
'Bound Futures: Patent Law and Modern Biotechnology' *Boston University Journal of Science and Technology Law* **9**(2) (2003): 326
Pink, D. H., *Drive: The Surprising Truth About What Motivates Us* (New York: Riverhead, 2009)
Plomer, A., 'Towards Systemic Legal Conflict: Article 6(2)(c) of the EU Directive on Biotechnological Inventions', in A. Plomer and P. Torremans (eds), *Embryonic Stem Cell Patents: European Law and Ethics* (Oxford University Press, 2009), ch. 7
'Human Dignity, Human Rights, and Article 6(1) of the EU Directive on Biotechnological Inventions' in A. Plomer and P. Torremans (eds), *Embryonic Stem Cell Patents: European Law and Ethics* (Oxford University Press, 2009), ch. 8
Plomer, A. and Torremans, P. (eds), *Embryonic Stem Cell Patents* (Oxford University Press, 2009)
Pogge, T., *World Poverty and Human Rights* (Cambridge: Polity Press, 2002)
'The Health Impact Fund: Better Pharmaceutical Innovations at Much Lower Prices', in T. Pogge, M. Rimmer and K. Rubenstein (eds), *Incentives for Better Global Public Health: Patent Law and Access to Medicines* (Cambridge University Press, 2010)
'Human Rights and Global Health: A Research Program' *Metaphilosophy* **36** (1–2) (2005): 182–209
World Poverty and Human Rights: Cosmopolitan Responsibilities and Reforms (2nd edn, Cambridge: Polity Press, 2008)
Polanyi, M., *Personal Knowledge: Towards a Post-Critical Philosophy* (Chicago University Press, 1962)
Popper, K., *The Poverty of Historicism* (London: Routledge, 1957)
Porter, G., 'Human Embryos, Patents and Global Trade: Assessing the Scope and Contents of the TRIPS Morality Exception', in A. Plomer and P. Torremans (eds), *Embryonic Stem Cell Patents: European Law and Ethics* (Oxford University Press 2009)
Posner, R., 'The Law and Economics of Intellectual Property' *Daedalus* (Spring 2002): 5–12
Pottage, A. and Sherman, B., *Figures of Invention: A History of Modern Patent Law* (Oxford University Press, 2010)
Powell, G. B., *Elections as Instruments of Democracy: Majoritarian and Proportional Visions* (New Haven, Conn.: Yale University Press, 2000)
Proudhon, P. P., *Les majorats littéraires. Examen d'un projet de loi ayant pour but de créer au profit des auteurs, inventeurs et artistes, un monopole perpétuel* (Brussels: Office de la publicité, 1862)
Radin, M. J., 'Property and Personhood' *Stanford Law Review* **34**(5) (1982): 957–1015, at 986

Reinterpreting Property (University of Chicago Press, 1993)

Contested Commodities: The Trouble with Trade in Sex, Children, Body Parts and Other Things (Cambridge, Mass.: Harvard University Press, 1996)

Raustiala, K. and Munzer, S. R., 'The Global Struggle over Geographic Indications' *The European Journal of International Law* **18**(2) (2007): 337–65

Ravvin, M., 'Incentivizing Access and Innovation for Essential Medicines: A Survey of the Problems and Proposed Solutions' *Public Health Ethics* **1**(2) (2008): 110–23

Rawls, J., *A Theory of Justice* (rev. edn, Oxford University Press, 1999)

Political Liberalism (New York: Columbia University Press, 1993)

Justice as Fairness: A Restatement (Cambridge, Mass.: Belknap Press, 2001)

Raz, J., *The Authority of Law: Essays on Law and Morality* (2nd edn, Oxford University Press, 2009)

The Morality of Freedom (Oxford: Clarendon Press, 1986)

Reiss, H. (ed.) and Nisbet, H. B. (trans.), *Kant: Political Writings* (Cambridge University Press, 1991)

Regner, T., 'Innovation of Music', in W. Gordon and R. Watt (eds), *The Economics of Copyright: Developments in Research and Analysis* (Cheltenham: Edward Elgar, 2003)

Resnik, D., *Owning the Genome: A Moral Analysis of DNA Patenting* (Albany: State University of New York, 2004)

Richards, D. A. J., 'Rights and Autonomy', in J. Christman (ed.), *The Inner Citadel: Essays on Individual Autonomy* (New York: Oxford University Press, 1989)

Richardson, H., *Practical Reasoning about Final Ends* (Cambridge University Press, 1994)

Ridley, D. B., Grabowski, H. G. and Moe, J. L., 'Developing Drugs for Developing Countries' *Health Affairs* **25**(2) (2006): 313–24

Rimmer, M., *Intellectual Property and Biotechnology: Biological Inventions* (Cheltenham: Edward Elgar, 2008)

Risser, R., 'Determinism, Creative Works and Proprietorship' *The Monist* **93**(3) (2010): 353

Ritvo, H., 'Possessing Mother Nature: Genetic Capital in eighteenth century Britain', in J. Brewer and S. Staves, *Early Modern Conceptions of Property* (London: Routledge, 1996), pp. 413–26

Romer, P., 'Endogenous Technical Change' *Journal of Political Economy* **98** (1998): 55–79

Rose, S., *Lifelines: Life Beyond the Gene* (London: Vintage, 2005)

The Making of Memory: From Molecules to Mind (London: Vintage, 2003)

Rosen, R., 'The Economics of Superstars' *American Economic Review* **71** (1981): 845–58

Rosenberg, A., 'On the Priority of Intellectual Property Rights, especially in Biotechnology' *Politics, Philosophy and Economics* **3**(1) (2004): 77–95

Royal Society, 'Innovative Mechanisms for Tackling Antibiotic Resistance' *RS Policy Document 14/08* (London: Royal Society, 2008)

Rubenfeld, J., 'The Freedom of Imagination: Copyright's Constitutionality' *Yale Law Journal* **112** (2002): 3–60

Ruse, M., *Science and Spirituality: Making Room for Faith in the Age of Science* (New York: Cambridge University Press, 2010)

Sag, M., 'Copyright and Copy-Reliant Technology' *Northwestern University Law Review* **103** (2009): 1607

Samuelson, P., 'The Story of *Baker v. Selden*: Sharpening the Distinction Between Authorship and Invention', in J. C. Ginsburg and R. C. Dreyfuss (eds), *Intellectual Property Stories* (New York: Foundation Press, 2006), pp. 159–193

'Why Copyright Law Excludes Systems and Processes from the Scope of Its Protection' *Texas Law Review* **85** (2007): 1921

Sandel, M. J., *Liberalism and the Limits of Justice* (Cambridge University Press, 1982)

Sarkar, S., 'Biological Information: A Sceptical Look at some Central Dogmas of Molecular Biology', in S. Sarkar (ed.), *The Philosophy and History of Molecular Biology: New Perspectives* (Dordrecht: Kluwer Academic Publishers, 1996), pp. 187–232

Satz, D., *Why Some Things Should Not Be For Sale: The Limits of Markets* (Oxford University Press, 2010)

Scanlon, T. M., 'Rights, Goals, and Fairness' *Erkenntnis* **11**(1) (1977): 81–95

Schrödinger, E., *What Is Life?* (Cambridge University Press, 1944)

Schultz, M. F., 'Copynorms: Copyright Law and Social Norms', in P. Yu (ed.), *Praeger's Intellectual Property and Information Wealth: Issues and Practices in a Digital Age* (London: Praeger Perspectives, 2006), vol. I, available at ssrn.com/abstract=933656

'Fear and Norms and Rock & Roll: What Jambands Can Teach Us About Persuading People to Obey Copyright Law' *Berkeley Technology Law Journal* **21** (2006): 651

Scott, D., Oliver, A. and Ley Pineda, M., 'Trade Marks as Property', in L. Bently, J. Davies and J. Ginsburg (eds), *Trade Marks and Brands: An Interdisciplinary Critique* (Cambridge University Press, 2008), pp. 285–306

Selgelid, M., 'A Full-Pull Program for the Provision of Pharmaceuticals: Practical Issues' *Public Health Ethics* **1**(2) (2008): 134–45

Sen, A., *Inequality Reexamined* (Cambridge University Press, 1992)

Development as Freedom (Oxford University Press, 2001)

'What do we Want from a Theory of Justice?' *The Journal of Philosophy* **103**(5) (2006): 215–38

Shaffer Van Houweling, M., 'Distributive Values in Copyright' *Texas Law Review* **83** (2005): 1535–79

Shapiro, C., 'Navigating the Patent Thicket: Cross Licenses, Patent Pools, and Standard Setting' *Innovation Policy and the Economy* **1** (2000): 119–50

Sher, G., 'Ancient Wrongs and Modern Rights' *Philosophy & Public Affairs*, **10** (1980): 3–17

'Three Grades of Social Involvement' *Philosophy and Public Affairs* **18**(2) (1989): 133–57

'Transgenerational Compensation' *Philosophy and Public Affairs* **33** (2005): 181–200

Shiffrin, S. V., 'The Incentives Argument for Intellectual Property Protection', in A. Gosseries, A. Marciano and A. Strowel (eds), *Intellectual Property and Theories of Justice* (London: Palgrave Macmillan, 2008), pp. 94–105

'Lockean Arguments for Private Intellectual Property', in S. R. Munzer (ed.) *New Essays in the Legal and Political Theory of Property* (Cambridge University Press, 2001)

Silbey, J., 'Harvesting Intellectual Property' *Notre Dame Law Review* **86** (2011): 2091

Silver, L., 'Life 2.0', *Newsweek*, 4 June 2007: 41–5, at 44

Silver, P. A., 'Making Biology Easier to Engineer' *BioSocieties* **4**(2–3) (2009): 283–9

Singer, J. W., *Property Law: Rules, Policies and Practices* (New York: Aspen Law & Business, 1997)

Smiers, J., 'The Abolition of Copyrights: Better for Artists, Third World Countries and the Public Domain', in R. Towse (ed.), *Copyright in the Cultural Industries* (Cheltenham: Edward Elgar, 2002), pp. 119–39

Solow, R., 'Technical Change and the Aggregate Production Function' *Review of Economic Statistics* **30** (1957): 214–31

Solum, L., 'The Future of Copyright' (Review of L. Lessig, *Free Culture*) *Texas Law Review* **84** (2005): 1137

Sonderholm, J., 'Paying a High Price for Low Costs: Why there should be no Legal Constraints on the Profits that can be made on Drugs for Tropical Diseases' *Journal of Medical Ethics* **35**(5) (2009): 309–13

'A Reform Proposal in Need of Reform: A Critique of Thomas Pogge's Proposal for How to Incentivize Research and Development of Essential Drugs' *Public Health Ethics* **3**(2) (2010): 167–77

'Intellectual Property Rights and the TRIPS Agreement: An Overview of Ethical Problems and some Proposed Solutions' *Policy Research Working Papers* (Washington, DC: World Bank, 2010)

Spellberg, B., Miller, L. G., Kuo, M. N., Bradley, J., Schild, W. M. and Edwards, J. E., 'Societal Costs versus Savings' *Infection* **35**(3) (2007): 167–74

Spence, M., *Intellectual Property* (Oxford University Press, 2007)

'The Mark as Expression/the Mark as Property' *Current Legal Problems* **58** (2005): 491–515

Stadler, S., 'Copyright as Trade Regulation' *Pennsylvania Law Review* **155** (2007): 899

Starling, E. S., 'The Croonian Lectures on the Chemical Correlation of the Functions of the Body. Lecture I' *The Lancet* **4275** (1905): 339–41

Statman, D. (ed.), *Virtue Ethics: A Critical Reader* (Edinburgh University Press, 1997)

Stenson, A. and Gray, T., 'An Autonomy-Based Justification for Intellectual Property Rights of Indigenous Communities' *Environmental Ethics* **21** (Summer 1999): 177–90

Sterckx, S., 'The European Patent Convention and the (Non)Patentability of Human Embryonic Stem Cells – the WARF Case' *Intellectual Property Quarterly* **4** (2008): 478

(ed.), *Biotechnology, Patents and Morality* (Aldershot: Ashgate, 2000)

Sterne, J., 'Is Music a Thing?', in J. Sterne, *MP3: The Meaning of a Format* (Durham, NC: Duke University Press, forthcoming)

Stewart, F. C., 'Letter to M. H. Coulston, President of the Patent Office Society' *Journal of the Patent Office Society* **2**(1) (1919): 73–5

Stiglitz, J. E., 'Scrooge and Intellectual Property Rights' *British Medical Journal* **333** (2006): 1279

Strahilevitz, L., 'Charismatic Code, Social Norms, and the Emergence of Cooperation on the File-Swapping Networks' *Virginia Law Review* **89** (2003): 505

Strevens, M., 'The Role of the Priority Rule in Science' *Journal of Philosophy* **100** (2) (2003): 55–79

Sulston, J. and Ferry, G., *The Common Thread: a Story of Science, Politics, Ethics and the Human Genome* (Washington DC: John Henry Press, 2002)

Sunder, M., 'IP3' *Stanford Law Review* **59** (2006): 257–322

Sweeney, M., 'Global recorded Music Sales fall almost $1.5bn amid Increased Piracy', *The Guardian*, 28 March 2011, available at www.guardian.co.uk/business/2011/mar/28/global-recorded-music-sales-fall

Tanford, C. and Reynolds, J., *Nature's Robots: A History of Proteins* (New York: Oxford University Press, 2001)

Taubman, A. and Leistner, M., 'Traditional Knowledge', in S. von Lewinsky (ed.), *Indigenous Heritage and Intellectual Property: Genetic Resources, Traditional Knowledge and Folklore* (2nd edn, The Netherlands: Wolters Kluwer, 2008), pp. 59–179

Taylor, C. *Hegel and Modern Society* (Cambridge University Press, 1979)

The Sources of the Self (Cambridge, Mass.: Harvard University Press, 1989)

The Ethics of Authenticity (Cambridge, Mass.: Harvard University Press, 1991)

Multiculturalism and the 'Politics of Recognition' (Princeton University Press, 1992)

Thambisetty, S., 'Sufficiency of Disclosure in the Common Law: Complexity, Divergence and Confusion', in C. Ng, L. Bently and G. D'Agostino (eds), *The Common Law of Intellectual Property: Essays in Honor of Professor David Vaver* (Oxford and Portland, Oreg., Hart Publishing, 2010), pp. 199–217

Thomson, J. J., *The Realm of Rights* (Cambridge, Mass.: Harvard University Press, 1990)

Torrance, A. W., 'Synthesizing Law for Synthetic Biology' *Minnesota Journal of Law, Science and Technology* **11**(2) (2010): 629–65

Torremans, P., 'The Construction of the Directive's Moral Exclusions under the EPC', in A. Plomer and P. Torremans (eds), *Embryonic Stem Cell Patents: European Law and Ethics* (Oxford University Press, 2009)

Towse, R. (ed.), *Copyright in the Cultural Industries* (Cheltenham: Edward Elgar, 2002)

Treiger-Bar-Am, L. K., 'Kant on Copyright: Rights of Transformative Authorship' *Cardozo Arts & Entertainment Law Journal* **25**(3) (2008): 1059

Tsosie, R., 'Reclaiming Native Stories: An Essay on Cultural Appropriation and Cultural Rights' *Arizona State Law Journal* **34** (Spring 2002): 299–358

Tushnet, R., 'Gone in Sixty Milliseconds: Trademark Law and Cognitive Science' *Texas Law Review* **86** (2008): 507–68

Vaidhyanathan, S., *Copyrights and Copywrongs: The Rise of Intellectual Property and How It Threatens Creativity* (New York University Press, 2001)

Van den Belt, H., 'Philosophy of Biotechnology', in A. Meijers (ed.), *Philosophy of Technology and Engineering Sciences* (Amsterdam and London: Elsevier, 2009), pp. 1301–40

van Hooft, S., *Understanding Virtue Ethics* (Stocksfield, UK: Acumen 2006)

Video clip of Arnold Schwarzenegger and Jackie Chan: www.youtube.com/watch?v=cKPs06vFihI

von Caemmerer, E. and Schlechtriem, P. (eds), *International Encyclopedia of Comparative Law* (Tübingen: Mohr Siebeck and Leiden and Boston: Martinus Nijhoff, 2007), vol. X (*Restitution/Unjust Enrichment and Negotiorum Gestio*)

Waelde, C., 'Copyright, Corporate Power and Human Rights', in F. Macmillan (ed.), *New Directions in Copyright Law* (Cheltenham: Edward Elgar, 2006), pp. 291–309

Waldron, J., *The Right to Private Property* (Oxford University Press, 1988)

'Superseding Historical Injustice' *Ethics* **103** (1992): 4–28

'A Right to do Wrong', in J. Waldron, *Liberal Rights* (Cambridge University Press, 1993), ch. 3

'From Authors to Copiers: Individual Rights and Social Values in Intellectual Property Law' *Chicago-Kent Law Review* **68** (1993): 841–87

'Property and Ownership', in E. N. Zalta (ed.), *The Stanford Encyclopedia of Philosophy* (Winter 2010 edn.) http://plato.stanford.edu/archives/win2010/entries/property/

Warren, S. and Brandeis, L. D., 'The Right to Privacy' *Harvard Law Review* **4** (1890): 193

Warren-Jones, A., 'Identifying European Moral Consensus: Why are the Patent Courts Reticent to Accept Empirical Evidence in Resolving Biotechnological Cases?' *European Intellectual Property Review* **29** (2006): 26

'Vital Parameters for Patent Morality – A Question of Form' *Journal of Intellectual Property Law & Practice* **2** (2007): 832

'Finding a "Common Morality Codex" for Biotech – A Question of Substance' *IIC* **39**(6) (2008): 638

'Morally Regulating Innovation: What is "Commercial Exploitation"?' *Intellectual Property Quarterly* **2** (2008): 193

Weinrib, E. J., 'Correlativity, Personality, and the Emerging Consensus on Corrective Justice' *Theoretical Inquiries in Law* **2** (2001): 107–59

'Corrective Justice in a Nutshell' *University of Toronto Law Journal* **52** (2002): 349–56

White, S. K., *The Cambridge Companion to Habermas* (Cambridge University Press, 1995)

White, S. 'Trade Unionism in a Liberal State', in Amy Gutmann (ed.), *Freedom of Association* (Princeton University Press, 1998), pp. 330–56

Wilkinson, S., *Bodies for Sale: Ethics and Exploitation in the Human Body Trade* (London: Routledge, 2003)

Williams, G., 'Kant's Account of Reason' in E. Zalta (ed.), *The Stanford Encyclopedia of Philosophy* (Summer 2009 edn)

Williams, M. S., *Voice, Trust and Memory: Marginalised Groups and the Failure of Liberal Representation* (Princeton University Press, 1998)

Wilson, E. B., 'Biology'. Lecture delivered at Columbia University in the Series in Science, Philosophy, and Art, 20 Nov. 1907 (New York: Columbia University Press, 1908)

Wilson, J., 'Rights', in R. Ashcroft, A. Dawson, H. Draper and J. McMillan, (eds), *Principles of Healthcare Ethics* (London: John Wiley & Sons Ltd., 2007)

'Towards a Normative Framework for Public Health Ethics and Policy' *Public Health Ethics* **2**(2) (2009): 184–94

'Could There be a Right to Own Intellectual Property?' *Law and Philosophy* **28** (4) (2009): 393–427

'Ontology and the Regulation of Intellectual Property' *The Monist* **93** (2010): 450–63

and Dawson, A., 'Giving Liberty its Due, but No More: Trans Fats, Liberty, and Public Health' *The American Journal of Bioethics* **10**(3) (2010): 34–6

Wong, D. B., 'On Flourishing and Finding One's Identity in Community', *Midwest Studies in Philosophy Volume XIII. Ethical Theory: Character and Virtue*: **13**(1) (1988): 324–41

Young, I. M., *Inclusion and Democracy* (Oxford University Press, 2002)

Zimmerman, D., 'Copyright as Incentives: Did We Just Imagine That?' *Theoretical Inquiries in Law* **12**, (2011): 29

Index

Cambridge Intellectual Property and Information Law

Titles in the series (formerly known as *Cambridge Studies in Intellectual Property Rights*)

Brad Sherman and Lionel Bently *The Making of Modern Intellectual Property Law*
978 0 521 56363 5

Irini A. Stamatoudi *Copyright and Multimedia Products: A Comparative Analysis*
978 0 521 80819 4

Pascal Kamina *Film Copyright in the European Union*
978 0 521 77053 8

Huw Beverly-Smith *The Commercial Appropriation of Personality*
978 0 521 80014 3

Mark J. Davison *The Legal Protection of Databases*
978 0 521 80257 4

Robert Burrell and Allison Coleman *Copyright Exceptions: The Digital Impact*
978 0 521 84726 1

Huw Beverly-Smith, Ansgar Ohly and Agnès Lucas-Schloetter *Privacy, Property and Personality: Civil Law Perspectives on Commercial Appropriation*
978 0 521 82080 6

Philip Leith *Software and Patents in Europe*
978 0 521 86839 6

Lionel Bently, Jennifer Davis and Jane C. Ginsburg *Trade Marks and Brands: An Interdisciplinary Critique*
978 0 521 88965 0

Geertrui Van Overwalle *Gene Patents and Clearing Models*
978 0 521 89673 3

Jonathan Curci *The Protection of Biodiversity and Traditional Knowledge in International Law of Intellectual Property*
978 0 521 19944 5

Lionel Bently, Jennifer Davis and Jane C. Ginsburg *Copyright and Piracy: An Interdisciplinary Critique*
978 0 521 19343 6

Megan Richardson and Julian Thomas *Framing Intellectual Property: Legal Constructions of Creativity and Appropriation 1840–1940*
978 0 521 76756 9

Dev Gangjee *Relocating the Law of Geographical Indications*
9780521192026

Andrew Kenyon, Megan Richardson and Ng-Loy Wee-Loon *The Law of Reputation and Brands in the Asia Pacific Region*
9781107017726

Annabelle Lever *New Frontiers in the Philosophy of Intellectual Property*
9781107009318